Strategic Workforce Planning

THE SIOP PROFESSIONAL PRACTICE SERIES

Series Editor
Douglas Reynolds

TITLES IN THE SERIES

Performance Management Transformation: Lessons Learned and Next Steps
Edited by Elaine D. Pulakos and Mariangela Battista

Employee Surveys and Sensing: Challenges and Opportunities
Edited by William H. Macey and Alexis A. Fink

Mastering Industrial-Organizational Psychology: Training Issues for Master's Level I-O Psychologists
Edited by Elizabeth L. Shoenfelt

Mastering the Job Market: Career Issues for Master's Level Industrial-Organizational Psychologists
Edited by Elizabeth L. Shoenfelt

The Age of Agility: Building Learning Agile Leaders and Organizations
Edited by Veronica Schmidt Harvey and Kenneth P. De Meuse

Overcoming Bad Leadership in Organizations
Edited by Derek Lusk and Theodore L. Hayes

Talent Assessment: Embracing Innovation and Mitigating Risk in the Digital Age
Edited by Tracy M. Kantrowitz, Douglas H. Reynolds, and John C. Scott

Becoming a Talent Magnet: Lessons from the Field on Attracting and Recruiting Great People
Edited by Mark A. Morris

Strategic Workforce Planning: Best Practices and Emerging Directions
Edited by Marc Sokol and Beverly Tarulli

Strategic Workforce Planning

Best Practices and Emerging Directions

Edited by

MARC SOKOL AND BEVERLY TARULLI

OXFORD
UNIVERSITY PRESS

Oxford University Press is a department of the University of Oxford. It furthers the University's objective of excellence in research, scholarship, and education by publishing worldwide. Oxford is a registered trade mark of Oxford University Press in the UK and certain other countries.

Published in the United States of America by Oxford University Press
198 Madison Avenue, New York, NY 10016, United States of America.

© Society for Industrial and Organizational Psychology 2024

All rights reserved. No part of this publication may be reproduced, stored in a retrieval system, or transmitted, in any form or by any means, without the prior permission in writing of Oxford University Press, or as expressly permitted by law, by license, or under terms agreed with the appropriate reproduction rights organization. Inquiries concerning reproduction outside the scope of the above should be sent to the Rights Department, Oxford University Press, at the address above.

You must not circulate this work in any other form
and you must impose this same condition on any acquirer.

Library of Congress Cataloging-in-Publication Data
Names: Sokol, Marc Barry, 1956- editor. | Tarulli, Beverly, editor.
Title: Strategic workforce planning : best practices and emerging directions / edited by Marc Sokol and Beverly Tarulli.
Description: New York, NY : Oxford University Press, [2024] |
Series: The SIOP professional practice series |
Includes bibliographical references and index.
Identifiers: LCCN 2023051073 (print) | LCCN 2023051074 (ebook) |
ISBN 9780197759745 (hardback) | ISBN 9780197759769 (epub) | ISBN 9780197759776
Subjects: LCSH: Manpower planning. | Strategic planning.
Classification: LCC HF5549.5.M3 S743 2024 (print) | LCC HF5549.5.M3 (ebook) |
DDC 658.3/01—dc23/eng/20240124
LC record available at https://lccn.loc.gov/2023051073
LC ebook record available at https://lccn.loc.gov/2023051074

DOI: 10.1093/oso/9780197759745.001.0001

Printed by Integrated Books International, United States of America

Contents

List of Figures — vii
List of Tables — ix
Foreword — xi
Acknowledgments — xiii
About the Editors — xv
Contributors — xvii

Introduction: Strategic Workforce Planning: Embracing Best Practices While Reimagining Our Potential — 1
Marc Sokol and Beverly Tarulli

1. Strategic Workforce Planning: How Can Our Legacy Frame the Future? — 15
Dan L. Ward

2. A Practitioner's Guide to Maturing Strategic Workforce Planning in Your Organization — 27
Tanya Moore

3. Practitioners' Perspectives on Operationalizing Strategic Workforce Planning: Data, Analytics, and Beyond — 48
Sheri L. Feinzig

4. Strategic Workforce Planning in the US Federal Government — 76
Laura Knowles and Samantha Adrignola

5. The History of the Workforce at Saudi Aramco: Opportunities for I-O Psychology — 99
Christian Hobson and Paul van Katwyk

6. Agile Workforce Planning — 116
Adam Gibson and Nicola Oldroyd

7. Strategic Workforce Planning for Growth: Strategies and Technology for Multispeed Growth — 140
James D. Eyring, Andrew P. Newmark, and Sunil Setlur

8. Enabling Strategic Workforce Planning Through Skills, Artificial Intelligence, and Internal Talent Marketplace   164
   Brian Heger

9. Strategic Work-Task Planning   198
   David Creelman, Alexis A. Fink, and David Ulrich

10. The Job as Work Role and Profession: It's More Than Skills   216
    Andrea Fischbach and Benjamin Schneider

11. Beyond the Theory: Adaptive Workforce Planning Approaches That Are Business-Led   241
    Adam McKinnon and Kanella Salapatas

12. The X-Factor in Strategic Workforce Planning: For CEOs, Context Is King   260
    David Reimer and Adam Bryant

13. Scenario Planning: The Secret Sauce to Making Strategic Workforce Planning Agile   282
    Edie Goldberg

14. Moving Mountains: Stamina and Resistance in Just Workforce Planning   300
    Juliet R. Aiken and Tori Glascock

15. Zero Hour for Jobs: How One Company Helped Others Adapt Their SWP when COVID Roiled the Planet and Learned to Adapt Itself   316
    Michael N. Bazigos

16. Teaching Strategic Workforce Planning: Hit the Ground Running   349
    Steve Weingarden, Nikita Arun, and Juliet R. Aiken

Conclusion: A Call to Action for Rethinking Workforce Planning   371
Beverly Tarulli and Marc Sokol

Index   389

Figures

1.1	Human resource planning process flow	20
1.2	Human resource planning process	21
1.3	Strategic workforce planning process	21
2.1	Stronger business outcomes with workforce planning	30
2.2	Levels of workforce planning maturity	31
2.3	Outperforming companies leverage artificial intelligence	33
2.4	The M. C. Dean approach to integrated strategic workforce planning	41
4.1	Finding the best level for workforce planning analysis	84
5.1	Workforce planning maturity model	106
5.2	Assessing and managing to leadership level transitions	111
6.1	The seven "rights" of workforce planning	117
6.2	The three horizons of workforce planning	118
6.3	The agile workforce planning cycle	124
6.4	Workforce drivers and model levers	131
6.5	Traditional (6.5a) versus agile (6.5b) approach to gap analysis	133
7.1	Talent strategies, growth, and key outcomes	147
7.2	Growth leader assessment styles and strategies development matrix	159
8.1	Internal talent marketplace concept and outcomes	170
8.2	Four strategic workforce planning capabilities enabled by ITM	171
8.3	Strategic workforce planning domino effect on other talent capabilities	175
8.4	Three artificial intelligence-based capabilities for enabling strategic workforce planning	176
8.5	Summary results for the platform that performed best	181
10.1	The culture and climate for professionalism is comprised of three interacting attributes	219
11.1	What needs to change?	244
11.2	A social network analysis of inventors listed on patents	254
11.3	Network analysis of IPC codes to identify domains and technologies	255
13.1	Scenarios for the future	285

13.2	Organization capability assessment	291
13.3	Options to bring in talent: buy, build, rent, or borrow	295
15.1	Workforce increases and reductions by company as of April 8, 2020	319
15.2	Screenshot of detailed O-NET tasks	326
15.3	Illustrative task decomposition of O-NET role	329
15.4	Percentage of tasks performable remotely with and without additional technological support	333
15.5	Illustration of a skill-based near-fit role analysis	335
15.6	Skills for impact as an organizational analytics practitioner	338
16.1	Model of an evidence-based organizational diagnostic process	351
C.1	A common strategic workforce planning methodology	382
C.2	A four-step approach to strategic workforce planning consulting	384
C.3	Technical and consulting model for strategic workforce planning	384

Tables

I.1	Different ways I-O psychologists engage in strategic workforce planning	4
3.1	Strategic workforce planning potential data sources	54
3.2	Types of analytics used in strategic workforce planning	59
4.1	Representation of employment statistics in the US federal government in recent fiscal years	77
6.1	Traditional versus agile workforce planning	120
7.1	Challenges and strategic focus in low- and high-growth environments	143
7.2	Implications of growth and strategy on strategic workforce planning and talent strategies	151
7.3	Sample strategic workforce planning and talent strategies for multispeed hospitality growth	155
8.1	Sample challenges and questions for implementing artificial intelligence technologies	167
8.2	Five questions for pilot study to help answer	177
8.3	Data sources for inferring employees' skills and job and learning opportunities	179
9.1	Comparing workforce and work-task planning	199
9.2	Keys for implementing a work-task agenda	214
10.1	Examples of professional behavior	217
10.2	O*NET listing of work styles that can characterize work roles	218
10.3	Hypothesized links between the five-factor model of personality and O*NET work styles	225
10.4	Climate and culture for service: employees speak	235
12.1	Helping CEOs plan for the future: A playbook for strategic workforce planning professionals	280
13.1	Sample capabilities assessment	292
14.1	Guidelines for Just workforce planning (JWP)	313
14.2	What next?	314
C.1	Areas of competence for industrial-organizational (I-O) psychology graduate programs defined by Society for Industrial and Organizational Psychology (SIOP, 2016) and relevant to strategic workforce planning (SWP)	379

Foreword

Strategic workforce planning (SWP) has evolved from a mere financial and headcount exercise into a dynamic and ongoing process that organizations need to adopt to keep up with rapid change and growing challenges. It is no longer sufficient to focus solely on the number of people and required skills. Instead, organizations must consider the complexities of automation versus human work, optimal skill utilization across the enterprise, and efficient organizational structures.

Traditionally, SWP has not been considered a core area of expertise in industrial and organizational (I-O) psychology. Similarly, SWP professionals have not fully embraced the knowledge, skills, and insights that I-O psychologists can provide. Both sides lack awareness of the potential contributions they can make to each other, even though I-O psychologists touch on various aspects of strategic workforce planning through their work on selection processes, work design, and development programs, among other areas.

For I-O psychologists to contribute effectively to strategic workforce planning, we need to adopt a broader organizational perspective and consider multiple levels of analysis, including the individual, team, and organizational levels. While some I-O psychologists already approach their work with this mindset, many focus on individual-level programs and functions. This book argues that I-O psychologists can have a more significant impact and gain more recognition by understanding and embracing the concepts, language, and mindset of SWP. Similarly, SWP professionals can greatly benefit from leveraging I-O psychology insights and methodologies.

This exceptional volume, edited by Marc Sokol and Beverly Tarulli, aims to bridge the gap between I-O psychology and SWP by providing insights into opportunities for integration. It targets both I-O psychologists and SWP professionals, aiming to enhance their understanding of how each discipline can positively influence the other. The editors, prominent organizational consultants and thought leaders with expertise in both SWP and I-O psychology, have drawn from their extensive global experience to create this book. They have gathered notable experts and curated relevant topics to offer valuable insights and future opportunities for both disciplines.

The development of an edited *Professional Practice Series* book such as this requires a substantial amount of effort and dedication. I want to express my deep appreciation to Marc, Beverly, and the chapter authors for their significant contributions and the time they devoted to this project. Their efforts will undoubtedly enrich the fields of I-O psychology and SWP. My hope is that readers will find inspiration in this volume, broadening their perspectives on the combined contributions that I-O psychology and SWP can make and enhancing the impact of their own work.

—Elaine D. Pulakos, Series Editor
July 2023

Acknowledgments

We wish to acknowledge the SIOP Professional Practice Publications Committee and its members for encouragement and input on the planning for this volume: Elaine Pulakos, Alison Eyring, Bill Gentry, Rose Hanson, Derek Lusk, and Shreya Sarkar-Barney. We also have benefited from external reviewers whose comments on the initial prospectus reinforced the directions being proposed for this volume and provided useful suggestions. Last, we remain indebted to family, colleagues, and contributors to this volume for their ongoing enthusiasm and support.

About the Editors

Marc Sokol, President of Sage Consulting Resources, has worked in large and small firms, public and private sector, in internal and external roles, and across 25 countries. He consults to boards, CEOs, and C-level executives, helping them extend impact across the firms they lead. Past executive editor of *People + Strategy*, he serves on the editorial boards of *Consulting Psychology Journal* and *Organization Development Review*. Co-author of several books including *Negotiation: Creating agreements in business and life*, he is past president of Minnesota Professionals for Psychology Applied to Work and 2024 president for the Society of Consulting Psychology. A fellow of the American Psychological Association (APA) and two of its divisions—Society for Industrial Organizational Psychology and Society of Consulting Psychology—he teaches Strategic Workforce Planning and Development for the American Bankers Association, Stonier Graduate School of Banking. Marc earned a PhD in industrial-organizational psychology from University of Maryland, College Park.

Beverly Tarulli is Clinical Assistant Professor at New York University, leading the Human Capital Analytics and Technology master's degree program within the School of Professional Studies. She is passionate about shaping the practice of human resources (HR) today and the HR leaders of tomorrow. She is also the founder of Novius Consulting, LLC, which helps organizational leaders with talent strategy, people analytics, and strategic workforce planning. Dr. Tarulli has worked in talent management, employee development, HR business partner, talent strategy, and people analytics roles at BellSouth (now AT&T) and PepsiCo and as a human performance consultant at Accenture. Her 35-year career has allowed her to develop and apply a broad, strategic perspective on how human resources contributes to organizational outcomes. Dr. Tarulli's professional interests include talent strategy, career development, diversity, support of STEM education, pay equity, employee reskilling, and workforce development. She has published in both academic and professional publications throughout her career. She earned a PhD in industrial-organizational psychology from The University of Akron.

Contributors

Samantha Adrignola is Program Manager at the US Office of Personnel Management (OPM) and leads the Strategic Consulting program in Human Resources Strategy (HRS) and Evaluation Solutions. The team consults with federal agencies in the areas of strategic workforce planning, succession planning, and workforce analytics. In previous roles in OPM HRS, Samantha served as a team lead in the Human Capital Industry Solutions (HCIS) program office, assisting federal agencies in accessing top private-sector human capital contractors. Samantha received her bachelor of arts in psychology from Truman State University and a master of science in industrial-organizational psychology from Missouri State University. Samantha lives in Kansas City, Missouri, with her husband Tony and sons (Nino, Leo, and Lorenzo) and family pets Silvio (cat) and Dread Pirate Roberts (dog).

Juliet R. Aiken, PhD, is a consultant with Volta Talent Strategies and the Head of Consulting at Conducere. Juliet holds a PhD in I-O psychology with a specialization in selection, equity and inclusion, statistics and measurement, and aligned strategic change management. At Volta, Juliet develops and validates competency models and assessments to enable law firms to hire, integrate, and retain diverse top talent. In all her work, Juliet serves as a trusted advisor to help organizations pivot during uncertainty, supporting them in developing systems for hiring, training, promoting, and retaining talent. She has more than a decade of experience in government, private-sector, and nonprofit sectors and has served as an expert witness around discrimination in hiring. Juliet has received the 2017 IPAC Innovation in Assessment Award for "Hiring Quickly and at a Low Cost Under a Consent Decree" and the 2020 Society for Industrial Organizational Psychology (SIOP) Early Career Award in Practice.

Nikita Arun is Program Director and a faculty member in the University of Maryland (UMD) industrial-organizational psychology master's program. She received her PhD in I-O psychology from Virginia Tech. She is passionate about training students in the field of I-O psychology and developing opportunities for I-O students to grow their knowledge, skills, and experiences. She has a special interest in implementing a universal learning approach and is currently teaching Introduction to I-O Psychology and Organizational Change. Dr. Arun is currently leading several program development initiatives to make the UMD I-O program more accessible and build opportunities for students. Prior to joining UMD, she worked in applied research and the corporate sector in the areas of employee engagement, data analytics, action planning, selection and assessment, test development, and workforce training.

Dr. Arun's past research has focused on motivation, self-regulatory processes, and goal setting.

Michael N. Bazigos, an ardent advocate for evidence-based organizational transformation and change, has dedicated his career to highlighting the quantifiable impact of talent, leadership, and culture and to designing performance-enhancing interventions. His innovative, data-driven approach led to quantitative business results at the organization level, persuading business executives and organizational psychologists alike to value these softer business aspects. As global Managing Director and de facto CEO of Accenture Strategy's organizational and talent analytics business, Dr. Bazigos built a successful practice that seamlessly integrates organizational psychology into business operations. His career spans leadership roles at McKinsey & Co., KPMG, IBM, and PwC, balancing these with academic commitments as an adjunct faculty at Columbia University. He also founded Pace University's Center for Urban Education. Guided by innovation, evidence-based management, and a culture of kindness, Dr. Bazigos has consistently delivered quantifiable results, underscoring his belief in the transformative power of people in achieving organizational success.

Adam Bryant joined The ExCo Group, a senior leadership development and executive mentoring firm, as Managing Director in 2017, after a 30-year career in journalism, including 18 years at *The New York Times*. In addition to his roles there as a reporter and editor, he created the weekly "Corner Office" column in 2009 and interviewed 525 CEOs and other leaders over the course of a decade. He has written four books based on the themes that emerged from those interviews, including his latest: *The Leap to Leader: How Ambitious Managers Make the Jump to Leadership* (Harvard Business Review Press). Since joining The ExCo Group, he has started popular interview series on LinkedIn with board directors, CEOs, CHROs, and prominent Black leaders, and he writes a monthly column on leadership for *Strategy + Business* magazine. Adam also is the senior adviser to the Reuben Mark Initiative for Organizational Character and Leadership at Columbia University.

David Creelman is CEO of Creelman Research. Based in Toronto, Canada, he consults around the world and has particularly close ties to Malaysia and Japan. He is well-known for his books and articles on the most interesting topics in human resources. He is a fellow of the Centre for Evidence-Based Management and is a winner of the Human Resources People + Strategy (HRPS) Walker Award. Currently, David focuses on the impact of generative artificial intelligence on HR, analytics, and reporting on human capital to investors.

James D. Eyring is CEO of Organisation Solutions, a global consulting company. He has more than 25 years of experience, specializing in executive coaching, leader assessment, leader development, team performance and change and transformation. James was the lead developer of the Growth Leader Assessment and 360 as well as Organisation Solutions' Personal Training methodology for coaches. He oversees all psychometric assessments and intellectual property development at Organisation

Solutions and is now Chief Science Advisor for Produgie, a B2B SaaS company. His current research interests focus on leadership and company growth. James has worked in HR leadership positions for PepsiCo, Dell, and Motorola. He now works with global Fortune 500 companies to help their executives and leadership teams perform, energize their teams, and transform their businesses. James holds a PhD and MA in industrial-organizational psychology from the University of Houston and has lived in Singapore for more than 20 years.

Sheri L. Feinzig, PhD, is Global Head of Workforce Planning & Analytics for Marsh McLennan. She is an experienced executive with a history of successfully leading teams through a range of business challenges, transformations, and growth, applying her expertise in HR research, analytics, and business transformation. Focus areas include people analytics, workforce planning, diversity, equity and inclusion, ethical AI, and employee experience. Sheri recently served as an adjunct professor for New York University's Human Capital Analytics & Technology master's program. She speaks frequently on various HR-related topics and is an author of numerous publications, including the critically acclaimed workforce analytics book *The Power of People*.

Alexis A. Fink, PhD, is Vice President, People Analytics and Workforce Strategy for Meta and the President-Elect for the Society for Industrial and Organizational Psychology (SIOP). She has been in practice in I-O psychology for more than 30 years and previously held leadership roles at Microsoft and Intel. Alexis is a Fellow of SIOP and a frequent and engaging speaker on people analytics topics. She has authored multiple books and scores of articles and chapters. Alexis earned her PhD in industrial and organizational psychology from Old Dominion University.

Andrea Fischbach is Full Professor of Social, Work, and Organizational Psychology at the German Police University, Münster. She received her diploma in psychology at Goethe-University, Frankfurt, Germany; her PhD at Georg-August-University, Göttingen, Germany; and she has held a Junior-Professorship for Organizational Psychology at Trier University, Germany. She has published more than 65 professional journal articles and book chapters on emotional labor, job crafting, organizational justice, and work diversity (age/gender/culture), and their implications for both performance and worker health. She has led several funded research projects (1 + Million Euros) including one 3-year project on emotional labor in retail stores. She co-edited with Benjamin Schneider the Special Issue of the *Journal of Service Management Research*, Emotional Labor and Service. Her research focuses on the dynamics of work conditions, leadership, and HR management to help understand what makes people engaged, motivated, and healthy at work.

Adam Gibson is a global leader in workforce planning, creator of the Agile Workforce Planning methodology, and a popular keynote speaker. He advises company executives on how to create a sustainable workforce that increases productivity and reduces cost, and has successfully implemented and transformed workforce planning and analytics in public- and private-sector businesses across the world. He has held senior roles in Ernst & Young, PricewaterhouseCoopers, the London Metropolitan Police, and Capita. Prior to his current career in business, he served in the British Army as a commissioned officer in the infantry and served on the front lines of Afghanistan and Iraq. Adam is an alumnus of the University of Sheffield and Stratford Business School. He is a Chartered Fellow of the Chartered Institute of Personnel and Development and a Fellow of the Chartered Management Institute. His book, *Agile Workforce Planning*, was published in 2021.

Tori Glascock is an organizational psychology doctoral student at the Graduate School of Applied and Professional Psychology (GSAPP) at Rutgers University and holds a Master of Applied Psychology, also from GSAPP. Currently, Tori is the Research Project Coordinator for the Division of Student Affairs at Rutgers University. In this role, Tori collects and analyzes data to ensure that student resources are reaching program goals and serving students in an inclusive and equitable way.

Edie Goldberg, PhD, is the founder and President of E. L. Goldberg & Associates in Menlo Park, California. She is a nationally recognized expert in talent management and the future of work. Her practice focuses on designing HR processes and programs to attract, engage, develop, and retain employees. Prior to starting her own firm more than 20 years ago, Edie was a global thought leader in the Human Capital Practice at Towers Perrin. She has a PhD in I-O psychology from the University of Albany, SUNY. She is a SIOP Fellow and is the Chair of the SHRM Foundation Board of Directors.

Brian Heger is an internal Human Resources practitioner with multi-industry experience, including pharma, retail, and telecom, having worked with Bristol-Myers Squibb, Hudson's Bay Company/Saks Fifth Avenue, and AT&T, respectively. His background encompasses roles as a Center of Expertise (COE) Lead in strategic workforce planning, talent management, talent acquisition, learning and development, and organizational effectiveness, as well as an HR business partner and consultant. Brian is also the publisher of *Talent Edge Weekly*, a weekly newsletter that provides HR practitioners with curated insights about the world of work, the workplace, and the workforce. He also shares HR and talent management ideas and resources at brianheger.com. Brian holds an MA in industrial psychology and BA in psychology from Fairleigh Dickinson University.

Christian Hobson currently serves as the head of Executive Talent Management within the Executive Development and Compensation (ED&C) team at Saudi Aramco, based in the Kingdom of Saudi Arabia. This ED&C team provides oversight of the leadership pipeline for the top 300+ leaders, including the C-suite, global affiliates, and their boards. He previously worked in the financial services sector located in London, Singapore, and Dubai. Christian was educated in the United Kingdom and is a chartered psychologist with the British Psychological Society.

Laura Knowles is Program Manager at the US Office of Personnel Management (OPM). She currently serves in the HR Solutions (HRS) organization and supports early career and cyber workforce initiatives, including Scholarship for Service, a program designed to recruit and train the next generation of cyber talent to meet the needs of federal, state, local, and tribal governments. In previous roles, Laura managed workforce planning, reshaping position management and classification functions in OPM HRS, and she provided consultative support to agency partners across government. Laura joined OPM in 2009 from the private sector as a research analyst. She holds a master of science in industrial-organizational psychology from Missouri State University, a bachelor of arts in psychology from the University of Northern Iowa, and is a certified project management professional. Laura lives in Kansas City, Missouri, with her husband, Chris, and sons, Cooper, Teddy, and Peter.

Adam McKinnon is currently the people data and analytics leader at Reece Group. Prior to returning to Australia in 2020, he worked internationally for 13 years delivering advanced people analytics and HR innovation projects for a variety of organizations. Drawing on a multidisciplinary background in psychology, IT, epidemiology, and finance, Adam is an advocate of asking two questions in his work: "So what?" and "Now what?"

Tanya Moore is Chief People Officer at West Monroe, a digital services firm that helps businesses not only do digital, but be digital. Prior to West Monroe she was the Chief People Officer at M. C. Dean, an organization that designs, builds, operates, and maintains engineering solutions for complex, mission-critical organizations. Ms. Moore also spent 20 years with IBM, where she served as Global Director of Career & Skills with responsibility for envisioning and executing a new career and skill acceleration experience for the IBM workforce. During her time at IBM, she served as a partner in IBM's Talent & Transformation consulting organization, bringing the best practices and lessons learned from her internal role with IBM to lead clients in their HR transformations. Ms. Moore regularly speaks on the topics of skill transformation and using digital technology to advance your workforce transformation, leadership, and employee experience.

Andrew P. Newmark is CHRO for Marriott International in the APEC region. He has more than 30 years of experience in the hotel business and human resources. Andrew has held generalist HR and COE leadership roles throughout his career. Over the past 10 years, he has led the region's HR function through the varied dynamics of M&A, the COVID pandemic, evolving talent and customer needs, and expansive business growth. He is committed to leading an HR function that partners and aligns its priorities with the business strategy and brings value to employees and the organization. Andrew holds an MBAX in change from the University of New South Wales/Australian Graduate School of Management and has lived in Singapore for the past 7 years.

Nicola Oldroyd is a strategic workforce planning consultant at Ernst & Young (EY), focused on public- and private-sector markets in the United Kingdom. Since joining EY in 2020, Nicola has been engaged in a number of organization and workforce transformation projects with clients from across the globe. A published academic, Nicola completed her undergraduate degree in chemistry at the University of Oxford, followed by a PhD from the University of Bristol prior to transitioning into consulting. As an enthusiastic athlete, Nicola enjoys running and has competed in multiple marathons and an ultra-marathon. Nicola also spends time volunteering at her local running club and community running events.

David Reimer is Group CEO and Managing Partner of The ExCo Group. Primarily focused on CEO succession and the fast-tracking of senior executives into new roles, David brings his clients an operational and GM lens as they consider the operational, cultural, and leadership requirements of their strategies. Prior to joining The ExCo Group in 2010, Reimer helped lead a turnaround under private equity ownership of Drake Beam Morin's (DBM) Asia Pacific and North American businesses, which included consulting to the three largest financial services integrations during the financial crisis. Reimer serves as Executive Editor of the journal *People + Strategy*, and his work and writing have appeared in publications such as the *New York Times*, *Strategy + Business*, *Fortune*, and *Inc*.

Kanella Salapatas currently holds the position of Global Head of People Data & Analytics at QBE Insurance. With more than 15 years of experience in various roles within the financial and health services sector, she has helped organizations mature and uplift their data and analytics strategies and services. Kanella has successfully led global teams in providing valuable insights through data, establishing global reporting solutions, championing the exploration and embedment of advanced analytics techniques while ensuring the prioritization and continued focus on the importance of data governance and management. Kanella's responsibilities include directing QBE's strategy for continuous listening by leveraging new technology to create and deliver employee voice as well as being accountable for implementing a global approach for financial planning and strategic workforce planning within the organization.

Benjamin Schneider is Professor Emeritus of Psychology at the University of Maryland (UMD) and Affiliate Research Scientist at the Center for Effective Organizations (CEO), the University of Southern California. Ben has published more than 125 professional journal articles and book chapters and 13 books. Ben's interests concern organizational climate and culture, service quality, work engagement, staffing organizations, and the role of personality in organizational life. Since retiring from UMD, he has worked with several research and consulting organizations (CEO, Valtera, CEB, and PDRI) helping organizations identify how they are handling these human issues. Ben has won distinguished contributions awards from the HR and Organizational Behavior (OB) Divisions of the Academy of Management,

SIOP, SHRM (the Losey Award), and the Services Interest Group of the American Marketing Association. Ben has also served as President of the OB Division of the Academy of Management and SIOP. More details are available at www.DrBenSchneider.com.

Sunil Setlur has spent nearly two decades at the intersection of people, organization, strategy, and culture. He is a technology optimist who is on a mission to build organizations that inspire people to do their best work every day. Sunil is the founder of Cognisen, an advisory practice specializing in organizational strategy and culture. He concurrently serves on the Board of Commissioners for Electrum, an Indonesian Electric Vehicles Company. Prior to his current role, Sunil was an advisor to the Group CEO at the GOTO group and venture portfolio advisor at Go-Ventures. Most notably, he was Global Chief People Officer (CHRO) at Gojek. Earlier in his career, Sunil held HR and HR business partnership roles with Google, Amazon and Accenture. Sunil holds a bachelor's degree in industrial relations, economics, and sociology from Bangalore University, India, as well as a postgraduate certificate in human capital management from XLRI Jamshedpur, India

David Ulrich is Rensis Likert Professor at the Ross School of Business, University of Michigan, and partner at the RBL Group. He has written more than 30 books and hundreds of articles, consulted with half of the Fortune 200, and spoken in more than 90 countries on topics related to human capability (talent + leadership + organization + HR). He has received a variety of recognitions and awards for his insights on theory, research, and practice.

Paul van Katwyk currently serves as Head of Assessment & Coaching within the Executive Development and Compensation (ED&C) team at Saudi Aramco, based in the Kingdom of Saudi Arabia. Previous to this role, he spent 25 years in a global consulting company where his roles included being a leader in both the executive assessment and the global leadership development practice areas. He also spent over a decade based in Asia as the managing director of Greater China business and then as the Asia-Pacific regional consulting director. Educated in the United States, Canada, and Hong Kong, he was awarded a PhD in industrial-organizational psychology by the University of South Florida. He has written book chapters and published articles in leading journals on topics ranging from succession management, workforce aging, assessment, the measurement of work affect, and the impact of leadership experience.

Dan L. Ward is Chief Workforce Economist for RevTek Solutions. Semi-retired and based in the Washington DC area, he was most recently employed full time by NASA. He previously provided support to federal government agencies while at the MITRE Corporation. Dan has a passion for workforce analytics, people strategy, program management, and scenario planning. Prior to his public-sector work, Ward served in leadership roles at EDS, Texaco, GTE, and AT&T. His accomplishments in business strategy, resource planning, knowledge management, and workforce analytics led to receiving HR People & Strategy's Lifetime Award. Dan has regularly provided support to the American Productivity & Quality Center (APQC), the Human Capital Institute, The Conference Board, and the RAND Corporation on advanced people resource strategy initiatives. He was project lead or principal on a dozen future workforce mobilization projects.

Steve Weingarden has dedicated his professional career to guiding senior executive leaders through the processes of organizational change, culture-building, and organizational growth. Currently CEO of Innovators of Change, he has worked in external and internal consulting for more than 25 years. He has extensive experience teaching undergraduate and graduate students, including course content related to organizational theory and change and social aspects of the workplace. Steve has developed and implemented leadership architectures and development programs with an emphasis on enhancing culture onboarding and promoting understanding of the strategic impact and design of organizational functions. Prior to achieving his doctorate at Wayne State University, Steve worked in the radio industry as a newscaster, producer, and sports talk show host. He maintains a specialized interest regarding the effects of executive leadership on baseball team performance. His passion integrates with his home life when he applies SWP principles to coaching fastpitch softball.

Introduction

Strategic Workforce Planning

Embracing Best Practices While Reimagining Our Potential

Marc Sokol and Beverly Tarulli

Strategic workforce planning (SWP)—the process of looking forward, assessing how to compete and win in your chosen market or business arena, and linking those insights to your existing and potential future workforce—is core to any institution that aspires to sustain itself over time. This volume presents best practices and emerging directions from those who embrace these activities.

There is often a backstory to a book, whether a set of experiences or a realization that provides the motivation to propose a new volume. We begin with a few of our own stories, as these set the tone for a journey that we hope you, the reader, will join us in.

Anticipating the future (one of Marc's stories). Jason is a long-term consulting client. He moved into a new role as the head of wealth management, a business unit that provides financial advisory services for affluent customers. This is a highly competitive market and an important line of business for his organization, and we were discussing how the industry was changing and what that might mean for him as an executive. He was focused on a baby-boomer megatrend expected to occur over the coming decade. As women statistically outlive their male spouses, the transfer of wealth would be unprecedented, estimated in the tens of trillions of dollars. This meant a significant shift in who would become their primary customer, and Jason had been absorbing all the related research, particularly research that indicated that these customers would likely be less tolerant of wealth advisors relying on old-school approaches and more receptive to advisors who were attentive to their needs and expectations. It signaled for him a change in how his business would need to compete. Retention of existing accounts and capacity to compete for new clients would require a shift in style of advising and even in the type of advisor who might be more successful. As he deepened his thinking, he could see implications for whom he needed to recruit and hire, how he might develop and manage advisors, even what type of manager of advisors will be needed in the future. His thinking then shifted to the question: Why wait for attrition of the existing team to embrace the future? How could he get to the future more quickly? He was, in fact, engaging in an SWP thought exercise without using that precise language.

Leveraging SWP to drive organizational change (one of Beverly's stories). I took over the leadership of a people analytics, SWP, and talent strategy team at a Fortune 50 company. The existing team was talented, and the SWP methodology was sound. The quality of the analyses the team conducted was high, as were the strategic workforce plans they produced in conjunction with our business partners. But two things occurred to me shortly after taking the role. First, there was little in the way of evaluation and follow-up once the SWP plans were handed over to the business and human resources (HR) business partners to execute, so we never had a view of how good our plans really were. Second, the organization had a robust enterprise business strategic-planning process, but SWP was not a part of that process, and our methodology did not map directly to the enterprise business strategy process, timing, or language. In addressing these gaps, I began to see SWP as part of implementing broader organization change and how SWP data and analytics were just part of our efforts to consult to and add value to the business. With this realization, I had taken my strong "I-side" (industrial psychology) approach to SWP and now found greater traction by combining it with an equally strong "O-side" (organizational psychology). From that point forward, I began to think about SWP in entirely new ways and saw much greater opportunity to have an impact.

Joining forces. As executive editor of *People + Strategy*, a professional publication, I (Marc) would search for salient topics and themes on the minds of senior executives. At one point I spoke with senior leaders in the pharma and biotech industries about the challenge of retaining and securing pivotal talent: they were especially concerned about increasing legal hurdles for obtaining visas to bring foreign researchers into the United States and maintaining visas for those already here. Beneficial as it may be to co-locate scientists and researchers in the United States, they were actively exploring more globally dispersed hubs as a hedge against political winds and constraints. Around the same time, I found myself in other conversations with talent professionals who were wondering how their companies would embrace and manage the impacts of the growing gig economy, especially in the information technology (IT) arena. Could they analyze a subset of company jobs, reduce them to sets of tasks, and then more efficiently outsource portions of the work? Would they need to find new ways to ensure that contract employees embraced their company culture? What implications, they wondered, might this have for establishing a sufficient pipeline of employees who would move up into managerial and other coordinating organizational roles? In response to these and other conversations, I dedicated an issue of *People + Strategy* to the topic of modern workforce planning (Sokol, 2019). Among the many experts who contributed to this issue was Beverly Tarulli, who, at the time, led advanced analytics and SWP at a Fortune 50 firm. Our ongoing conversations, even after that special issue was published, led to new questions about the potential role of SWP, as well as to our eventual framing of this volume.

Why This Book in the SIOP Professional Practice Series?

We believe that practitioners who engage directly in SWP have special insights to offer for the rest of I-O psychology. Other I-O psychologists certainly incorporate thinking that is associated with SWP within their everyday consultation activities, but they don't have a complete language or realize that there are integrating concepts that can help them more fully leverage their insights with clients. Many I-O psychologists do not yet get to see the full potential of SWP as an application of our body of knowledge and skills. If we consider SWP using the classic parable of blind men who are first encountering an elephant, then it can be said that many I-O psychologists routinely touch different parts of this animal (job analysis, selection, job design, talent development, and so on) but rarely see the whole of it—unless they happen to work with a company that has a functional unit devoted to SWP and is staffed with I-O psychologists. HR business partners may see the whole of SWP for a line of business, and the chief HR officer (CHRO) may see the whole of it for an enterprise, but unless the I-O psychologist has moved into one of these roles, they likely miss the opportunity to influence SWP practices and decisions. We believe that many of us, in our work advising clients and organizations, can be even more influential to the extent we seize the concepts, language, and mindset of SWP.

Here we look at the different ways and vantage points from which I-O psychologists engage in SWP and the emphasis surrounding each type of involvement (see Table I.1). I-O psychologists, if they are in the role of CHRO or lead a SWP center of excellence (COE), for example, are more likely to consider the overall architecture of how SWP functions while also guiding the senior executive team about the role of workforce planning. If there is a formal SWP COE, the I-O psychologists who are team members will be attentive to data collection, analysis, and reporting, and managing the complexity of SWP across the enterprise. HR business partners, on the other hand, provide internal consultation to business line and functional leaders. I-O psychologists who have taken up such an organizational role may be able to offer deep practical and strategic expertise to their clients, but they may sometimes find themselves as more like a pair of hands if their clients only ask them to focus on resource planning and reactive staff replacement.

Table I.1 Different ways I-O psychologists engage in strategic workforce planning

Type of SWP involvement	With emphasis on	Typically found among
Strategic architecture, methodology, and organizational guidance	Design and tailor the framework of SWP to support company strategy; guide senior executive team	CHROs, heads of SWP COEs
Analysis and plan development	Data collection, analysis, and reporting; manage complexity of SWP across the enterprise	Members of designated SWP COE; HR data analysts
Internal SWP consultation	Support and advice to line of business and function leaders	HR business partners
Link other HR and business service to SWP; draw from SWP to enhance value of HR services	Leadership development, selection, organizational development, diversity, total rewards, learning, change management, talent management, and other COEs who work in parallel to SWP COE and customize their focus based on SWP insights	Organizational design and transformation consultancies; internal HR specialists, such as leadership development curriculum design
Implications of SWP beyond any single organization	Researchers, academics, and practitioners who look at broader industry, workforce, national, and international trends	Academics, think tanks (e.g., The Conference Board), research consortiums

Within the HR function, I-O psychologists can be found among COEs, such as leadership development, talent acquisition, talent management, change management, and total rewards. The question is whether these professionals work in close collaboration with the SWP COE, if they adapt any of their own practices based on SWP insights, or if they work in silos, as if SWP has no impact on the work their COE performs for the company. I-O psychologists concerned with SWP might also be found at universities, in think tanks and research consortia, and in larger consultancies, where they attend to industry, national, and international trends with implications for the workforce and organizations of the future. It is here that we also see I-O psychologists pushing the envelope of SWP, addressing larger societal issues or how SWP thinking can be a positive response to world events.

We further believe that senior leaders, the combined executive committee, and board discussions can benefit from real-time interaction with I-O psychologists who understand SWP and its potential to provide competitive advantage to the company. I-O psychologists can create more traction for the many services we offer when we organize our thinking around concepts such as SWP.

I-O psychology brands itself as a "science for a smarter workplace." What, then, is the role and potential of applied psychology to enhance SWP? Most likely, it is a psychology drawing from many streams and subdisciplines, and it requires multiple levels of thinking and analysis. Applied psychology can support SWP because it draws on what we know about assessment of people, jobs, and organizations, as well as about recognizing different stakeholders and fostering their alignment, implementing change, and establishing processes that sustain new practices, roles, and behavior. We approached this volume with these questions in mind, asking contributors to say how we can articulate current best practices in SWP and at the same time continue to evolve—even reimagine—SWP using our experience to better learn together.

There are a few books on workforce planning; some reflect the personal approach of a single author and practitioner whereas others, such as Dan Ward and Rob Tripp's 2013 book, *Positioned*, capture a breadth of perspectives from a management and HR perspective. Adam Gibson (2021) offers a cutting edge perspective in his book, *Agile Workforce Planning*, that is consistent with our own thinking as he considers ways SWP helps any company better compete in its chosen arena. Dan and Adam are each among our contributors, sharing their more recent thoughts and experience on SWP.

Three Areas of Focus Readers Will Find Throughout This Volume

As we initially spoke with our contributors, we found three issues that repeatedly surfaced. First, there are many best practices for conducting SWP. Some involve the tactics of data collection and analysis, while others are guidelines for accessing and managing data in less than perfect settings. Additional areas of best practices include the consulting approach taken with different clients and the challenge of framing this work within any enterprise. Not surprisingly, these best practices often emerge as the result of time-tested experience, and we benefit from each contributor's willingness to share the evolution of their thinking and approach.

A second issue was that many of our colleagues felt they had come to reimagine SWP as an outgrowth of their work, sometimes leading them to generate new terminology to better capture the evolution of their thinking and aspirations. Like Beverly, some reimagine SWP as a process embedded within company strategy and organizational design and development and as an iterative consulting process that benefits from both planning and action. Other contributors have come to see SWP as relevant to new ways of working and addressing broader topics ranging from pressing societal issues to being an accelerator of a multicompany, multi-industry pandemic response.

Within this volume the reader will note a variety of terms that capture for different authors their reality as they go beyond traditional frameworks. Expect to read well thought out descriptions of workforce planning practices that increase impact to the extent they are "agile" (Gibson and Oldroyd), "adaptive" (Salapatas and McKinnon), "scenario-based" (Goldberg), moderated by a "high or low speed of business growth" (Eyring, Newmark, and Setlur), or focused on "work-task" rather than "workforce" (Creelman, Fink, and Ulrich). We even encounter "just workforce planning" (Aiken and Glascock), where the modifier "just" doesn't refer to simplicity but to "fairness" and addresses workforce planning in the broader context of justice, equity, diversity, and inclusion. We see such terminology as a welcome advance. It is not so much individual rebranding of existing concepts but rather a recognition that the traditional frame is no longer sufficient to keep pace with our changing circumstances and the changing world of work.

The third issue common among our contributors is that, in some manner, they all recognize tradeoffs in the practice of SWP. For us, underlying a comprehensive SWP approach is the act of embracing the "both/and" of various choices. This is captured in questions such as the following:

1. When should the priority be on the data collection and analysis aspects of SWP, and when should the consulting focus take precedence? How do you assess the quality and maturity of each aspect of your SWP approach?
2. As we consider the maturity of SWP practices, to what extent do we bias our view toward having a well-integrated set of analytics tools and processes, *and* to what extent do we see maturity as the capability to work with incomplete, inconsistent datasets, creating workarounds that provide enough insights to keep moving forward?
3. When is it more appropriate to approach SWP as an opportunity to disaggregate jobs and roles into tasks and skills that can be segmented and potentially outsourced or automated, and when is it more appropriate to approach SWP from the standpoint of intact roles and jobs?
4. How do we balance short-term workforce and resource management with longer-term planning for the future of the business? On what time frame should SWP focus? What aspects of short-term workforce planning are real strategic differentiators for the business?
5. What aspects of context matter most for SWP? Is it the surrounding culture and climate for the roles being addressed; or is it the larger business environment of the firm? If your response is yes to the first two, how do you tailor and differentiate your SWP approach based on this context?
6. From a consulting standpoint, when are SWP practitioners best leveraged as a pair of hands and a reactive service, helping their client or executive team sustain the existing business and talent supply, and when are SWP practitioners best leveraged as proactive agents of company competitiveness, such as informing deliberation on potential acquisitions? One of our contributors, by the way, actually applies SWP insights as a resource to his company's decision process for mergers and acquisitions.

Our hope for the impact of this volume is, first, that readers will increase their awareness of how I-O psychology can have a greater voice in SWP practice. We also hope that SWP practice and practitioners will take on more of the mindset of I-O psychology. And, finally, we hope that SWP thinking will be applied to topics bigger than any single business unit or enterprise. We aspire to see SWP thinking prove helpful to issues related to the recent pandemic; to organizational justice, equity, diversity, and inclusion (JEDI); to business sustainability; to how we address the growing gig economy; and to the question of how quickly emerging technologies like generative artificial intelligence (AI) will change work. For graduate students and those new to SWP, this volume offers a degree of conversational competence that they can bring to their work and professional conversations. For those already working in SWP, this volume offers an array of best practices, methodologies, and emerging directions to advance their own thinking and practice.

What the Reader Should Look for from Contributors to This Volume

When we approached professionals we knew working in this arena, we framed their contributions as an opportunity to write for other professionals as well as a chance to strike a collegial rather than academic tone. We invited them to share rich case illustrations and accompany them with their insights and lessons learned. In many cases, readers will get to see the story behind the story, even the type of personal reflection one might hear in a private one-on-one conversation but which is often not provided in a formal article.

Several took up our challenge to describe how their professional training helped in pursuit of SWP practice, along with what they had to learn above and beyond their initial professional training. In all cases, contributors offer practical advice for those advising companies, whether as an internal or external practitioner.

We hope that this volume increases the enthusiasm for SWP fundamentals, awareness of best practices in design and delivery of SWP practices, and a curiosity about emerging directions that can lead one experiment with approach and perspective.

Overview of This Volume

The following is an overview of the chapters and topics covered in the pages ahead. Sixteen different contributions reflect the evolution of SWP thinking, variations of practice in large and small firms, SWP here in the United States and elsewhere around the world, lessons acquired over decades of practice, and practices for teaching this domain to graduate students.

We begin by providing some historical perspective. If you want to imagine the future, it sometimes helps to first consider the past. In Chapter 1, Dan Ward, whose workforce planning experience spans companies such as MITRE, EDS, NASA, Texaco, and GTE, recounts the origins of workforce planning, how it morphed to take on both HR and strategic nomenclature, and how models of the approach for this developed over several decades.

Tanya Moore, Chief People Officer for West Monroe and a veteran of HR centers of excellence at IBM, adds to this picture in Chapter 2 by presenting a maturity model of workforce planning. Each level represents a different set of characteristics of the SWP approach, moving from budget-driven, financial-headcount thinking, to a broader view of overall talent planning, to the deeper focus on analytics that capture both supply of and demand for needed talent, and finally to the incorporation of SWP into enterprise business rhythms with involvement from both HR and business leaders. Her case examples bring different stages of workforce planning maturity to life, along with some of her own lessons learned over time.

Sheri Feinzig, drawing on her experience as global head of workforce planning and analytics at Marsh & McLennan Companies and previously at IBM, incorporates ideas found within Dan's evolution of SWP and Tanya's maturity model to describe the current state-of-the-art practice in her overview of the role of data and analytics in SWP. In Chapter 3, she offers practitioners' perspectives on what it looks like to do SWP well, the types of internal and external sources of data one ideally seeks to capture, and how to remain ethical and responsible in the management of so much data, as well as an overview of the types of analytics one might desire to perform on the data obtained. She then takes this a step further, highlighting what one might look for among an internal SWP team and the skills necessary for such professionals. Sheri doesn't limit her focus to data and analytics: she also walks us through the consulting side, building buy-in from key stakeholders, implementing and following through on SWP initiatives, and addressing emerging issues.

What might SWP look like on a really large scale? We are fortunate to have two such contributions in this volume, one representing the U.S. federal sector and the other reflecting SWP evolution in a large enterprise outside the United States.

With millions of employees organized across multiple agencies and organizations, the U.S. federal government is almost in a class by itself. How would you embrace SWP for the overall enterprise and at the same time support each agency to manage its own SWP needs and approach? In Chapter 4, Laura Knowles and Samantha Adrignola, both from the U.S. Office of Personnel Management, help us see how professionals strive to balance enterprise decisions with agency-specific needs. Among their insights are the balancing act of rigor and practicality, long-term strategic planning and immediate tactical support, guiding agencies via common best practices and respecting the autonomy of individual agencies. They advise I-O psychologists of ways we can influence and improve workforce planning in the public sector.

Saudi Aramco is a global leader in the energy industry. Workforce planning goes hand in hand with the 80-year evolution of this company. In Chapter 5, Christian Hobson and Paul van Katwyk, who are each senior talent professionals at Aramco, share how national strategies and aspirations have always been fully embedded within SWP in this enterprise. They describe the historical and future role of I-O psychologists at special enterprises such as this one, providing personal advice that has served them well in this unique setting. I-O psychologists who aspire to work on a multinational and cross-cultural level will benefit from their experience and reflections.

The more someone stays engaged in the practice and delivery of SWP, the more likely they will see places where traditional approaches (i.e., how they were told the practice works) no longer fit the situations encountered over time. Adam Gibson, leader of SWP at EY in London, and EY colleague Nicola Oldroyd, provide one such contrast as they guide us through how they have come to think about "agile workforce planning." Building off Adam's book of the same name, in Chapter 6, they share case examples of what agile workforce planning looks like and the principles underlying their approach.

It's one thing to imagine the evolution of SWP approaches over time or to develop a maturity model, but how do you flex SWP for different organizational conditions? Would you employ the same game plan with every organization? In a large diverse enterprise, would you want to use an array of plans, tailoring each to the maturity and situation of the business? In Chapter 7, James D. Eyring, CEO of Singapore-based Organisational Solutions; Andrew Newmark, from Marriott International's APEC region; and Sunil Setlur, a strategy and culture advisor and former chief people officer of Gojek in Southeast Asia, look at the different challenges stemming from high- and low-speed growth environments. Their distinction guides the tailoring of an SWP approach for companies in the same industry that have different growth speeds. The plan may vary even for different business units within the same enterprise. The implications of their framework extend from SWP to talent management strategies, as well as to how you assess and then address questions of key talent changes based on growth trajectory.

Technology developments continue to reframe our approach to many aspects of work and life, and SWP is no exception. Brian Heger from Bristol Myers Squibb, long a practitioner of SWP, shares stories and insights of how SWP can be better enabled through a combined concentration on skills and AI and the cultivation of an internal marketplace. In Chapter 8, he describes the opportunities and challenges of artificial intelligence (AI) for SWP today, walks us through how his company took a deep dive into application, and how they translated lessons learned into actionable insights. For those planning to follow a similar route, this chapter will be of tremendous value. Brian leaves the reader with advice for mobilizing support of AI-enabled SWP, evaluating vendors as some components of this work are outsourced, and how to strengthen the relevance of AI applications as well as overcome nontechnological barriers to creating an internal marketplace that aligns with SWP. Finally, he offers a personal perspective on how to better tap the expertise of I-O psychologists to increase the likelihood of success in these endeavors.

The changing nature of work—where work occurs, how it is accomplished, and how organizations configure themselves—is partially enabled by the evolving world of technology. In Chapter 9, David Creelman, at Creelman Research; Alexis A. Fink, vice president of people analytics and workforce strategy at Meta; and Dave Ulrich, professor at the University of Michigan Ross School of Business and principal of RBL Group, describe an emerging perspective on SWP, one that many companies and practitioners are also exploring. They see a shift from strategic *workforce* planning to strategic *work-task* planning. Note the explicit change in language. Rather than assume the work revolves around and reinforces headcount, locations, levels, positions, and jobs as we have traditionally conceived of them, these contributors analyze work to the level of tasks, increasing options for companies to contract out or automate certain tasks.

Whereas some contributors to this volume are breaking SWP down to the task level and skills and then applying technology and AI to innovate new opportunities, other contributors look at SWP as competitive differentiation around the full role, especially for professionals. Andrea Fischbach, of the

German Police University, and Benjamin Schneider, University of Maryland emeritus professor and organizational research consultant, look at SWP as it intertwines with the culture and climate for professionalism in firms. The inherent ambiguity and level of discretionary action embedded in most professional roles require a different type of workforce planning. In Chapter 10, they describe leadership, HR management, and job design practices that, in combination, define the organizational culture and climate for professionalism that will inevitably lead SWP practices to succeed, to limit success, or to outright fail over time.

In shaping this volume, we had a personal network of SWP professionals we could contact. We also searched for others we did not know to find those who were actively sharing their insights via conferences and social media. We are fortunate to have met Adam McKinnon, people data and analytics leader of Reece Group, and Kanella Salapatas, group head of people data and analytics at QBE, two Australian professionals, each with unique SWP experience. As they share their respective stories and insights, in Chapter 11, a set of "adaptive" workforce planning approaches becomes apparent. They have their own perspective on the maturity of workforce planning, and SWP is only midway along their continuum. In addition to data quality and the overall process, they consider the user experience of workforce planning. They also have some novel applications of SWP, including helping to enhance how a company approaches mergers and acquisitions.

Just how do CEOs view SWP? David Reimer, CEO, and Adam Bryant, senior managing director, both from The ExCo Group and longtime C-suite consultants, highlight a notable contrast: for all the discipline and rigor that strategic workforce planners bring to their work, the CEO's own ideas and blind spots represent a huge variable in an organization's ability to embrace wise counsel. In Chapter 12, they provide us with a playbook for better engaging this key stakeholder, even noting ways that many CEOs have shifted their own mindsets about SWP since the onset of the pandemic.

Whereas Reimer and Bryant broadly advise us about CEOs and the C-suite, Edie Goldberg, of E. L. Goldberg & Associates, has discovered a niche within SWP that readily draws executive attention. She works with fast-moving startup companies, where change is rapid internally and externally and where a disruptive future can be just a day away. In Chapter 13, she shares her scenario-based planning approach to SWP, which stays close to competitive positioning of the firm and therefore is never just another HR practice but is core to the viability of the firm.

In our contemplation of what topics to include in this volume, we wondered about the intersection of SWP with equity, diversity, and inclusion (EDI). We know a good number of professionals working in the SWP arena and many also working in the EDI area, but how many are simultaneously working on these together? What blind spot might be reflected in the lack of overlap and combined practice? In Chapter 14, Juliet R. Aiken and Tori Glascock, of Conducere Consulting, deliver a powerful story of what happens when these two domains are explicitly addressed at the same time. They take one EDI variant—justice, equity, diversity, and inclusion (JEDI)—and combine it with SWP, presenting a novel conception of "just workforce planning." The word *just* isn't about simplifying workforce planning: it is an explicit intent to instill concepts of JEDI into SWP thinking, process, and impact. In this framing of SWP, we see a path to address long-standing EDI issues in the ways we imagine the future, which will allow us to design novel collaboration across HR practices and take a stand on what it means to really do the work of enhancing diversity and inclusion.

For those who have ever privately wondered how their graduate training and subsequent experience as an I-O psychologist help address life's really big issues, the next contribution may supply inspiration. The COVID-19 pandemic was a worldwide event, and it continues today to impact people, jobs, and companies everywhere and all at once. In Chapter 15, Michael Bazigos, managing director of strategy consulting in the talent and organization practice of Accenture, shares a special story of how one company enlisted others and together adapted SWP approaches to respond to a global crisis, building solutions across companies, industries, and competitors at a time when the world needed novel approaches and practical actions. In doing so, the focal company increased its capacity to rapidly build out a suite of related SWP solutions—that is, skill proximity, a process other companies can learn from.

Most contributors told us how they learned about SWP after graduate school. They may have had a great foundation and developed analytical skills in their formal training as I-O psychologists, but the practice of SWP was an on-the-job experience for them. We wondered if and how some I-O psychologists might be teaching SWP today, and we identified three colleagues who were already teaching SWP in graduate programs for I-O psychology. Two are practitioners who teach as adjunct faculty; one is a full-time faculty member. Steve Weingarden, CEO of the consulting firm Innovators of Change; Nikita Arun, director of the Masters in I-O Psychology program at the University of Maryland, College Park; and Juliet R. Aiken, head of consulting at Conducere Consulting, collaborated in Chapter 16 to distill their experience teaching SWP at the graduate level. In addition to sharing some of their own lessons learned as faculty teaching this topic, they reached out to alumni of their programs to capture insights from the perspective of recent graduate students, now early-career practitioners.

In our concluding chapter, we look to the emerging directions of SWP, building on best practices and applied psychology and incorporating insights across our contributors, and we offer a final set of recommendations for practitioners and students of this work. We make several challenges to elevate the potential for impact. As you read the various chapters, we encourage you to be alert for

1. *Best practices* you might import into your own work, department, or consulting approach.
2. *Emerging directions* that not only expand application of SWP practices but even transform the language you can use to shape your work.
3. *Competing values* that underlie SWP, how you can recognize these, and the inherent tensions around what type of work you focus upon.
4. *Insights* that will help you tailor your own mental model to recognize what is really strategic, what the appropriate time horizon is for your SWP efforts, and when your SWP perspective might center on tasks, roles, people, organizational units, society at large, or some combination.

References

Gibson, A. (2021). *Agile workforce planning: How to align people with organizational strategy for improved performance*. Kogan Page Limited.

Sokol, M. (2019). Can strategic workforce planning still guide us toward the future? Executive editor introduction: Modern workforce planning. *People + Strategy, 42*(4), 4.

Ward, D., and Tripp, D. (2013). *Positioned: Strategic workforce planning that gets the right person in the right job*. AMACOM.

1

Strategic Workforce Planning

How Can Our Legacy Frame the Future?

Dan L. Ward

In 2016, HR People & Strategy Association gave me a Life-Time Achievement Award. The accompanying citation noted my 40+ years in the forefront of shaping and sculpting the practice that has become known as *strategic workforce planning* (SWP). It was a career pinnacle moment.

One week later, a local reporter suggested taking photos of me holding the award in front of the MITRE Corporate Headquarters. After a few standard snapshots, he said, "I've got a great idea" and grabbed the award out of my hands. The crystal was heavier than he anticipated. He lost his grip, and I watched in stunned horror as this coveted award hit the bricks and smashed into a hundred fragments.

This may be a near-perfect metaphor for working in SWP. From a peak summit to smashed on the rocks in only a week. Like mountaineers, we have struggled to find a workable route to mission success in the quest to better align people resources with organizational mission. Sometime, havoc awaits us on our return. (On a happier note, HRPS soon provided a replacement copy.)

History suggests that success has many parents while failure is typically an orphan. Variations of this truism can be found in almost any culture, including professional association meetings whenever the topic of SWP has emerged. To fully understand how the field has evolved and why so many efforts failed or succeeded spectacularly, it can be helpful to consider the evolution of the field. I close the chapter with reflections about how our legacy of SWP can frame our future.

Dan L. Ward, *Strategic Workforce Planning* In: *Strategic Workforce Planning*. Edited by: Marc Sokol and Beverly Tarulli, Oxford University Press. © Society for Industrial and Organizational Psychology 2024.
DOI: 10.1093/oso/9780197759745.003.0002

My Professional Orientation

Serendipity plays a role in every career. My good fortune was to attend one of three universities that was funded by the US Department of Labor to grow "manpower economists" (Columbia University, University of Houston and the University of North Texas). Workforce economics added sociology and demography to a strong labor economics foundation, balancing the statistical "what, when, and how" analytics with "who" and "why" insights.

My good fortune continued as a management scientist when my very visible forecast of future college recruiting needs precisely hit the actual requirements. Wise enough not to admit my success was due to errors that cancelled each other out, I was able to move to another position before the opportunity to fail occurred.

The educational background I gained provided a rich toolkit of statistical and analytical methods. Supportive leaders provided opportunities to explore and learn from mistakes. Formal and informal networks provided a community of peers from many disciplines. While we did not always agree on methods, we shared a common vision for improving the alignment of people resources with organizational mission and doing so in ways that provided enriched career opportunities for employees.

Ancient Roots

Some have suggested that Samuel Pepys opened the door to formalize people planning in 1676, when he called for more effectively planning the development of a future officer cadre for the Royal Navy. During a series of conference dinners in the early 1980s, James Walker, Thomas Bechet, Bill Maki, Rob Tripp, and I regularly debated the origins of people planning. We eventually agreed it probably had Stone Age roots. There seemed nothing theoretical about it—the very survival of the tribe or clan depended on applying their best resources to providing food, clothing, and shelter. Better hunting and gathering practices were passed down verbally from one generation to the next via myths and legends.

The Pyramids, the Great Wall of China, and the Roman Army are among the greatest human endeavors of their time. Each demanded massive numbers of workers to achieve the intended result. Unskilled slave labor was key to the bulk of these feats, but each required people with specialized skills—architects, stone masons, riggers, engineers, builders, planners, etc. All these had to be found, trained, deployed, and maintained. The creation of specialized capabilities took place over scores, even hundreds of years; the need for specialty labor had to be anticipated.

Successful practices resulted in growth and expansion. Geographical expansion often resulted in conflict with other groups. Hunting skills were adapted for defensive and offensive purposes. Gathering evolved into logistics. The need for better shelter evolved into more sophisticated types of construction. Working together, our species moved from leveraging natural rain shelters and windbreaks to simple housing to homes, villages, walls, roads, bridges, religious sites, etc. A tribe could not just wake up one morning and build Stonehenge, the Pyramids, or the Great Wall of China. Enduring collaborative community efforts require some sort of thinking ahead (e.g., serious planning). As fourth-century BC Chinese philosopher Kuan Chung Tzu noted, "If you want to plan for a lifetime, develop men."

Formalizing SWP

The 1950s, '60s, and '70s

In 1967, Eric Vetter published *Manpower Planning for High Talent Personnel*. Eric defined the challenge as "getting the right person at the right place at the right time." From his perspective, the "right" person implied an adequately capable and affordable individual. In 1967, the right place did not include a virtual workplace. The right time reflected a work environment in the early stage of transitioning from the Industrial Age to the Information Age. Of course, people also immediately began tweaking his simple definition, but variations of right person, place, and time have endured.

Eric's work was of course rooted in earlier thinking: in the mid-1950s and into the late 1960s, a number of European social scientists published articles focused on labor movement within organizations. Typically referred to as "flows," a common theme was to separate the analysis between the movement of the demand for workers, the movement of the supply of workers, and the movement of the interaction between supply and demand.

London School of Economics professor D. J. Bartholomew was prolific as an individual author and in accumulating collections of the works of others. Bartholomew's articles on the prediction of labor turnover dating from the mid-1950s set the stage for future actuarially based studies. His *Manpower planning* anthology, published by Penguin books in 1976, offers a great collection of works from the late 1960s and early 1970s for those interested in digging more deeply into this period.

Primarily focusing on balancing the overall talent supply and demand, it is interesting that some of these earlier studies also looked for what were considered the social consequences of staffing cycles. Michael Lewis, A. R. Smith, A. Young, and others analyzed more than 100 years of Royal Navy promotional practices. They noted promotion and staffing practices during periods of growth were not scaled back during periods of staff reductions. This resulted in top-heavy organizations and reduced spans of control. This effectively devalued the higher-level positions because routine work still needed to be done, and it migrated upward. This became known as the *Bardot-Braddock cycle*. Few organizations have the multiple-century tenacity of the Royal Navy, but it is interesting that contemporary organization development studies have largely missed or ignored these earlier insights about the consequences of not maintaining proportionality between leaders and subordinates.

In 1969, James W. Walker's *Harvard Business Review* article, "Forecasting manpower needs" brought formalized people planning to a much broader business audience. Walker and Elmer H. Burack co-edited a collection of articles entitled *Manpower planning and programming*, describing the state of workforce planning practices across industry. Walker founded the Human Resource Planning Society (HRPS) in 1977, and he organized its first annual conference in Atlanta in 1978, with 225 attendees. (HRPS eventually became HR People & Strategy and is now the executive networking arm of the Society of Human Resource Management [SHRM].)

Big Models

Much was written during the late 1960s and early '70s on defining ways to anticipate future workforce opportunities. Despite this passion for growing and developing the workforce, the stimulus that really accelerated growth in the field came from litigation rather than goodwill. AT&T lost a major class action race discrimination challenge in the mid-1970s. As part of the settlement, the AT&T Bell Labs subsidiary developed a massive time share mainframe workforce analysis and modeling package called the *Interactive Flow Simulator* (IFS). Written in FORTRAN, IFS users commonly quipped that it was "user-hostile software." For those who mastered the tedious programming interface, however, IFS offered a discrete flow renewal model well capable of simulating and anticipating future workforce flows (losses, transfers, promotions, hires, leaves of absence, etc.).

A typical IFS model generated several hundred pages of output, perhaps of dubious accuracy, but the historical workforce analysis generated transition tables on a scale not available previously. Analysis was based on better-documented historical movement of staffs and provided insights needed to define improved utilization of staffing opportunities for the future. Much of 21st-century workforce data analytics was foreshadowed by this seminal 1970s tool. The tool was not as user friendly as modern analytics packages, however, and the robust analytical methodology was so tedious that it was not for the faint of heart.

Little Models

By the early 1980s, a variety of workforce models became commercially available. Simple *Markov manpower models* were particularly easy to implement as Excel spreadsheets and quickly displaced the more cumbersome simulation approach. In conference presentations, Dr. Michael Hawkins suggested that manpower models were either demand/pull or supply/push. Vacancies or opportunities occur either because someone created a new position due to growth or restructuring or else an incumbent was lost from a current position. The loss of an incumbent could be due to an exit from the organization (attrition) or due to internal movement such as a transfer or promotion. Promotion or transfers typically follow historical patterns based on tradition and policy/practice. These movement paths could be modified to anticipate a policy/practice change. Skilled users could offer insights into the impact of policies.

A variety of workforce modeling and forecasting tools evolved, and each had its advocates. Once again, litigation prompted another breakthrough in approach. *Roberts v. Texaco*, in 1995, was a race discrimination case resulting in a $177 million settlement against Texaco—the largest settlement in history up until that time. Part of that settlement required Texaco to plan and achieve strong positive progress in minority representation across all management levels.

Leveraging the workforce modeling techniques pioneered in AT&T's IFS approach, Texaco developed *JOBFLO*. The new model provided

IFS-like capabilities by stacking simplified Excel models on personal computer platforms. Working under a court-directed consent decree, Texaco allocated 50% of all anticipated future staffing opportunities to members of protected classes. The model's simulation examples enabled staffing strategies so that Texaco met the court-mandated representation goals in less than 4 years.

Texaco's accomplishments were more remarkable because they occurred during a business decline cycle. Overall headcount declined in each of those years. Other employers had routinely used declining headcounts as a rationale for not meeting workforce inclusion goals, but Texaco proved progress was possible via better planning. Other employers, including Motorola, Mobil, and Coca Cola, had similar litigation challenges in subsequent years and adopted similar workforce models leveraging Texaco's successful example.

A Standard Approach

By the mid-1990s, most workforce planning practitioners were using variations of what Tom Bechet called his *human resource planning process flow* as shown in Figure 1.1.

Bechet's approach was adapted and modified by numerous practitioners, such as the evolved variation used at Texaco in the late 1990s, shown in Figure 1.2.

It continued to evolve, as seen in the process used by EDS in the early 2000s, shown in Figure 1.3.

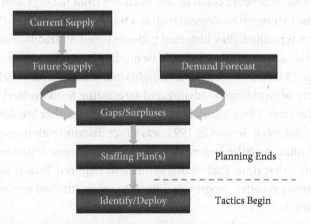

Figure 1.1 Human resource planning process flow.
Adapted from Bechet (2008)

STRATEGIC WORKFORCE PLANNING 21

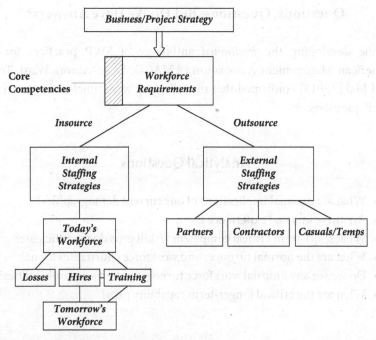

Figure 1.2 Human resource planning process.
Used at Texaco.

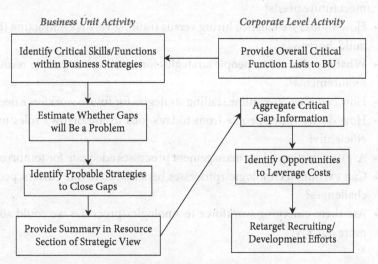

Figure 1.3 Strategic workforce planning process.
Used at EDS.

Questions, Questions: But Do We Have Answers?

While developing the *Positioned* anthology of SWP practices for the American Management Association (AMACOM), co-editors Ward, Tripp, and Maki (2013) confirmed that the following were timeless key executive SWP questions.

Analytical Questions

- What are unusual implications of our current demographics?
- Are there unusual experience gaps?
- What short-term critical competency/skill gaps do we anticipate?
- What are the normal turnover and workforce churn rates for us?
- Do we see any unusual workforce turnover patterns or probabilities?
- What are the critical longer-term capability gaps?

Strategy Questions

- Does our organizational structure align with our operational reality?
- Are our existing staffing/recruiting/outplacement practices sufficient to meet future needs?
- How should we balance hiring versus training versus contracting (buy, build, borrow?)
- What are alternative people strategies for meeting our people resource requirements?
- How could we streamline staffing strategies for future workforce needs?
- How do we move people from today's jobs to tomorrow's roles more efficiently?
- Are our existing talent management processes adequate for tomorrow?
- Can existing technologies/processes better address our current people challenges?
- Are there emerging workforce technologies/processes we could adopt more quickly?

In developing these questions, I had the advantage of having participated in a series of EDS senior leadership meetings in late 2001 and early 2002.

Consultant Ram Charam suggested "the world is full of planners, but very few who can execute." Analysis paralysis can be real. Too often, people planners offer reams of data that are perceived by leaders as little more than interesting trivia and of limited tactical or operational values.

In one of these meetings, EDS CEO Dick Brown complained that people wanted to show him the organization is in trouble by using "fancy" charts and graphs. In frustration, he said "Don't show me I am in trouble with a prettier shade of red. Give me something that helps me find the path to green!" This charge is often levied at the current state of practice in "data analytics." More sophisticated machine learning and artificial intelligence (AI) practices have increased the volume of analysis. We bring volumes of data, but do we bring new insights to find the path to green? A Pareto analysis might question whether the incremental value exceeds the incremental cost.

Shortly before she retired as the resident workforce planning subject matter expert for The Conference Board in 2019, Mary Young told me that she was dismayed at the number of practitioners whose data analytics seem never to move beyond descriptive statistics. It is not sufficient to simply describe the current or near-term future situation. To be effective and truly have impact, SWP must be able to *inform strategy and action.*

Communities of Practice

Early HRPS conference attendees were often evenly split between math-oriented model builders and career designers. The former focused on building better analytics tools and forecasting models. The career management community saw the challenge as better understanding career paths and providing methods for individual developmental planning. During the conferences, there were occasionally heated exchanges, with one camp suggesting the others should go to a more appropriate venue, but mostly it was a shared journey of exploration.

Many early members were active in multiple professional communities. This included the American Society for Personnel Administration (ASPA), the American Society for Training and Development (ASTD), The Institute for Management Sciences (TIMS), the Operations Research Society of America (ORSA), Human Resource Systems Professionals (HRSP), various other programming and information sciences disciplines, systems engineering, industrial engineering, engineering management societies, statistical and/or mathematical subgroups, and even early AI groups. Perhaps the greatest contribution of HRPS was in providing a venue for sharing SWP experiences among those whose primary interests lay elsewhere.

As the HRPS annual conferences became more generic to reach a broader audience, some hard-core workforce planners decided to meet separately from the formal events. The first SWP Advanced Practitioners' Colloquia was an invitation-only event. A dozen of the "best" people in the field attended.

It became an annual event, each hosted by a member. The host provided a meeting room and snacks, but otherwise the attendees covered their expenses. The formal "cost" of attending was to make a detailed and candid presentation on latest practices. Attendees agreed no one would cite another person or organization's work without specific pre-approval. As a leading-edge technology/process exchange meeting, this approach more quickly spread better practices among the leaders in SWP. It specifically avoided the normal restrictions on freely sharing proprietary information typically encountered when sharing information in a "public" venue such as a conference or journal publication. Hosted as a working session at a business location, it avoided the "boondoggle" label that often made it difficult to attend an event at an "executive retreat" location during the late 1990s. The last colloquium was in 1999, although other groups evolved in the early 2000s, targeting subtopics such as attrition and retention.

The original HRPS meetings mellowed over time. In time, HRPS became part of SHRM, and the focus of meetings shifted away from SWP. Per the HRPS website, it is now the "executive networking" arm of SHRM. The Society for Industrial Organizational Psychology (SIOP) was well established as a welcoming home for people who focused on strategically anticipating future workforce challenges and championing an integrated approach for people planning. One could easily argue that SIOP is much closer today to the original intent of growing a SWP discipline than is HRPS or any other professional group.

Advice for Those Seeking a Career Embracing SWP

Early to mid-career builders often ask: "How can I get a seat at the table?" The "table" in this context is figurative, referring to how one can make sure he or she will be included when important decisions are made: A cynic could note that being in the room when important decisions are made is not the same as being an important decision-maker. A perhaps wiser approach is to worry less about being in the room and more about being known as the person who always brings something of value to any discussion about the workforce. It is better to be sought out to be at the table instead of insisting on simply being present.

Parting Thoughts

The practice of SWP has seen a continuous succession of various tools and methods. Practitioners sometimes become so enamored with a "flavor of the month" that they risk losing sight of what their executive customer demands. There are exceptions, but most senior leaders look to SWP to help inform better decision-making and not to usurp their own executive leadership prerogatives. If I had to choose between data science expertise versus management consulting skills, the later would win. This is perhaps the primary reason SIOP members have generally been more successful in SWP than those who depended only on number crunching skills. Effective SWP requires a blend and is perhaps best executed with a partnership that provides both.

I leave the reader with several time-tested lessons, ones that stayed with me and which I believe offer value to the next generation of those who continue to grow and evolve SWP:

1. Being mindful of history helps us to recognize old wine in new bottles and avoid chasing distractions that have already proved to be ineffective in the past.
2. A blend of analytic and consulting skills will outperform excellence in only one of these skills.
3. Individual accolades, like my lifetime achievement award, will all be forgotten someday, but passing along insights to the next generation of professionals is timeless.
4. Great conversations about workforce planning stand the test of time—listen, learn, and lead the way

References

Bartholomew, D. J. (1976). *Manpower planning: Selected readings*. Penguin.

Bechet, T. P. (2008). *Strategic staffing: A comprehensive system for effective workforce planning*. AMACOM/SHRM.

Vetter, E. W. (1967). *Manpower planning for high talent personnel*. University of Michigan Press.

Walker, J. W. (1969). Forecasting manpower needs. *Harvard Business Review*, 47(2), 152–164.

Walker, J. W., and Burack, E. H. (1972). *Manpower planning and programming*. Allyn & Bacon.

Ward, D. L., Tripp, R., and Maki, B. (2013). *Positioned: Strategic workforce planning that gets the right person in the right job*. AMACOM.

2
A Practitioner's Guide to Maturing Strategic Workforce Planning in Your Organization

Tanya Moore

At a recent conference, I was speaking on the topic of *strategic workforce planning* (SWP) and started out by asking the audience a few questions:

- How many people in the audience know—consistently and accurately—how many employees you have working for you? *Approximately half of the room raised their hand.*
- How many people in the audience know—consistently and accurately—how many employees you have working for you, and the roles they are in in? *A bit fewer than half of the room raised their hand.*
- How many people in the audience know—consistently and accurately—how many employees you have, what roles they are in, and what skills they have? *About an eighth of the room raised their hand.*
- How many people in the audience know—consistently and accurately—how many employees you have, what roles they are in, what skills they have, and the expertise level of those skills? *One gentleman raised his hand.*

I shared with the audience that their responses were very consistent with organizations across the globe. In fact, only 28% of organizations leverage data-driven insights to create proactive, enterprise-level human capital strategies (Harris, 2022). Even fewer plan and execute a workforce strategy centered around business-critical skills. I congratulated the gentleman who had raised his hand and asked how many people were in his company. He replied: "Two." We all got a good laugh.

The reality, however, is that this topic is no laughing matter.

Tanya Moore, *A Practitioner's Guide to Maturing Strategic Workforce Planning in Your Organization*
In: *Strategic Workforce Planning*. Edited by: Marc Sokol and Beverly Tarulli, Oxford University Press.
© Society for Industrial and Organizational Psychology 2024. DOI: 10.1093/oso/9780197759745.003.0003

Navigating Uncharted Waters

Changing demographics, global tension, inflation, and the pace of technology advancements have resulted in all organizations working under unprecedented workforce circumstances.

A Global Labor Shortage

- By 2030, there will be a global human talent shortage of more than 85 million people, or roughly equivalent to the population of Germany. Left unchecked, in 2030, that talent shortage could result in about $8.5 trillion in unrealized annual revenues (Franzino et al., 2023).
- Long-term supply dynamics will continue to be a major force that creates a persistent gap between employer demand for new hires and the supply of candidates, resulting in a global labor shortage for years to come (Bremen, 2023).

A Global Skills Crisis

- Three hundred million workers globally will need to switch jobs and/or learn new skills as digitization, automation, and advances in artificial intelligence (AI) disrupt the world of work (Toh, 2023).
- Skill sets for jobs have changed by approximately 25% since 2015. By 2027, this number is expected to double (LinkedIn Learning, 2023).

A Continued Recalibration of What Workers Value in Their Work Experience

- Employee well-being, hybrid work, skills-based career growth, and being with a company whose values match their own all top the list of employee demands for their work experience (Kropp and McRae, 2022).
- Forty-four percent of employees are "job seekers," according to Willis Towers Watson's 2022 Global Benefits Attitudes Survey (Iacurci, 2022).

While one of these circumstances in isolation is not unusual throughout history, it is a new dynamic to have them all happen at once. A labor and skills shortage in a highly competitive business environment while people make an active decision to sit out of the workforce—and while the employee has the upper hand to dictate what they want from their work experience—is like nothing we have seen before.

These factors—especially in concert—result in a highly complex talent landscape that requires an entirely new level of proactive, data-driven analysis to understand the areas of greatest talent risk and develop targeted talent strategies that will have real business impact. Along with data and technology, it also requires a more human connection between employers and employees. The greatest challenge of all is that this requirement comes at a time when more than half of organizations struggle to execute even the most basic level of workforce planning (Harris, 2022).

Strategic Workforce Planning Defined

SWP is the process of ensuring that the organization has the right number of people with the right skills and the right expertise level of skills, in the right place, at the right time, to deliver on current and future business outcomes.

At the core, the steps of SWP have not changed: understand your current talent needs, understand future talent needs, and close the gaps.

What has changed is the *how*. Gone are the days of Finance and/or human resources (HR)-driven headcount reports and spreadsheets. To move with the speed and scale that today's competitive landscape requires, companies are now required to have a robust strategic workforce plan that (1) is seen as a vital business function versus an HR-only activity, (2) has skills at the core of the strategy, and (3) is heavily informed by data and enabled by technology.

Stronger outcomes are achieved when SWP is implemented (Figure 2.1). A 2022 research report from Sapient Insights Group found an increase in business outcomes, HR outcomes, and talent outcomes when workforce planning is implemented (Harris, 2022). Specifically, on a 5-point scale, talent, HR, and business outcomes average 2.8 when no workforce planning is executed. With the implementation of basic headcount or labor-based workforce planning, outcomes increase. Outcomes jump to an average of 3.10 when SWP is implemented. In addition, Sapient Insights' 2022 Annual HR Systems Survey found that workforce planning that included business data

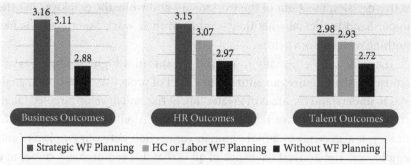

Figure 2.1 Stronger business outcomes with workforce planning.

and position management was the second highest positive correlating factor to making HR a strategic business function.

> **Practitioner Tip!**
>
> Convincing stakeholders of the importance of SWP can be challenging at times. Identify a business problem, start small with a pilot, and demonstrate small wins.
> Alternately, in a tight talent market, if you're one of the companies that is losing about as many people as you're hiring, leverage that data to start a new narrative!

Workforce Planning Maturity Model

There are four levels of the workforce planning maturity (Figure 2.2).

Level 1

Budget-driven planning, often from a financial headcount perspective. How many people do we need to execute the work, now and in the future? This

MATURING STRATEGIC WORKFORCE PLANNING 31

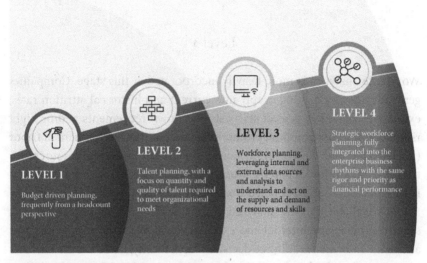

Figure 2.2 Levels of workforce planning maturity.

methodology tends to be short-term focused, reactive, and lacks detail and insights to make meaningful decisions.

Level 2

Talent planning, with a focus on quantity and quality of talent required. In this level of maturity, companies look not only at headcount, but also incorporate methodologies such as a "9 Box" talent management model to determine the quality of talent within the company. These "9 Box" talent discussions lead to conversations and actions around promotions, development opportunities, performance counseling, critical skill gaps, and succession planning. While this level starts to incorporate longer-term concepts, this approach continues to be primarily short-term based.

At this level of workforce planning, companies often look to standardize their role and skill taxonomy, recognizing that this standardization is a prerequisite to progressing to more mature stages of workforce planning. In this work, companies develop a common and consistent role and skill structure throughout the company which builds a critical foundation for future workforce efforts.

Level 3

Workforce analytics is more heavily incorporated at this stage. Companies generally start by digging deeply into current and historical attrition rates, exit survey data, key project starts/stops, known retirements and/or flight risks, learning consumption, promotion rates, etc. The Department of Labor (for US data) and the World Economic Forum can be helpful resources for this level of workforce analysis. Modern technology tools are often procured in this phase to support detailed workforce analysis at scale.

Once available data are analyzed, companies at this level of maturity will secure and evaluate internal and external workforce data to draw insights and make informed workforce decisions. Specifically, based on the business strategy and outlook, what is the *demand* for people with specific skills—both now and in the future? How many people are required, in what specific roles, and with what specific skills and competencies? In what location(s) are they needed? Can the role be hybrid or remote? Is demand for specific roles and skills in the business growing or declining? What HR actions and programs are required to prepare?

What is the *supply* of resources with specific skills available—both internally within the company and externally in the market? How many people are available with required levels of skills and competencies, and in what locations/markets? Organizations often leverage data services from companies such as Gartner, Lightcast, and LinkedIn to understand the external supply of roles and skills in the market. With this level of workforce supply and demand data, highly targeted HR programs and actions are developed and executed for maximum impact.

Level 4

SWP is fully incorporated into the enterprise business rhythms, led by HR and with highly active involvement from business leaders, finance, operations, and IT. Workforce planning is no longer seen as an HR process, but

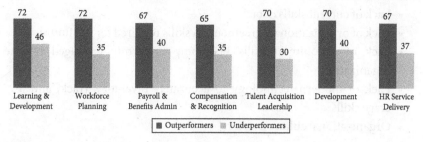

Figure 2.3 Outperforming companies leverage artificial intelligence.

instead is seen as a business process vital to the enterprise and reviewed with the same level of rigor and priority as financial performance.

Both short and long terms are evaluated and planned. Analysis is at the skills level, with data insights informing all pieces of the HR strategy and actions, including recruiting, training, reskilling, moving employees between projects, workforce optimization, high-potential programs, succession management, and compensation. Scenario and "what if" planning is incorporated.

As shown in Figure 2.3, organizations that outperform their peers in revenue and profit leverage AI to predict workforce needs and close talent gaps. As an example, 35% of underperforming companies leverage AI in their SWP efforts, compared to 72% of outperforming companies. The same applies to other areas of the HR portfolio such as learning and development and talent acquisition (IBM Institute for Business Value, 2017).

Skills Are the Heart of Strategic Workforce Planning

All companies—regardless of industry—are required to navigate an ever-changing external landscape to achieve business outcomes. This requires people with relevant skills. The challenge, however, is that skilled resources can be hard to come by in this increasingly competitive labor market, and the skills required to succeed change almost daily with accelerating changes in digital technology. In addition, the workforce now demands investment in keeping their skills current with industry trends as a key part of their employee experience. The complexity of shifting to a skills-based workforce strategy can be challenging. Common roadblocks include:

- Lack of current skills data
- Lack of organizational agreement on skills required for the future
- Lack of a common skills taxonomy uniformly leveraged by the organization
- Lack of modern technology to accurately inventory, track, and leverage skills
- Organizational culture barriers

To progress a skills-based workforce strategy, organizations must develop and leverage a common skills taxonomy. This work is hard, and the rewards are not often seen until after the work is complete, but it is critically important to build a common skills foundation that can be used as the core data element for all people-related processes. This core data element is also critical for companies to benefit from the myriad of solutions available in the market that leverage AI and machine learning that will help drive a modern SWP program as well as provide a personalized employee experience around recruiting, learning, internal mobility, career growth—even compensation. Bottom line: it's a critical foundational step that cannot be skipped.

What Is a Skills Taxonomy?

A *skills taxonomy* is part of an overall job architecture. In a job architecture, a company defines the jobs across the enterprise and then organizes them into job families (a group of jobs that involve similar work and require similar training and expertise). As an example, Finance is a job family. This job family could then be broken down into subfamilies of Accounting, Budget, Financial Operations, etc. Within each of these subfamilies there are specific jobs that an employee could perform, such as Accountant, Controller, Financial Specialist, etc. Each of these specific jobs would require certain skills.

A skills taxonomy is a hierarchical system of classification that can categorize and organize skills. A skills taxonomy includes technical skills, leadership/management skills, and "soft skills" (also called "success skills" or "professional skills"; e.g., communication, creativity, problem-solving). A skills taxonomy will name the skill, define the skill, define proficiency levels for the skill, and define which skills are required for which jobs. A skills taxonomy also provides the capability to assess current skills, signal future required skills, and define skill gaps—at both an individual and summary levels.

> **Practitioner Tip!**
>
> Many external vendors are experts in the field of job architecture and skills taxonomy. These vendors provide taxonomies available for purchase that are kept up to date with changing industry trends. While most of the taxonomy will be useful right out of the box, you are able to easily customize this for your organization.
>
> Many organizations I've worked with try to create a homegrown system and find that years later they are no farther than when they started. Leverage the experts in this space!

Sources of Data to Inform Strategic Workforce Planning

SWP requires an understanding of the present and the future, from both an internal and external perspective.

> **Practitioner Tip!**
>
> Identifying and communicating data can have a significant impact.
>
> When I was leading Career and Skills at IBM, I realized that we were doing a very good job communicating to the workforce that they needed to continually grow their skills to keep pace with changes in technology. I also realized that we needed to do a better job in transparently sharing with the workforce the roles and skills that mattered most to the future of IBM and our clients.
>
> We started by sharing a list of roles and skills that were growing in demand. Sharing this data alone was highly impactful. Over time, we shared additional information, linking the list of roles and skills to available training offerings and open positions.
>
> Sharing this information resulted in a significant increase in the number of employees who sought out in-demand skill-building opportunities.
>
> Don't underestimate the power of sharing data!

Examples of Internal Data Sources

Business strategy and competitive landscape:

- Business goals, priorities, and performance results
- Business strengths, weaknesses, opportunities, threats
- Business-critical roles and skills
- Key business unit/or organizational needs
- Primary competitors and their business goals, priorities, and results
- Current client/or customer satisfaction and future looking customer expectations

Talent acquisition:

- Hires per year demographics
- Hire acceptance rates, including reasons for candidates declining offers
- Time and cost to hire
- Retention of new hires in first 90, 180, and 360 days
- Candidate experience ratings
- Employee value proposition

Learning and development:

- Learning consumed and in what areas
- Percent promotions per year in what roles/skills
- Percent involuntary exits per year in what roles/skills
- Emerging skills required
- Training spend

Workforce profile:

- Workforce demographics (headcount, cost, diversity, location, etc.)
- Skill demographics
- Attrition rates and reasons
- Competitors losing talent to and why
- Employee engagement rates
- Retirement profile
- Market competitiveness of compensation
- External workplace perception (e.g., Glassdoor, Indeed, etc.)

Compensation:

- Compensation demographics by job classification, location, performance
- Compensation competitiveness with market

Examples of External Data Sources

Government data:

- Graduation rates
- Employment rates
- Economic indicators
- Macroeconomic trends
- Occupational outlooks
- Relevant and/or new regulations
- Industry trends

Competitor information:

- Annual report(s)
- Industry report(s)
- Merger and acquisition information
- News and press
- External workplace perception (e.g., Glassdoor, Indeed, etc.)
- Competitor benchmarks (turnover, cost per hire, time to fill, etc.)

Research and professional services companies:

- Industry benchmarks
- Industry trends
- Labor market competition reports
- Talent availability by skill and geography

Getting Started

With more than half of organizations struggling to execute even the most basic level of workforce planning, getting started can be a daunting challenge. Below are several examples to demonstrate how various companies are making progress. Note that while starting at different points and using different levels of technology, with the right focus every company can make significant progress that can then be matured over time.

Dutch Railway

The Netherlands has one of the top railroad infrastructures in the world, supporting both passengers and cargo. To meet future demand, Dutch Railway will need to increase capacity by 30%, which will require new technology to automate large parts of the current traffic control processes. This new automation will also require new workforce skills. The railway partnered with Bright & Co. to understand the impact on the workforce and what decisions and actions would be required to align the workforce with its future operational model (van Dijk, 2022).

HR established a core team with HR business partners, HR data analytics & operations, and people strategy and analytics experts from Bright & Co. This core team took a data-driven approach to estimating the availability and composition of the workforce based on currently available personnel data. These data were then reviewed extensively with managers and subject matter experts to evaluate factors that could influence workforce demand.

> **Practitioner Tip!**
>
> Don't underestimate the power of starting with low-tech tools like Excel and maturating as you go. With strong Excel skills, you can uncover meaningful insights and identify where you want to know more for the future as you progress.
>
> Also, be innovative in your gap closure solutions. Many companies tend to rely on a build (internal workforce development) or buy (talent acquisition) strategy.
>
> Consider other options:
>
> *Borrow*: Hiring contractors, outsourcing, gig workers
> *Bind*: Retaining key employees
> *Boost*: Accelerating planned promotions
> *Bot*: Identifying activities that can be automated
> *Bounce*: Removing low-performing employees

While the analysis was conducted in an Excel-based SWP tool, the outcome was powerful. Data analysis showed that natural turnover due to retirements would exceed the projected reduction in required operators. This, combined with the reduced number of operators required due to technology improvements, reduced the need for a major layoff and highlighted the specific time periods where reskilling and hiring would be required as well as what changes would be required to the rail operations processes and workstations. Through this project, the company achieved a shared understanding and a proactive plan to build the workforce of the future.

M. C. Dean

When looking to improve HR outcomes, many enterprises launch organization-wide initiatives to address specific areas of the talent lifecycle. Examples include modernizing the enterprise role/skills taxonomy, developing career paths, and developing a high potential (HIPO)/and succession management program. Each initiative is normally planned and executed for the workforce at large: one initiative to modernize the enterprise role/skills taxonomy, one initiative to develop/modernize career paths, one initiative to develop and deploy a HIPO and succession management plan. This approach often leads to significant, siloed initiatives—executed in a serial fashion—that can take a great deal of time to plan and implement for the entire workforce.

At the same time, research shows that in a typical organization, 5% of roles carry 95% of the business impact (Mankins, Garton, and Schwartz, 2021). With this in mind, M. C. Dean started SWP efforts by

1. *Identifying two roles critical to business outcomes*: While every single role at M. C. Dean contributes to business objectives, two roles in particular—project leaders (PLs) and engineering leaders (ELs)—are responsible for business development, the project/technical approach, project delivery, client management, and team leadership. Knowing that these two roles have significant impact on revenue, profit, client satisfaction, and employee engagement, we started with these two roles.
2. *Strengthening strategic workforce planning programs across the entire talent lifecycle*: Specific to the PL and EL roles, an integrated team of HR and business unit leaders from across the organization partnered to:
    - Understand the company strategic vision and how this vision would impact the capacity and capabilities required for these two roles.

- Define the skills, experience, and credentials required for now—and the future.
- Define the role and skills taxonomy, including alignment of current staff to the new taxonomy.
- Define the career and learning paths.
- Train leaders on best practices to conduct meaningful career conversations while training employees on how to prepare for a meaningful career conversation with their managers.
- Define the promotion guidelines and processes.
- Identify HIPO employees, defining a pipeline of future leaders for succession management.
- Refine internal processes to promote internal mobility across the organization.

> **Practitioner Tip!**
>
> Strategies to identify areas of focus:
>
> - Identify the roles that are most critical to business outcomes
> - Identify key roles with the biggest skill gaps
> - Identify a business unit with a leader who demonstrates interest and is willing to partner with you on a pilot
> - Identify the top talent risks most likely to impact the successful execution of a specific product, project, and/or the business strategy

As a result of this methodology, instead of assessing and improving each HR program and process in a silo, M. C. Dean leveraged the two priority roles to evaluate all key HR programs and policies relative to the PL and EL employee experience, thus accelerating the entire HR portfolio of solutions (Figure 2.4).

This approach allowed M. C. Dean to accelerate the modernization of all key talent programs while creating an integrated strategic workforce plan for two roles critical to business outcomes.

3. *Scaling the methodology*: This methodology, as well as the programs that were developed through the PL/EL process, is being leveraged for other roles throughout the organization.

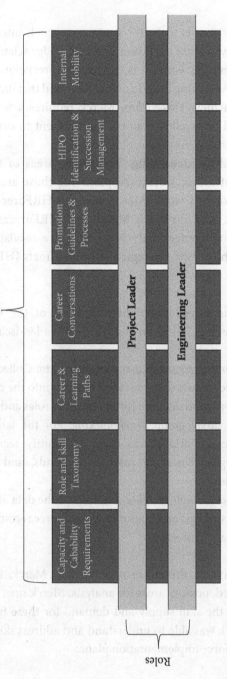

Figure 2.4 The M. C. Dean approach to integrated strategic workforce planning.

Merck Group

Merck Group's vision is to be the premier research-intensive biopharmaceutical company and use the power of leading-edge science to save and improve lives around the world. It is this deep appreciation for life that leads Merck to focus everything they do on people—and that includes their 68,000 employees. To achieve this vision, Merck requires a workforce with the highest standard of excellence and a commitment to continuous learning and innovation.

Merck started by identifying "must-win" areas of the business and then building strategic workforce plans for these areas. Knowing the critical nature of this work, Merck selected HRForecast as their consulting partner. The approach Merck and HRForecast took included deep market intelligence analysis to ensure a robust, data analytics-driven approach to their strategic planning efforts (HRForecast, 2022). Specifically, the team

1. *Defined the target group*: Identification of the target roles/skills for analysis was based on the competitive landscape for the "must win" areas
2. *Collected and analyzed macro-economic data*: Collection and analysis of macro-economic data provided insights into the current and future market supply and demand for the targeted roles and skills
3. *Conducted target group benchmarking*: For the target roles, leading practice benchmarking was done to identify recruiting and location strategies, emerging roles, skill trends, and future organizational models
4. *Developed actionable insights*: Analysis of the data and the creation of actionable strategic and operational workforce recommendations were developed and delivered

Instead of looking at the entire organization, Merck, like M. C. Dean, identified targeted, priority areas for analysis. Merck then gathered external data to evaluate the skill supply and demand for these target areas. Using these data, Merck was able to understand and address skill gaps and create actionable workforce implementation plans.

> **Practitioner Tip!**
>
> Merck accelerated its progress and outcomes by partnering with an external consultancy skilled in this space. This work can be challenging because there are many expert firms in the talent space. It is important to leverage an external consulting partner with a track record of success to guide and accelerate your transformation journey.
>
> Merck's HR team also focused on partnering with business leaders throughout the initiative to educate the SWP team on evolving business priorities while also bringing the business leaders along in understanding and championing leading people practices.

IBM

IBM, a leader in cutting-edge HR and talent strategies, has been operating at the highest level of SWP maturity for several years. While this state of workforce planning didn't happen overnight, IBM was—and continues to be—heavily committed to a business and people strategy centered around skills. Today, IBM regularly collects and analyzes role and skill supply and demand using both internal and external data to inform state-of-the-art gap closure strategies (Moore and Bokelberg, 2019). As examples, IBM developed an AI system that can infer employee skills and skill proficiency levels based on the digital footprint of each employee in the enterprise. IBM then leverages this knowledge to provide personalized learning recommendations and encourage each employee to continue growing their skills in the areas that matter most. IBM deployed AI-based career coaching tools that help each employee navigate job opportunities, learning, and career paths by providing personalized recommendations. Finally, a machine-learning model is used to inform salary decisions, reinforcing the skill-based strategic workforce strategy with both managers and employees.

At this level of SWP maturity, the outcomes are notable. Employees proactively dove head-first into learning opportunities and proudly displayed recognition of their learning and career growth. Lagging indicators, such as hours of training per employee and courses completed, rose. Over time, leading indicators, such as sales revenue and employee engagement, also rose. IBM was later named by Forbes as one of the 10 best employers in the world for 2022 (Fernandez, 2022).

> **Practitioner Tip!**
>
> Don't underestimate the power of starting small and building from it.
>
> While the Global Leader of Career & Skills at IBM, one of the things I noticed is that we were doing a good job communicating to the workforce that everyone needed to upskill, but we needed greater transparency with the workforce about the roles and skills that were most important to IBM and our customers.
>
> We started by working with business leaders to create a list of roles and skills that were growing in market demand. The list was organized by business unit and geography. We put the list on the intranet. Communicating to the workforce the skills that the market valued was a big win with the employees, even if it was presented in a low-tech manner for version 1.
>
> We then built on it each year, tying these "hot" roles and skills to learning, digital badges, open roles, career conversations, and more.

Keys to IBM's Skill-Based Workforce Strategy

Predicting skill supply: Using advanced analytics, AI, and machine learning, IBM invented a state-of-the-art, objective, and efficient method to predict and infer skill supply. This approach assesses and measures the skills—and skills depth—of the workforce on a regular, automated basis. The outcome is a reliable baseline to monitor the skill position over time and provide needed details for targeted workforce planning.

Personalizing gap closure recommendations: By understanding the skills each employee has and the skills they need, learning and skill growth recommendations are personalized to each employee and presented to them in a highly engaging experience. IBM is a learning organization, facilitating continuous learning that is supported by the organizational culture as well as by advanced AI solutions, such as job alerts that promote internal mobility, peer-to-peer coaching, and real-time feedback.

Signaling to the workforce the skills that matter: IBMers are transparently led to roles and skills that are growing in market demand through digital badging. IBM's approach to digital badging is robust, signaling to the workforce the skills that matter in the market.

Making skills a currency: AI and predictive analytics help managers make better-informed decisions about promotions, compensation, and project assignments. Compensation decisions include factors such as employee's performance, salary competitiveness, and market demand for skills. The quality of manager/employee skill and compensation discussions has also improved, positively impacting employee engagement and retention.

Lessons Learned

Moving up the SWP maturity curve is no small feat. Here are a few top lessons learned.

1. *Start*: Over the past several years, companies have focused on their customers, revenue, and cost containment to remain competitive in the ever-changing market. As a result, many companies are behind on the modernization of their HR function and struggle to know where to start in SWP because there is so much ground to be made up. The bottom line here is to start. Start small. Pick one part of the organization, one line of business, or one project. Just start and then build capability over time.
2. *Assess*: Every organization does not need to immediately move to Level 4. Determine the stage of maturity required for your business based on the competitive need, data and technology availability, and organizational readiness for change. In some cases, your competitive environment may not provide the luxury of time; in these cases, strong consulting companies that have proven experience in modern strategic workforce planning can help to accelerate outcomes. In other cases, significant value can be created at Levels 2 and 3 while readying the organization to mature further in the future.
3. *Focus*: Remember that 5% of roles have 95% of business impact. Don't try to do the entire organization all at once. Focus on the role(s) that have the greatest business impact or on an area of the business that is a

pain point. Partner with HR, Finance, and Operations to demonstrate positive business outcomes and expand from there.

4. *Develop*: This approach to SWP requires new expertise and skills from the HR team. Develop your HR team through both talent acquisition of HR professionals and training of your existing staff. Business acumen; data science; analytics; enterprise design thinking; and modern learning, skill gap closure, and employee experience approaches will also be critical.

5. *Invest*: With the shortage of talent, a highly competitive job market, and roles that continue to change, a workforce strategy that relies primarily on talent acquisition will not succeed. Data shows that 60% of future roles can be filled by current employees if the company has the right programs in place (HRForecast, 2022). Invest in the development of career progression and the engagement of your current workforce.

Organizations are progressing in this space—and you can, too! Start today.

References

Bremen, J. (2023, January 30). Why talent shortages persist—Moving beyond the Great Resignation and quiet quitting. Forbes. https://www.forbes.com/sites/johnbremen/2023/01/30/why-talent-shortages-persist-moving-beyond-the-great-resignation-and-quiet-quitting/?sh=26168ff97139

Fernandez, C. (2022, October). Costco moved up, Amazon dropped off: These are the 10 best employers in the world for 2022. CNBC. https://www.cnbc.com/2022/10/18/best-employers-in-the-world-forbes-survey.html

Franzino, M., Guarino, A., Binvel, Y., and Laochez, J. (2023). The $8.5 trillion talent shortage. Korn Ferry. https://www.kornferry.com/insights/this-week-in-leadership/talent-crunch-future-of-work

Harris, S. (2022, March 1). A how-to guide for workforce planning beyond the Great Resignation. Human Resource Executive. https://hrexecutive.com/a-how-to-guide-for-workforce-planning-beyond-the-great-resignation/

HRForecast. (2022). Merck gained transparency on global labor market skills to inform strategic workforce planning decisions. https://hrforecast.com/portfolio-item/merck-workforce-planning-solutions/

Iacurci, G. (2022, March 22). The Great Resignation continues as 44% of workers look for a new job. CNBC. https://www.cnbc.com/2022/03/22/great-resignation-continues-as-44percent-of-workers-seek-a-new-job.html

IBM Institute of Business Value. (2017). Extending expertise: How cognitive computing is transforming HR and the employee experience. https://www.ibm.com/downloads/cas/QVPR1K7D

Kropp, B., and McRae, E. (2022, January 13). 11 trends that will shape work in 2022 and beyond. Harvard Business Review. https://hbr.org/2022/01/11-trends-that-will-shape-work-in-2022-and-beyond

LinkedIn Learning. (2023). 2023 Workplace Learning Report: Building an agile future. https://learning.linkedin.com/resources/workplace-learning-report

Mankins, M., Garton, E., and Schwartz, D. (2021, September-October). Future-proofing your organization. Harvard Business Review. https://hbr.org/2021/09/future-proofing-your-organization

Moore, T., and Bokelberg, E. (2019, Fall). How IBM incorporates artificial intelligence into strategic workforce planning. SHRM Executive Network. https://www.shrm.org/executive/resources/people-strategy-journal/Fall2019/Pages/moore-bokelberg-feature.aspx

Toh, M. (2023, March 29). 300 million jobs could be affected by the latest wave of AI says Goldman Sachs. CNN Business. https://www.cnn.com/2023/03/29/tech/chatgpt-ai-automation-jobs-impact-intl-hnk/index.html#:~:text=300%20million%20jobs%20could%20be%20affected%20by,of%20AI%2C%20says%20Goldman%20Sachs&text=As%20many%20as%20300%20million,according%20to%20Goldman%20Sachs%20economist

van Dijk, R. (2022). Case study: Strategic workforce planning for rail infrastructure managers. Academy to Innovate HR. https://www.aihr.com/blog/case-study-strategic-workforce-planning/

3
Practitioners' Perspectives on Operationalizing Strategic Workforce Planning
Data, Analytics, and Beyond

Sheri L. Feinzig

Indisputably, data and analytics are essential elements of successful strategic workforce planning (SWP). In any analytical endeavor, the data chosen for analysis must be highly relevant and of sufficient quality to yield reliable and valid results, and SWP is no exception. Similarly, the methods of analysis must be fit for purpose: appropriate for the data to which it is applied and aligned with the objectives of the analysis. When analyzing data in an organizational context with the intent of effecting some sort of action—a decision to stay the course, reallocation of investments, and so forth—the ability to communicate the results of the analysis in a way that is easily understood and embraced by the target audience is also of utmost importance. The following foundational propositions underline this chapter's point of view about data and analytics for SWP:

- Smaller, targeted, high-quality datasets are superior to larger, diffuse data of unknown quality
- External data sources are valuable; internal data (people-related and financial) are indispensable
- Qualitative insights from highly knowledgeable subject matter experts should be relied on to complement, inform, and provide context for quantitative data
- Simpler analyses are generally preferable to more complex and harder-to-explain techniques

Furthermore, SWP requires much more than data and analytics. Those foundational components must be integrated into a larger system of planning and operations, aligned with the organization's broader strategic and financial planning, and explicitly linked with the human resources (HR) processes and systems that bring SWP guidance and recommendations to fruition. SWP is also an iterative process that must be reevaluated and adjusted at regular intervals and in response to the dynamic environments in which organizations operate. Ideally, forward-looking scenario planning will be incorporated as part of the process, anticipating potential disruptions and enabling the appropriate response. Recognizing this broader systems context, the goal of this chapter is to provide guidance, based on current practitioner practices and anticipated future direction, for selecting datasets and applying analytical techniques to guide successful SWP (see Box 3.1).

Box 3.1 The Practitioner Perspective

To inform this chapter's content, we interviewed about a dozen SWP practitioners across a range of industries, including retail, professional services, life sciences, technology, industrial products, consumer packaged goods, and engineering/industrial project management. Topics ranged from high-level questions around the definition of workforce planning and the importance of doing it well, to details around data sources, analytical methods used, planning time horizons, and scope. We touched on team, skills, and organizational structure and the specific software used for planning. We probed on the impact of the COVID-19 pandemic, if any, on workforce planning efforts and top challenges and benefits of SWP. We are grateful to all the participants for candidly sharing their experiences and expertise. Some have requested anonymity and, to those, we thank you privately. For the others, we publicly thank the following: Dr. Stefanie Becker, James Bryce, Rene Gessenich, Dr. Wendy Hirsch, Blair Hopkins, Dr. Michael Kannisto, Sarah Kelly, and John Whelan. Special thanks to Dr. Nigel Guenole for his invaluable assistance with the interviews, and to Dr. Steven Katzman for his expert insights and highly valuable recommendations. And to all, we reiterate our gratitude for sharing your time and your expertise that brought this chapter to life.

This chapter includes the following topics:

- *The big picture*: Defining SWP, and the importance of doing it well
- *Data, analytics, tools*: Data sources, ethics, analytical methods, headcount vs. skills focus, nonanalytic methods, scenario planning, and tools
- *Operationalizing SWP*: Scope, team structure and skills, time horizon, buy-in and influence, implementation and follow-through
- *Additional considerations*: SWP challenges, impact of COVID-19, and looking to the future

The Big Picture

Defining Strategic Workforce Planning

We asked practitioners to share their perspective on how they define SWP and how their definition has been operationalized in their respective organizations. We found quite a bit of variability in how SWP is defined and implemented, which in itself is instructive in understanding the current state of the field as well as future potential. Among the practitioners we spoke with, the practice of SWP varies along several dimensions including: simple versus complex analytics, broad versus narrow scope, the planning time horizon, and the relative importance of quantitative versus qualitative methods. Considered in total, these varying perspectives suggest a potentially rich and robust domain with substantial opportunity to positively impact both business outcomes and the workers comprising those businesses.

In its broadest terms, SWP can be defined as a process that enables an organization to have "the right people in the right place at the right time" to meet business objectives. For many, the "strategic" aspect of SWP necessarily translates to long-term planning, whereas others see a somewhat artificial distinction between "strategic" and "tactical," given the need to act with speed to meet both near-term and longer-term talent needs and to operationalize the planning into actions that drive results. An important point highlighted by some was the notion that, when done correctly, SWP is a gradual approach that avoids large, disruptive changes to the business and workforce. Effective SWP utilizes readily available information and highlights trends that can be identified and acted on with enough advance warning to be addressed in a methodical, planful, and nondisruptive way (circumstances such as the COVID-19 pandemic notwithstanding).

Another important point highlighted by several practitioners is the value of aligning SWP with the organization's existing strategic and financial planning processes, which enables the consideration of workforce dynamics and talent requirements as necessary for realizing planned business outcomes. Similarly, SWP practitioners should strive to align financial metrics with people metrics such that all parties are "speaking the same language" and agree to a set of actions and accountabilities for outcomes.

Additional variations in emphasis and focus included whether the analysis focuses on job roles (typically, a small number of critical roles) or skills (which might be considered independent of role, for example, looking at future trends and anticipating the need for certain skills based on labor market projections and overall hiring patterns). Another variation was the extent to which the SWP scope includes following through on tactical actions to operationalize the planning (e.g., the proverbial "build/buy/borrow" type of decisions) and linking directly with functions such as talent acquisition and procurement to ensure implementation.

> **Practitioner Tip!**
>
> For us, it's more about what we need for innovation, future-proofing, staying on top of industry trends, and then hiring the talent from other companies or building it within.

Importance of Doing SWP Well

To further understand practitioners' experiences with SWP, we asked them to explain the importance of doing it well. Again, responses varied but collectively speak to the potential value SWP brings when done effectively. Some described SWP as the "glue" between business strategy and talent planning and how that connection is necessary for business success.

Having the right talent in place is notably essential in industries such as pharmaceuticals and life sciences, where the research and development performed by select highly skilled individuals directly drives the ability of the organization to succeed. Also noted was the reciprocal relationship between business strategy and people, where broader external factors can drive employee requirements for things like flexible working conditions, which in turn have implications for company processes and infrastructure.

> **Practitioner Tip!**
>
> SWP provides a competitive advantage. External forces are impacting workforce availability for all organizations, and the only lever to differentiate is the talent you are able to hire. Understanding the talent you need in advance of when you actually hire is the ultimate competitive advantage.

Finally, high-quality and well-executed SWP prevents unnecessary disruptive actions associated with short-term reactions to unplanned events, which impede the business and, importantly, negatively impact the workforce. Proper planning can foresee many such events and allows for a more gradual, less disruptive response.

Data, Analytics, and Tooling

Data Sources

As with any data analytical endeavor, SWP practitioners should always follow standard scientific practices when selecting their data sources: formulate hypotheses to guide data selection, choose datasets highly relevant to the organization and its workforce, select the best quality datasets available (versus the most convenient), recognize your data's gaps and limitations and temper your conclusions accordingly, triangulate with multiple sources of data where possible, and "sense check" and replicate findings as feasible. All datasets have inherent limitations and recognizing them allows the practitioner to move forward responsibly with analysis, reach useful conclusions, and bring value to the organization.

> **Practitioner Tip!**
>
> We try to be selective in the data we focus on, based on what makes the most sense for the business. We have to consider the business context. It's easy to become overwhelmed with the amount of data available.

For SWP, data are an absolute necessity, and practitioners described various relevant data sources that fall into two broad categories: data created and housed within the organization (internal) and data procured from outside the organization (external). Within each of these broad categories is a multitude of potential data sources. Many of these sources are, unsurprisingly, quantitative in nature, although important insights gleaned from qualitative information should not be overlooked and were described by some as pivotal for informing SWP priorities and guiding analyses.

Table 3.1 summarizes SWP data sources by category. Within the *internal* category is a wide array of human resources data from a variety of sources. Current workforce details are essential for understanding the makeup of the existing workforce within the organization, encompassing both regular employees (where data are likely housed in an HR information system) as well as contingent workers (where the data likely reside in procurement systems).

Relevant workforce data elements include various employee demographic categories (such as gender, race, age, disability status, veteran status, and so forth), job role history, compensation, tenure, time in role, and more. Other relevant workforce data will likely be stored in different systems and databases and include performance data, employee career aspirations, leadership potential, employee survey data, skills information, and various workforce dynamics (such as promotion rates and turnover).

In addition to accurately profiling the current workforce by collating HR data, successful SWP requires analyzing the HR data in relation to business metrics. To that end, participants highlighted the importance of the organization's financial data (such as revenue, cost, currency, and productivity metrics) and of framing the analyses in the context of qualitative leadership insights about the business (including knowledge of local markets, competitors, key performance indicators, strategy, and goals).

External data sources provide essential context for understanding local labor markets and trends, necessary for informing assumptions around workforce supply and anticipated demand from other organizations competing for talent. Labor market data are available from vendors such as Lightcast (formerly Emsi Burning Glass) and Gartner TalentNeuron, as well as from government sources such as the US Bureau of Labor Statistics. External labor market data can be very powerful when used to query the business plan owners about how their plans address challenges indicated by current and future workforce dynamics. Broader economic trends, and the organization's brand perception, were also highlighted as relevant external data sources.

Table 3.1 Strategic workforce planning potential data sources

Internal sources	
Human resource data	**Examples**
Current workforce details	Demographics; job families/functions; stratification levels; portfolio of skills; tenure; time in role; time to retirement; date of availability for new role
Employee performance	Annual performance appraisal ratings
Employee career aspirations	Career path preferences
Employee leadership potential	Manager ratings (e.g., 9-Box)
Employee engagement/ experience	Employee survey data
Employee skills	Skill proficiency ratings
Workforce dynamics	Promotion rates; retention rates
Contingency labor	Number/percent of contingent workers relative to regular employees
Financial data	
Revenue	Total revenue; revenue per employee
Cost	Salary; incentive pay; benefits
Currency	Revenue and cost expressed in local currency; currency dynamics
Productivity	Sales per employee/role/business unit
Qualitative business data	
Leadership insights	Knowledge of local markets; competitive insights
Business priorities	Revenue and profit goals; strategic investments
External sources	
Labor market tends	
Lightcast (formerly Emsi Burning Glass)	
Gartner/talentneuron	Employment trends; local employment rates; population dynamics, other companies' hiring activity; job post scrapings for roles/skills trends
Linkedin Insights	
Job advertisements	
US Bureau of Labor Statistics	
Economic trends	
Country/industry/trade reports	Country GDP; inflation rates; supply shortages
Brand perception	
Customer experience	Net promoter scores; social media trending topics

Working with HR Data Ethically and Responsibly

Working with HR data requires special care due to the often personal and sensitive nature of the information. HR datasets generally contain personal information about employees, referred to in the United States as *sensitive personal information* (SPI), with similar designations in other countries. This is information that, if compromised or disclosed, could result in damaging situations and legislative violations such as unwanted disclosure of personal information, identity theft, or discrimination. It is essential that proper data handling procedures be adhered to by SWP practitioners, ensuring compliance with local country legislation as well as the organization's own standards for data collection, access, usage, and storage.

This requires a clear understanding of all relevant data legislation, regulations, and guidelines, which have evolved over time and will continue to do so. Organizations often have functions such as a Chief Privacy Office that can serve as an important resource for SWP practitioners, ensuring appropriate use (and avoiding misuse) of the organization's workforce data.

It's important to keep in mind that data collected for some purposes cannot always be analyzed for other purposes. For example, data collected via employee surveys and intended to understand workers' attitudes and perspectives at the group level should never be used for identifying specific employees who expressed negative opinions and subsequently taking an action that impacts those individuals based on their scores.

Data policies and regulations exist for good reason: to keep all members of society (including workers) safe from data misuse, fraud, and unethical activity. As important and necessary as this is, government legislation to protect individuals consistently lags the development of technologies that can cause individuals harm, and this is very much the case when it comes to accessing and analyzing personal data. Therefore, rather than simply adhering to existing legislation, SWP practitioners should strive to be ahead of legislation and follow a higher standard of data ethics. As a guiding principle, even if you *can* analyze available data, that does not mean you should.

Role of Analytics in Workforce Planning

As with data, analytical methods for analyzing those data are essential for SWP and should always be chosen to fit the objectives of the analysis and the datasets being analyzed. Analytics build credibility with business leaders, and they form the basis for rich and valuable discussions yielding important qualitative insights and commitment to action. That said, complex and sophisticated analytics are not a necessity. Often, simple and straightforward methods that are easy to explain are quite effective and impactful. For example, simply summarizing the number of people staffed in critical roles, along with the turnover and promotion rates for those roles, can be sufficient for driving action. Simple analyses can also be a starting point subsequently built upon with more complex techniques as appropriate. Continuing with the critical roles example, *if-then scenarios* can be used to model the impact of an action (such as hiring more or fewer people into those critical roles) on business outcomes (such as change in revenue or productivity).

Practitioners highlighted the power of connecting workforce planning with the organization's existing strategy planning and business processes and methodologies to demonstrate analytically and render explicit the connection between workforce actions and business outcomes. Strive to use similar terminology as well. One practitioner described a successful example where the SWP team was able to show statistically that better performing business units were characterized by better people management practices.

Practitioner Tip!

Synchronize workforce planning with business strategy planning and align where the money needs to be spent so the financial plans line up. By adapting to existing processes, it avoids people having to learn a brand-new process.

One word of caution is to avoid appearing overly academic when discussing analytics with business leaders. It's important to know your audience and strike the right balance between thoughtful analysis and business relevance. Also noted was the risk of being overly focused on statistics, to the extent that they get in the way of understanding important nuanced experiential insights from members of the workforce. People are complex and cannot always be reduced to a set of numbers.

Types of Analytical Methods Used

In addition to choosing analytical methods that are fit for purpose and matched appropriately with the type of data being analyzed, it's important within a business context that the analytical results can be communicated to and understood by the intended audience (business leaders), accepted as credible, and acted on. As such (and as mentioned above), many practitioners err on the side of simplicity in choice of analytical methods. A useful approach for determining the value of newer, more complex analyses is to test empirically whether they yield superior outcomes to more traditional, tried-and-true methods. Experience suggests that often the simpler, time-tested approaches are more effective.

> **Practitioner Tip!**
>
> The predictability of outcomes from overly complex models is not as good as the conversations we have with business leaders.

Many rely on basic computational analyses available in spreadsheet applications to compute descriptive statistics, providing the fact base necessary for describing the current workforce along multiple dimensions. These types of foundational analyses should routinely be the first step because getting the basics correct and verified is necessary before moving on to more sophisticated techniques.

In addition to a current snapshot of the workforce, these analyses can show historical trends and noteworthy workforce dynamics, such as increases or decreases in the number of people holding specific roles and indicators of emerging roles and skills. Big-picture summary statistics of the current state can also prompt a fruitful discussion on what the future will look like if the organization continues on its current course and speed in terms of workforce decisions and actions. Showing leaders a picture of that future state and explicitly asking "is this what we want the organization to look like in three to five years?" can serve as a useful catalyst for prompting much needed decisions and actions.

Building on or supplementing these basics, practitioners described analytics for predicting turnover, modeling succession planning, estimating the impact of expected retirements, and estimating the impact on various outcomes if the number of employees in each role was to increase or decrease by different percentages. Guided by well thought out hypotheses, these types of analyses and more can yield very useful insights for building workforce plans.

To better understand observed workforce dynamics and guide future actions, practitioners employ correlational and regression analyses to help explain relationships among multiple factors, forecasting and simulations to predict workforce requirements for the future, and network analyses (based on email connections or employee surveys of colleague interactions) to understand working patterns and relationships. The types of analyses described by practitioners are summarized in Table 3.2.

Even with more sophisticated analyses, practitioners are advised to err on the side of relative simplicity. As one practitioner warned, large models with multiple scenarios can quickly become unmanageable, and skepticism from any one stakeholder can result in loss of credibility for the entire analysis.

Privacy and ethics are important considerations as well. While it may be tempting to use techniques such machine learning to predict behaviors, such as the probability that specific individuals will leave the organization, practitioners should consider whether this is a violation of individuals' rights to privacy. For example, increased activity on websites and apps such as LinkedIn could indicate a person is looking for a new job. However, it could also be the case that the person is researching information for a work-related project or perhaps simply staying informed of work-related trends to guide skill development decisions. Given the different meanings a behavior can have for any given individual, the practitioner should question whether machine learning techniques are appropriate and ethical in this context even if they are highly predictive on average.

Given the vast amount of relevant data available for SWP, even simple analyses can become overwhelming for the intended audiences. While the SWP team should analyze all relevant data thoroughly, they should be selective in what to share with business leaders, provided the selected information is sufficiently reflective of the whole analytical effort and accurately conveys the information needed to drive appropriate action. Understanding the business context is essential, and analytical findings must be explained in a way that the business can understand (and act on).

One practitioner cautioned against the use of "Big Data" analytics due to the challenges with determining causality and the risk of spurious findings. While such analyses can potentially be useful for informing hypotheses for more systematic investigation, well-planned analytics using carefully curated datasets will serve SWP practitioners well.

Accuracy of Workforce Planning

When asked about the expected accuracy of workforce plans, practitioners indicated that SWP is less about precision and more about producing credible plans that are directionally correct and, ideally, identifying actions to account

Table 3.2 Types of analytics used in strategic workforce planning

Types of analysis	Why conduct this analysis	Example data sources	Example methods	Example information/insights
Description	Understand the current states of the organization's workforce and historical internal workforce dynamics	Internal HR and contingent workforce data	Frequency Distributions, Means, Variance (e.g., standard deviation)	How many people do I have in each of our critical roles? What is our diversity mix? What have our retention rates been for the past two years? What are our promotion rates and velocity, by job role? What is our average tenure with the organization? What is the range of proficiency levels for our critical skills? Will decreasing birth rate trends impact our ability to hire in specific regions?
	Understand the external labor market and historical trends	External labor market data	Difference Tests (t-tests, ANOVA)	Does our offer acceptance rate differ by recruiting source? Do our employee engagement sources differ significantly for different gender and racial groups?
	Understand socioeconomic and industry trend and associate workforce implications	External industry reports	Organization Network Analysis	What will be the impact if a key, well-connected employee leaves the organizations? Are there information "bottlenecks" inhabiting effective collaboration within and among teams?
Associative	Explore the strength and nature of relationships among variables	Internal HR and contingent workforce data Internal financial data Customer experience reports	Correlation coefficients (for continuous variables) Chi-Square (for categorical variables)	Do better management practices correlate with stronger business unit performance? Is level of educational attainment associated with retention?

(*continued*)

Table 3.2 Continued

Example Analytical Method use in Workforce Planning

Types of analysis	Why conduct this analysis	Example data sources	Example methods	Example information/insights
Predictive	Estimate future workforce requirement and the likelihood of future outcomes	Quantitative business Data Leadership and subject matter expert insight, business objectives and priorities)	What-If Analysis	How many incremental people in key roles will be needed to increase sales by 15% year-over-years? What is our expected hiring target for the next 2–3 years if we improve retention by two percentage points?
		Internal HR and contingent workforce data	Linear Regression (continuous outcomes variables)	How will do our current selection tools predict employee performance? Will increasing employment rates and other labor market trends affect our ability to fulfill hiring demand?
		Internal financial data	Logistic Regression (continuous outcomes variables)	Which employees are most likely to stay or leave the organization in the next 12 months? What are the top drives of retention?
		External labor market data	Demand forecasting	How many people with sufficient skill proficiency will be needed in each region to meet business objectives? How can we quantify risk across a distribution of possible outcomes?
		External industry reports Base demand forecasting models Repeated randomly generated sample datasets	Monte Carlo Simulations	What is the best estimate of our future workforce requirements, accounting for various uncertainties that could impact supply and demand?

for the inevitable uncertainty. For example, if ultimately more employees than originally planned for will be needed, the plan can include a provision to fill any gaps with a larger number of contingent workers as needed.

> **Practitioner Tip!**
>
> You can't really predict the future, so you'll never come to accurate numbers, but you can predict trends, which is quite important.

Recognizing that workforce planning will not be precisely accurate in forecasting future needs, it is important to periodically review the assumptions that went into the modeling and revise recommendations accordingly. The focus should be on predicting trends and having a regular monitoring cycle to validate the company's direction. One practitioner described stress-testing the plans by thinking through different scenarios of how things could go wrong, with a focus on not losing money on the planned investments. Changes should be expected, detected, and acted upon.

Rather than broad-brush headcount forecasting across the organization, most practitioners are focused on either the job roles deemed critical for achieving the organization's strategic objectives or the skills anticipated to be essential for future success. For those focused on roles, some are striving for overall trends regarding anticipated increases or decreases, while others pursue additional precision by defining tiers of critical roles, forecasting the numbers needed for those roles with the expectation that the forecasts will be directionally correct, and identifying actions for successful hiring and retention. For those focused on skills, the planning efforts attempt to discern what skills will be needed for future success and to invest in those skills accordingly, even if it is not yet clear exactly how those skills will be used.

A governance process should be put in place for holding the SWP team and the business accountable for the workforce planning effort, including agreed metrics and a process for measuring success. Align on key performance indicators (KPIs) and set target levels, then track progress relative to those targets. Example KPIs include budgets, headcount, and skill gap closure. Another useful practice is to overlay the previous year's plans with the current year's plans and then facilitate a conversation around why any planned actions differed from what actually occurred. Finally, recognize that getting traction with SWP takes time, perhaps 2 to 3 years as described by an experienced practitioner. This ramp-up time should be taken into account when setting initial targets.

Headcount Versus Skills Focus

As mentioned, some practitioners focus their planning efforts on anticipated headcount requirements (often segmented by job role), whereas others focus on specific skills that will be needed. To a certain extent, a job role may imply a certain skillset, and, among practitioners currently focused on headcount, many aspire to a skills-based approach although challenges have proved formidable. For example, a necessary initial step is having clarity around the current skills profile of the workforce, ideally by levels of proficiency. A precursor to that current-state view is agreement on a skills taxonomy, and many organizations struggle with even that foundational level of information.

> **Practitioner Tip!**
>
> We're focused on numbers for specific critical roles. We haven't focused on skills in the past but we're moving in that direction.

For those finding success in a skills-based approach, the key seems to be limiting the scope to a relatively small number of skills that are most important for achieving the organization's strategic objectives. This requires maniacal focus, dogged discipline, and steadfast agreement among stakeholders and the recognition that "directionally correct" versus "precisely accurate" will often need to suffice. All that said, we anticipate continued movement toward a skills-based approach to SWP.

Nonanalytical Approaches

Data and analytics are cornerstones of SWP, but we clearly heard from all practitioners that numbers alone never tell the whole story. It is essential to understand the business context for which you are planning from the perspective of the organization's leaders as well as the employees. Nonanalytical approaches to SWP are as necessary as the data and analytics.

> **Practitioner Tip!**
>
> The numbers never tell the whole story. You need the context. The numbers are the things we can argue over, but context tells us what to care about.

Relationship building, change enablement, stakeholder management, and top leadership support are musts. Effective interactions with leaders and other stakeholders not only provide the context that SWP practitioners require, but they also afford the opportunity to secure buy-in and support. Listening to leaders and employees also provides much needed guidance when changing conditions demand a change in strategy and actions.

A starting point for SWP should be gaining agreement on the top priorities to address as well as aligning on what success looks like (which should then be translated to KPIs, as discussed previously). These fundamentals should not be overlooked. Conversations and qualitative data gathering can take the form of interviews with people at all levels of the organization, workshops to identify critical roles and discuss labor market and industry trends, and roundtable discussions about topics such as hiring strategies and succession planning. Data and analytics can be extremely useful in grounding and focusing these conversations.

> **Practitioner Tip!**
>
> The qualitative component is very important to workforce planning. It makes it real, and it helps leaders to operationalize and move in the right direction. It's an important part of the value proposition.

One practitioner described strategy maps for understanding the business priorities and customer value proposition, then working out the talent implications. This allows for a deep understanding of the business imperatives and what that means in terms of people, process, and technology, and the recognition that sometimes the pain points are specific to process and technology. While HR might not own or champion those aspects, the impact on workforce planning is significant and needs to be addressed (Box 3.2).

Box 3.2 Identifying Critical Roles

Given the reality that most SWP practitioners and the organizations they support do not have unlimited resources at their disposal, it's typically necessary to prioritize the work of the SWP team. This often takes the form of identifying those job roles that are the most critical for the organization, those that disproportionately contribute to achieving the strategic objectives. Identifying critical roles translates to singling out those with highest business impact, for example, by identifying those most likely to contribute to sales and revenue growth, improve profitability, or increase customer retention, to name a few. Identifying the most impactful roles requires first understanding the business strategy and objectives. Armed with that knowledge, SWP practitioners will then rely primarily on nonanalytical approaches—interviews and working sessions with leaders and subject matter experts—to identify the roles that will have the most influence on whether the business objectives are achieved.

To facilitate the interviews and working sessions, SWP practitioners can frame the question in terms of impact on the value chain, which involves understanding what the main and supporting processes and activities are that enable the organization to achieve its core strategic objectives and then identifying the roles and skills needed to successfully execute those processes and activities. Prioritize based on which roles are contributing most (i.e., which have the biggest impact on success versus failure). For example, if growth of new products is a key strategic objective, you would prioritize the specific sales, marketing, and customer support roles associated with the new products (as opposed to the entire salesforce, marketing organization, and customer support organization).

Another technique is to determine which roles, if insufficiently staffed, would have the most negative impact on the organization's ability to operate and thrive. SWP practitioners could facilitate the conversation with leaders and SMEs by asking the following hypothetical question: If everyone in the organization took a week off from work, the absence of which roles would be most disruptive? This has the benefit of potentially revealing jobs that could be overlooked but are essential to day-to-day operations, such as more junior-level roles (Sparkman, 2018).

Use of Scenario Planning

The term "scenario planning" is used frequently in the context of SWP, and it can mean different things to different practitioners. For some, scenario planning refers to what-if queries posed to a workforce plan: for example, what if headcount increases 20% in the next 12 months—what will be the impact on cost and revenue? This is essentially a forecasting tool for planning workforce headcount, typically for a subset of roles or business units within the organization. This provides a methodical way for making intentional decisions around the amount of investment the organization is willing to make and what the expected outcomes are based on historical patterns.

For other practitioners, scenario planning involves ad hoc scenario modeling using sophisticated methods such as Monte Carlo studies to quantify risk across a distribution of possible outcomes. A *Monte Carlo study* is a probability-based mathematical technique used for estimating the likelihood of multiple possible outcomes for an uncertain event by recalculating results thousands of times within a defined range of values (IBM, www.ibm.com). These analyses can be difficult to explain and require careful interpretation and quantification of bottom-line impact, but they can be very powerful for informing a course of action.

Still others consider scenario planning an even broader concept, one that requires research and facilitated discussions to identify a range of future possibilities and be prepared to respond to what unfolds. It's "a way of rehearsing the future to avoid surprises by breaking through the 'illusion of certainty'" (Garvin and Levesque, 2006). This approach can help organizations break out of constraining mental models and think differently. For example, it can help challenge long-held assumptions regarding what worker attributes are truly needed for success and then identifying traditionally untapped sources of talent based on that new way of thinking. In a highly competitive talent market, such thinking can provide a unique competitive advantage.

Practitioner Tip!

Workforce planning is really a forecasting exercise—it's typically, we're going to go up 5%, down 5%, or stay level—that's the mental model. Scenario planning allows you to step outside that mental model and think differently.

All these approaches and methods are useful, albeit very different tools, for SWP. The approach described by Garvin and Levesque is rather uncommon in practice. Due to the commitment in time and resources required as well as the hypothetical nature of the exercise, few companies are likely to embark on this type of work effort. For organizations that do embrace the methodology, it's much more likely to be used as an overall strategic business planning tool versus strictly focused on workforce planning. But it can be a highly effective SWP tool as well. In one example described by a practitioner, the approach was used as part of workforce planning and resulted in a decision to keep specific strategic capability in-house and therefore retain the people with the very specific skills needed. While rare and labor intensive, there is much potential benefit to be derived from this approach, particularly in light of the COVID-19 pandemic and the instantaneous reactions required of organizations to a previously unthinkable occurrence.

Tools

The software tools used by SWP teams range from simple to sophisticated, although this variability does not appear to be associated with effectiveness and impact. Rather, it's a matter of choosing the tools most suitable to the team's skills and the types of datasets available for analysis. On the simpler end of the spectrum, spreadsheet software (such as Microsoft Excel) is quite prevalent. Some practitioners are planning to migrate from spreadsheets to statistical analysis tools such as R and Python, to increase repeatability and efficiency.

Given the central importance of trusted internal HR data to SWP, teams rely heavily on core HR information systems such as Workday or SAP as the backbone to their analytics work. Database tools that can aggregate data from multiple sources are extremely useful, as are visualization tools such as Power BI or Visier for navigating and interacting with data.

Other useful tools mentioned by practitioners include organization design and organization charting software, succession planning capability, Draup for skill adjacency analysis, SAP Analytics Cloud planning module, SuccessFactors for skills analysis, Alteryx for data transformation, and scenario planning capability in Excel and Python.

Looking to the future, a data management and governance technology that is beginning to gain traction is "data fabric," an architectural approach to data management that provides safe, secure, self-serve access regardless of where the data reside. Given the importance of data privacy and integrity and the highly sensitive nature of HR data, this is a promising technology for easing access to multiple sources of essential data for the SWP function while protecting the individuals represented by the underlying data.

Prior to choosing and investing in a particular technology, as one practitioner advised, it's important to first think about the future you want to create. As with any organizational process and tooling, the business objectives and supporting technical requirements should be clearly understood, with appropriate tools selected to support the work that's needed to achieve those goals. Given limited budgets, cost-benefit tradeoffs will need to be considered as well.

> **Practitioner Tip!**
>
> Don't think first about a tech solution. Rather, think about the model and the type of impact you want to create. Then, choose technology that can make it easier and help you scale.

Operationalizing SWP

Scope of Workforce Planning

Another point of variation is in the scope of SWP. For some organizations, the business units (countries, divisions, etc.) conduct their own planning, with headquarters performing some level of aggregation. In other cases, the process is driven globally. As pointed out by a practitioner with experience across a variety of industries, the scope and scale depend on where the power center is for making decisions and taking actions.

> **Practitioner Tip!**
>
> The scale depends on the organization. You scale to wherever the power center is for making decisions and taking action, and this varies by organization.

In some cases, the global or headquarters team serves as an aggregator of business unit plans, and, in other cases, it takes a more active, consultative role: providing frameworks, centralized datasets, training, guidance, and best practices and running pilot initiatives with the units. In these models, the central team may or may not aggregate the business unit plans. One practitioner described a centrally driven process executed by the business units and aggregated at the enterprise level, identifying company-wide issues to address (such as imminent retirement of a large proportion of the workforce). In this case, approximately 80% of the planning is performed at the business unit level, given the depth of knowledge and unique strategies and dynamics, while 20% will be elevated to the enterprise level.

SWP Team and Skills

Among the practitioners we spoke with, their SWP teams were quite small, ranging in size from one senior person relying on a matrixed structure to execute the work, to teams of five to ten people. All described their functions as a *center of excellence* (CoE). The teams tend to consist of a combination of business-facing, consultative roles and analytical roles. Both skillsets are deemed essential—specifically, the ability to translate business strategy into workforce implications and the ability to properly analyze and interpret the numbers.

> **Practitioner Tip!**
>
> If you have all data scientists it won't help with the art side of things. If you just have consultants, they want to do therapy. If you don't have a good data engineer, you can't get the data in the format that you need it in.

Small teams also rely heavily on other resources throughout the business. For example, HR business partners (HRBPs) can be essential for helping to translate workforce plans for the business leaders. For the leanest of teams, internal or external consultants can be called on to work through deliverables and enable HRBPs to assist.

In terms of specific skills, in addition to being able to translate planning output into business terms, the SWP team requires strong people skills and relationships skills for navigating the organization's political landscape. SWP has been described as a combination of art and science requiring a broad spectrum of skills: data scientists, data engineers, and consultants. Having a proper balance of these skills is a key to success.

Time Horizon for Workforce Planning

The time horizon for SWP is typically thought of as longer-term, perhaps as long as 5 years out or further. However, most practitioners indicated that shorter-term horizons are much more practical and necessary, particularly given unprecedented disruptive events such as the COVID-19 pandemic, supply chain issues, climate events, and war in Eastern Europe.

> **Practitioner Tip!**
>
> It depends on the business context. Currently we can't plan too far out. We can look 1 year into the future, and even with that we have to adjust every 6 months.

The specific time frame varies by industry, with those industries (such as retail) most acutely impacted by surrounding events requiring shorter-term planning, as short as a 1-year outlook with checks and adjustments every 6 months. Practitioners in consumer-packaged goods and software technology described aspirational time horizons of 3 to 5 years, but acknowledged that 1 to 2 years is more realistic, even in times of less uncertainty. In a private equity environment, time horizons are even shorter, with rolling quarterly planning a necessity.

The longest time horizons were described for industrial products (3 years maximum), professional services (3–5 years), and engineering/project management (3–5 years, given the long-term nature of many of the projects). Across industries, the most typical planning horizons are about 1½ to 2 years. This reinforces the notion that the distinction between strategic and tactical is not clear-cut, and workforce planning needs to encompass both aspects.

SWP Buy-In and Influence

Given the criticality of leadership participation and ownership for SWP, we asked practitioners to share their experiences with securing buy-in and building credibility and influence. One important point is to start, where possible, with leaders who already want to implement workforce planning, rather than trying to convince those who do not. With that group, identify pilot projects, learn from those pilots what will work within the organization, and then move on to the next area to build momentum. If leadership has already bought in to SWP, bring in new ideas that leadership had not considered previously.

> **Practitioner Tip!**
>
> It's important to know the organizational context and work within that context. Never try to force your way in if you don't have support of the power base.

Several practitioners indicated that buy-in comes from delivering high-quality work and demonstrating the financial benefit of people-related actions such as changing the hiring flow or taking actions that increase retention. Strive to explicitly link HR practices to business priorities. A powerful example shared by a practitioner was being able to demonstrate the extent to which workforce dynamics are associated with the success of acquisitions and divestitures.

> **Practitioner Tip!**
>
> It comes down to the money—if I can prove that by tweaking a part of our hiring flow it translates to money, that's powerful. New hire failure rate is another example—losing 60% of new hires in their first year—that's a huge cost. If I can get that down to 7–8%, it's a tremendous savings.

Adoption and participation will be stronger when SWP is integrated into existing business strategy planning and implementation processes. Working closely with individual business units to provide them with valuable guidance can create champions for the work of the SWP team. Finally, the analytics themselves—having a data-based approach to planning—adds credibility to the team's work.

Implementation and Follow-Through

Data and analytics will have no impact on an organization unless action is taken as a result. SWP practitioners need to be mindful that whatever they recommend in their workforce plans must be implemented by the organization if it is to bring value. Practitioners can enable implementation by establishing strong connections with the stakeholders and processes needed to turn the planning actions into reality (e.g., talent acquisition and talent management teams). Through these stakeholder relationships, practitioners can assist in working through potential barriers up front. As an example, if workforce planning includes a workforce reskilling component, successful implementation will require current managers to release their people for new roles; for this to happen, the financials should be worked out in advance to keep managers whole in terms of headcount. These are the types of logistics that should be taken into consideration when building plans and determining their feasibility. Again, the value of SWP is determined as much by the actions taken to implement the planning as it is by data and analytics.

> **Practitioner Tip!**
>
> Many SWP practitioners expect the implementation to go on managers' regular operational workloads, but those plans will always be sidelined. If you want an SWP plan to work, you need as much focus on delivery as on the analytics.

Additional Considerations

The Biggest SWP Challenges

Even the most experienced SWP practitioners have experienced challenges along the way, and they have generously shared their words of wisdom.

First, SWP must be led by business leaders, and it can be challenging to keep leaders' focused on the long-term given near-term financial objectives. The challenge for the SWP practitioner is demonstrating how SWP will be beneficial to leaders so they take full advantage of all it has to offer. A related challenge is dealing with conflicting priorities among stakeholders. Ensure you are sufficiently knowledgeable about each business unit, and work beyond individual silos when feasible.

Patience and skill are required for enabling experienced, successful leaders to be comfortable with new metrics and embrace new ways of looking at problems. And care must be taken in communicating analytical results and the meaning and implications of the findings, including any limitations. This is of utmost importance to avoid unwarranted conclusions and misguided actions.

> **Practitioner Tip!**
>
> It needs to be business-led. If it's HR-led, it will stall.

Among the more tactical challenges, it can be easy to get caught up in the process and lose focus on the outcome you are trying to achieve. Strive to be efficient with your time and energy to ensure your efforts are focused on the most impactful areas. A natural tension may exist between striving to maintain a targeted focus that delivers quick results and wanting to spend time learning more and more. Similarly, while the entire talent "value chain" is interconnected (hiring the right people, setting them up for success, retaining them, enabling them with the right processes and technology, etc.), it is not feasible to try to change everything at once. Pragmatism should be a guiding principle. Recognize the messiness of data, highlight any gaps in information required for answering foundational questions (such as skills of the current workforce), and secure commitment to close the most problematic gaps.

Impact of COVID-19 on Planning

The COVID-19 pandemic has had an enormous impact on businesses and their workforces, with sudden shutdowns imposed to minimize viral spread prior to vaccine availability, followed by substantial layoffs of millions of workers, and then a surprisingly fast turnaround of strong hiring demand and a shift in the power dynamic that became generally favorable toward workers. These dynamics helped to demonstrate what was possible in terms of transitioning to remote work virtually overnight and in what workers were willing to demand and often received (including more favorable working conditions, better compensation, and more flexibility). As with almost all aspects of work, SWP practitioners adjusted their efforts accordingly. And among practitioners interviewed, demand for their work remained high throughout the pandemic and generally increased in urgency, albeit with a shift in focus.

In some cases (notably retail), more near-term planning was required. Others emphasized the need to change assumptions around physical locations and workspace requirements; for example, shifting from numerous small locations to a small number of hubs. Some practitioners saw an increased demand for data to make immediate decisions and an increased emphasis on analyzing worker behaviors (e.g., number of meetings attended) to guide actions for improving worker well-being.

> **Practitioner Tip!**
>
> Workforce planning is one of the ways we maintain the "True North." It will morph and adapt, but it's not going away.

One positive result from the shift to remote work is that new labor markets opened up for sourcing workers to fill demand; this proved especially valuable for the life sciences industry, where specialized skills are critically important. On the flip side, some traditionally stable markets in terms of workforce dynamics suddenly became less predictable, with worker resignations in countries that traditionally have had very low turnover.

The fast-paced changes and uncertainty caused some practitioners to become more flexible and to have different scenarios in place to allow for quicker responses to a work environment in flux. Interest in attrition modeling increased for some, and new opportunities emerged for the SWP team to help navigate the uncertainty and market dynamics. Even in industries that should not have been as impacted given the long-term nature of their business projects, it was necessary to react (e.g., to enable social distancing for employees at physical work locations).

> **Practitioner Tip!**
>
> For better or for worse, plans are changing due to the uncertainty in our environment, but we still maintain our organizational priorities, and workforce planning continues to play an important role.

Looking to the Future

Some practitioners offered their thoughts on where they see SWP headed in the future. It was noted that workforce analytics overall has been on a long journey, and a next step will be applying it more quickly for faster results, given the preponderance of data available and capabilities for analyzing it. Also noted was the missed opportunity among many organizations of failing to prioritize workforce planning as a core HR function and therefore foregoing the many benefits afforded those organizations that have integrated SWP into their broader enterprise planning processes. More focus is expected on agile planning, allowing organizations to respond more quickly to market changes while remaining flexible for iterating and reworking plans as needed. Finally, as the world continually becomes more pervasively data-enabled, practitioners will be challenged with how to use data and analytics for societal good.

> **Practitioner Tip!**
>
> The next step for workforce analytics will be going faster and determining its role helping business in the broader societal context.

Conclusion

Effective SWP can yield tremendous benefits, to the organization as well as the people in its employ. As attested to by practitioners, thoughtful, intentional, and well-executed SWP enables the business to run more smoothly, supports employee well-being and happiness, and makes clear the linkage between workforce actions and business effectiveness. And, by thoroughly analyzing potential future scenarios, organization will be prepared to act in ways that provide a distinct competitive advantage.

References

Garvin, D. A., and Levesque, L. C. (2006). A note on scenario planning (Case #9-306-003). Boston, MA: Harvard Business.

IBM (2023). What is Monte Carlo simulation? https://www.ibm.com/cloud/learn/monte-carlo-simulation. Retrieved November 12, 2023.

Sparkman, R. (2018). Strategic workforce planning: Developing optimized talent strategies for future growth. Kogan Page Limited.

4
Strategic Workforce Planning in the US Federal Government

Laura Knowles and Samantha Adrignola

How do you tackle strategic workforce planning (SWP) in the federal government? From multiple angles. The federal government workforce tends to be misunderstood by those not working around or in it, either thought of as a monolith ("the government") or conflated with the visible work of the legislative branch. As of the writing of this chapter, the executive branch of the US government is composed of 15 cabinet-level departments and 108 independent agencies and commissions, with more than 270 large subagencies or components, all with unique missions including areas like transportation, labor and trade, public lands, food safety, agriculture, public health, and defense. According to the Office of Personnel Management (OPM), the federal workforce is composed of an estimated 2.1 million civilian workers (Congressional Research Service, 2022, see Table 4.1), which equates to roughly the population of New Mexico.

This chapter addresses SWP within the federal government setting. We, the authors, serve agencies as advisors and human capital service providers, and our context is that there is no single "owner" of SWP across the federal enterprise. Most agencies operate independently of each other, much like private-sector organizations operating in a similar space. Although generally driven by a common set of employment regulations, agencies have a lot of autonomy regarding their strategic initiatives and decision-making structures.

In this chapter, we will set the stage for SWP in the federal public sector and then describe the common strategies and challenges of SWP in the federal government. Then we make a case for the increased engagement of I-O psychologists in federal SWP, leveraging the unique skillsets of the field to address the critical need for strategic, data-driven workforce management decision-making in the complex environment of the government (Table 4.1).

Table 4.1 Representation of employment statistics in the US federal government in recent fiscal years

Federal civilian employees on board personnel, 2014–2021

	2014	2015	2016	2017	2018	2019	2020	2021
United States	2,003,713	2,029,293	2,054,135	2,045,458	2,056,092	2,087,269	2,134,575	2,144,744
US territories	11,809	12,311	12,046	12,276	14,386	14,246	14,896	15,288
Foreign countries	29,260	29,168	29,938	29,085	29,360	30,027	30,200	29,509
Unspecified areas	925	944	919	928	964	1,2z70	1,435	1,470
Total	2,045,707	2,071,716	2,097,038	2,087,747	2,100802	2,132,812	2,181,106	2,191,011

Each total is an "on-board" count for September of the year noted. Current coverage does not include the Board of Governors of the Federal Reserve, Central Intelligence Agency, Defense Intelligence Agency, foreign service personnel at the State Department, National Geospatial-Intelligence Agency, National Security Agency, Office of the Director of National Intelligence, Office of the Vice President, Postal Regulatory Commission, Tennessee Valley Authority, U.S. Postal Service, White House Office, foreign nationals overseas, Public Health Service's Commissioned Officer Corps, nonappropriated fund employees, selected legislative branch agencies, the judicial branch, or the military.

It's Big and It's Complicated

Due to the size and scope of functions performed by federal employees, workforce planning in the federal government has never been more critical, or more challenging. Agencies regularly respond to evolving threats, opportunities, and commitments, and to meet the needs of the public there is a relentless tension between agility and bureaucracy. On one hand, government agencies must be responsive to emerging issues (e.g., natural disasters, public health crises), but on the other, there can be arduous vetting and approval processes to navigate.

> **Practitioner Tip!**
>
> The budget cycle can also present a challenge to accessing outside resources/contractor support. Agencies who anticipate needing SWP help may hold out on procuring assistance until they have confirmed funding. Due to contracting timelines, this can put an organization even further behind if they don't have the internal resources to do SWP for themselves.

To illustrate this tension, consider the dynamic between budget and hiring. Federal agencies are bound to a workforce size and composition based on a highly structured budget and appropriations process. After budgets and staffing levels are approved, filling staff roles is incredibly important, not only to carry out the work of an agency, but to demonstrate a need for the positions (i.e., if you don't fill a vacancy, you run the risk of losing the slot). When the appropriations process drags out, agencies often do not confirm budgets until well into the fiscal year. In the meantime, they do the best (and most) they can within existing staffing levels. "Use that time to plan," one might say, and yes, that is absolutely what we like to hear, but it's complicated. Imagine waiting months to get your budget approved for five top priorities that you estimate will require new positions. While you wait, you confirm the talent you'll need, and you create a recruitment plan to hire people with the necessary knowledge, skills, and abilities. You wait not days or weeks, but months, and finally get your approval. Your budget has been approved for two of the five priorities, and one that you hadn't planned on. Did the planning help? Of course! But now you need to adjust, and the race is on to get people hired. This environment can create a reactive cycle where, despite best planning intentions, agencies may stall, or even worse, rush to fill vacant positions.

This plays out in the two scenarios described below. Let's imagine there are two agencies, similar in size and structure. Each has roughly 5,000 employees, multiple occupational families, and office locations across the country.

Agency 1 stood up in response to an administration priority and was quickly hit with multiple high-visibility priorities and initiatives. It needed to staff up quickly to respond to mounting requests and requirements. In lieu of establishing a workforce plan to determine the number of full-time equivalent employees (FTE), skillsets, or structure of their workforce, they held surge hiring fairs and picked up as many competent and qualified bodies as they could. The agency struggled with onboarding due to undefined roles and the high number of incoming staff, including new supervisors with limited resources to help their own new hires. Staff ranged from being absolutely overworked to not understanding their roles. Responsibilities across teams became unclear, and issues emerged around who was doing what. Work units started to compete for resources, and the culture suffered. The agency experienced issues with morale and retention. Years later, the agency was combined with another subagency in hopes of boosting performance, and they had to lay off hundreds of employees through federal reduction-in-force (RIF) procedures.

Agency 2 also stood up in response to an administration priority and was immediately under substantial scrutiny. Because of the urgency and pressure, it established a human capital office with operational human resources (HR) and SWP capabilities and established a plan with the leadership team to prioritize position and skill needs. Position descriptions were created to accurately capture duty and knowledge requirements. Recruitments were based on these descriptions, and tailored assessments were used to get the right people in the right jobs. Hiring addressed different career levels and position types, which helped to ensure work was aligned to positions and grade levels. Both hiring and onboarding were managed in waves, based on criticality of the positions determined during initial staffing planning and SWP activities. Workload remained a challenge, but team members understood their roles, and performance standards aligned to the work they were doing. The agency experienced measured growth that allowed them to meet mission demands while building capacity for expanded impact and public assistance.

These scenarios, inspired by actual situations, illustrate the themes we develop in this chapter:

- Tactical SWP decisions can influence the degree to which organizations achieve their missions.
- Professional SWP procedures in the federal space align with many evidence-based practices familiar to I-O practitioners and researchers in terms of both micro (individual employee-level) and macro (organizational strategy-level) interventions.
- Federal agencies have the latitude to enact their own SWP procedures.
- SWP requires the ability to diagnose challenges and prioritize actions to address immediate needs as well as long-term goals.

Timely response on a nationwide scale, within the bureaucratic system, takes a lot of discipline and coordination. Agencies must be deliberate about the initiatives they prioritize as well as the investments made to *meaningfully* act. If workforce planning is overlooked, it can compound and/or create long-term challenges. Realistically, many agency environments represent a mix of both scenarios described above. When an agency or subagency is created, or if an existing agency needs to reconfigure activities to respond to a high priority, there is always urgency and a need for smart talent decisions. A strategic workforce plan doesn't remove the urgency in these cases, but it does prepare an agency to quickly make the best talent decisions based on business need, and it mitigates the risk of bad workforce investments. Due to the size and scale at the federal level, risks and costs can multiply quickly.

> **Practitioner Tip!**
>
> Key takeaway: SWP is a set of evidence-based practices aimed at ensuring the right people are in the right roles at the right time. SWP is a critical practice for federal agencies to be good stewards of public funding, but forward-looking SWP is challenging due to the number of agencies that make up the federal government, their capability to act independently, and the bureaucracy associated with decision-making and oversight systems. Without workforce planning, agencies can lose sight of who (and how many) are doing what, which can lead to costly decisions around hiring, training and development, and performance management. To be responsive to emerging requirements, organizations need to establish stable and consistent SWP practices that can be sustained even in times of uncertainty.

It's the Same... But Different

> **Practitioner Tip!**
>
> How this can play out: Some organizations have "shadow" HR staff working within mission-critical work units to advance their specific needs. For example, a law enforcement division may have HR staff providing dedicated support separate from or outside of the HR department. This reinforces the need to talk with stakeholders across roles and organizations to understand the variety of efforts that may be underway.

In many ways, workforce planning challenges facing the US government are what you'd encounter in a large corporation. When conceptualized as a conglomerate, the US government is the nation's largest employer. However, to allow for distinctions in mission and operations, agencies across the US government do not function as a single corporate entity when it comes to SWP. The massive scale and complexity of work requirements and workforce characteristics magnify the common challenges of forecasting workforce needs and implementing changes to address gaps. Stakeholders (like the public and Congress) rightfully want agencies to run effectively and efficiently, and workforce planning is the best way to meet work demands and mitigate risks of wasted resources. Unlike a large corporation, the US government can't have a single workforce plan that adequately represents its workforce needs. Even if a single workforce plan could cover the entire government, HR functions operate autonomously in each department, making it close to impossible to coordinate the effort necessary to analyze and react to federal workforce needs meaningfully or accurately. Interestingly, functional (mission-critical) areas of agencies often spearhead SWP activities, rather than HR (mission-support) departments. Workforce planning, then, is left to the departments, agencies, and subcomponents. This patchwork quilt of practices across the federal government presents numerous challenges to understanding the state of workforce planning and the common trends and needs of the workforce.

The remaining sections summarize the most common workforce planning approaches federal agencies deploy to overcome these challenges, the need for scalable workforce planning tools and activities, and how I-O psychologists play an important role in workforce planning in the government.

Balancing Enterprise Decisions and Organization-Specific Needs

Much like many private-sector companies, the federal government has the challenge of planning for an uncertain future by taking into consideration factors like strategic priorities, budget, existing talent, and the labor market. With that in mind, the government could be considered akin to a large corporation with multiple brands—each brand has its own targeted activities with tailored goals and performance measured at the brand level. It could be argued that departments or even agencies operate similarly, except their "brands" can be subdivided and sometimes resemble full corporations in terms of size and scope. For example, the Food and Drug Administration (FDA) is an agency within the Department of Health and Human Services (HHS) and is made up of multiple Centers (e.g., Centers for Medicaid and Medicare, Center for Drug Evaluation and Research, Center for Devices and Radiological Health). Planning for human capital needs in one Center may look substantially different from planning for human capital needs across the entire Department. If each Center has its own set of processes and inputs for workforce planning, consolidating even at the FDA level would be difficult. Expand that out across all HHS agencies and components and it becomes even harder. Expand that out to all of government? You see where this is going.

On the other hand, understanding the current capacity and challenges across agencies and components provides a huge advantage. If one component needs to increase bandwidth in a certain occupation, and you know another component excels and has robust resources in that occupation, you can leverage one to help another for the greater good of the whole. Additionally, adopting more proactive, evidence-based SWP methods provides agencies an advantage for benchmarking or aggregating across other organizations versus a more reactive or ad hoc approach. Like the old "garbage in, garbage out" adage, the quality of SWP methods matters greatly if you want to use the data to make inferences across agencies.

This balance between tailoring processes to meet unique needs of a few and standardizing processes to meet the general needs of the whole is long felt. There is a historical pattern of agencies shifting between decentralization and centralization of processes and operations. The symptoms and benefits tend to be as follows:

Decentralized approach: If an agency has the resources to invest in its own SWP infrastructure (typically staff and technology), it can create internal data standards, collection methods, education/liaising capabilities, and reporting to pull information together for its specific needs. This works best when there is consistent participation and application of rules and best practices. In addition, regular communication needs to happen across all stakeholders—up, down, and all around. Problems arise when there are not adequate resources (typically money) to staff and establish this infrastructure. If there are adequate resources in one part of an agency, you can't assume there are in all, and, if out of balance, aggregate "enterprise" plans can become disconnected or get bounced back by Headquarters. The worst-case decentralized scenario is that there are no resources to put toward SWP efforts, and the function languishes.

Centralized approach: If an agency decides it wants one strong and guiding "owner" of SWP, it may create internal data standards, collection methods, oversight capabilities, and reporting to compile and assess information from all of its components. This works best when the rules provide guardrails while still meeting the needs of the various programs within the agency. The benefit of centralizing the information, assuming the data are valid, is the opportunity to make enterprise decisions based on the results. Leveraging training resources at the HHS level, for example, can be more efficient and cost-effective than HHS subagencies separately contracting for the exact same training course. It requires a balance between structure and flexibility so that rules can be applied while unique perspectives are reflected. The biggest complaint here is that the process becomes a generic data call and box-checking exercise. The worst-case centralized scenario is that specific component and program needs are not adequately captured.

Practitioner Tip!

Analysis is needed at different levels to provide the best possible information to address questions about the workforce.

In our experience, the key is balancing the characteristics of the centralized and decentralized approaches to maximize the overall benefit. This capitalizes on different levels of proximity, influence, and control in an organization to establish a responsive workforce planning system. In lieu of a dichotomous view, we use the analogy of a dial—finding the right level of analysis based on the problem or question at hand. For example, if asked by Congress, a department must have an answer for how it will modernize the skillsets in its IT positions. Likewise, at the work unit level, a manager must be prepared to answer why they need x number of employees with xyz skillsets to accomplish the work. To answer these types of questions from the most appropriate vantage point, SWP mechanisms must be set up at multiple levels. We envision four levels (Figure 4.1):

Level 1: Supervisors and managers on the ground have the skills and tools to regularly evaluate the gaps in their work unit. Supervisors should be having regular conversations with their employees about development, career growth, and, of course, performance. This level also includes regular activities around staffing planning and assessing training needs or skills gaps, with those inputs coming directly from the supervisors and managers.

Figure 4.1 Finding the best level for workforce planning analysis.

Level 2: The subagency, or agency, level is where data and information are most often aggregated. Often the responsibility for the workforce planning function lies heavily on this level. If there is little coordination of workforce planning at higher levels, agencies or subagencies often establish these practices on their own to improve their organization's strategic planning capabilities. If there are department-wide processes already in place, at this level agencies or subcomponents are often trying to determine how best to implement policies and processes in their unique environment.

Level 3: Departments, the highest organizational unit in federal structures, are most likely to be evaluated for how well workforce planning is being done and whether there is a department-wide workforce plan. However, they often have little control over how workforce planning activities are being conducted at lower levels. Departments often have the best access to personnel data and trends, but necessary contextual information needs to be passed up and down through levels 1 and 2.

Level 4: Government-wide workforce planning generally takes two forms. The first involves analyses focused on specific, common, mission-critical positions—like information technology (IT) roles. The second involves examining specific data points, like representation of diversity across positions and agencies.[1] The insights gleaned from data at this level are not necessarily used to make decisions about workforce resources in departments or agencies, but to influence the direction of policy, the appropriated budget process, and government-wide strategy.

These levels each play a role in ensuring that agencies have the workforce they need to accomplish their missions. Sustainment of a workforce planning function and responsibility for related activities are usually most effective at the subagency or agency level because this level has the insight needed to more accurately identify workforce needs and the influence over budget and decision-making to address gaps. But this can also be the stickiest level depending on where the department or agency is on the decentralization scale. A subcomponent might not have authority or access to the data that it needs to conduct robust workforce planning. To be most effective, workforce planning functions need to be defined across levels in the organization layers. This creates accountability, reduces duplication of effort (or counterproductive efforts), and creates a workforce planning infrastructure that supports the activities where they are needed. No one single workforce planning system or approach can work for every department, but the level of analysis should be dialed in based on the organization's critical workforce questions and the structure and flow of data and information in the organization.

> **Practitioner Tip!**
>
> Coordinated approaches to strategic workforce planning are critical no matter if the function is centralized or decentralized within an organization. The breadth of federal departments, agencies, subagencies, and work units is enormous, which makes this challenging, but not impossible. Workforce planning mechanisms must exist at multiple levels within the organization, with consideration of stakeholder perspectives and available data at each level.

Federal Strategic Workforce Planning Guidance

If it is big, complex, and there are countless combinations of how to do it successfully, you may be wondering how you formalize SWP in the federal government? The answer is, "broadly." All agencies view themselves, their structure, and positions as unique, but there is a widely shared set of workforce management parameters and budget constraints that impact most. As such, agencies want guidance that meets government-wide standards and regulation (5 CFR Part 250, Subpart B, 2016) but that also accounts for the nuances of their agency. According to the Federal Human Capital Business Reference Model (OPM, 2017) maintained by the US Office of Personnel Management, "workforce planning" is defined as:

> A systematic and continuous process in which all levels of an organization's leadership and management teamwork in coordination with their Chief Human Capital Officer (CHCO) to identify the size and composition of a workforce needed to achieve its goals and objectives. The process incorporates the practice of business intelligence to identify the knowledge and skills required (now and into the future) to assess its current workforce to calculate the organization's skill gaps. The outputs of the workforce

planning process will inform the formulation of a budget justification, personnel investigation and vetting forecasting, and the design/implementation and monitoring of agencies' human capital strategy to enable the organization to be agile, resilient, and able to respond to current and future impacts.

Conceptually, workforce planning is easily recognized and understood as something an organization should do. But figuring out how to make it work in a complex, layered, and distributed workforce can be daunting. This is why workforce planning is a recognized need within the federal government, and it has made its way into multiple US Government Accountability Office (GAO) reports for agencies.

The GAO states two critical needs that define strategic workforce planning:

1. Align the human capital program with emerging mission goals; and
2. Develop long-term strategies for acquiring, developing, and retaining staff to achieve programmatic goals.

Throughout its recommendations, GAO identifies three leading practices for workforce planning:

1. Determine needed skills and competencies and develop strategies to address gaps;
2. Monitor progress toward human capital goals and assess the effectiveness of human capital strategies; and
3. Develop strategic workforce plans to coordinate human capital activities and align them with agency-wide goals.

Practitioner Tip!

Agencies want guidance that meets the government-wide standards and regulation, while accounting for the nuances of their agency. Federal SWP guidance exists but is broad to allow for tailoring to meet agency and organization needs. When operationalizing leading practices, organizations need to consider their stakeholders, existing processes, and infrastructure.

> **Practitioner Tip!**
>
> - *Make SWP activities approachable.* So often we see organizations introduce a tool that will make planning "easy," but instead it makes planning painful due to jargon, complicated instructions, and formulas.
> - *Keep it simple.* When engaging stakeholders from different levels of the organization, use terms that will resonate and keep the level of effort as minimal as you can.
> - *Don't let perfection get in the way of progress.* The landscape of a workforce changes daily. Measure what you can as consistently as you can.

We often observe that the challenge organizations struggle with isn't identifying best practices but operationalizing how to best implement them. There is a lot of flexibility in how agencies can make workforce planning work for them. Our most successful projects have been with smaller organizations, often subagencies that see the potential of workforce planning to positively impact their mission capabilities. The first step is usually to align whatever SWP standard operating procedure (SOP) is being created to existing processes like strategic planning, staffing planning, budget formulation, etc. Additional steps involve identifying ongoing targets for that organization (mission-critical occupations [MCOs], career paths, positions that are hard to fill, known retention risks). Many agencies struggle with the workforce assessment piece—how to measure skills gaps appropriately and swiftly within the workforce. Determining measurement strategies often requires consideration of potentially competing factors (e.g., union agreements, scale of the data collection, time available for workforce participation, availability of assessment tools). The general minimum steps involve some sort of assessment of supply (workforce skills/composition/market) as compared to the demand (mission needs). The mark of successful SWP is that strategies and plans can be meaningfully implemented, and results can be measured. The measurement aspect of strategic workforce planning has traditionally been the common connection point for I-O psychologists.

Advancing SWP and I-O Psychology

In a sector as large and diverse as the federal government, there is no shortage of opportunities for I-O psychologists to advance the field. Against the backdrop of the material and examples presented in this chapter, we now offer perspectives on how I-O practitioners—and those with adjacent skillsets—can contribute to professional SWP practice based on our experiences in the public sector.

Broadening Connections

As we have described, SWP is a web of interconnected activities and factors with many facets well suited for I-O psychologists: identifying, collecting, and accessing the most appropriate data points; analyzing and interpreting data; creating reports and visualizations to tell a compelling story about workforce needs; prioritizing gaps as they align to mission needs; developing strategies and actions that are realistic; communicating with and educating stakeholders; executing strategies and actions. I-O psychologists can fill many different roles when contributing to workforce planning in the federal government. Often there are personnel with similar (or even the same) backgrounds in I-O psychology conducting similar work but under different job titles and occupations, including management analysts, program managers, HR generalists or specialists, and/or personnel research psychologists, among others. The I-O community can support its talent by acknowledging the contributions made from various roles in government and promoting continued collaboration, training, and development. Strengthening collegiality across I-Os in different roles presents a tremendous opportunity to advance professional standards and positively influence the federal sector. And, just as there are opportunities to strengthen ties between I-Os in different roles, there is an opportunity for I-Os to partner more closely with stakeholders in areas like HR information technology (HRIT); operational HR; training; diversity, equity, inclusion, and accessibility (DEIA); budget; and performance and evaluation functions (among others). Especially as it relates to SWP, investing in these connections improves understanding of available data and tools and may unlock solutions that can be more readily scaled, executed, and sustained.

Technical and Practical Competency Development

In addition to building connections across the I-O community, investing further into scientist-practitioner perspectives is key. The Society for

Industrial Organizational Psychology (SIOP)'s competency model for training and education of I-O psychologists (SIOP, 2017) includes many competencies that are directly relevant to workforce planning. To keep up with ever-emerging trends in human capital, it helps to consider the practical scenarios these competencies often help address and the questions routinely faced.

Workforce Assessment and Analytics
SIOP's competency model includes "Statistical Methods/Data Analysis" with the following as part of the definition, "the various statistical techniques that are used in the analysis of data generated by empirical research." In federal workforce planning, a foundation in statistical design for empirical research is a hugely beneficial skillset that I-O psychologists bring to the table. Arguably just as valuable is the ability to maximize the use of existing data for broader applications (e.g., OPM using Fedscope data to identify high-risk occupations across government). Time and resources to design and execute research studies are luxuries many agencies believe they lack (or actually do lack). This becomes one of the tougher assessment and analytic challenges to balance: What is the appropriate level of rigor to make sound, data-driven workforce decisions? And how can existing data be more effectively leveraged? I-O psychologists can bring data- and evidence-based inference to the table, which is critical for providing insight and influence to senior decision-makers in agencies.

Agencies regularly seek benchmarking information to help make decisions, and while it can be very valuable, there are often multiple caveats to how data were collected, metrics captured, sample size, purpose of the study, etc. that raise questions of whether the data are useful at all or whether the results generalize to any other setting. So how can we tell? Based on our I-O training, we know the importance of research methods, but there is an inherent tension between the desire to research further and the need to make a decision using the information available. The ability to leverage enterprise-level data, existing datasets, and workforce data trends within the parameters of what is statistically and analytically sound has become increasingly important to make timely and informed decisions. As practitioners and management consultants, I-O psychologists are well positioned to guide the use of these data to achieve practicality and validity.

> **Practitioner Tip!**
>
> An added obstacle to robust workforce planning is the variety of personnel data systems that don't connect. There is no central owner of all federal workforce data, and while sources like Fedscope.gov (which provides access to employment statistics) are incredibly valuable, data modernization is a known need and an area of focus for the federal government. Currently there are massive investments around data and planning to support DEIA; the future of work, including hybrid and remote work trends; emerging occupations and broadening career fields, including cyber, artificial intelligence, and automation. Data modernization efforts have the potential to vastly improve how we link human capital metrics and planning to program goals.

Job Analysis/Competency Modeling

Job analysis is a core aspect of I-O psychology and, at the heart of workforce planning, is competency modeling and gap analysis. The "robustness" of these activities can vary, which is where balancing the role of scientist and practitioner is key.

Consider a common scenario: an agency receives funding to tackle a national priority (e.g., global pandemic, housing crises, infrastructure). The agency needs to mobilize existing staff with specific skill sets to meet this priority, *and* it needs to fill the remaining workforce gap by hiring the best and the brightest. But how does it know where (or if) these skillsets exist within its workforce? Does it have staff who could be trained to support the effort? Which positions does it prioritize for hiring? What jobs does it need? Scientists? Administrative support? Analysts? Does the agency need entry-level positions? Expert-level? How many of each?

In an ideal world, the agency would know which gaps to prioritize based on existing workforce planning, competency modeling, and gap analysis results; it would work with its training and development team to establish curricula and work with its hiring team to craft recruitment packages targeting those areas of greatest need. But many agencies do not have individual- or even work unit-level details on existing skillsets or proficiency levels. Many don't have competency models for all mission-critical occupations due to the time and investment it takes. This becomes more difficult to keep up with as occupations and job families evolve.

Often agency leadership, even in HR, may feel like a better move is to act quickly with limited information on training, development, or hiring priorities compared to fully developing and validating competencies and conducting a gap analysis. As I-O psychologists, we might feel tempted to stand our ground on the need for rigor in these situations, but that does not help agencies address their short-term needs. This presents an opportunity for I-O psychologists to participate in, or even direct, efforts to identify appropriate and scalable approaches to job analysis and competency modeling. To do so requires weighing risk factors, establishing thresholds for how results can be used, and leveraging available data to guide decision-making. In the face of imperfect data, I-O practitioners are uniquely able to explain the caveats and guide the interpretation of the data.

Consulting Skills

Workforce planning is an opportunity for I-O psychologists to inform and influence leaders' strategic decisions about where resources are deployed, how budget is spent, and how best to manage workforce programs. To effectively sit at the decision-making table, or even influence the conversation, consulting skills are incredibly important. Most masters' level I-O programs design curriculum to train students as applied practitioners, highlighting how to:

- Assess the needs of a customer
- Establish a consultative relationship
- Promote the benefits of approach/methodology
- Solve complex problems

Many I-O programs also provide opportunities to practice consulting skills in real-world scenarios through case studies, practica, internships, etc. Expanding this tradition, I-O programs could integrate more workforce planning scenarios into the curriculum. Workforce planning challenges present the opportunity for I-O students to apply knowledge across many common organization planning processes, synthesize multiple data sources, and identify where new data should be collected to add to the understanding of the issues. SWP also presents a unique intersection between the individual and organizational "sides" of the discipline.

Organizational Theory

There are aspects of individual assessment in workforce planning in addition to examining workforce gaps in aggregate at the organization level. I-O psychologists are generally skilled in "understanding the complex nature of organizations," which is foundational to workforce planning. The study of organizational theory should include systems such as structure, process, technology, culture and climate of a team or organization, leadership, and management. These I-O skills can be used to ultimately assess the overall performance and health of an organization to determine workforce needs.

Practitioner Tip!

The field of I-O psychology has a huge opportunity to influence and improve workforce planning within the public sector. I-O psychologists can help solve some of the most common challenges in federal workforce planning by focusing on how to:

- Build connections within the field and collaborate with human capital partners in HRIT, DEIA, operations, performance, and budget.
- Identify and leverage available enterprise data sources.
- Balance rigor and practicality to make meaningful improvements.
- Engage in long-term strategic planning activities while contributing to regular tactical resource planning and management.

I-O psychologists possess a unique mix of competencies to meaningfully execute the individual parts of workforce planning and also the holistic strategies that must be implemented with a consultative approach. Current workforce planning practices could benefit from the contributions of I-O psychologists who are comfortable working in applied settings with applied methods and willing to look for creative solutions to balance rigor and realism.

Leading Practices

Given the substantial challenges in federal workforce planning and the capabilities of I-O psychologists to make a positive impact on these processes and outcomes, there are multiple lessons learned and potential actions to recommend.

Recommended Practices for I-O Programs and the Field

While I-O practitioners have skills well-suited for workforce planning programs and activities, workforce planning training or curriculum is still lagging for most programs. More focused attention on workforce planning in I-O programs would position the field to make a significant impact on SWP practices and allow for additional modes of influencing leadership decision-making about workforce issues. There is room to improve how I-O programs prepare students for the agility required in this critical area. Some areas worth further exploration by I-O programs include:

- Explore frameworks for workforce planning and how SWP practices can drive organizational performance.
- Identify ways to adapt the scale or methods for competency modeling and job analysis, as may be necessary with vague occupational categories and the massive size of the federal workforce.
- Determine how to maintain rigorous methods in situations where time and existing research is limited.
- Explore ways to enact SWP activities while concurrently addressing urgent operational needs.
- Account for the variety of factors impacting workforce planning and how they can quickly evolve.
- Emphasize data visualization and highlight techniques that can be used to support a business case and inform organizational decision-making.
- Conduct and apply different types of analyses, including trend analysis and predictive analytics to capture change over time and projections for the future.
- Introduce students to professional associations in addition to SIOP that are recognized by I-O psychologists in government (e.g., International Personnel Management Association [IPMA], Association of Talent Development [ATD], and Society for Human Resources Management [SHRM]).

- Identify SWP-relevant coursework in adjacent academic departments to make these opportunities known and available to students.

Practices for Agencies

Agencies engaging in workforce planning or hoping to begin planning have an enormous opportunity to determine the practices that work best for their unique situations. The workforce planning space can become confusing because so many of the terms and labels are used interchangeably—and, as a field, I-O psychology tends to set strict boundaries around its work. We would argue that distinguishing between staffing or resource planning and SWP is perhaps less important than agencies making progress on gathering data and making informed plans for their workforce needs. Better yet, progress can be made in both the operational and strategic tracks simultaneously, with efforts at the four different levels described earlier in this chapter. The connections between the strategic and operational activities happening at various levels are key so that efforts are aligned toward a common purpose.

> **Practitioner Tip!**
>
> Whether a work unit needs a staffing plan or an agency needs an enterprise strategy to close skills gaps, workforce planning is under way.

The broad steps of SWP apply to any industry, so that part is easy. In fact, one of the best workforce planning courses we send our new employees to is not government-specific. The foundations are the same. The challenge lies in helping departments, subagencies, or work units develop an agile, easily repeatable, and sustainable process, one that helps them drive mission outcomes and is not a check-the-box activity. Scaling SWP activities to the right level is a persistent challenge. The challenges we've outlined regarding size, bureaucracy, and variety within federal workforce planning highlight the need to translate policy and guidance to "real-world" solutions. This is necessary for policy creators and agencies to understand. Policymakers must design guidance that can be applied across the wide breadth of agency needs, with an eye toward how agencies are expected to act on that guidance.

Agencies themselves need workforce planning talent and the resources to develop tools and implementation approaches that will work within their operating environment. An understanding of varying HRIT systems, reporting cadences, and priorities is needed to translate policy into successful practice.

Across government, there are many bachelor's, master's, and doctorate-level I-O practitioners well-suited to work in workforce planning. Our advice for best utilizing I-O psychologists in SWP across the federal government? Broaden your team: there are likely talented people with I-O (or related) backgrounds in different parts of your HRIT, data, HR operations, performance, and strategic planning teams. Network with other agencies' workforce planning teams to compare methods and challenges. Join communities of practice, like the OPM's listserv, to stay current on leading practices that are working across government agencies.

Practices for Future I-O Psychologists in Workforce Planning

The workforce planning space has so much to offer an I-O psychologist, particularly one interested in addressing ever-changing challenges, and the opportunity for broad organizational impact is immense. Workforce planning in the federal government offers the added benefit of meaningful, mission-focused work and helping agencies smartly plan for their workforce needs into the future. Our advice for preparing to go into workforce planning in a federal agency? Be ready to broaden your approach and think outside the box to make common methods work in the real world. You will apply your knowledge of rigorous assessment methods, but you'll want to be open to different ways of attacking the challenges facing your agency. In any of your courses, consider the implications to the workforce and workforce planning processes. Are you studying job analysis methodology? How could that be applied to determine the workforce necessary for the future? Are you studying training development or evaluation? How could that be used in the workforce planning process to address skill gaps in the organization? Studying performance appraisals and management? How would organizational performance metrics (or key performance indicators) inform workforce planning needs? If necessary, seek out additional training that will make you even more marketable as a workforce planner, such as a workforce planning-specific course, advanced predictive analytics, or data visualization.

Conclusion

There are extraordinary opportunities for the field of I-O psychology and its skilled practitioners to have a positive impact on federal government SWP. With its vast size and scope of work, the federal government needs research, benchmarking, and connection points across government agencies, which I-O psychologists can help facilitate. Individual departments and agencies need customized processes and tool development to help execute strategic workforce planning and more tactical activities, such as assessing the workforce, identifying broader workforce needs, and designing a process that accounts for an annual planning cadence for budget and strategic planning. I-O psychologists are uniquely positioned to design those processes and create momentum for improved workforce management practices based on sound practices in assessment, interpretation of data, and consulting skills. Federal managers, supervisors, and staff need guidance, training, information, and tools to embed workforce planning and career development in day-to-day operations. In so many federal organizations, the priority to execute on mission with lean resources takes precedent over long-term planning. I-O psychologists can help balance the scales, equipping those managing the mission-critical work in agencies to meaningfully plan for the most critical resource in government—its people.

Practitioner Tip!

We all play a part in strengthening strategic workforce planning.

I-O Programs:
- Recognize and reinforce the critical role of SWP within I-O programs and curricula.
- Build strategic workforce planning skillsets in future and current I-Os through enhanced learning opportunities.

Agencies:
- Promote a comprehensive workforce planning ecosystem with mechanisms for evaluating and building workforce capacity at multiple levels.
- Engage a broad set of stakeholders to create and implement workforce planning programs that meet unique organization needs.

Future I-O Psychologists:
- Think broadly and consider unique applications to methodologies and approaches you learn.
- Embrace both scientist and practitioner perspectives to discover sound and practical solutions.

Authors' Note

The discussion presented in this chapter represent the views and experiences of the authors and do not necessarily represent those of the US Office of Personnel Management.

Note

1. The Chief Human Capital Officers Council website is a resource for OPM memorandums to Chief Human Capital Officers, HR Directors and Heads of Agencies: https://www.chcoc.gov/transmittals

References

Congressional Research Service (2022, June 28). *Federal Workforce Statistics Sources: OPM and OMB (R43590)*. https://crsreports.congress.gov/product/pdf/R/R43590/20

Strategic Human Capital Management, 5 CFR part 250 subpart B (2016). https://www.ecfr.gov/current/title-5/chapter-I/subchapter-B/part-250/subpart-B

U.S. Office of Personnel Management (OPM). (2017). *Human Capital Business Reference Model.* https://www.opm.gov/services-for-agencies/hr-line-of-business/hc-business-reference-model/hc-brm-interactive-model.pdf

Society for Industrial and Organizational Psychology, Inc. (2016). *Guidelines for education and training in industrial-organizational psychology.* Bowling Green, OH: Author. Retrieved November 13, 2023, from https://www.siop.org/Events-Education/Graduate-Training-Program/Guidelines-for-Education-and-Training

5
The History of the Workforce at Saudi Aramco
Opportunities for I-O Psychology

Christian Hobson and Paul van Katwyk

As a global leader in the energy industry, Saudi Aramco has dramatically evolved since its founding more than 80 years ago to become one of the most highly valued organizations in the world. This chapter examines the history of Aramco, its workforce, and, in turn, the role of strategic workforce planning (SWP). This case study begins by exploring the history of this organization because it illustrates the unique workforce planning implications of operating as the steward of the vast oil and gas resources within the Kingdom of Saudi Arabia. Then an overview is provided around the company's efforts to make workforce planning more strategic and relevant to the businesses within Aramco. From this discussion will emerge opportunities for roles that the field of industrial-organizational (I-O) psychology has and could play in the future of SWP in companies like Saudi Aramco.

History of Aramco and Its Workforce

Historical Context Around Workforce Planning

Aramco was founded in 1933, with an agreement between the newly established Kingdom of Saudi Arabia and the US company Standard Oil of California (SoCal) to support exploration for oil. The discovery of oil in 1938 brought in a new era for the Kingdom, in part because of the significant demands created for assuring a capable workforce. Early efforts at workforce planning placed a heavy reliance on contractors and an external workforce that included many Americans. However, the more strategic thrust at

Christian Hobson and Paul van Katwyk, *The History of the Workforce at Saudi Aramco*
In: *Strategic Workforce Planning*. Edited by: Marc Sokol and Beverly Tarulli, Oxford University Press.
© Society for Industrial and Organizational Psychology 2024. DOI: 10.1093/oso/9780197759745.003.0006

workforce planning at this US-based organization focused on forecasting and responding to the training and education requirements needed to develop a pool of skilled Saudi national workers (Pledge, 1998). Unique from most other companies and tied to its commitment to the Kingdom, Aramco worked with the government by taking a pivotal and direct role in building and supporting schools for the development of an educated population from which to draw, which began with a focus on basic skills including literacy and core math skills.

In terms of forecasting, even in these early decades, predictions of the required workforce were challenged by market volatility as world oil producers evolved and changed. For example, in 1949, with a reversal in the trend of oil production, given external demand challenges, the workforce was reduced from 20,254 to 16,084, which included many from the expatriate pool (Pledge, 1998). Furthermore, entering into the 1950s, the oil trade forecast was that Aramco had grown as large as it could, with a peak of 532,000 barrels/day. This prediction contrasts starkly to today's reality in that Aramco recently announced the 2022 results noting an average production of crude oil at 10.47 million barrels per day.

Saudization as a Strategic Workforce Priority

The 1950s also presented a new and visible workforce planning challenge, one unique from many other organizations across the globe. Specifically, serious planning began for Saudi nationals to provide the majority of skilled roles and take leadership positions in the company (Pledge, 1998). Therefore, Personnel Planning Committees were tasked to assure the training plan needed to prepare a workforce for tomorrow. Part of this included the Aramco Production Training Program, which called for intensive on-the-job training for 8,000 unskilled Saudi workers, with the goal of raising half of the Saudi workforce to skilled and semiskilled levels by 1954. The associated workforce planning objective was labeled the "Saudization" of Aramco's workforce and consisted of an organized, company-wide effort to qualify large numbers of Saudis for jobs being performed by expatriates.

Between 1949 and 1953, the number of employees surged from 15,314 to 24,120 (Pledge, 1998). However, this workforce size would not be achieved again for 25 years as the US-based company focused on reducing its workforce through greater productivity and efficiency. In turn, efforts at Saudization were mixed as the percentage of Saudis rose from 59% in 1952 to only 65% by 1960 as the employee base dropped to just over 15,000. Yet on the leadership front there were successes in that, by the early 1960s, around 50 of the senior staff were Saudi, up from only 3 a decade earlier. Saudi nationals also held one-third of supervisory roles, with 467 out of the 1,416 positions. Efforts at reducing the illiteracy rates of the Saudi workforce had successfully dropped it to 40% from 85% a decade earlier. Much of this reduction in illiteracy was supported by Aramco's efforts between 1949 and 1954 to take on significantly more responsibility for the well-being and education of Saudi employees.

As part of the effort to build its skilled workforce, after an agreement with the government in 1953, Aramco also built government schools and paid for their operations with government-supplied curriculum and teachers. This included significant investments that continue to this day in sponsoring key technical talent and those with leadership potential within Saudi Aramco for education at leading global universities. Aramco also played a key support role in providing the land, buildings, and core funding toward the establishment of a College of Petroleum and Mining. Founded in 1963, the King Fahd University of Petroleum and Minerals (KFUPM) has a current enrollment of more than 10,000 students with a ranking among the top 200 universities worldwide (Quacquarielli Symonds, 2021), and it was 14th in 2020 among universities granted US patents, with 1,500+ patents (National Academy of Inventors, 2021). In 2021, the university admitted its first female students into its undergraduate engineering programs, which aligns with Saudi Aramco's current efforts to diversify its workforce. To this day, sponsorship programs of thousands of promising Saudi high school students for an education at universities like KFUPM have been core to Aramco's effort in building its workforce for tomorrow.

"Mega" Projects and the Nationalization of Aramco

In terms of workforce growth, while the workforce forecast in 1970 was that the ongoing reductions would continue from about 10,000 to as low as 5,000 by 1980 (Pledge, 1998), a number of factors have influenced Aramco's growth to more than 70,000 direct employees today (not including the more than 60,000 employees in global affiliates and many thousands more who are full-time contractors). One factor has been the growth in oil demand, which began to explode in the early 1970s, with countries like the United

States dramatically increasing their imports. Saudi Aramco saw overall production double in a year. The workforce demand has also been spurred by the introduction of significant "mega projects" such as the Master Gas System, which marked a growing trend in multibillion dollar projects. The workforce impact was that, within 4 years, the workforce doubled to 19,467 employees in 1975 (Pledge, 1998). Contrasting this to the original workforce forecast in 1970 of a 50% reduction over the coming decade, this is an example of how organizations like Aramco operating within a globally dynamic and highly politized environment (e.g., Organization of Petroleum Exporting Countries [OPEC]) struggle to provide reliable workforce forecasts. In turn, the workforce planning efforts were again insufficient to meet demand, which resulted in a movement to hire increasingly from foreign markets. Expatriate growth added 11,800 expats and only 3,360 Saudis between 1975 and 1978. This resulted in an overall decline in the Saudization of Aramco as a percentage of the total workforce.

The year 1980 was a pivotal moment in Aramco's history as the Saudi government took over full ownership of Aramco. With this transition, Saudi nationals took control of workforce planning and key activities like ensuring the training and development of employees. The nationalization of Saudi Aramco and renewed efforts at Saudization had moved the percentage of Saudi nationals in the workforce to 65% by 1985, with almost a 10-fold increase over the previous decade to 1,700 Saudis being classified as professionals (Pledge, 1998). Yet still workforce planning efforts only continued around the Saudization of Aramco because only 21% of professional positions and 18 of the 31 executive management positions were held by Saudis. The impact of this continued focus was that, by its 60th anniversary in 1993, Saudi Aramco had 46,000 employees, of whom 75% were Saudi nationals with almost a completely Saudi executive management team.

Aramco Looks Forward

In the 30 years since its 60th anniversary, workforce demands have had to further evolve as the Kingdom's demands on Aramco have significantly expanded in the 21st century. A prime example is the Kingdom's ongoing focus and commitment to realizing its stated Vision 2030. This vision highlights a strategic framework for reducing the nation's reliance on oil production. Yet, ironically, diversification into other industries relies on Aramco to play a key role in the realization of this vision through initiatives to drive a more thriving economy supported by a vibrant society. One significant change this brought to Aramco was the decision to privatize the company in 2019, which provided a source of funding for the Kingdom's significant development projects.

A related effort to Vision 2030, which brings significant workforce planning implications, is an aggressive goal to localize all of Aramco's spending on goods and services from 35% in 2015 to 70% by 2030. This ongoing effort has involved supporting the establishment of new supplier industries and businesses within the Kingdom (e.g., shipping, steel plate manufacturing, industrial 3D printing, advanced chip and smart sensor manufacturing). On top of these national demands are the SWP challenges associated with the overall transformation in the oil and gas industry. Aramco, like many of its peer companies, is transforming into an energy company that includes diversification into downstream businesses and significant investments in realizing new technologies (e.g., blue hydrogen, renewable energy). All of these demands require significant investments and partnerships by Aramco to ensure the necessary skilled workforces for itself *and its local suppliers*. This has resulted in targets such as graduating up to "360,000 young Saudi men and women in a wide range of disciplines" (Saudi Aramco, 2016).

Integrating Diversity in the Saudization of Aramco

Vision 2030 also brought forward another significant consideration and change in the targeted composition of the national workforce. As outlined earlier, the Saudization of talent has been a priority over the decades and has met with success in that, today, Saudis hold most all key business and professional leadership roles across levels and business lines. In recent years, a focus on the diversity of Saudi talent has gained increased attention. Specifically, the diversity focus has been on women and those with disabilities. Strategic goals now include the hiring of diverse talent throughout the workforce and diversity in leadership at all levels. Currently within Saudi Aramco, the percentage of women is 4.5% of the 70,000+ workforce, with a target of 12.5% by 2030.

In the Aramco context, when focusing on talent within the Kingdom, there are workforce challenges similar to other engineering-focused companies. Specifically, while female participation in postsecondary education is greater than 70% in Saudi Arabia and has recently become higher than males

(UNESCO, 2022), their studies are focused more on education, social sciences, or specialized areas like law versus training for engineering-focused professions. An additional challenge in Saudi Arabia is that, despite having a highly educated female population, there is a relatively low participation rate of women in the workplace, which just passed 20% in 2020 (International Labour Organization, 2022).

With the aspirations of Vision 2030 have come policies that support increased participation by females in the workforce (e.g., allowing driving licenses for women) and highly visible actions such as a royal princess as the first female ambassador to the United States. As well, the efforts to support a more diverse working environment within Saudi Aramco and its workforce planning efforts have seen significant increases in women's participation in the workforce. Yet, for a range of factors, at more senior leadership levels, women have very limited presence, with only two females in the top 300+ leadership roles at the writing of this chapter. To address this challenge, workforce planning efforts include the establishment of internal career paths, development resources, and building a more inclusive culture to support reaching the stated targets at all levels of leadership. These efforts have involved departments like a devoted Diversity and Inclusion Division as well as other groups like Executive Development, where there are I-O psychologists engaged in these initiatives. As well, consistent with past workforce efforts, Aramco has partnered closely with the government to support its own and the broader diversity goals of the Kingdom. These efforts have included evaluating and reclassifying roles that females have traditionally not been allowed to fill (e.g., roles in remote locations) and opening attendance to universities traditionally limited to males, thus creating doors to new careers (e.g., engineering, IT).

The Unique Nature of Workforce Planning at Aramco

Overall, this case description of Aramco's history illustrates the unique workforce planning implications of being a part of this national company. Some of the most significant and potentially unique workforce planning considerations are:

- A high priority on supporting national interests including but not limited to having direct involvement in the education of the local population;

- A predominant focus on internal development in assuring a pipeline of future talent especially at the leadership levels; and
- Challenges in forecasting when operating in a globally complex and highly politized industry such as oil and gas (and now more broadly energy).

In the next section, a closer look at the evolution of SWP within Aramco and the roles I-O psychologists have played and could play is covered.

The Evolution into Strategic Workforce Planning

Drivers for Strategic Workforce Planning

Like any robust SWP approach, the driver for Aramco's SWP is the company strategy. Aramco plays a systemic role not only in the energy sector but also in the global markets and trade corridors into Saudi Arabia. The Kingdom has a population of 37 million, 70% of whom are younger than 35 years, and, central to the Kingdom's Vision for 2030, are economic reforms with diversification and sustainability at their core. This serves and supports a generation that will rely less on hydrocarbons to secure their future. More than ever, this means treating oil and gas as scarce and finite commodities, as exemplified by the "liquid to chemicals" program, which at its heart is the technology to remove or streamline several conventional industrial processes resulting in chemicals and plastics that are less expensive to produce while at the same time creating a significantly reduced carbon footprint.

Outside of the conventional sector, Aramco is focused on the emerging technologies of the Fourth Industrial Revolution along with logistics, industry, and services that are developed and established to serve both the Kingdom's and Aramco's vast and dynamic ecosystem. Such diversification layers complexity onto an approach to SWP and offers several challenges for the company. These can be summarized as (1) understanding requirements and impact of investment and strategic pivots, (2) estimating workforce requirements and capability gaps, and (3) quantifying workforce cost implications—ranging from education, training, salary costs, transportation, to employee housing.

Steps in the Evolution

This has driven a rapidly maturing approach to SWP over recent years. Initially, SWP could be positioned at an operational end of a continuum characterized by headcount projections and a reliance on retrospective data and static reporting and ultimately aligned with budget-driven headcount planning. Figure 5.1 illustrates the levels and how the approach at Aramco has had to progress rapidly to address the impact and workforce capability implications of progressive corporate strategic shifts and external disruptors in the workforce. A major step change was the application of an advanced predictive analytics framework to produce accurate, consistent, and comprehensive workforce planning for both the short-term cycle (3 years) and long-term investment plan (10 years and beyond). Other industries may focus on shorter time frames for workforce planning, given the volatility and uncertainty of their markets. Yet while unpredictable volatility and uncertain futures are part of the oil and gas industry, the scale and time frames associated with new strategic priorities and projects (e.g., building of a refinery, opening up new fields) typically demand at least a decade from planning to realization. Thus this structured approach is critical to managing risks in terms of exposing potential capability gaps and informs appropriate human resources (HR) measures and a range of interventions, such as mobility, training, development, and recruiting before integration and re-entry into the Corporate Planning process.

It is important to note that the talent strategy at Aramco has for many years been a predominantly build-only approach with a very limited and measured augmentation of specialized non-Saudi "expat" talent. This is most acute at the leadership level, which is currently almost exclusively populated by home-grown Saudi talent from local universities and with

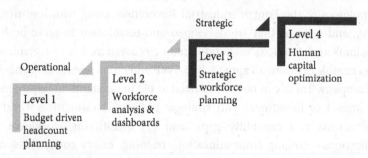

Figure 5.1 Workforce planning maturity model.
Adapted from Mercer, 2015.

engineering-related degrees. This has served the company well and is an indicator of the successful culmination of both internal workforce planning and the Kingdom's investment in the education and training that it has offered its citizens over many years.

Despite the stability and certainty this strategy offers (attrition is less than 2%) it does present some challenges. Assimilation into the organization and the high context culture perpetuate the build approach, making rapid acquisition and deployment of talent from the market less likely to succeed. The build approach is enabled by an education system within the kingdom which is unsurprisingly weighted toward science and engineering specialties and the structured development programs and cross-functional opportunities that the company offers. Hence the payoff from a robust approach to SWP is high and is regarded as a key HR strategic initiative, with a dedicated team of specialists drawn from various parts of the organization, not solely HR, into a multidisciplinary team.

One example of this relates to the ramp-up of corporate development and the need to build commercial skills. Building and managing companies that serve not only Aramco across the value chain but also the kingdom's needs has been a major pillar of Aramco's strategy in recent years. However, finding commercially savvy dealmakers in a company mainly populated by high-end engineering graduates is a challenge. However, many engineers understand the fundamentals of the sector, are exceptionally numerate, are problem-solvers, and have the relationship skills and agility that enable them to pivot to these new roles. The I-O psychologist sits across the business lines and can understand the skills and provide rigorous assessment and conduct talent reviews that will identify and draw from this nascent talent pool. Subsequent training delivers either sustained or temporary commercial deal teams to capitalize on strategic opportunities.

The approach was introduced with pilots focused on critical work segments. The identification of such segments need not be complex. An analysis of the capabilities that have highly significant strategic impact, coupled with either a high-change or high-growth environment or a significant talent challenge (such as high demand or scarce capability), has often proved sufficient. One example is the impact of digitization on the role of the HR business partner or advisor. This we regard as a critical work segment, not least because the role is rapidly changing as the business lines becomes more global, empowered, and digitally enabled. The HR business partner role is transitioning to manage divergent stakeholder relationships and influence strategy rather than simply being the strategy executor. Digitization supports this transition; it drives efficiencies and removes human interaction with many routine transactions, leaving space for more complex and higher-value work falling to the business partner. This leaves us asking questions regarding the shape and size of the HR business partner talent. We analyze what capabilities remain, what is to be added, and, crucially, what will be jettisoned. In our experience, clarity regarding the elements of a role that are to be removed are often underestimated as blockers for a successful implementation of the workforce plan. Many professionals naturally feel comfortable maintaining some of the core skills that have enabled their success in the past, and giving these up can be a challenge. As we will explain, the I-O psychologist can play a valuable role in smoothing this transition.

The Value of I-O Psychology

The professional value that I-O psychologists bring is evidenced by intervention at various points in the process, ranging from the analysis and categorization of capabilities, assessment, evaluation of engagement and job design, and reskilling to ensure meaningful work in an environment where people want to perform at their best and feel they belong.

More fundamentally, the training that an I-O psychologist undertakes is especially beneficial in such a company at such a pivotal inflection in its history. Domains spanning job evaluation and compensation through to individual assessment and criterion theory all go into making a broad toolbox that can be deployed by the practitioner in the field. In Saudi Arabia, our experience shows that understanding attitude theory and culture as applied to organizational development is key. The impact of culture and change in such high-context environments is an important consideration when embarking on the planning process. Although the Kingdom is changing rapidly, there prevails a diffuse yet rule-bound and hierarchical culture. At Aramco this is overlaid on a scientific research and engineering approach, together with the collective culture of the region.

Armed with this knowledge and understanding, the question is how this affects the I-O psychologist's approach. A clue may be found in how Vision 2030 has galvanized the people of Saudi Arabia and, in turn, the purpose of Aramco: comprehensive tangible programs communicated in a manner that all can relate to and understand their impact. The growth and diversification agenda that is core to Aramco's strategy is now increasingly reliant on imperatives that build for scale: a perspective that considers the whole ecosystem, technology platforms that allow data to be the core business, and an experiment-and-learn-fast environment (McKinsey, 2021). These are the considerations when embarking on any SWP approach and are often in contrast to more traditional static SWP approaches. Questions we ask are how do we harness the whole of the organization's vast array of networks? How do we support growth and innovation through data-rich technology? And how do we ensure nimble and constant adaptation? These are not straightforward questions but wrestling with them early on in the process is, in our experience, time well spent.

The Historical and Future Role of the I-O Psychologist

Turning to a more specific example of how the impact of the I-O psychologist at Aramco has been acutely felt, we focus on their influence on the future leadership pipeline, where there has been a substantial legacy of credibility and delivery. For many years the company has employed a cadre of I-O psychologists who have advised and built assessment and development practices with future capabilities in mind. The role's impact is amplified in environments where certainties of the future are less clear. This was observed during the preparation for Aramco's listing in 2019 on the Saudi Stock Exchange, the Tadawul. Like most public companies, investors and stakeholders are looking to understand how talent is identified, developed, engaged, and deployed to ensure the company is well managed and its people risks understood and mitigated. Clearly, the lessons learned from numerous corporate failures across the world have led to greater scrutiny and tighter evaluation of companies' leadership and succession management practices as part of broader environmental, social, and governance (ESG) goals.

The I-O psychologist brings a unique skillset to this situation. Defining capabilities and investing in robust success profiles has been a most worthwhile activity at Aramco, and yet a common challenge is to ensure there is enough clarity regarding the role such that it is not only applicable to a cluster of jobs but also sufficiently future-proofed that it will be appropriate for evaluating and developing talent for tomorrow's challenges. Guidance lies in the company's strategy, and the value the I-O psychologist brings is to translate this into a success profile by looking at the company "from the outside in" (Kenny, 2019). The I-O psychologist is well trained in supporting the translation of future capability demands into success profile components that include valid behavioral competencies and the associated personality, cognitive, and motivational preferences that can guide effective HR solutions. As we often see in discussions on future potential, the I-O psychologist can provide a relevant voice in conversations around talent requirements where the aspirational (e.g., "We need people with charisma") and the propositional (e.g., "He reminds me of when I was a young leader") may not correspond to what data-based research on talent would suggest.

Supporting a data-based approach to talent has been the assessment strategy at Aramco, one that is fully integrated into the talent management strategy. The leadership journey is well defined in terms of both development activities and assuring assessment data at the right time for the right purpose. The performance management process is the first filter, and those with a strong performance track record and good delivery against defined key performance indicators, together with desired leadership behaviors, are then evaluated regarding potential. This is defined in terms of personality, intelligence, and motivation (Macrae, Furnham, and Reed, 2018), and the trajectories of potential are again anchored on the defined leadership level. The question of whether the leader has the ability to progress one leadership level or two needs to be answered. The leader may also have plateaued, and development will continue at his or her current level. Beyond two levels, we become less sure and thus assessments are repeated as the leader progresses up the hierarchy, typically at an interval of 4–7 years.

Readiness and alignment with succession management follows. Significant focus is given to the readiness assessment, where assessment centers are used at key levels of leadership as shown in Figure 5.2.

These assessment centers of readiness are built on Aramco's core competency model and leverage customized simulations, interviews, and testing to provide internally or externally benchmarked evaluations. In the past 21 years, more than 7,500 leadership readiness assessments have been conducted, and these have been integrated into Success Factors to provide a rich database to be leveraged on top of data including performance evaluations, potential scores, acting assignments, completed development programs, and a range of other insights into the individual and their career history. It is at this point that the value of the I-O psychologist becomes more apparent to business leaders, where counsel, grounded in this data, stewards the decision to appoint an individual to a particular position.

A leadership journey aligned to the success profile minimizes risk, and all leaders are expected to have progressed along this journey to be ready for the transition. The journey comprises experiences and developmental programs which are grounded in the success profile and in service of accelerating readiness. With readiness assessed and development gaps closed, the subsequent

THE WORKFORCE AT SAUDI ARAMCO 111

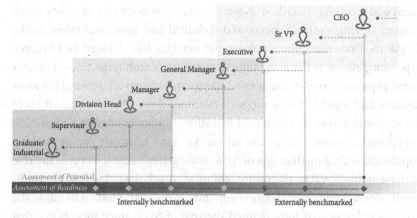

Figure 5.2 Assessing and managing to leadership level transitions.

promotion into the next leadership level is relatively smooth. This placement decision, owned by the business leader but informed by I-O psychologists, ensures carefully managed and risk-mitigated succession. It is this practical and data-driven approach, one grounding the future to the present, which Aramco seeks from its I-O psychologists. They have undoubtedly contributed to building the leadership pipeline needed for the most reliable, profitable, and largest companies in the world.

Before we examine the impact that I-O psychologists will have in the coming years on the company's SWP, it is worth summarizing the historical role these professionals have played in Aramco. Over the decades, their expertise either as external consultants or as employees has helped ensure that Aramco has a tremendously efficient method of identifying and developing talent to meet future demands. Most often I-O psychologists have been involved in the assessment component (e.g., staffing selection, readiness assessment). However, I-O psychologists working within Aramco have often found themselves seated alongside other HR experts, playing roles instrumental in ensuring that the right capability has been deployed in the right place at the right time (e.g., talent advisors, senior HR professionals) as well as in more specialized roles (e.g., assessment heads, career management, coaching, talent data analysis).

Future Impact of I-O Psychologists

Major priorities are likely to arise that will further shape the I-O psychologists' role at Aramco. First, there will be a rebalancing of the supply-and-demand talent equation. As described above, Aramco was once one of a very small number of employers of specialized technical and industrial talent in the Kingdom. Since then, the employee marketplace has changed and become hypercompetitive at the same time that Aramco's ambitions toward greater global expansion and an accelerated energy transition will demand the most valuable and highly diverse range of talent available. The diversification of the economy driven by significant investments associated with Vision 2030 has created a strong and diverse job market for a relatively young working population with a median age of 31.8 (www.statista.com). In turn, the role of those doing SWP in the future will need to acknowledge that the traditional worker–employer relationship has been disrupted. Although the two major forces that have defined the role of SWP since inception—that being balancing the future demands of the business strategy against the dynamics of the available talent market—still remain, the relationship between the people and the company will be increasingly personalized. We see this across many organizations, arguably because of the pandemic and the subsequent increased importance of the human element at work. This dynamic has created an opportunity for I-O psychologists to focus their remits and reinforce the connection of business strategy to people strategy.

Aramco has come to see empowering its people with agency and choice must be at the heart of how it plans and designs jobs in the future. This is where the I-O psychologist has a unique role to play, one potentially more complex than in the past, but more holistic and with far greater impact on the success of the company. The talent at Aramco are expecting their professional lives to feature careers that are no longer solely vertical but that are paths providing meaning and variety. The challenge for the I-O psychologist is to work seamlessly with business leaders to design jobs, workspaces, and careers that optimize both company and employee needs. Additionally, Aramco will continue to see a shift from an SWP approach centered on current capabilities to a focus on potential. "Know how" becomes "learn how," and the I-O psychologist is uniquely placed to assess not only the agility and potential to thrive in such an environment, but also the values and drivers that align with the company's vision and strategy. In an environment of engineers who focus on what can be measured today, assuring they can understand how to focus on potential will present questions the I-O psychologist is well positioned to address.

The whole has always been greater than the sum of the parts at Aramco. As the challenges and global context becomes more complex, solutions will rely on interdisciplinary and geographically dispersed teams. In the context of SWP, this presents measurement challenges in predicting workforce requirements at the team level, which involves more than targeting a set number or mix of individuals. The I-O psychologist has for many years studied team effectiveness. However, it will require an even greater shift in focus from the measurement of individual performance to team-level performance and that considers the effects of variables like diversity and collaboration. Clearly, the recognition and incentivization associated with such team-based performance measurement will be a key consideration. However, from team configuration and performance assessment through to companywide organization design, the skills of the I-O psychologist will be invaluable to the company's ability to meet the challenges of the future (Box 5.1).

> **Practitioner Tip!**
>
> **Advice That Has Served Us Well**
> - *Start small, think big.* Regardless of your company's size, you are unlikely to need to plan for the whole workforce. Prioritize and look for where you will have the most impact, start small, and then zoom out. If it's overwhelming, then take a deep breath and pare it back. However, considerations of the organizational culture and that of the wider talent market are key. Think deeply about some of the diverse political, economic, social, technological, legal, and environmental (PESTLE) forces influencing your company and the talent dynamics (i.e., political, economic, sociological, technological, legal, and environmental).
> - *Bring others with you.* The aim of SWP is to deliver business results, and although the I-O psychologist has a unique perspective, our work needs to be collaborative and embedded in business strategy. Articulate the problem, what you can bring to help solve it—and what you need from your colleagues. In our experience, once others see credible versions of the future, they become exited, engaged, and want to be part of shaping it.
> - *Be directionally right, not precisely wrong.* SWP is not about the numbers of people and hiring targets. It's about a strategic direction—or directions. If you are getting deep into numbers, then you may be missing the bigger picture.
> - *Review and refine.* It is not necessary for the planning to be right the first time. It will go through iterations and change as your knowledge, context, and, potentially, the facts change. Partnering with your business leaders to help inform and support them will allow you to refine to the point of viable delivery.

Conclusion

This case study has looked at the unique history and dynamics associated with the growth and evolution of a Middle East national oil company into a leader in the global energy market. From this historic overview came the unique workforce planning demands associated with a company that is expected to play a central role in responding to the needs and vision of the country. Key implications include playing significant roles in developing and enabling the national workforce, which includes funding schools for future employees to supporting the SWP requirements of their local suppliers. An overview of the ongoing evolution of SWP highlighted the implications of key trends, such as an increasingly competitive and diverse employment market that also requires new ways of thinking as the employee–employer relationship changes. This evolution presents new challenges that I-O psychologists are well positioned to address.

Looking to how we will evolve in years to address these opportunities, there are several tenets that we hold firm and which will support the unique role that the I-O psychologist can play in SWP. Core is our focus on a "scientist-practitioner" perspective, one grounded in data and practical in implementation. As I-O psychologists we work alongside other professionals, and our training and discipline give us the confidence to view a problem from different angles. These views are no more relevant than our colleagues', but they are different. The challenge presented to our profession is the need to view the world through a broader lens, one that includes the perspective of the individual within the company and the numerous communities and societies that it touches. This expanded view considers culture, generation, gender, and background and brings these together into action with positive intent.

The challenge for the I-O psychologist is not just our own. It also requires organizations to actively see and support the role of the I-O psychologist beyond their traditional roles in areas such as assessment, performance appraisal, and succession management. Our experience has been that the windows for "rebranding" our profession are opening as the demands on SWP professionals require a more sophisticated consideration of variables, including retention risk, employee value proposition, potential capabilities, strategically pivotal capabilities, and the predictive evaluation of different SWP strategies. Ironically, as we look to our future role as industrial psychologists within this company, there is arguably a parallel in the journey of Saudi Aramco with that of our profession. Saudi Aramco, in its relatively short history, has needed to evolve from an oil and gas company into a global energy leader by leveraging its distinctive technical capacities and its strong engineering culture. So, too, as a relatively young profession, we are being asked to evolve to meet the emerging complexity of SWP demands and play a broader role that leverages our deep technical capabilities grounded within our strong scientist-practitioner culture. For our team of I-O psychologists across Saudi Aramco, this provides a rich and promising professional future as we work to effectively respond to the call offered in meeting the SWP needs of this company.

References

Arab News. (2021, December 14). Education takes biggest chunk of Saudi public spending in 2022. https://www.arabnews.com/node/1986011/business-economy

International Labour Organization. (2022). Labor force, female (% of total labor force)—Saudi Arabia. data.worldbank.org. https://data.worldbank.org/indicator/SL.TLF.TOTL.FE.ZS?locations=SA

Kenny, G. (2019). *HBR guide to thinking strategically*. Harvard Business Press.

MacRae, I., Furnham, A., and Reed, M. (2018). *High potential: How to spot, manage and develop talented people at work*. Bloomsbury.

McKinsey. (2021). Organizing for the future: Nine keys to becoming a future-ready company. 2021-01-11. Retrieved 2023-12-24. https://www.mckinsey.com/capabilities/people-and-organizational-performance/our-insights/organizing-for-the-future-nine-keys-to-becoming-a-future-ready-company

National Academy of Inventors. (2021). Top 100 worldwide university granted U.S. utility patents, 2020. National Academy of Inventors; Tampa, Florida. https://academyofinventors.org/publications/top-100-2020/

Pledge, T. A. (1998). *Saudi Aramco and its people: A history of training*. Aramco Services Company.

Quacquarielli Symonds. (2021, June 8). QS World University Ranking 2022. qs.com.

Saudi Aramco. (2016). Saudi Aramco reaffirms its commitment to its flagship localization initiative—iktva. December 15, 2021. iktva.sa. Retrieved April 17, 2022. https://www.eyeofriyadh.com/news/details/iktva-a-cornerstone-of-saudi-vision-2030

UNESCO. (2022). School enrollment, tertiary (% gross) for females and males data as of June, 2002. data.worldbank.org. https://data.worldbank.org/indicator/SE.TER.ENRR.FE?locations=SA&view=chart

6
Agile Workforce Planning

Adam Gibson and Nicola Oldroyd

Introduction

The worst thing that can happen when you invest time in learning something new is finding that it does not work in the real world. Agile workforce planning grew out of tripping over the practical application of traditional approaches to strategic workforce planning (SWP). This chapter lays out the limitations of traditional approaches before introducing the agile workforce planning approach. It lays out the principles of the approach and steps through the methodology using multipart business case studies. Throughout the chapter, we make specific callouts to the experiences of a new practitioner in the workforce planning field.

What Is Workforce Planning?

Fundamentally, workforce planning is a systematic and data-led approach to ensure an organization has the right workforce to achieve its business objectives (Figure 6.1). At the core of the right workforce is the need for the right capability, and that capability connects across six further dimensions.

1. *Right size*: Is there enough capability?
2. *Right shape*: Is there the right mix of capabilities?
3. *Right location*: Is that capability in the right geographic and structural location to do the work?
4. *Right time*: Is capability available at the time it is needed and for the duration it is needed?
5. *Right cost*: Are we paying the right cost for capability; does it provide value for money?
6. *Right risk*: Does the capability mitigate the impact or likelihood of a surplus or deficit in our workforce?

Adam Gibson and Nicola Oldroyd, *Agile Workforce Planning* In: *Strategic Workforce Planning*. Edited by: Marc Sokol and Beverly Tarulli, Oxford University Press. © Society for Industrial and Organizational Psychology 2024. DOI: 10.1093/oso/9780197759745.003.0007

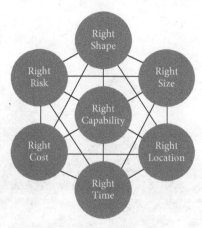

Figure 6.1 The seven "rights" of workforce planning.

Limitations of Traditional Strategic Workforce Planning

Siloed Approach to Workforce Planning

Traditional SWP is one of three broad planning horizons that are traditionally considered in silo. These horizons relate to how far into the future we are looking, as opposed to when changes to the work or workforce may take place (Figure 6.2).

SWP is the long-term horizon and is a top-down approach to planning that focuses on understanding and actioning the changing workforce requirements across multiple years to understand what people (both capacity and capability) are needed to accomplish long-term business strategies. *Resource planning* focuses on the current year and is also known as *tactical workforce planning, capacity planning, scheduling,* or *resource management*. It is a bottom-up approach that relates to managing day-to-day staffing needs and usually translates into a schedule showing who is doing what and when. *Operational workforce planning* focuses on planning the workforce to achieve business objectives in the next financial year. Operational workforce planning is commonly run by the finance function as part of budget planning activities and is based on a performance management framework.

Each of the three planning horizons has the potential to provide benefits to an organization when incorporated into a workforce plan. However, the

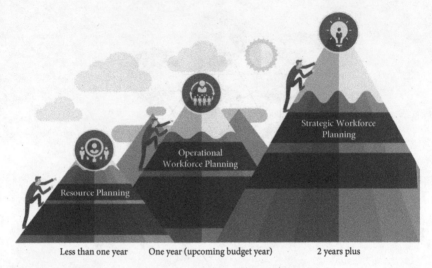

Figure 6.2 The three horizons of workforce planning.

siloed approach of treating each of the horizons independently is itself a limitation: namely, that there is a disconnect with the other horizons and the additional benefits that they could bring if incorporated into the workforce plan are not being realized. Failing to recognize the connection between the strategic planning horizon and the tactical and operational horizons typically results in a disconnect between how work is done day to day, the operational strategy, and the longer-term organization goals.

Failing to consider the tactical planning horizon means that organizations are not presented with actionable steps that employees can take on a daily basis to support the organization in achieving its strategic goal. A focus on the long-term timeline and ignoring the operational planning horizon can prove detrimental if the organization does not meet the budget and performance requirements of each intervening financial year.

Five D's of Traditional Strategic Workforce Planning

The limitations of traditional SWP result in an experience called the "five D's":

1. *Digest*: The SWP project team digests business strategy, objectives, and workforce data.
2. *Deliver*: A workforce plan is created and delivered to the organization.

3. *Depart*: Once the plan has been delivered, the project ends, and the team departs or moves to a new project or business-as-usual activity.
4. *Disrupt*: The organization is disrupted by either internal or external factors which negatively impact the execution of the plan, whether that be late delivery, different results, or being cancelled altogether.
    a. Examples of internal factors are budget underestimation, shifting business priorities or a change in leadership, businesses not realizing the potential benefits and not backing the case for change, disconnect between the strategy and way in which work is done, and failure to achieve the expected benefits from a planned transformation
    b. Examples of external factors are market shocks (recession), legal (regulatory changes), and competitive forces (new products).
5. *Disregard*: The workforce plan is deemed no longer fit for purpose and is disregarded. At this point, the organization can either reengage with the project team, come up with a new plan, or do without a plan

The product of traditional workforce planning is typically delivered as a workforce plan. It is then the responsibility of stakeholders within the organization to implement that plan. The presence of a plan alone is not enough to change behavior, and often the organization does not have the capability to deliver the plan and ultimately realize its benefits. This can be attributed to the plan being "owned" by human resources (HR), which presents issues with prioritization because the tendency is for HR to treat all areas equally, and also it is senior stakeholders within the business that have the real authority to implement change (Sullivan, 2002a, 2002b).

Poor Target Setting

Traditionally, workforce plans consisted of targets that were often either too narrow and/or ambitious, with a lack of best- and worst-case scenario planning. When internal or external factors differ from the predictions, the workforce plans were viewed as inflexible documents, rather than a way of thinking to be used as a decision filter. The combination of these factors resulted in goals being missed, frustrated stakeholders, and reduced confidence in the organization of workforce planning as a critical success factor.

An Agile Approach to Workforce Planning

The potential benefits of SWP can be lost in traditional approaches. Traditional approaches to SWP are focused on crafting a plan based on a single planning horizon. *Agile workforce planning* (Gibson, 2021) moves away from the siloed approach of treating each planning horizon independently and plans and executes across each of the horizons simultaneously. Solving the short-term problems will feed into creating a strategic workforce plan that is successful in delivering a long-term solution. The agile workforce planning methodology goes a step further than producing a plan for the organization. There is also a shift to ensuring the organization uses the plan and implements the suggested actions as a success factor for delivery (see Table 6.1).

Table 6.1 Traditional versus agile workforce planning

Traditional strategic workforce planning	Agile workforce planning
Considers a single long-term planning horizon in silo, which can lead to disconnections and reduced benefit realization.	Executes across each of the planning horizons simultaneously to solve short-term problems and deliver a long-term value.
The plan is based on either a single gap of current supply vs future demand or the supply vs demand gap at the end of the planning horizon.	The plan is based on studying the evolution of the supply vs demand gap over the planning horizon.
The plan focuses on talent management interventions, which can erode potential benefits.	The plan focuses first on demand optimization, before considering talent management interventions.
The final product is the delivery of a workforce plan which is not necessarily implemented.	The final product is the delivery of an action plan to achieve the desired business outcome.
Workforce plan is inflexible, scenarios may feature in planning but not as part of the execution.	Consideration of a range of scenarios from best to worst case with flexibility for the plan to be revised as and when circumstances (internal and external) change.
The plan is considered final, which risks it being unworkable if the organization is disrupted.	The plan is considered a working document, a minimum viable product, with an expectation of ongoing iteration.
Strategic workforce planning is considered a one-off activity for the whole workforce or a segment of the workforce.	Workforce planning is an ongoing activity, starting with a segment of the workforce and scaling to incorporate the whole workforce.
Strategic workforce planning activity is limited to a core team of practitioners.	Workforce planning is done with an agile team, led by a workforce planning practitioner and drawing on wider organizational expertise.
The plan is treated as a glossy brochure published for shareholders.	The plan is treated as an operational plan with specific accountabilities to execute.

The values, principles, and methodology of agile workforce planning stem from those of agile software development first outlined in the *Agile Manifesto* (Agile Alliance, 2001) in 2001. It is based on using an iterative approach to deliver a project throughout its lifecycle and is designed to be adaptable in an increasingly volatile, uncertain, complex, and ambiguous (VUCA) world where the pace of change and complexity of problems that businesses face are increasing. This manifesto listed four core values.

Agile Values Applied to Workforce Planning

Agile is based on four values, and each of these values has been incorporated into the agile workforce planning methodology.

Agile Value 1: Individuals and Interactions over Processes and Tools

The recent boom in people analytics has been accompanied by an expansion of technologies to support SWP. Although these technologies can provide value to SWP, they are not a standalone tool. Delivering true value in SWP relies on practitioners with an understanding of the methodology, principles, and techniques, able to interact with each other and the stakeholders to extract appropriate insights and translate this into an effective plan.

Agile Value 2: Working Software over Comprehensive Documentation

In workforce planning, it is more important to deliver the right workforce than it is to have a glossy plan. Many businesses engaging in SWP have prioritized the creation of a flashy document that can be shared with shareholders or alliance partners. It is much more important to have a minimally viable plan that can be delivered and to iterate and refine that plan over time.

Agile Value 3: Customer Collaboration over Contract Negotiation

Regular collaboration with stakeholders throughout the process to determine changing requirements is more critical for success than being able to define the exact future state at the beginning. The basis for planning will be several possible futures hanging on a wider range of assumptions. Recognizing this, workforce planning seeks meaningful collaboration with stakeholders across the organization to provide the best possible inputs and involve them as the plan is refined over time.

Agile Value 4: Responding to Change over Following a Plan
The plan is not the aim of workforce planning: the plan is a vehicle to create the right workforce. Change is inevitable, so the workforce plan must be flexible to respond to those changes. The expectation is of ongoing iteration of that plan to reflect reality, rather than sticking rigidly to a one-off plan based on assumptions that have long since changed.

Principles of Agile Workforce Planning

The agile workforce planning methodology is based on seven principles that stem from the most recent developments in agile.

Principle 1: Start with why. The phrase "start with why" was coined by Simon Sinek (2011). The first stage of developing a workforce plan must include understanding the "why" of the organization. It is important to understand the current nature of the organization (what it is, what it does, and why it does those things) and its ambition (the strategic business plan).

Principle 2: Be flexible. As noted above, a significant limitation of traditional project management and traditional workforce planning is the lack of flexibility. Agile workforce planning places flexibility at its core, and the principles and methodology allow it to be executed across all organizations and time horizons. Value can be achieved in both the current year and future years using the same workforce plan.

Principle 3: A team of teams. Success in workforce planning needs to be more than just a "them" (stakeholders) and "us" (workforce planners) siloed approach. A cross-functional team and collaboration with experts who hold the specific expertise to develop and build on ideas are crucial. For example, facilities will be able to provide input on the *right location*; finance may provide input on the *right cost*, procurement input on the levels, and pipeline of contingent labor; and HR business partners provide invaluable insight when working with unfamiliar areas of the business.

Principle 4: Iterative planning. Agile workforce planning is an iterative approach. Plans are executed based on the most likely scenario, but contingencies are created for the best and worst cases. There is flexibility for plans to be revised and actions altered as and when circumstances change.

Principle 5: Incremental problem-solving. The problems that will give the greatest return or are easiest to understand and resolve are a priority for focus. An initial focus on these problems will provide the organization with value early in the workforce planning process and will help deprioritize other more complex business challenges and improve the chance to demonstrate impact.

Principle 6: Always be learning. Workforce planning problems are not usually labeled as such. Workforce planning experts must undertake continuous development to learn about the workforce, organization, customers, market, industry, and the wider landscape intertwined within it to make the biggest impact.

Principle 7: It is about the workforce. The aim of workforce planning is not to create a workforce plan; the aim is to create the right workforce to deliver the desired business outcomes.

> **New practitioner point of view (part 1 of 4): Agile versus waterfall**
>
> I (Nicola) recently transferred to workforce planning from working in a chemistry research laboratory. My lived experience is that practical research is unpredictable and consequently it is not possible to have a long-term plan with a set deadline. When faced with a "chemical" problem to solve, the solution (or importantly how to get there) was seldom immediately obvious to me. I found that working within a collaborative team that understood the breadth of techniques, equipment, materials, and methods available was key to creating an initial roadmap to the solution. I learned that research can be unpredictable and to expect the unexpected. Understanding of the chemical properties and systems are continually developing based on intermediate results, and developing the final solution was very much an iterative process that required an ability to respond to changes in the original plan.
>
> The "experimental" approach of agile versus waterfall is aligned with my ways of working from the research environment, hence following this approach to problem-solving was a natural transition.

Agile Workforce Planning Framework

This six-stage framework forms a new basis for SWP. In this section, we talk through each of the six stages, highlighting these with reference to three client case studies (Figure 6.3).

124 STRATEGIC WORKFORCE PLANNING

Figure 6.3 The agile workforce planning cycle.

Stage 1: Baseline

In this phase, the first action is to establish the nature of the organization, its ambition, and the factors that may impact it.

What Does It Look Like?
Understanding an organization's business model and the activities through which it creates and captures value is important for understanding the way it operates in relation to external markets and internal operations.

What Is It Trying To Achieve and Why?
Successful workforce planning must be aligned and connected with overall HR and business strategies. This involves gaining an understanding of the organization's strategic framework that connects the "why" with the way work is done through mission, goals, objectives, strategy and execution.

Environmental Scanning
It is also important to understand factors that may impact or change the organization. This encompasses both opportunities and threats and is commonly described using the political, economic, social, technological, legal, and environmental (PESTLE) approach. Understanding the internal context and factors is best done before scanning the external environment.

Understanding the Workforce

Understanding the workforce is the next baseline activity. This requires translating raw data into information which can be used to provide insight into the current state of the "seven rights" within the organization. The insights gathered can be used to suggest future trends and activities (Walker, 1992). As a caveat it is important to consider the quality and reliability of any data sources and any assumptions that are made to plug data gaps—there is no such thing as perfect data.

The workforce, at a glance, is large and homogenous—too big to assess as a whole at the first attempt. As a result, we break the workforce into segments to achieve a better understanding. Financial structures (such as profit or cost centers) and operational structures (such as geographies or functions) are the most common segmentation criteria. Segmentation can be used to identify critical roles where the biggest return on investment for workforce planning can be achieved. Critical roles generally share some of the following characteristics:

- They are critical to achieving the business strategy (in terms of both development and execution).
- They provide an organization's current comparative advantage.
- They will provide an organization's future comparative advantage.
- They comprise a meaningful number of roles. For example, at least 50 heads for an organization of 1,000 heads; however, this cannot be too stringent to avoid excluding total workforce sizes that do not reflect this scale.

Whereas workforce supply data are usually readily available within an organization, reliable demand data are harder to obtain. For this reason, calculating a demand baseline to be used for forecasting future demand is done as part of the demand stage.

Case Study 1

A global technology client was struggling to deliver a quality service through one of its back-office functions. As part of the baselining process, we conducted "voice of customer" interviews with senior stakeholders, which confirmed that the services provided by the function were critical to the business achieving its growth aspirations. One capability was consistently highlighted as a key success factor: having a deep knowledge and understanding of the business and employees it served. Within the function, conversations with stakeholders identified one specific role as critical for delivering the service in the future due to that role's having the highest level of unique knowledge through being proximate to the business and employees.

Gain Stakeholder Buy-In

The final action within the baseline phase is to gain buy-in from stakeholders, and it is essential to agree on the terms of reference for the workforce planning exercise. Stakeholders must be identified and mapped prior to engagement. There is a tendency for stakeholders to favor a particular course of action before the problem is fully understood and a workforce plan created. Consequently, a key challenge for workforce planning practitioners when engaging with stakeholders is to provide a firm evidence base for decision-making without the stakeholders exhibiting any cognitive biases.

These understandings of the baseline phase provide the basis for all subsequent workforce planning activities.

New practitioner point of view (part 2 of 4): Understand the problem

The first step I had to undertake when faced with a "chemical" problem was to spend time understanding it in as much detail as possible. This included familiarizing myself with related work, the properties of the materials, and how this problem connects to the wider research field. This knowledge is gained through reviewing relevant literature and communicating with experts in the field. This is synonymous with the baseline stage of agile workforce planning. It was natural to me that, before proceeding to the next stage, the full context of the problem within the organization needed to be understood because there may be factors that affect decision-making later down the line.

Within the research environment, I learned that a combination of time, material, and financial constraints meant that it was not possible to explore every possible pathway from the problem to the solution. Starting

> with a deeper understanding of the problem aided with articulating an appropriate hypothesis to agree with stakeholders prior to beginning experimental work. This is like agreeing on the terms of reference—for example, the business area that will be the focus of workforce planning activity.

Stage 2: Supply

This phase focuses on what workforce an organization has, and will have, to service the demand. Looking at workforce evolution is key to being able to forecast the workforce of the future. *Organizational churn* is the movement of the workforce in, around, and out of the organization through recruitment, internal mobility, and turnover, respectively. Because recruitment and internal mobility are controllable factors it is recommended that the modeling and forecasting of supply be carried out using turnover data. This will give the clearest view of the inevitably declining supply over time.

The effect of megatrends, such as migration, an aging workforce, or talent shortages also impact the evolution of the workforce.

Historical internal turnover trends, overlayed with external megatrends and a consideration of performance over time, can be plotted against the baseline of the workforce as supply.

> **Case Study 1**
>
> The supply profile for the function was captured using a mixture of interviews, focus groups, workshops, and data analysis. The rate of attrition for the critical roles within the function was 25%, much higher than the rate for other back-office functions. This gave the clearest view of the inevitably declining supply over time, which was proving unsustainable.
>
> Demand is serviced through the performance of the workforce, not just having the workforce in place. Because workforce performance is the supply side of productivity, insights into the productivity of the function were obtained.
>
> Employees within the function were consistently working a 44-hour week, higher than the 35-hour week to which they are contracted, and

without overtime pay. Therefore, supply was being stretched by 26% to achieve the current levels of service and was viewed as a key driver of high turnover and sickness rates.

If working hours were to match the contract, we needed to unpick their productivity:

1. *Available time is less than the contracted time.* Annual leave was accounted for as a reduction from contractual time to available time by 14%. That absence must be covered by other members of the team.
2. *Not all available time is productive.* Available time can be split into productive time (time operating at the processing speed required on core tasks), shrinkage time (deduction from available time due to non-core internal activities such as training, or external drivers such as sickness), and lost productivity (underperformance in new starters as they build knowledge).

Across all areas of the function, productive time (as a percentage of available time) was calculated at 77%, with 18.2% lost to shrinkage and 4.7% lost productivity. Ultimately, only 66% of contractual time (23.1 hours per week) is available to complete the core activities of the function. Stage 5 of the framework (action plan) focuses on defining a solution using various levers to minimize shrinkage time and lost productivity, therefore increasing productive time.

Stage 3: Demand

Demand can take on many meanings, but, in the context of workforce planning, it is understood to be the requirement for a workforce as a result of consumer demand; this can be referred to as *derived demand* (Marshall, 1997). Demand can either be a pull model where the output target is predetermined, such as production, or part of a push model where customer requirements derive the demand, such as service delivery.

As mentioned in the baseline section, reliable demand data are usually harder to obtain than that of the workforce supply, hence calculating a demand baseline to be used for forecasting future demand is done as part of this stage rather than in the initial baselining stage.

Demand at a certain point in time can be calculated using the relationship between input, workers, and output. This will translate into the baseline workforce required today to achieve a particular outcome. This may not necessarily equal the workforce supply baseline (i.e., you might not have the right workforce now to achieve the outcomes expected today). Once a demand baseline has been established, as with supply, forecasting of future demand must be carried out. Multiple change factors can impact demand. These can be internal factors stemming from the organization's strategic plans, or external factors (see PESTLE analysis above). The demand forecast will ultimately result in quantification of the seven rights (capability, size, shape, location, time, cost, and risk). The forecast represents the target at each stage of the workforce planning horizon.

Case Study 2

A media giant was facing challenges with its workforce as it transformed on a multiyear journey. Supply and demand drivers were evaluated to analyze future capacity and capability requirements. This was a forecasting exercise to predict the future shape of a critical operational department and provide high-level recommendations.

Capacity. Baseline demand was established using current vacancy data. A series of workshops with key stakeholders were conducted to understand demand drivers impacting the workforce over a 5-year horizon. Several factors contributing to changes in demand were highlighted as a result of these stakeholder discussions.

Expansion into new territories was a key factor expected to increase demand. On the other hand, convergence and consolidation of operational activities were expected to create efficiencies that would reduce demand over time.

Our team drew on EY industry subject matter professionals from across the globe to review this initial scenario and help craft a second that would factor in additional key trends facing the sector. The outside-in view of the SMEs considered that, within the sector, digital transformation will cause an initial increase in demand, which over time will decrease due to optimization of technology and processes. It was also suggested that the department would need to invest in specific capabilities that they did not have, such as change specialists to deliver transformation. Ultimately, this contributed to the demand profile of the second scenario being higher than when purely considering the demands arising from stakeholder discussions. The demand profile modeled for each scenario was presented to the client, broken down by function, subfunction, and role.

Capability. To accompany the capacity demand analysis, external market insights were used to identify key capabilities of critical roles (predetermined by stakeholder discussions). EY's proprietary Workforce Blueprint technology was used to understand the demand profile from a skills perspective through the generation of a series of success profiles using market intelligence benchmarks. For each critical role, a success profile highlighted the skills identified as trending with competitors; classified them as knowledge, tool, or skill; and categorized them as declining, maintaining, or emerging. Furthermore, natural language processing was used to associate a proficiency level (entry, intermediate, advanced, mastery) with each identified skill.

Gaining an understanding of future capability requirements, in particular identification of emerging skills within the marketplace, is essential for organizations to maintain a competitive advantage (e.g., by preparing the existing workforce by providing training or making external hiring decisions).

Case Study 3

A multinational telecommunications company faced an ongoing skills challenge that had not been addressed by its existing planning capabilities. A robust, standardized, and scalable SWP approach was required to inform the reshaping of the business over the next 3–5 years to achieve a balance of capacity, capability, and cost to meet strategic needs.

Thirteen key roles considered core to business delivery were selected as roles of interest for initial SWP. The 13 roles comprised a critical mass of employees, had anticipated skills and industry changes over the next couple of years, were considered core to business delivery, had available job descriptions and demographic data, and had stakeholders who were available and willing to engage in the process.

The use of a skills artificial intelligence (AI) tool to analyze job descriptions allowed detailed analysis to be done on skills at the role level. The data provided valuable insight into the emphasis the client was putting on each skill against those of its competitors and an "optimum skills profile." The AI tool allowed the current level of skill to be inferred to a high degree.

A combination of quantitative data (from existing systems and plans) and qualitative data (stakeholder discussions on existing on expected trends) was collated and consolidated to give five macro drivers impacting the future skills profiles and the supply and demand of the workforce. The macro drivers were simplification, channel shift, growth ambitions, product strategy, and people. A follow-up workshop was held to validate and agree on a scenario range to be modeled by defining assumptions and determining the likely outcomes. The macro drivers were translated into model levers, with the possibility that one lever can be influenced by multiple macro drivers (Figure 6.4).

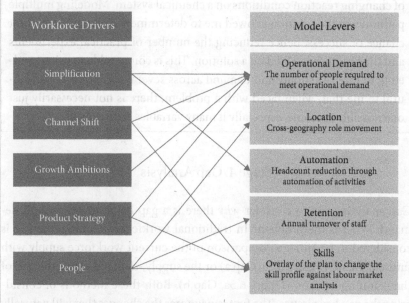

Figure 6.4 Workforce drivers and model levers.

> The model levers were then fed into the SWP model, and the output was a forward projection of how the skills profile for each role will change over the next 5–10 years; the skills that will be needed in the future could be clearly articulated.

> **New practitioner point of view (part 3 of 4): Data and modeling**
>
> The research that I carried out was underpinned by data. To be credible, all results and analysis had to be supported by accurate data. Although the concept of using modeling to forecast supply and demand made sense to me, I struggled at first to accept that there were cases where approximations and/or assumptions had to be made. For example, one particular organization could not provide a full breakdown of employee locations. My advice for scenarios where approximations and/or assumptions must be made is to validate them with the appropriate stakeholders and/or SMEs prior to incorporating them into the modeling.
>
> Within my research, I used computational studies to predict the effect of changing reaction conditions on a chemical system. Modeling multiple pathways to the solution allowed me to determine which has the highest chance of success, hence reducing the number of practical experiments and time required to land on a solution. This is comparable to using modeling to forecast supply and demand across several scenarios. It was natural to me that, when faced with a problem, there is not necessarily just one possible outcome, especially if many variables are involved.

Stage 4: Gap Analysis

Gap analysis aims to consider *why* there is a gap between supply and demand: What is the problem? In traditional workforce planning, the gap is considered to be either a comparison of the current workforce supply with future demand (Figure 6.5a, Gap a) or the supply–demand gap at the end of the planning horizon (Figure 6.5a, Gap b). Both these methods of considering the gap have issues. The first gap ignores the changes that will naturally occur to a workforce to reduce supply, such as turnover of staff, and results in

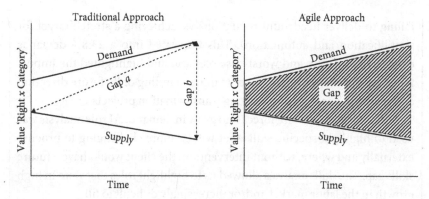

Figure 6.5 Traditional (6.5a) versus agile (6.5b) approach to gap analysis.

decisions to remove workers that would have naturally departed during the planning horizon. As the current workforce supply is not a constant there is no real merit in comparing current workforce supply with future demand. The second gap overlooks any changes in demand (e.g., due to the achievement of goals and objectives over the planning horizon) and is a common problem of being able to translate workforce plans into action.

In contrast, in agile workforce planning, the area of the gap over the planning horizon is analyzed (Figure 6.5b) rather than making a point-to-point analysis. This focuses on the whole evolution of supply and demand, rather than a comparison of just two data points (e.g., today vs. 10 years). This enables the identification of both key risks and opportunities for the future. As supply and demand will be affected differently by different identified scenarios this will lead to differing gaps to consider.

The final step in the gap analysis phase is to re-engage key stakeholders and communicate the impact and corresponding business problem of not closing the gap. Storytelling is important here to influence the stakeholder and gain their support for change.

Case Study 3

We forecast that, despite the introduction of operational efficiencies and demand reductions, attrition was expected to lead to a headcount gap across all roles. For each role, there were a large range of possible outcomes for the headcount gap due to a lack of clarity on business changes. (e.g., failing to deliver headcount reductions vs. achieving a stretch target for simplification and automation). This translated into a 23.8% deviance between a best-case and worst-case scenario and highlighted the importance for the client of tightening its understanding of its future direction and realizing benefits from existing transformation projects.

Although all roles were forecast to grow in demand, AI role analysis was used to highlight specific skills that will be more challenging to procure externally and where, without intervention, the client would have a future skills gap. The skills analysis allowed us to highlight roles that were in high growth in the labor market and/or increasingly difficult to fill.

Stage 5: Action Plan

This phase is based on defining a solution that will close the future gap in workforce supply and demand. It is unlikely that a perfect solution will be discovered, but the goal is to produce an action plan to give the best possible solution that balances long-term gain against short-term risk.

Seven B's of Action Planning

Agile workforce planning uses the seven B's of action planning as levers to close the supply–demand gap. Brief definitions are outlined below, with specific examples called out in the following case study.

The first two are demand optimization levers. The focus of these levers is to ensure that demand is optimized before committing human resources to avoid wasting workforce cost and efforts. Demand optimization has not been included in traditional workforce planning:

- *Balance*: Ensure demand levers, such as location, processes, and operating models, are correctly aligned and balanced throughout the organization to enable the most effective use of supply.
- *Bot*: Implement automated technology to augment or replace existing capacity or capability. This can be through initiatives such as data center automation, robotic process automation, or artificial intelligence. The industry in which it operates, the business model, and operational maturity of the organization will determine the extent to which enhancement technology can be implemented. Using tools and technology

where appropriate can free up time for the team to focus on strategic, high-value activities.

The final five points are talent management levers. These levers enable an intervention in the flow of the workforce into and out of the organization:

- *Bind*: Prevent the loss of capability by binding it in place. Although organizational churn has its advantages—in particular through avoiding an organization becoming stagnant—it comes at the cost of performance and administration.
- *Bounce*: Move a capability around or exit it from the organization. This, with the Bind action, can fundamentally change the churn of the workforce.
- *Buy*: Purchase and acquire a permanent capability. Talent can be bought as either experienced hires who have the skills and knowledge to perform in the role immediately or as progressive hires who are chosen based on their potential.
- *Build*: Build a capability from existing capacity within the workforce. This lever is essential when bringing in new capability to an organization. The primary interventions are delivering learning and development, giving the employees the opportunity to acquire knowledge and skills, and enhancing an employee's career through progression via a change in role.
- *Borrow*: Acquire temporary capability by borrowing from elsewhere. This is typically at a higher cost than the more permanent levers; however, it has the advantage of allowing the organization to only pay for what they need at that moment in time. Talent can be borrowed using contingent labor, professional services firms, or alliances.

When creating an initial action plan, we do so at the level of these levers and not below for three reasons. The first is that multiple levers may need to be used in succession to deliver an outcome, and the second is that initiatives to close the gap may cross several of these levers. For example, a salary increase for new joiners could help with buying and binding new talent but may lead to increased bounce of long-term employees. The third reason to base the initial plan on these levers rather than focus on a specific initiative is that the workforce planners and the senior stakeholders do not have all the solutions. It is important to have the opportunity to collaborate on the details with experts who sit outside the workforce planning team once the end-to-end plan is in place. This is an effects-based approach; giving the organization an effect to achieve rather than prescriptive instructions on how to get there.

Following collaboration with experts, specific initiatives to close the workforce gap will have been proposed. The initiatives are the ideas, and they are subject to cost-benefit analysis to determine whether each initiative is worthwhile and will contribute to business objectives.

Only once the workforce levers and corresponding initiatives have been established can a workforce plan be created. Given infinite time and money, a perfect workforce could be generated; however, this is not realistic. The workforce plan will be a compromise of time and cost to meet the *right* risk, and it must align with the organization's strategy.

An effective workforce plan will articulate the baseline, highlight outcomes and timelines, describe the journey, and assign responsibility. The plan may contain details on aspects such as demand management, recruitment and procurement, redeployment and promotion, learning and development, change projects, and contingencies.

Case Study 3

The gap analysis over 5 years highlighted a startling gap between supply and demand that was nearly a third bigger than the entire current workforce. Several initiatives across the seven B's were proposed to bridge the gap.

Balance. Several activities were identified that could aid with achieving the most effective use of supply:

- Replacing a repeatable in-person activity with a pre-recorded video.
- Identifying specific areas where technology adoption or lean processes would release capacity.
- Moving suboptimal processes to the process owner in a different function to properly optimize the end-to-end activity.
- Reducing hierarchies toward a flatter structure to reduce the time lost to management activities and speed up decision-making. The

roles and responsibilities for each level would have a much clearer delineation of responsibilities.
- Identifying a few activities where cost and capability could be better aligned to release capacity for critical roles, for example, offshoring lower-impact activities.

Bot. No single identified process was identified that could be automated entirely; however, a small number of activities were identified where automation could form part of the process and augment the workforce to release capacity.

Bind. The identified critical role had to be a target for reduced attrition. An employee value proposition was created to improve the retention of high performers and develop specialist knowledge within the role. Aspects such as reward, employee experience, and development were considered.

Bounce. Not every position in the current model mapped directly to a future role. Those in positions that would become redundant were a focus of skills analysis to map to other parts of the business.

New practitioner point of view (part 4 of 4): Solving the problem

My research often revolved around plugging a gap between the current properties of a system and the enhanced, or more desirable, properties of a system that was yet to be developed. There were often multiple possibilities in the process and route that could be used to optimize the current system to the enhanced future system.

I found that being familiar with having to select which method(s) to use from several possibilities was analogous to the agile workforce planning levers. In research, starting with experiments that are predicted to bring the biggest benefits, regularly reviewing results to understand the scale and direction of any property changes, and methodically adjusting reaction conditions will facilitate the most efficient route to the solution. The same logic can be applied to agile workforce planning when choosing levers to use to close the supply–demand gap.

Stage 6: Deliver

Whereas in traditional workforce planning creating the plan is the final step, agile workforce planning views the creation of the plan as part of the journey, not the end state. What matters is executing a workforce plan that delivers the right workforce to achieve the desired business outcomes. To deliver effectively in agile workforce planning, we must concern ourselves with the management of a living plan.

- *Communication*: It is crucial to remember that a strategic workforce plan is not a glossy document to send to shareholders or place on a website. A strategic workforce plan is an operational document detailing the actions required to build a workforce. If a glossy document is required, that is a separate communications document. Communication of the plan is a key step in galvanizing support to enable success, so we consider the different stakeholders with whom we need to communicate the plan.
- *Managing quality*: The success, or failure, of creating the right workforce will often lie at the lowest levels of project execution. Having the right governance in place at project, program, and portfolio levels is vital to ensure the quality of dependencies is managed, that anticipated benefit realization is achieved, and that a timely intervention is applied if outcomes are not progressing as expected.
- *Managing risks and assumptions*: It is in the management of risks and assumptions where we see one of the biggest departures from traditional SWP. Capturing risks and assumptions throughout the agile workforce planning process allows us to move faster, rather than having to wait for perfect data. In delivery, we continue to monitor those risks and assumptions and adjust the plan accordingly as the data improve or forecasts get tighter.

If we treat this initial workforce plan as a minimally viable product, then we can satisfy two of the key principles we discussed earlier: iterative planning and incremental problem-solving. As we deliver the workforce, we create a new baseline for the organization and workforce. In a VUCA world, we can iterate the plan to respond to internal and external changes. We are also able to add to the plan, considering additional segments of the workforce or conducting greater investigation into assumptions in the plan to identify underlying sources of causation.

Conclusion

At the start, we posited that the worst thing that can happen when you invest time in learning something new is finding that it does not work in the real world. We talked about what workforce planning is, how SWP fits into it, and where more traditional approaches have broken down. We then introduced agile thinking and went through the six-stage approach with client examples and the reflections of a new practitioner.

Agile workforce planning is not about a rigid process or something that is heavily overengineered and will rile stakeholders when we force it through. Agile workforce planning is a way of thinking. It is a methodology that is designed to be flexible across all organizations and all planning horizons, where you can move to fast results and value creation. When you do that, not only will you create value for your business, but you also will demonstrate to your many stakeholders the true potential of workforce planning to create a better working world.

References

Agile Alliance. (2001). Home page. https://www.agilealliance.org/
Gibson, A. (2021). *Agile workforce planning: How to align people with organizational strategy for improved performance*. Kogan Page.
Marshall, A. (1997). *Principles of economics*. Prometheus Books.
Sinek, S. (2011). *Start with why: How great leaders inspire everyone to take action*. Penguin.
Sullivan, J. (2002a, August 12). Before you try it, understand why workforce planning fails. https://drjohnsullivan.com/articles/before-you-try-it-understand-why-workforce-planning-fails
Sullivan, J. (2002b, August 19). Why workforce planning fails, part 2. https://drjohnsullivan.com/articles/why-workforce-planning-fails-part-2/
Walker, J. W. (1992). *Human resource strategy*. McGraw-Hill.

7
Strategic Workforce Planning for Growth
Strategies and Technology for Multispeed Growth

James D. Eyring, Andrew P. Newmark, and Sunil Setlur

Long-term revenue growth is critical to firm survival. Companies that sustain growth attract greater investment, create greater shareholder value, attract better talent, and, at a societal level, improve people's income and well-being (Ahlstrom, 2010). Companies that fail to grow fast enough lose market capitalization, have higher borrowing costs (Ahlstrom, 2010), and are five times more likely to fail before the next business cycle than their higher-growth counterparts (Smit, Thompson, and Viguerie, 2005). Because of this, growth goals are a central component of company strategy, and obtaining these goals is a key to company survival. Strategic workforce planning (SWP) acts as a key enabler to these growth goals by ensuring the organization has the right capacity and capabilities it needs in the right locations. Strategic workforce plans are most effective if they use company growth targets as an important contextual factor throughout all stages of the SWP process, including analytics, forecasting, workforce segmentation, organization design, and talent development and management.

The link between a company's growth goals and the SWP process is often strong in the initial stages of planning. For example, approximately 89% of companies link their SWP to their business planning process, and most companies use forecasted growth as part of their supply-and-demand forecasting (Tucker and Morgan, 2021). Done well, these initial links to company goals can result in a SWP that directs resources, capabilities, and needed human resource processes to fast-growing product or service areas while redeploying or automating resources in slower growth areas. Many companies experience this multispeed growth, in which some areas of the company are growing quickly and other areas are growing slowly or are shrinking. To address this challenge, SWPs must adapt to allow redeployment of resources to high-growth areas while reducing workforce costs in

James D. Eyring, Andrew P. Newmark, and Sunil Setlur, *Strategic Workforce Planning for Growth*
In: *Strategic Workforce Planning*. Edited by: Marc Sokol and Beverly Tarulli, Oxford University Press.
© Society for Industrial and Organizational Psychology 2024. DOI: 10.1093/oso/9780197759745.003.0008

lower-growth areas. Unfortunately, many SWPs may fail to address these multispeed growth challenges. For example, 49% of SWPs are either designed to be top-down plans or are not integrated across divisions/regions within the enterprise (Tucker and Morgan, 2021). Top-down plans may result in one-size-fits-all strategies that fail to differentiate the needs of high- versus low-growth product or service areas. Plans that are not integrated across the enterprise may result in SWP inefficiencies or a failure to allocate resources to areas of the company that most need support to fuel growth. The link between SWP and growth may be even weaker in later stages of planning. For example, approximately 70% of companies do not fully adapt or evolve their practices to changes in workforce or market needs (PwC, 2019). This can result in implementation of practices or processes that do not meet the needs of a changing marketplace and do not adapt to the growth needs of different parts of the business.

Linking growth goals to the entire SWP process is important as the pace of growth can impact a company's approach to talent management and even its philosophy of talent (Eyring and Eyring, 2013). For example, high-growth companies often select different approaches to talent than do their lower-growth counterparts. Companies that choose to standardize their approach to talent may ultimately stymie growth in some parts of their business. Worse, companies selecting the wrong talent strategy based on industry "best practices" may implement practices that do not enable their unique growth objectives. Ensuring that growth and SWP strategies, tactics, and practices are linked more explicitly will help practitioners make better decisions to help their organizations achieve their growth goals. In other words, understanding the context of growth may help practitioners identify the right strategies and practices needed to meet the demands of growth.

This chapter addresses this issue by first exploring the challenges of growth in both high- and low-growth environments and the implications of these challenges on the SWP process. The chapter then turns to explore how growth impacts company selection of talent management strategy and development practices and the impact of these practices on organization outcomes. This model offers practitioners a framework to make better SWP and talent decisions to close workforce gaps. Finally, the chapter explores two company cases that highlight different strategies that enable growth. The experience of Marriott International highlights how a company can adapt SWP and talent processes to meet the needs of multispeed growth. The experience of Gojek highlights how hypergrowth in a technology start-up challenges SWP processes and how to use technology to build core leader capabilities. The chapter closes with tips and suggestions for practitioners to make decisions to better enable growth in their companies.

Challenges of High and Low Growth

Growth of any speed comes with challenges, and these challenges are compounded in large companies with "multispeed growth," where some divisions may be growing fast while other divisions are slower in growth. The challenges of growth also depend on other factors such as size and age of the company, industry type, and the company's competitive positioning. Understanding these challenges and the impact they have on SWPs is an important first step in making better decisions to support company growth. For simplicity, this section focuses on contrasting the challenges of high- and low-growth environments and how each might impact different aspects of SWPs. These challenges are based on two sources of information. First, this section draws on qualitative research with division-level CEOs from high- and low-growth multinational companies operating across Asia, Africa, and Europe (Eyring and Lim, 2014). These CEOs managed large countries, regions, or divisions within global multinational companies and had to manage the challenges of growth within this context. Second, this section draws on experience working with high- and low-growth companies, including high-tech start-ups and larger multinational companies in more mature industries.

In the Eyring and Lim (2014) study, slower-growth companies averaged 2.5% year-over-year revenue growth. Because of this low growth rate, their key business challenge was to accelerate or enhance growth to return greater value to shareholders and remain competitive. Their high-growth counterparts grew revenue at an average of 23% year-over-year. Their key challenge was to scale their organizations to continue to grow while keeping pace with the demands this growth places on the company. These business challenges shaped their growth strategies, which in turn shaped the strategy enablers they pursued and the skills and processes they built to drive their strategies (see Table 7.1).

The impact of growth is highlighted by how these companies focused on different growth strategies. For example, although innovation is a key strategy for both high- and low-growth companies, lower-growth companies

Table 7.1 Challenges and strategic focus in low- and high-growth environments

	Low growth	High growth
Business challenge	Accelerate growth	Scale to keep pace with growth
Key growth strategies	Innovate new products and services Expand geographically Add new distributors or channels	Innovate new products and services Expand geographically Inorganic growth Inclusive growth
Strategy enablers	Hire and develop right talent Build culture for growth	Focus and align to growth goals Manage key stakeholders
Skills	Growth mindset Innovation Agility and speed	Managing people Developing others Aligning the organization
Processes	Need to adapt/transform	Need to build
People risks	Burnout from pace of transformation Turnover due to lack of career growth	Burnout from pace of job demands and growth

Note: This table represents the challenges and focus of CEOs and leaders in high versus lower growth environments and is adapted from cross-company qualitative research (Eyring and Lim, 2014).

were more likely to focus on innovating new products or services (Eyring and Lim, 2014). This is not surprising as innovation is a key driver of company growth (Bahadir, Bharadwaj, and Parzen, 2009; Junni et al., 2013) and companies looking for new sources of revenue are likely to leverage this strategy. Lower-growth companies were also more likely to try to expand sales by entering new geographies and/or by expanding their distributor or channel networks. Although high-growth companies in the study also pursued innovation and geographic expansion, they did so at a lower frequency than their low-growth counterparts. In part, this was because many high-growth companies in the study were growing organically and were less reliant on new innovations for growth. Instead, high-growth companies were more likely to focus on inorganic growth, specifically to help them enter challenging markets by acquiring companies or creating joint ventures to gain access to customers and talent. High-growth companies were also more likely to focus on inclusive growth strategies whereby they built partnerships with customers, governments, and universities to have greater social and business impact in targeted markets. Each of these strategies has implications for SWP processes. For example, a focus on innovation may result in investments in product or research and development groups, while a focus on inclusive growth strategies may require building new partnership capabilities. Geographic expansion may result in adding resources in new regions or countries.

These challenges and strategies shaped the people strategies these companies pursued and the skills and processes they developed. Leaders in lower-growth companies reported that they relied on hiring and developing the right talent and building a culture of growth to enable their growth strategies (Eyring and Lim, 2014). These companies, especially those with a history of lower growth, did not have the skills they needed to innovate and expand. Moreover, they felt that current employees did not have the right mindset for growth. Some leaders in companies with a history of slow growth report that their organizations are bureaucratic and lack the agile and entrepreneurial capabilities needed to respond quickly to the market, innovate, and drive growth. Because of this, they often try to build skills and a culture in the areas of growth mindset, innovation, and agility. When the need to change is great, companies also may transform their organization structure and processes to respond more quickly to external challenges. A high rate of transformation and change can lead to lower employee motivation and a higher risk of burnout due to the pace of change. A low rate of transformation also has risks. With low growth and a lack of change, employees may leave the company because of slow career growth.

Leaders in higher-growth companies reported that focusing and aligning all employees and managing key stakeholders were the top people enablers of growth (Eyring and Lim, 2014). High growth meant that these companies were regularly adding new employees and were promoting individual contributors into manger jobs quickly. As the organizations grew, they needed to ensure all employees and departments were focused and aligned to the most critical growth priorities. Managers also needed to build relationships with global stakeholders to gain their support and obtain needed resources. These growth dynamics also impacted the skills the organizations needed. Many managers were new to management or new to the company. Those in management roles found that their job scope expanded quickly, with managers potentially going from a team of 5 to a team of 200 over the course of 2 years. Because job scope changed so quickly, these companies focused more time building core management skills. They needed to help managers lead teams, develop team members, and collaborate with stakeholders across the organization. High-growth companies also cited the need to build new processes to help their teams standardize work. Because of rapid headcount growth, they had to build processes that enabled them to deliver consistent results as teams grew. Without building these skills and processes, these companies ran the risk of burning out employees due to the pace of growth.

Although high-growth companies also focused on hiring and developing talent to fuel growth, lower-growth companies were twice as likely to cite this area as a key enabler for growth. When discussing this area, high-growth company CEOs focused more on the need to find technical talent or talent that could fit into their cultures long-term. Low-growth CEOs focused more on the need to upgrade talent and bring new skills (e.g., innovation) into the organization. This implies that although hiring and developing is important in high-growth companies, lower-growth companies may have a more urgent mandate to leverage this strategy to kick start growth by upgrading talent. This dynamic is frequently played out in companies with very low or negative growth. CEOs or senior leaders are replaced as part of a new strategy, which often results in hiring new talent with different skills lower in the organization.

These high- and low-growth dynamics also impact a company's approach to SWP. For example, companies with the highest growth rates often create workforce plans on a quarterly basis. Growth of the business requires constant revaluation of headcount needs. Because of this, the scope of their SWP process is much more focused on forecasting overall headcount needs and headcount in job categories that are important for growth (e.g., software engineers in technology firms). These companies need a SWP process with a broad annual plan and quarterly quick and agile adaptations because their time is limited and focused on enabling growth. When costs, efficiency, or other issues become problematic, high-growth companies shift their attention to address location strategies, workforce segmentation, mobility, or other aspects of SWP. Once the problems are addressed, they return to a more rapid and agile approach to SWP. In extreme growth cases, SWP focuses on how many employees to hire and where and how to use contract labor if hiring does not meet these needs quickly. All other aspects of SWP are ignored until needed.

Lower-growth companies often take a different approach to SWP. The SWP process is longer, includes more data analytics, and covers more SWP strategies. If cost and productivity are challenges, SWP may include organization and job structure changes to shift more work to shared service centers, automate work, or shift headcount to lower-cost locations. Because the workforce changes more slowly, these companies can examine a broader array of job categories and can create strategies (e.g., development, benefits) for different employee segments.

Because the approach to SWP varies so much by growth rate, companies experiencing multispeed growth often struggle. Higher-growth divisions or geographies find that slow and unchanging SWP processes are insufficient for their needs. One good example of this is found in companies with new venture groups. These groups are designed to spark entrepreneurial growth, but the systems provided by their slower-growth parent companies are often designed to prevent this. Highly structured compensation systems, tools that are designed to find talent that can succeed in large companies, performance management systems, and other policies all can slow and stifle growth in these ventures. Although venture groups are not that common, this example highlights the need for large companies to take a different SWP approach that better enables growth in high- and low-growth divisions.

These examples illustrate how growth can impact company strategy, strategy enablers, and even a company's approach to the SWP process. Growth rates also likely shape talent management and development strategies, which is explored more in the next section.

Talent Strategies and Practices for Growth

Companies often adopt their talent strategies based on best practices or from current fads and thinking on talent (Gallardo-Gallardo and Thunnissen, 2016). For example, General Electric was an icon for talent management practices for decades until company performance declined (e.g., Forbes, 2012). PepsiCo has continued to be known for its practices, while Google has become a more recent favorite (e.g., Business Insider, 2022) Some research (Meyers et al., 2020) also suggests that a human resources (HR) manager's selection of talent strategy is influenced by their country's culture. Companies adopting practices based on best practice or cultural values may ignore the potential importance of growth on selection of talent strategy. As an example, Google's revenue grew 60% year-over-year over a 5-year period (Macrotrends, 2022a) and their talent practices and outcomes are likely influenced by this. A slower-growth company may not benefit from adapting these practices. Some research (Eyring, 2014; Eyring and Eyring,

2013) indicates that companies do adopt different talent strategies based on their revenue growth. More importantly, this research finds that the approach taken to talent drives differential outcomes. Linking these decision choices to growth strategies more explicitly may help practitioners and companies select the right practices to enable their strategies.

Building on a framework originally proposed by Iles, Chuai and Preece (2010), Eyring and Eyring (2013) examined company talent strategies along two dimensions. Companies could be either broad or narrow in how they target their talent strategies and could be focused on either positions or people. Companies with broad strategies focused their efforts on many positions or people, and those with narrow strategies focused on fewer people or positions. Companies with position strategies focused on key roles or job groups, and those with people strategies focused on key people. These dimensions and the four talent strategies they create are shown in Figure 7.1. Follow-up analysis (Eyring, 2014) found that the average company growth rate varied by each

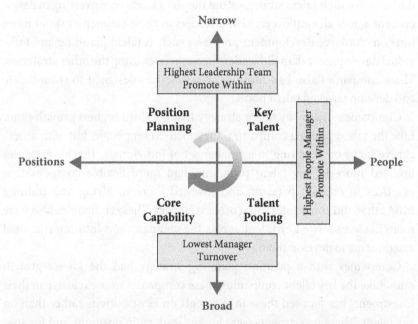

Figure 7.1 Talent strategies, growth, and key outcomes. This figure illustrates four talent strategies companies leverage. Company revenue growth is lowest in the Position Planning quadrant and increases in each quadrant in a clockwise progression with the highest growth in the Core Capability quadrant. Key outcomes from different strategies are represented in shaded boxes.

strategy selected. Companies in the Position Planning quadrant had the lowest growth rates. Companies with a Key Talent strategy had 11% higher growth than those with a Position Planning strategy; Talent Pooling companies had 26% higher growth, and Core Capability companies had 80% higher growth rates when compared to companies in the Position Planning quadrant.

Companies with a core capability strategy had the highest growth rates. These companies developed core capabilities or skills (e.g., customer service orientation) across positions in the company to differentiate themselves from their competitors and keep pace with growth. These companies often did not have key talent development programs and did not use sophisticated selection tools or compensation strategies. Some participating companies reported that they did not have time to invest in HR processes due to the pace of growth, but instead focused on hiring talent and developing skills important to the company.

Companies with a talent pooling strategy had the second highest growth rates. Like the core capability companies, these companies also were broad in the target for their talent strategies, but they had a focus on investing in development across all employees. Senior leaders in these companies spent more time on employee development processes such as talent planning and individual development than did leaders in companies using the other strategies. These companies also had more flexible practices designed to compensate and develop targeted talent pools.

Companies with a key talent strategy had the third highest growth rates. Like the talent pooling companies, they focused on people, but with an exclusive focus on investing in a smaller set of individuals. These companies invested more in key talent programs, had more flexible compensation practices to retain top talent, and invested more in hiring and training MBAs than did companies using other strategies. These companies also were more likely to move key talent across the company and into international assignments to develop them.

Companies with a position planning strategy had the lowest growth rates. Like the key talent companies, these companies were exclusive in their investments but focused these investments on key positions rather than on key talent. These investments were for key leadership positions and for specialty roles, such as key R&D or marketing jobs. Company practices were more flexible when it came to creating attractive offers for external hires for targeted job groups. They also were more likely to implement formal mentoring programs for individuals in key jobs.

As expected, companies using these strategies experienced different outcomes. Companies leveraging a position planning or key talent strategy invested most in key talent or key positions, which resulted in the highest number of senior leadership team members being promoted from within the company. Companies leveraging key talent or talent pooling strategies invested in talent at all levels in the organization, which resulted in the highest number of people managers promoted from within the company. Finally, companies with a talent pooling or core capability strategy invested resources across more people or positions within their companies, resulting in lower manager turnover. Turnover among managers in position planning companies was 43% higher than in core capability or talent pooling companies, which may indicate that differential investment in targeted positions may have a negative effect on managers not in these positions.

In addition to outcomes, the selection of these strategies may impact other decisions. For example, companies with key talent and talent pooling strategies focus more effort on building talent pools within and outside the organization. Inside the organization, these companies focused more on assessing potential and developing and actively moving talent. Companies with key talent strategies focused on a relatively small set of talent, while companies with position planning strategies focused on a large set of talent. For example, some companies had key talent pools that exceeded 40% of their target managerial populations. Outside the organization, key talent and talent pooling companies also were more likely to focus on mapping, identifying, and tracking external talent pools to bring in new talent. Companies with position strategies were less likely to use these strategies and had less focus on talent pools. Growth may have influenced these approaches. For example, position planning companies had the lowest growth. These companies may not have needed to utilize talent pools to fulfill their talent needs. Contrary to this, core capability companies had the highest growth. Focusing on talent pools may not have been sufficient to fulfill their talent needs, leading them to focus on building core capabilities. Regardless, growth seems to shape overall talent strategy, which then shapes focus and investments in specific talent tactics.

Although this study is limited in scope, it highlights an important link between growth rates and talent strategies. Companies with high growth may need to develop the skills of large groups of employees to build the capabilities or skills needed to fuel growth while slower-growth companies may be able to focus on a much smaller set of positions or individuals to meet their growth needs. Companies in the study reported that some of their strategies varied between high- and low-growth markets, which supports the argument of differentiating strategies based on multispeed growth. For example, position planning may be a useful strategy when growth is slower and talent is only needed in key positions. Position planning also may be useful when the company can find talent easily in the external marketplace. A key talent strategy may be useful when the company needs relatively few managers to prepare for next-level jobs. Lower growth and low manager turnover may mean that a company can meet its needs by investing in a small key talent pool. As growth increases, a talent pooling strategy may be required to broaden the key talent pool to prepare individuals for an increasing number of management positions. Finally, a core capability strategy may be required when growth is very high and the company needs to develop core capabilities to meet its needs. Companies may benefit by more consciously adapting their talent strategies for divisions or markets with different growth rates.

An initial model of how SWP and talent strategies may change based on growth rates is provided in Table 7.2. This is for illustrative purposes because the strategies selected will vary based on a company's or division's business strategy, industry type, business model, company maturity, and employee turnover. However, the table may provide insights into adapting SWP strategies for multispeed growth. For example, a slower-growth division may need to focus its SWP on productivity, location, or automation strategies to reduce costs (see Position Planning in Table 7.2). Due to low growth, its talent pipeline needs are low, and a succession planning strategy for key positions may sufficiently meet its needs. At the same time, it has a growth challenge to ignite new growth. This may result in additional SWP strategies to drive innovation or cultural transformation. As growth increases, it may then need to adapt to a key talent approach. Divisions in the key talent quadrant may need to employ more SWP strategies because they need to both improve organization efficiency and future-proof their business to enable future growth. Due to higher growth, their talent pipeline needs are higher, and a key talent planning approach may sufficiently meet their needs. Each quadrant has unique growth challenges that may shape a division's overall SWP. For high-growth companies, this may even mean slowing growth to put the processes and culture in place to execute well before growth causes significant operational issues.

These strategies and approaches to talent management are illustrated below in two cases. First, a case from Marriott International's Asia Pacific

Table 7.2 Implications of growth and strategy on strategic workforce planning and talent strategies

Position planning	Key talent

Growth: Negative or flat; growth slower than overall economic growth
Strategic Workforce Plan
   Focus: Productivity, location strategies, automation, etc.
   Frequency: Yearly
Talent strategy: Succession planning (hire or develop) for key positions (e.g., CEO, CFO, etc.)
Growth challenge: Need to ignite growth, which may greatly impact SWP and talent strategy
	Growth: At and above overall economic growth (e.g., 5–15%)
	Strategic workforce plan
	   Focus: Segmentation, organization design, talent pools, productivity, etc.
	   Frequency: Yearly
	Talent strategy: Identify and develop key talent to ensure leader bench strength
	Growth challenge: Future-proof the business and enable this with new skills (e.g., digital)

Core capability	**Talent pooling**

Growth: Very high (e.g., 25%+)
Strategic Workforce plan
   Focus: Forecasting overall headcount growth and growth in key skill pools
   Frequency: Quarterly forecasts, agile and adaptable processes
Talent strategy: Develop core skills across employees and/or in key job groups
Growth challenge: Need to build culture and processes; may need to slow growth at times
	Growth: High (e.g., 15–25%)
	Strategic workforce plan
	   Focus: Forecasting, segmentation, and job design; building future skill pools
	   Frequency: Biannually or quarterly
	Talent strategy: Develop large pool of talent to keep pace with growth with ability to ramp-up or ramp-down
	Growth challenge: Need to manage high growth and prepare to ramp up if growth increases

Note: This table illustrates how growth and strategy may impact strategic workforce plans and talent strategies. Other factors (e.g., growth strategy, turnover rates, industry) may impact strategy choice.

region highlights how SWP and talent processes can be adapted to meet the needs of multispeed growth, and how these can be further adapted when challenged with a global pandemic. Second, a case from Gojek, a hypergrowth technology start-up, highlights the challenges of high growth and how this impacts SWP processes and talent management practices.

Marriott: Multispeed Strategic Workforce Planning

Marriott International is a multinational hospitality company that manages, franchises, and owns hotels under a portfolio of 30 brands, including The Ritz-Carlton, Sheraton, and Westin hotels. Altogether, as of 2022, they manage more than 8,000 properties and more than 1 million rooms across 134 countries and territories. Between 2009 and 2016, Marriott revenue grew approximately 6% per annum (Macrotrends, 2022b). Marriott then acquired Starwood Hotels and Resorts Worldwide, increasing its annual revenue by approximately 30%. Quarterly global revenue growth slowed between 2017 and 2019, and then, in 2020, plummeted as the global travel and hospitality sectors were impacted by COVID-19 (Gursoy and Chi, 2020). These growth dynamics impact global SWP strategies and approaches. However, differential growth by region also impacts Marriott's SWP. While global growth slowed between 2017 and 2019, Marriott's Asia Pacific business grew rapidly. In 2017, Marriott Asia had approximately 500 properties in the region. Despite a pandemic slow-down, in 2022, Marriott in Asia has more than 900 open properties with close to 690 in the pipeline. Because of this growth, Marriott in Asia needed to adapt its approach to SWP and its approach to talent. They had to further modify their SWP to manage the impact and challenges of COVID-19.

At a global level, Marriott International provides SWP frameworks and processes that are then executed at regional and local levels. Their philosophy is that the markets know how to best grow their businesses. They enable market growth by providing performance management, talent review, talent acquisition, and employer branding tools. This allows each level in the organization to adapt its SWP and approach to talent to meet its growth needs. For example, at a global level, Marriott uses a key talent approach to talent management. This reflects the relatively slower overall global growth rate and a focus on developing talent for a smaller set of senior level jobs. At a hotel property level, Marriott uses a core capability approach to talent management. Its SWP efforts focus on forecasting, hiring, and developing talent below a certain level of management. Because turnover in some roles can be high and each market has different labor dynamics, this approach ensures a fit-for-purpose SWP for each property. At a regional level, Marriott employs multiple workforce strategies that reflect its strategic priorities, expected growth rates of different brands and geographies, and the shortage of talent in some markets.

Building Skills to Fuel Growth

Marriott International's Asia Pacific strategy includes working with developers and owners to open new properties across geographies, especially in high-growth markets such as China and India. Its strategy also includes focused development of properties within its luxury brands such as The Ritz-Carlton and St. Regis while also focusing on its premium brands such as Marriott and Le Meridien and select service brands such as Four Points and Moxy. These strategies shape Marriott's SWPs. To meet the demands of growth, it needs to forecast, hire, and develop staff for, on average, more than 100 new properties per year. At a management level, this means increasing experienced management headcount by greater than 10% in key roles across a variety of countries and locations. This is made more difficult because Marriott's brand segment growth strategies require it to develop leaders with the specific skills needed to manage different types of properties. For example, the competencies needed for leading in a luxury hotel are specialized and different from leading in other brand segments. Because of this, Marriott's SWP strategy requires it to hire and develop a large number of leaders to fuel its hotel development pipeline but with specific skills to meet the growth of each segment and job type (e.g., operations, food service, etc.).

These challenges are made more difficult because many of the markets in which Marriott is growing lack experienced talent in these segments and job types. To address these needs and to integrate the new portfolio of brands acquired in their purchase of Starwood, the company created the Marriott Development Academy. This initiative was designed to build leadership skills that would help individuals face the challenges of moving into a new job level or job type. To build a talent pipeline, Marriott uses workforce planning to identify staffing needs based on its strategic growth plans and then uses its talent review process to identify leaders who can be developed into these new roles. The Marriott Development Academy is used to help these identified leaders get ready for these roles. Developing internal talent cannot always meet its needs, so Marriott also maps external talent in targeted segments (e.g., luxury, food and beverage) within key markets. They proactively build relationships with these individuals and bring them on board as staffing demands increase.

Marriott's strategy can change by type of property, brand segment, level of leader, and country in which they operate. For example, Marriott opened a series of Fairfield hotels in Japan's Michi-no-Eki, or roadside service stations. These smaller select service hotels require fewer, multiskilled staff members and hands-on leadership, which required different skills and training compared to Marriott's traditional hotel employee. Because of their sometimes remote locations, they also had to partner with government and community groups to identify staff. Marriott is using a core capability strategy to meet the demands of this unique project and to help prepare for expected high hotel development growth.

Shifting Strategies Based on Business Needs

Although Marriott has high growth in Asia, it has used a key talent approach to develop more senior leaders because of the limited number of next-level roles and the lower turnover in some of these roles. However, Marriott shifted this approach during the pandemic. Leaders at these levels faced many challenges, including finding new sources of revenue, changing their business models, and managing staffing complexities. To support them, Marriott shifted to a talent pooling strategy to provide greater support for the group while building new skills. For example, it created the General Manager Certificate program to upskill and support General Managers (GMs) and soon-to-be GMs. Because travel was restricted and budgets were tight, the company created a program that included leadership assessment and workshops to build knowledge in the areas of business acumen and owner relation management and to discuss the challenges of leading through COVID-19.

Shifting to a talent pooling strategy meant that the company had to scale the program to more than 100 leaders at a time when revenues were under pressure from the pandemic. To provide a premium experience, Marriott leveraged Produgie, a SaaS platform designed to multiply the impact of leaders and teams. Leaders in the program used Produgie's leadership assessment to gain insight into skills they needed to develop. Produgie then recommended Development Sprints that leaders could execute and leverage to learn on the job while having greater impact. For example, given the demands of the pandemic, these leaders and their teams were under high levels of stress. Produgie included sprints to help leaders and teams improve their well-being practices, better craft their job by managing their work demands and resources, and learn how to build a resilient culture. Sprints guided their actions and stakeholders provided them development advice and feedback to maximize their learning. Leveraging technology enabled them to change their talent strategy and deliver a high-quality learning experience.

Marriott's experience highlights that SWP strategies should be adaptable and flexible. Within a company, some regions, business units, or segments

Table 7.3 Sample strategic workforce planning and talent strategies for multispeed hospitality growth

	Moderate growth	Higher growth
Business and growth challenge	Moderate expansion of luxury hotels within a competitive market	Rapid expansion of select service hotels in a new market
Implications on SWP	Yearly forecast of headcount growth and turnover by segment Identification of talent pools internally and externally to meet location strategy Identification of luxury trends impacting service skills needed	Continuous headcount forecasting based on hotel development pipeline Analysis of location and workforce dynamics and availability Design of critical jobs and identification of skills needed
Implications for talent strategy	Identification and development of key talent to open new hotels and staff operating hotels	Recruit and hire external talent Develop local partnerships to support staffing needs Develop talent in existing hotels prior to new openings

Note: This table represents how SWP and talent strategies may vary for moderate versus high growth in the hospitality industry.

may be growing faster than others, requiring different approaches to talent acquisition and development. At the same time, external events such as COVID-19 may require even more adaptation as goals of SWP shift from fueling a pipeline of talent to retention. This is illustrated further in Table 7.3, which shows how these strategies may change within a hospitality company. This highlights how needs and strategies may vary in a moderate- versus high-growth environment.

Gojek: Strategic Workforce Planning in a Hypergrowth Environment

Gojek is an on-demand, multiservice technology platform that provides users a Super App that includes ride sharing, food delivery, payments, and more than 20 other services. Gojek started in 2010, and it now operates across three countries. It was Indonesia's first unicorn, and, in 2021, the company merged with Tokopedia, an e-commerce platform. The combined entity known as GoTo then listed in an initial public offering (IPO) that raised more than US$1 billion and was valued at $28.8 billion in early 2022 (Forbes, 2022). In just over 10 years, Gojek transformed from a small call center with 20 motorcycle taxi drivers to launching its Gojek app in 2015, to a multiservice platform and IPO. Much of its high growth was fueled by expanding core services, launching new services, and expanding its geographic footprint. A scalable technology platform enabled much of this expansion. To fuel this hypergrowth, Gojek had to add staff, build new skills, and open new offices. This rapid growth has shaped Gojek's approach to SWP and talent management.

Strategic Workforce Planning in a Hypergrowth Environment

Traditional SWP processes were predominantly created in government agencies and large companies (Ward, 2012). Mature, slower-growth companies have more historic and stable data available for analytics and forecasting, their business strategy is more static, talent and performance management processes are routinely executed, and the job scope of employees is relatively stable. If the company is large, it also may have a larger employee and geographic footprint to drive new initiatives. Contrast this to a smaller technology startup where the employee base is small and historic trends are not relevant given dynamic change in the company. Strategies change quickly, requiring more agile planning because business needs for resources and skills are constantly in flux. As an example, within a few years of launching its app, Gojek added more than 20 services and created multiple partnerships, requiring it to integrate and develop new technology. Gojek had to scale its platform to manage more than 2 million drivers and more than 300,000 merchants, enable $2 billion in food delivery, and process more than 6 billion API transactions annually. This rapid and dynamic growth resulted in shifting priorities that challenged traditional SWP processes.

To address this, Gojek designed agile and scalable SWP and talent practices. Gojek wanted agile practices that were flexible, locally relevant to the business, and quick to change. For example, if a division was growing rapidly, it needed the flexibility to change its hiring forecast at any time, and it needed to hire talent ahead of its expected revenue growth curve. These decisions needed to be made rapidly at a business level to ensure quick execution. At the same time, Gojek wanted SWP practices to be scalable. For example, job and compensation structures and hiring processes had to be consistent across divisions to enable quick, centralized execution. As Gojek matured as a company, the balance between ability and scalability had to adapt.

Between 2018 and 2019, Gojek was growing very rapidly and its SWP practices focused more on agility. Because it was growing quickly, the company wanted to launch new services and build new technical skills. At the time, technical talent was becoming more difficult to find and hire. To address both needs, it acquired more than 15 companies in 2 years. This resulted in the launch of new services and operations as well as expansion into new countries such as Vietnam. Each business group operated as its own entity and had agency to make SWP decisions that met its local business needs. They could hire, forecast, plan succession, and manage job structures to meet their business needs. While this gave each business freedom to grow quickly, it also resulted in some fragmentation. Acquisitions were not initially well integrated, resulting in inconsistent HR and SWP processes. Gojek had agility but needed more scalability.

Between 2019 and 2020, Gojek accelerated integration and consolidation of these companies. To scale, the business focused on integrating its brand and technology architecture, and HR focused on standardizing more of its HR and SWP processes. However, HR wanted to balance the need to scale with being agile. They wanted businesses to have agency to make decisions locally and quickly. They also wanted standardized solutions that could scale and that were flexible. To accomplish both objectives, they introduced the idea of modular, iterative SWP and talent solutions. Solutions were modular in that they could be used in a plug-and-play manner to address issues or challenges in the business. Solutions were iterative in that they could be changed or updated at any time during the year to meet business demands. For example, they designed their performance management system to focus on employee impact on the business rather than on a particular goal (e.g., # of units produced). With this focus on impact, goals and metrics within the performance system could be easily changed throughout the year as teams and employees focused more on their overall impact on the company. Their compensation system was designed to allow salary and promotion changes every 6 months, but also allowed off-cycle exceptions to maximize the flexibility a business needed to reward or retain talent.

These principles were used as Gojek launched its first central workforce planning process in 2021. At the beginning of the year, each business provided a roadmap for its business forecast, product launch dates, and the impact this had on its people and capability forecast. This was scalable and used across the business to agree on a headcount plan for the year. As the year progressed and business requirements changed, each business could easily ramp its plan up or down to reflect the market situation. For example, if a competitor exited a market, a business was able to make decisions to change pricing, acquire new customers, or hire the competitor's staff. To enable this, HR adopted a 60/40 approach to SWP. The business could drive up to 60% of decisions needed to adapt quickly. The global team drove 40% of SWP processes. HR standardized modular processes that the business could use and maintained oversight on some decisions throughout the year to ensure alignment. If business slowed, this allowed the global team the flexibility to step in and provide more process checks and balances to support updated goals.

Scalable and Agile Core Capability Development

Gojek also applied this principle of being scalable and agile to building employee skills. To do this, the company focused on providing scalable and modular solutions to address the challenges and needs of employees. One example of this is the Gojek Growth Leader Journey, which was an initiative designed to understand and build core manager capabilities. Gojek built the program around Produgie to enable the company to scale tools across its managers. After an initial program orientation, managers used Produgie to complete the Growth Leader Assessment (GLA; Eyring, 2019). This assessment was designed to measure the skills leaders need to drive company growth. The Growth Leader Style assessment provides leaders insight into their slower-to-change traits, personality, and mindsets while the Growth Leader Strategies assessment provides leaders insight into the management practices that they employ on the job. Together, these assessments help leaders and companies identify skills to hire and/or develop. For example, the leader profile in Figure 7.2 indicates that the leader has relatively high scores in the Structure and Execute Growth Plan capability, which means they are both conscientious (style) and have good practices to focus their team and align stakeholders to support their goals (strategies). However, their Lead Innovation score shows that they are not very creative (style) but are moderately high in the practices they use to drive innovation with their

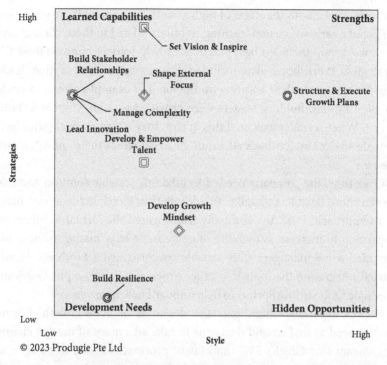

Figure 7.2 Growth leader assessment styles and strategies development matrix. This figure illustrates the relationship of Styles and Strategies. Each capability has a Style and Strategy measure. Build Resilience, for example, measures Composure as a style (i.e., emotional adjustment) and Adapt as a strategy (e.g., practices to adapt to stressful situations). This leader scores low in both areas, indicating a development need.

team (strategy). At a company level, these scores can be used to shape the SWP process. For example, a traditional logistics company used Produgie and the GLA to build innovation skills. The company used the assessment to identify individuals with strong innovation skills and had these individuals conduct Produgie innovation Sprints with their teams. This increased innovation projects in the company and built new skills on these teams.

For Gojek, this assessment helped leaders identify priority development areas to review with its managers. At a company level, this allowed Gojek to identify skill gaps across leaders. These gaps were similar to those listed in Table 7.1. Specifically, leaders needed to better drive performance through others by aligning efforts across groups, drive change in the organization, and cope better with the stress of high growth. To address these gaps, Gojek delivered a series of virtual learning webinars related to these content areas. Each workshop included best practices to help leaders improve their GLA Strategies. Workshops also included Development Sprints that leaders could use to apply their learning on the job. For example, after a workshop on aligning stakeholders, leaders were provided with an Align Stakeholder Sprint. When a leader executed this Sprint, they nominated stakeholders to provide advice and feedback via Produgie to help track their improvement in the area.

Over time, the company needed to take this scalable solution and make it even more flexible and agile. To address this, Gojek made a few changes in its approach. First, the company transformed the virtual webinars into e-learning to increase availability of content for busy managers. Second, it provided some managers with scalable coaching using Produgie. Third, it started integrating the tools into other processes. For example, Gojek used Produgie Onboarding Sprints to help onboard new managers.

Gojek's experience highlights the demands of hypergrowth. Business leaders need to make rapid decisions to take advantage of market changes. This meant that Gojek's SWP and talent processes needed to be agile and readily adaptable through the year. As the business grew, these processes also had to become scalable, and Gojek had to strike the right balance between the two approaches. Its experience also highlights the importance of a core capability talent strategy to build skills across managers. Using technology is one solution to help ensure this is done in a scalable and agile manner.

Actions You Can Take

Companies often use their strategy and revenue growth goals as part of the initial stages of SWP and forecasting. Although this is a good first step, they can go much further in using growth to shape their SWP and talent strategies. Consider taking these key actions to help you better drive growth through your SWP practices:

- *Identify the strategic impact of growth*: Explicitly identify how growth rates will impact your strategy and strategic enablers. Low-growth groups may have a more urgent need to focus on innovation, bring in talent with a growth mindset to transform the organization, or reduce

costs by offshoring. High-growth groups may have a greater need to align employees to key priorities or develop managers for the demands of growth. Take time to identify how growth rates will impact your growth strategies, strategy enablers, skill needs, and SWP practices (e.g., location strategies, job redesign, career planning, etc.).
- *Adapt for multispeed growth*: Move away from a one-size-fits-all approach to SWP. Higher-growth divisions or products may require more frequent SWP planning, different staffing processes, or more flexibility in their practices. Marriott's case highlights how agile a company can be in adopting different strategies. The company leverages different talent strategies at a global level (i.e., Key Talent), for its regions (e.g., Talent Pooling), and for different brands. More importantly, it changes these strategies as it adapts to changing market dynamics.
- *Be more strategic when adopting best practices*: Many companies adopt best practices based on the company's brand name or their beliefs about talent. Avoid this pitfall and consider instead your growth strategy and expected growth rates. For example, a slower-growth company or division may gain few benefits by adopting recruitment and development practices from a high-growth company. Likewise, a fast-growth company or division may fail to grow if they adopt succession planning, job design methodologies, or key talent programs from slower-growth companies. Pick the right best practices for your businesses' expected growth rates.
- *Build more agile SWP practices*: If you are in a slowly changing industry and a slow-growth company, a yearly SWP exercise may be sufficient for your needs. As the pace of external change and internal growth increases, consider more agile and more frequent SWP planning. Gojek's case highlights the value of doing this. To meet the demands of hypergrowth, Gojek used an iterative approach to forecasting that allowed it to shift its SWP priorities quickly. It also built agile practices that could meet local business needs but scale for the whole business.
- *Take SWP beyond forecasting and staffing*. Forecasting and staffing are important aspects of SWP. However, growth impacts leader priorities, behaviors, and the skills they need to succeed. Growth also impacts how fast jobs are changing, the speed at which employees need to develop to succeed, and the types of transformation the company is experiencing. Whether your company is growing slowly or fast, consider all these demands when implementing SWP practices.

- *Use technology to understand and develop workforce skills*: Technology has been used in SWP for forecasting, performance management, and succession planning. The Marriott and Gojek cases highlight how technology also can be used to understand and develop skills. Consider using technology to assess and pinpoint skill gaps across the organization. Then consider using technology to design scalable development programs that can reach more employees.

Ultimately, SWP should help a business achieve its growth goals. To do this well, growth rates should be considered throughout the SWP process, including the frequency of planning, strategies selected, practices used, and flexibility allowed in the planning process. Integrating growth more closely with SWP practices will help companies build the workforce they need to deliver against their strategies.

References

Ahlstrom, D. (2010). Innovation and growth: How business contributes to society. *Academy of Management Perspectives*, 24(3), 11–24.

Bahadir, S. C., Bharadwaj, S., and Parzen, M. (2009). A meta-analysis of the determinants of organic sales growth. *International Journal of Research in Marketing*, 26(4), 263–275.

Business Insider. (2022). The 25 most highly rated leadership teams at large companies. https://www.businessinsider.com/comparably-large-companies-highly-rated-leadership-teams-2022-7.

Eyring, A. R., and Lim, A. (2014). *Leading growth in Asia: A summary report*. Organisation Solutions Pte. Ltd.

Eyring, J. (2014). Talent management strategies for multi-speed growth: Getting your practices in the right gear. *People and Strategy*, 37(3), 30–35.

Eyring, J., and Eyring, A. (2013). Workforce strategies for high growth markets. In D. L. Ward and R. Tripp (Eds.), *Positioned: Strategic workforce planning that gets the right person in the right job* (pp. 93–109). AMACOM.

Eyring, J. D. (2019). *Technical report: Business unit leader style and strategy capabilities and year-over-year business unit performance*. Organisation Solutions Pte. Ltd.

Forbes. (2012). The world's best companies for leadership. https://www.forbes.com/sites/susanadams/2012/05/02/the-worlds-best-companies-for-leadership/?sh=38c47111ce6f.

Forbes. (2022). Indonesia's GoTo raises $1.1 billion and delays market debut. https://www.forbes.com/sites/yessarrosendar/2022/03/31/indonesias-goto-raises-11-billion-and-delays-market-debut/?sh=38a966e22c71.

Gallardo-Gallardo, E., and Thunnissen, M. (2016). Standing on the shoulders of giants? A critical review of empirical talent management research. *Employee Relations*, 38(1), 31–56.

Gursoy, D., and Chi, C. G. (2020). Effects of COVID-19 pandemic on hospitality industry: review of the current situations and a research agenda. *Journal of Hospitality Marketing and Management, 29*(5), 527–529.

Iles, P., Chuai, X., and Preece, D. (2010). Talent management and HRM in multinational companies in Beijing: Definitions, differences and drivers. *Journal of World Business, 45,* 179–189.

Junni, P., Sarala, R. M., Taras, V. A. S., and Tarba, S. Y. (2013). Organizational ambidexterity and performance: A meta-analysis. *Academy of Management Perspectives, 27*(4), 299–312.

Macrotrends. (2022a). Alphabet revenue 2010–2022. https://www.macrotrends.net/stocks/charts/GOOG/alphabet/revenue

Macrotrends. (2022b). Marriott revenue 2010–2021. https://www.macrotrends.net/stocks/charts/MAR/marriott/revenue

Meyers, M. C., van Woerkom, M., Paauwe, J., and Dries, N. (2020). HR managers' talent philosophies: Prevalence and relationships with perceived talent management practices. *International Journal of Human Resource Management, 31*(4), 562–588.

PwC. (2019). Workforce Strategy Benchmarking Survey industrial data sheet. https://www.pwc.com/gx/en/services/people-organisation/publications/assets/pwc-workforce-datasheet-global.pdf

Smit, S., Thompson, C. M., and Viguerie, S. P. (2005). The do-or-die struggle for growth. *McKinsey Quarterly, 3,* 35–45.

Tucker, E., and Morgan, L. (2021). Strategic Workforce Planning survey report. APQC. https://www.apqc.org/resource-library/resource-listing/strategic-workforce-planning-survey-report

Ward, D. L. (2012). How long has this been going on? In D. L. Ward and R. Tripp (Eds.), *Positioned: Strategic workforce planning that gets the right person in the right job.* (pp. 9–17). AMACOM.

8
Enabling Strategic Workforce Planning Through Skills, Artificial Intelligence, and Internal Talent Marketplace

Brian Heger

The global pandemic, economic climate, and social events of the past few years have forever transformed all aspects of work, the workplace, and the workforce. The impact has not only redefined what workers value, but has also altered where people work, how work is organized, who does the work, and how it gets performed. As organizations continue to adapt to this new paradigm, many are reimagining their talent strategies, practices, and technologies to follow suit.

One talent practice critical to the future of work is strategic workforce planning (SWP), yet many practitioners struggle to implement SWP in their firms. According to a Boston Consulting Group study (2021) of 32 human resources (HR) practices, SWP is among the top three practices with the largest gap between organizations' current level of capability and the importance they place on the topic. A Gartner survey (2022) found that fewer than 28% of surveyed Chief Human Resource Officers are confident in their organizations' approach to SWP. And Mercer's 2022 Global Talent Trends study shows that both business and HR leaders' top talent concern is improving workforce planning to better inform buy, build, and borrow strategies (Mercer, 2022). With the SWP capability gap continuing to widen in many organizations, firms are hindered in their ability to drive business performance through differentiated workforce strategies.

Why Is SWP Increasingly Difficult to Execute? Jobs and Skills

While there have always been barriers to implementing SWP (e.g., lack of alignment to business strategy, data quality, etc.), several factors are converging and making it increasingly difficult to implement. At the forefront of these challenges is that jobs—the cornerstone of legacy workforce planning—continue to shift at an accelerated pace. An analysis by Lightcast (2022) of 15 million online job advertisements posted between 2016 and 2021 found that nearly three-quarters of jobs changed more from 2019 through 2021 than in the previous 3-year period. The World Economic Forum (2020) notes that, by 2025, 85 million jobs may be displaced, but 97 million new roles could emerge. Given the speed at which jobs continue to change, thought leaders envision a future of work characterized as "work without jobs"—where jobs are deconstructed into tasks and used as the basis for workforce planning (Deloitte, 2021; Jesuthasan and Boudreau, 2021; Ulrich, 2020). And while workforce planning practitioners have begun to experiment with this next-generation approach to SWP, only 22% of organizations are effective at breaking down jobs into smaller tasks (Institute for Corporate Productivity, 2021b). At the current pace, it could take years until organizations fully develop the capability to fractionalize jobs into tasks and integrate them into SWP.

The challenge of knowing what jobs are needed, where, and when is one reason there has been a surging interest in skills-based workforce planning. As the name implies, skills-based SWP focuses on the skills an organization needs rather than jobs. Although business and HR leaders report a strong desire to shift from job-based to skills-based talent practices (Deloitte, 2022), fewer than one in five organizations have successfully adopted skills-based approaches to a significant extent. And according to the Conference Board (2022a), only 4% of respondent organizations have integrated skills across all talent practices. These organizations also report that the transition to skills-based talent solutions has taken longer than expected and is more complex than anticipated.

The shift to skills-based talent practices will be increasingly difficult to navigate considering that the average shelf-life of many skills is shortening from 5 to 2½ years (IBM Institute for Business Value, n.d.) and that 40% of current workers' core skills are expected to change between now and 2025 (World Economic Forum, 2020). Compounding this challenge is that many organizations do not have a skills taxonomy or common language for discussing skills. As reported by the Institute for Corporate Productivity (2021a) in their survey of more than 1,300 HR and business executives across 80 countries:

- Only 10% of respondents said their organizations have an employee skills database with profiles for understanding employees' skills.
- 53% said their organizations have insufficient data about the current skills of their workers.
- More than a quarter agreed that LinkedIn knows more about their organization's respective workforce skills than the organization does.

Although HR leaders rate workforce planning as the top talent practice for which skills-based talent solutions can yield the most value (Conference Board, 2022a), organizations must first overcome several obstacles to understanding the skills of their workforce before this value can be realized.

Artificial Intelligence Comes to the Rescue—Maybe

Despite the challenges to implementing skills-based SWP, practitioners have been encouraged by technology and artificial intelligence (AI) platforms intended to overcome these barriers. These technologies—sometimes referred to as *talent intelligence platforms*—leverage AI to enable skills-based talent practices. But, as pointed out by leading industry analyst Josh Bersin (2022), the skills-tech market is still emerging and is one of the most immature of all HR tech applications. Although a few early adopters (e.g., Unilever) of skills-based AI technologies have reported meaningful business outcomes empowered by these platforms (Nair and Pasala, 2021), many need more time for lagging indicators to catch up before long-term value and return on investment (ROI) is determined. And while the marketing and sales teams of these AI platforms might imply that their implementation is as easy as "plug and play," there are several deployment challenges that practitioners will need to evaluate and overcome as they mobilize AI-based talent solutions. These challenges extend beyond the technical components of AI implementation and encompass change management, data privacy and fairness, and user adoption, to name a few. Table 8.1 includes a few of these challenges and the questions they raise.

Table 8.1 Sample challenges and questions for implementing artificial intelligence technologies

Challenges	Sample questions to answer
Over 250 AI-based tools exist in HR alone (World Economic Forum, 2021).	Where do we start in determining which AI platforms to evaluate? Do we target a 'pure play' AI solution that focuses on a specific capability (e.g., internal mobility) or a human capital platform that offers a range of solutions as part of a broader suite?
Seven of 10 companies report minimal or no value from their "overall" company-wide investments in AI. (Ransbotham et al., 2019).	How do we get agreement and support from leaders, given the considerable time, costs, and resources required to shift to skills-based AI practices? How do we develop a business case that quantifies the potential ROI for the organization?
Data privacy (e.g., Europe's General Data Protection Regulation), fairness, and the responsible and ethical use of AI must be heavily considered and scrutinized.	How do we evaluate a platform's AI models for bias so that fairness and ethical AI are ensured? How can we critically assess these risks, especially when many vendors place limits on what they can share about how their AI works because of proprietary information?
AI-based platforms must integrate with an organization's core HR system, broader HR tech stack, and talent processes.	What if we want an AI platform that has the capabilities we need, but that doesn't fully integrate with our HRIS? Who has decision rights in selecting a platform? HRIT, SWP, LandD, or someone else? If it is a team decision, how do we handle cases when the team can't agree?
Successful implementation and user adoption could require extensive change management and a redesign of the employee experience.	What nontechnical barriers (e.g., policies, practices, processes, and mindsets) will we need to address to enable user adoption? Since many AI platforms are add-ons to an organization's core HR technology (e.g., HRIS, LMS, ATS), how do we integrate these platforms to provide a seamless employee experience?

Overall, while AI-based talent platforms can help overcome obstacles to skills-based SWP, these technologies are much harder to mobilize, implement, sustain, and show ROI than most organizations estimate. As a result, SWP practitioners must avoid the "bright and shiny object" trap when assessing these technologies and take an expansive and objective view of the multiple—and often less obvious—factors critical to AI evaluation and implementation.

Internal Talent Marketplace: Integrating Skills, AI, and SWP

Alongside skills and AI is a related topic that has received much attention in workforce planning and talent management: *internal talent marketplace* (ITM). An ITM—also called a *talent marketplace* or *opportunity marketplace*—is a technology-enabled platform that uses AI to match employees (and their skills) to opportunities in their organization. These opportunities range from full-time roles, part-time jobs, projects, temporary assignments, gig work, and various types of development and training. While ITM providers vary in how their AI matches employees' skills to opportunities, their recommendations are typically enabled by two components: (1) an employee skills profile and (2) an internal opportunities repository.

Employee Skills Profile

Although organizations try to build and maintain employee skill profiles, they often face challenges when doing so. First, employee skills information is usually fragmented in various places, such as an HRIS, employee resume, LinkedIn profile, talent management database, and employee development plan, to name a few. Having skills information in different locations makes it next to impossible for organizations—especially larger firms—to curate a holistic view of employees' skills. Second, even when employee skills are stored in one location, a lack of taxonomy or language for describing skills often results in inconsistent or overlapping skills. This approach leads to an inaccurate estimation of an organization's skill supply. The third challenge is that getting employees to maintain and update their skills profile is an arduous task. As a result, employee skill profiles can become outdated quickly, rendering them less useful for SWP and other talent practices.

To overcome these challenges, an ITM can import a variety of employee skill sources into its platform—enabling its AI to analyze these data and infer skills using a common language. And, as employees gain new skills through roles, projects, and development experiences, most ITM platforms prompt employees to add those skills to their profile with help from the AI's talent intelligence. This process results in a robust and up-to-date employee skills profile that provides the backbone for an AI engine that matches workers to internal opportunities.

Internal Opportunities Repository

Similar to how an ITM uses AI to infer internal skill supply, it can also help a firm organize, manage, and estimate its work demand. It does this by ingesting various opportunities (e.g., open jobs, projects, assignments, etc.) from multiple standalone platforms, such as an applicant tracking system (ATS), projects or gigs database, and learning management system (LMS). An ITM integrates each of these individual sources into its platform and curates a collective view of internal opportunities. Not only does it merge these opportunities into one platform, but it also uses its AI to identify the skills required for those opportunities. The result is an integrated and transparent view of an organization's current internal opportunities to which employees and their skills can be matched.

Altogether, an ITM is a two-sided marketplace that brings employees and opportunities together through a common skills language. It provides buyers of work within the organization (e.g., managers, workforce planners, recruiters, etc.) with access to qualified sellers (internal workers) who can be redeployed to relevant opportunities as work demands shift. This bidirectional approach unlocks several talent capabilities, from internal mobility, upskilling and reskilling, and agile workforce planning. Figure 8.1 illustrates how an ITM works and the outcomes it can produce.

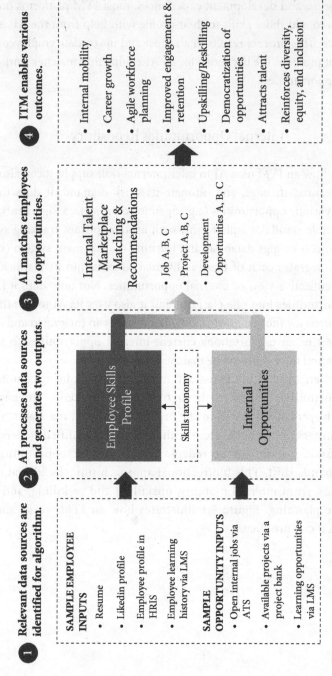

Figure 8.1 Internal talent marketplace concept and outcomes.

SWP Capability	Talent Challenge It Addresses	How ITM Enables SWP Capability
Broaden the internal talent pool.	Organizations express concern about not being able to attract and hire top talent in a competitive labor market.	Identifies "hidden" internal talent with the skills, adjacent skills, and the desire to take on new work opportunities.
Unlock workforce capacity.	Peaks and valleys in employee workload leads to the underutilization of internal talent and "trapped" capacity.	Releases "trapped" capacity—enabling workers to flow to wherever their skills and interests can add the most value.
Stabilize internal talent supply.	Lack of career growth and development is a top reason employees leave their organizations.	Stems unwanted turnover by making career opportunities more prominent, accessible, and transparent.
Accelerate upskilling and reskilling.	Organizations are concerned they are not upskilling and reskilling workers fast enough to pace with the needs of the business.	Uses organic opportunities for developing employees' skills and building organizational capability.

Figure 8.2 Four strategic workforce planning capabilities enabled by ITM.

Finally, while an ITM can fuel a broad range of talent outcomes, it can be especially powerful for workforce planning. An ITM can help balance work demand (e.g., jobs, projects, short-term assignments) and internal talent skill supply in a dynamic, scalable, and efficient manner. And although the internal workforce is only one of several sources for supplying work needs, it is a superior option for workforce planning since it enables multiple SWP capabilities that help hurdle various talent challenges. Figure 8.2 illustrates four primary SWP capabilities an ITM can support and the talent challenges they help to overcome.

Aside from these primary SWP capabilities, tapping into an internal workforce to meet an organization's work demands provides other benefits, such as:

- *Saving organizations money* by reducing the reliance on external recruiting and contracting.
- *Improving time to full productivity* because of shorter learning curves and reduced onboarding time.
- *Strengthening an organization's employment brand* as a developer of talent—increasing its ability to attract top talent.
- *Improving cross-functional collaboration* by facilitating new internal connections and relationships, which increases organizational capability.
- *Strengthening diversity, equity, and inclusion* by basing matches on objective skills criteria and work requirements.

In short, while SWP should include a combination of tactics (e.g., build, buy, borrow, bot, etc.) for supplying an organization's talent needs, the build component—or internal workforce—is an untapped lever that could release disproportionate value for many organizations.

The Challenge and Opportunity Ahead

The challenges and opportunities for delivering SWP in today's business landscape present SWP practitioners and their organizations with paradoxical considerations. On one hand, the obstacles to implementing SWP are greater than ever and more difficult to overcome. And while skills-based AI and ITM technologies provide a solution for overcoming these challenges, these platforms are difficult to implement and they come with risks. Yet failing to act will further widen the SWP capability gap and jeopardize organizations' business performance. With talent at the top of most CEOs' business priorities (Conference Board, 2022b; PwC, 2022), there is no better time than now to reimagine SWP and tap its potential as a source of competitive edge. The question for internal SWP practitioners to answer is: *How do we unlock the potential of AI, skills, ITM, and SWP to drive business performance while mitigating the risks?*

The remainder of this chapter offers an internal SWP practitioner's perspective on how organizations can answer this question. It draws from a "real-world" pilot study conducted in one of our business units at Bristol-Myers Squibb (BMS), where we evaluated two skills-based ITM platforms on their ability to enable SWP. This section covers three areas:

1. *The approach used for our pilot implementation.* This section begins with the business context for conducting this initiative and how it supports the organization's business strategy. We share how the pilot was mobilized by an internal team and how the team identified three AI and ITM-based capabilities that served as the pilot's focus. Tactics for gaining leadership support are covered, and we discuss our approach to identifying, evaluating, and selecting vendors. Since data are critical to this initiative, we share the five data sources that were used by the ITM platforms to generate AI-based inferences. This section also includes criteria used for pilot group selection and covers five questions for the pilot to answer.

2. *Results from the pilot.* In this section, we share quantitative and qualitative feedback from pilot participants and business leaders on how well the platforms performed on five measures. These measures include the ability to accurately infer employees' skills, effectiveness in matching employees to relevant jobs and learning opportunities, whether the outputs are useful for informing SWP, and user experience.
3. *Lessons learned and recommendations for practitioners.* The final section provides suggestions for practitioners to consider as they mobilize AI, skills, ITM, and SWP in their organizations. The insights are organized into five categories, including kickstarting the initiative, evaluating vendors and executing the pilot, strengthening AI's inferences to better enable SWP, addressing the nontechnological barriers to ITM, and how industrial and organizational (I-O) psychologists can help organizations overcome the challenges to implementing SWP through AI, skills, and ITM. The insights serve as a playbook that practitioners can use to mitigate risks and accelerate SWP in their organizations. I end the chapter with a personal reflection on how skills are an enabler—not the sole driver—of SWP.

While the topics of AI, skills, internal talent marketplace, and workforce planning can be covered in a book by themselves, let alone one chapter, this chapter provides an integrated view of how each of these components works together to drive SWP. And since a pilot informs this chapter's insights, organizations are provided with practical ideas for reimagining SWP and tapping its full potential as a source of competitive edge.

Pilot Study and Results

Background

BMS is a specialty biopharmaceutical company engaged in the discovery, development, licensing and manufacturing, marketing, distribution, and sale of medicines and related medical products to patients with serious diseases. The company's medicines span multiple therapeutic areas, such as oncology, hematology, immunology, and cardiovascular disease and include brands such as Eliquis (apixaban), Opdivo (nivolumab), Orencia (abatacept), Yervoy (ipilimumab), and Zeposia (ozanimod), to name a few. With an annual revenue of $46 billion and a global workforce of 32,000 employees, BMS combines the agility of biotech with the reach and resources of an established pharmaceutical company to create a leading global biopharma company.

In November 2019, BMS completed the $74 billion acquisition of Celgene, which represented the largest merger-acquisition transaction in the industry's history. As part of its post-acquisition integration planning, the newly combined organization set out to reimagine how it could optimize its business operations to accelerate the execution of the company's business strategy. Given that BMS's business strategy encompassed multiple late-stage pipeline product launches over a 12- to 24-month period, redefining its business processes, practices, and technologies could help to speed up the delivery of needed medicines to patients. To support this effort, BMS embarked on a company-wide initiative to identify how digital capabilities (e.g., technology, AI, etc.) could fuel the execution of six business capabilities, ranging from how clinical trials are conducted to how product supply is managed. An executive steering committee was formed to oversee this digital initiative, and six work streams (one for each capability) were established and charged with finding ways to unlock these capabilities through digital and AI-based technologies; one work stream focused on talent.

The Talent Capability Workstream

The remit of the talent capability team was to identify opportunities where AI and digital capabilities could improve the delivery of BMS's business strategy through talent. This effort began by bringing together a group of team members in HR—including talent management, talent acquisition, learning and development, people analytics, total rewards, HR business partners, HR information technology—and support partners such as procurement. Many of the team members understood the talent challenges facing BMS business leaders and offered a diverse perspective on how AI and technology could address those challenges and enable a competitive advantage.

Given that AI and technology transformation efforts often fail because implementation teams take on too much too fast, the team spent its first few meetings narrowing the initiative to the few talent capabilities that disproportionately affect BMS's strategic capabilities. Many of the talent capabilities that were identified—such as facilitating internal mobility and the faster redeployment of talent—hinged on the broader capability of SWP.

To illustrate how SWP enables multiple talent capabilities, one can draw from the metaphor known as the "domino effect," which describes how a chain reaction caused by one event produces a series of continuous actions until the last piece falls into place. As shown in Figure 8.3, SWP is the "lead domino" or the catalyst for enabling other talent capabilities, such as internal mobility, talent acquisition, and learning and development. Stated differently, the outputs of SWP are critical to informing the strategies and tactics of other talent practices. Although BMS implemented an SWP approach in 2019 without AI or technology (Heger and Aulbach, 2019), the organization knew it would eventually need a digital platform to strengthen its SWP and adjacent talent capabilities. The company's broader AI and technology initiative was the impetus that pushed the "lead SWP domino" into motion.

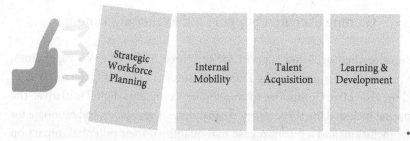

Figure 8.3 Strategic workforce planning domino effect on other talent capabilities.

Three SWP-Based AI Capabilities of Interest

The talent team identified three specific AI-based capabilities that presented the organization with the greatest opportunities to drive aspects of SWP at greater speed and scale: (1) infer employees' skills to develop an employee skills profile, (2) match employees to work opportunities, and (3) recommend learning and developing opportunities to employees. Figure 8.4 shows the three AI-based SWP capabilities and the targeted outcomes they help to achieve.

AI-Based SWP Capability	Description and Sample Benefits
Infer Employees' Skills and Form a Skill Profile	• Infer employees' current skills using a common skills language; employee can modify/add to the AI based profile; results in a robust employee skill profile. • Enables a collective view of the organization's skills—both strengths and gaps—which informs SWP activities.
Match Employees to Work Opportunities	• Recommend internal jobs, projects, and other work opportunities based on the degree of match between an employee's skills and the skills required of the opportunity. • Enables managers and workforce planners to dynamically flow internal talent to where their skills are needed and add the most value.
Recommend Learning and Development	• Proactively recommends targeted learning content to employees based on their current skills and career interests, and the needs of the business. • Uses organic opportunities for developing skills and increasing skills proficiency, maximizes learning time; builds organizational capability faster.

Figure 8.4 Three artificial intelligence-based capabilities for enabling strategic workforce planning.

Gaining Executive Support and Evaluating Vendors

To ensure alignment and support for the three AI-based SWP capabilities, we presented a proposal to the Human Resources Leadership Team (HRLT) and the Executive Committee overseeing the company's digital initiative. The proposal included the three targeted capabilities, the reasons and rationale for their inclusion, and a business case that quantified their potential impact on organizational outcomes (e.g., productivity, retention, cost savings, etc.). The proposal also painted a picture of how lacking these capabilities would impede the organization's ability to execute its business strategy over the next few years. Far too often business cases include the return on investment (ROI) projections of taking an action but don't augment this ROI with the cost of not acting. Including the cost of inaction helps to create a burning platform for articulating why the capabilities are needed. The HRLT and Executive Committee endorsed the proposal, and the talent capability team proceeded to identify and evaluate AI platforms that could enable the three SWP capabilities.

Using the three capabilities, the talent capability team worked with the internal procurement organization to translate the capabilities into a request for proposal (RFP). While 12 vendors responded with interest, six of them eventually dropped from consideration after realizing their platform did not offer the AI capabilities to the extent we required. The remaining six vendors were invited to demonstrate their platforms' capabilities to the talent team. Based on the results, two of the six vendors advanced in the process, which included additional discussions and an opportunity for the talent team to test both platforms. Both parts of this process resulted in satisfactory performance.

Using a Pilot to Test Proof of Concept

Far too often, technology purchasing decisions are made based on a vendors' demonstration of their platform to organizational decision-makers. And while these demos are informative and introduce the vendor's capabilities, they are insufficient by themselves for making decisions that carry significant financial investments that span multiple years. To test these platforms in our own business environment—using our own data, with our employees, and within our broader data and technology ecosystem—we developed a plan to pilot these platforms in one of our business units. The purpose of the pilot was to establish a minimal viable product that employees could test. Employee feedback on both platforms would serve as a critical input to making an informed decision on whether one of the platforms should be purchased and implemented across the company. Table 8.2 shows five questions and outcomes the pilot intended to answer.

Table 8.2 Five questions for pilot study to help answer

Focus	Question	Measurement
1. Skill inferences	Could the AI platform infer employees' skills with relative accuracy based on the data sources provided?	Survey feedback from employee
2. Job matching	Could the platform effectively match employees to relevant open BMS job opportunities based on employees' skills and the skills required for the job?	Survey feedback from employee
3. Development opportunity recommendations	Would the platform recommend relevant learning content based on the employee's skill profile.	Survey feedback from employee
4. Usefulness for workforce planning	Would the outputs be useful for informing various aspects of workforce planning?	Survey feedback and debrief discussion with business unit leaders, HR Centers of Excellence (e.g., SWP, talent acquisition, learning, etc.)
5. User experience	Would the platform be easy to use and provide an engaging user experience?	Survey feedback from employee and HR Center of Excellence leads.

While our original plan was to also test the platform's ability to recommend relevant project work—not just open jobs—we decided to forgo this option for the pilot since our organization did not have a systematic way of curating projects at the time of the pilot. And given that the AI job matching capability works in the same way as project matching, we were comfortable with only testing the job matching during the pilot.

Criteria for Pilot Group Selection

Although many business units and functions in our organization volunteered to take part in the pilot, our goal was to be intentional about pilot group selection. The following criteria informed selection:

- *Business need*: A part of the business where it has been challenging to attract, recruit, and retain needed talent
- *Business impact*: A part of the business that disproportionately affects the execution of the company's strategic priorities
- *Leadership support*: The business leader of the pilot group will prioritize and actively support the initiative
- *Ample work demand*: A business area with heightened work demand
- *Manageable organizational size*: The organization's size is no larger than 500 employees
- *US-based organization*: Most of the organization is based in the United States. (This decision was made because of the excessive time it would take to review the approach with Works Councils and gain their approval. We agreed to first test the platform in a US pilot group and then extend to non-US locations at a later stage if the original pilot was successful).

Based on the criteria, a business unit of 349 employees was selected. The goal was to have half of the group test one platform and the other half test the second platform. We considered having each employee in the pilot (all 349) test both platforms, but felt this added more complexity and was a big ask of the pilot participants. While the number of employees in the pilot group might appear small relative to the size of our organization, it was sufficient for making an informed decision while moving with speed.

Data Sources Used for the Pilot

To ensure we provided relevant data sources for each platform's AI engine, we worked with the vendors to determine which employee and organizational data would be most useful. Five data sources were identified, including three sources for inferring employee skills and two for matching workers and their skills to work opportunities and development suggestions. Table 8.3 provides a description of the data sources used.

Table 8.3 Data sources for inferring employees' skills and job and learning opportunities

Inference for	Data source	Description
Employee Skills Profile	Employee profile data in HR Information System (HRIS)	• Where available, career history, development goals, and skills information were used.
	Employee learning and development history from Learning Management System (LMS)	• Internal training and development that employees have completed (e.g., leadership programs, skill-building courses, etc.) • Courses that are compliance-driven (e.g., Code of Conduct) were excluded from the data transfer since they are less relevant to the pilot's purpose.
	Resume or LinkedIn profile	• Participants uploaded either a resume or a LinkedIn profile to the AI platform.
Internal Opportunity Matching	BMS Open Jobs via Applicant Tracking System (ATS)	• +1,500 open jobs for which BMS was actively recruiting for at the time of the pilot were used; transformed job titles and descriptions to AI platform from ATS.
	Available learning content in BMS's LMS	• All active courses and development program titles and descriptions were transferred courses that were compliance-driven were removed from the transfer since they were less relevant to the purpose of this initiative.

Sample Steps to Mobilize and Execute the Pilot

Although a full communication and engagement plan was developed and implemented for the pilot, a few of the plan's tactics included *attend the business unit's leadership team meetings* to answer questions about the pilot and how the results could be used to enable their business strategy; *attend the business unit's town hall meetings* to share the purpose of the pilot, generate excitement, and answer questions about how the pilot would be implemented; *provide each pilot group with a 12-minute video* (developed by BMS) on how participants can use the platform; and *conduct open office hours over a 3-week pilot period* to provide support to participants and answer their questions.

Results

A five-point rating scale (5 = Strongly Agree, 4 = Agree, 3 = Neutral, 2 = Disagree, and 1 = Strongly Disagree) was used to collect quantitative survey feedback from the pilot's participants. Participants also had the option to provide qualitative feedback. For the quantitative results, percent favorable refers to the total number of participants that responded with an "Agree or Strongly Agree." Results showed that one platform outperformed the other on the five criteria. Figure 8.5 shows the percent favorable scores for the one platform that performed best. The results are based on responses from 162 employees who piloted this platform. While not shown, statistical significance testing was performed to ensure the results were meaningful.

1. *Skills inferences*: Could the AI platform infer employees' skills with relative accuracy based on the data sources provided? Overall, 72% of the pilot group who tested this one platform felt the AI accurately identified their skills. A few verbatim comments from the survey include:
   - "Having the platform determine my skills as an initial first pass made it significantly easier for me to critically evaluate and think about the skills I have."
   - "I like how the platform recommended additional skills that I might have, which forced me to reflect and think about whether I possess those skills. I ended up adding a few of these 'less obvious skills' that I had but wasn't really aware of."
   - "It might have been helpful to have a proficiency rating for each skill, since there are certain skills on my profile that I am much stronger in than others. Nonetheless, the platform did a good job of estimating my overall skills."

Factor/Question	% Favorable
1. Skill Inferences Could the AI platform infer employees' skills with relative accuracy based on the data sources provided?	72%
2. Job Matching Could the platform effectively match employees to relevant open BMS job opportunities based on employees' skills and the skills required for the job?	53%
3. Development Opportunity Recommendations Would the platform recommend relevant learning content based on the employee's skill profile?	55%
4. Usefulness for Workforce Planning Would the outputs be useful for informing various aspects of workforce planning?	84%
5. User Experience Would the platform be easy to use and provide an engaging user experience?	70%

Figure 8.5 Summary results for the platform that performed best.

2. *Job matching: Could the platform effectively match employees to relevant open BMS job opportunities based on employees' skills and the skills required for the job?* Only 53% of the pilot group felt the platform recommended relevant BMS jobs. A few of the survey comments include:
    - "Job matches showed me jobs that were at my current job level; in some cases, it recommended jobs below my level."
    - "Job matches recommended jobs that are in a different function/area of the business that I am not interested in."
    - "Although I was recommended jobs that did not initially seem like a match, the recommendations provided me with ideas on career opportunities that I might want to consider."

3. *Development opportunity recommendations*: Would the platform recommend relevant learning content based on the employee's skill profile? Like the job matching results, only a little more than half of the participants (55%) believed the platform recommended relevant learning and development suggestions. A few comments from participants include:
    - "I like how the development suggestions provided me with insights into the skills I would develop by pursuing the development recommendation."
    - "Some of the development suggestions and recommended courses were more basic relative to my skill level and experience."
    - "It was unclear to me why the platform was recommending courses and how those courses were applicable to my current role and career goals."
4. *Usefulness for workforce planning*: Would the outputs be useful for informing various aspects of workforce planning? For this measure, a combination of survey feedback and discussions with the business unit's leaders and HR Centers of Excellence (e.g., SWP, talent acquisition, learning, etc.) were used. Regarding the survey, 84% of the respondents rated the platform and its outputs as being useful for workforce planning. A few comments include:
    - "It was great having a complete view of my organization's skills—both the strengths and gaps. As a leadership team, this helps us to make and prioritize talent investments in the right areas."
    - "Having a common language for understanding the skills in the organization provides us with actionable insights for how we drive our business strategy through talent strategy."
    - "It is amazing that we now have a clearer and more holistic understanding of our employees' skills. It will be interesting to see how we translate this into operational workforce plans."
5. *User experience*: Would the platform be easy to use and provide an engaging user experience? Seventy percent of the pilot participants responded favorably about the overall user experience. A few comments include:
    - "The platform was easy to use, intuitive, and had a good user interface."
    - "The tool saved me a lot of time by automatically populating information about my skills onto my profile. And I liked how the platform connected skills, job opportunities, and learning together to provide a holistic picture."
    - "While I like the tool, I still don't understand how this technology connects to other talent technologies we use in our company. Knowing

how these platforms work together—and which platform I should use for different purposes—would make for a better overall experience."

While there were additional analyses we conducted, the summary feedback shows that one platform outperformed the other relative to our criteria. It also showed in which areas the outperforming platform was strongest and where there are opportunities for improvement. As we reflect on the results and lessons learned, the section that follows provides insights and recommendations for practitioners to consider as they implement similar efforts in their organizations. The insights also address factors that may have impacted the pilot's results, such as the decision to include and exclude certain platform features from the pilot (e.g., skills proficiency, career interest, etc.).

Translating Pilot Results into Actionable Insights

This section is organized into five categories and provides a "menu" of considerations for practitioners to refer to as they develop their plans and approach to enable SWP through skills, AI, and ITM. The five categories and the questions they seek to answer are:

1. *Mobilizing efforts*: How do we gain momentum and internal support for enabling AI, skills, ITM, and SWP?
2. *Evaluating vendors and implementing a pilot*: What tactics help identify, evaluate, and select vendors with whom we can partner. What are the best practices for planning, executing, and assessing a pilot and its outcomes?
3. *Strengthening AI's inferences and relevance to SWP*: What factors will most likely improve the accuracy of the AI's inferences (e.g., skills and opportunities) so they are more useful for SWP?
4. *Overcoming nontechnological barriers to implementing an ITM*: What are a few of the nontechnological barriers to overcome to realize the full potential of an ITM as an enabler of SWP?
5. *Tapping the expertise of I-O psychologists to increase the likelihood of success*: How can I-O psychologists help organizations overcome the challenges to implementing SWP through AI, skills, and ITM?

As practitioners go through the list of insights, they can highlight those they want to pursue as a next step for their organization and/or include as part of their plan.

Mobilizing Efforts

How do we gain momentum and internal support for enabling AI, skills, ITM, and SWP?

Identify a person who will lead the organization's AI, skills, ITM, and SWP effort.	• While there are many people in an organization whose work relates to AI, skills, ITM, and SWP, it is important to identify one person as the lead. • The lead will oversee and coordinate the work through various team members and organizational stakeholders. • The person should have skills and knowledge that span various talent disciplines and understand the different parts of the organization and the talent challenges it faces. • Candidates for this lead role often reside in the SWP function, talent management, learning and development, and talent acquisition, to name a few.
Form an internal implementation team of 5–8 people who will be responsible for execution.	• Team members might be in roles related to HRIT, talent management, people analytics, learning, talent acquisition, HR business partner, procurement, and legal. • A critical first step for the team is to develop a business case that includes the initiative's purpose, scope, targeted capabilities, timeline for implementation, barriers to execution and plans to address, the resources required for execution (e.g., people, costs), and expected return on investment (ROI), such as cost savings, improved retention, and faster time to fill.
Present the proposal and business case to the executive team for feedback and support.	• Ensure the conversation in anchored in the business. Answer questions such as: *What business problems are we trying to solve? What talent capabilities will the AI platform enable? How will this initiative impact important organizational outcomes? How will it deliver value to internal and external stakeholders?* • Since vendors' ROI estimations of their platform tend to be on the higher end, it's recommended to be conservative when presenting estimations to the executive team. Use tactics such as: (a) presenting the ROI as a range (e.g., *We expect an ROI of X, but it can be as high as Y*); (b) showing how ROI accumulates over time (e.g., *Year 1 we expect an ROI of X, year 2 we expected an ROI of Y*). • This approach—which is still likely to provide a compelling business case—helps to establish credibility and reduces the likelihood of "overselling" the business case.

Identify a business leader and business unit who will sponsor a pilot implementation.	• Be deliberate and intentional about selecting a pilot group and a leader who will support the efforts. Selecting the right pilot group is important since the pilot's learnings will inform decisions that impact the larger organization. • Use clear criteria for pilot selection—similar to what was referenced in the experiment section of this chapter (e.g., business need, leadership support, etc.).

Evaluating Vendors and Implementing a Pilot

What tactics help identify, evaluate, and select vendors with whom we can partner? What are the best practices for planning, executing, and assessing a pilot and its outcomes?

Convert the list of desired AI capabilities into a request for proposal (RFP) that is used to identify suitable vendors.	• Refine the broader capabilities from the business case with details about the specific features the AI must have. *Will the platform need to allow for skill proficiency ratings? Will a definition be required for each skill?* • This level of specificity is necessary to draw qualified vendors to the RFP. The greater the clarity, the more likely unqualified vendors will select out of the process. • It's also essential for the RFP to state that the platform should have the capabilities as part of its current product offering rather than something planned for a future release.
Have qualified vendors demonstrate their platform and evaluate them on their capabilities.	• A 90-minute demonstration is sufficient for an initial review. • Make it clear that you want the vendor to spend most of the time demonstrating the capabilities outlined in the RFP. • Following the demo, have the internal implementation team complete an evaluation. Compile the results and conduct a debriefing session with the internal team to determine which vendors will proceed in the process.

Conduct a follow-up meeting to learn more about the vendors' product and organization.	• Ask questions that were not covered in the initial demonstration or that need additional clarification. • A few questions might include: *How many clients currently use your platform for these capabilities? What results have your clients achieved that can be attributed to the platform? What measures do you take to reduce and mitigate bias within your AI? What is your roadmap for how your platform will evolve over the next three years?* • Share questions in advance with vendors, so they are prepared to address them in the meeting. • Determine which vendors will advance in the process.
Have the talent capability team members test the platform.	• Partner with the selected vendor(s) to allow each member of the talent team to "test drive" the platform and further evaluate its capabilities. One week is sufficient for testing. • Based on the testing, determine the final two providers that will be part of the pilot. • You might find that some vendors may not want to be part of a pilot if they are being evaluated against another provider. Nonetheless, since your RFP should make it clear that your selection process includes a pilot—which could also involve other vendors—most providers won't have any issue with this approach.
Determine the type of employee and organizational data that will be imported to the AI platform.	• Ask vendors questions such as *Based on your previous implementations, which data sources have disproportionality influenced the AI's ability to accurately infer skills and match workers to relevant opportunities?* • A few examples of data sources include: (a) employee-related (e.g., employee skills profile in an HRIS, learning history, resume) and (b) organizational-specific (e.g., job descriptions, project descriptions, learning opportunities). • Audit the availability of data to determine gaps and designate someone within your organization (someone who has a good understanding of your organization's data) to work with the vendor on data transfer.

- Whatever time you estimate for a data transfer, it's likely to take twice as long. A few factors that delayed our own data transfer are (a) *educating vendors on various data fields and terminology that are unique to our organization* and (b) *gaining agreement and approval on the most secure and efficient way to transfer data.*
- You can minimize delays by asking vendors early in the process: *What barriers have your encountered when receiving a data transfer from clients? What can we do to avoid those barriers?*
- Transferring employee data from an organization to a third-party requires employee consent. We worked with our legal department and data privacy team to create a consent form. Consent was obtained electronically from employees.
- It's critical to involve your legal and data privacy teams in the process early; otherwise, you expose the organization and initiative to heightened risk.
- We stipulated in our vendor contracts that they are to purge the employee data from their platform within 30 days of concluding the pilot. They were also required to confirm in writing that the purge has occurred.
- Since our pilot was US based, we did not have to gain approval from works councils for this phase. However, our planning for the pilot factored in works councils so we would be better prepared when it is time for a global launch.

Generate awareness and excitement about the pilot.
- Use town halls, email communications, and video snippets to create anticipation and help the pilot group understand the purpose of the initiative, what to expect, and the personal benefit to them.
- It's important that the effort is not presented or perceived as an HR initiative, but rather as a business initiative. While the project team should work behind the scenes, the business leader should be the face and voice of the initiative.
- Regarding training and change management, we found that a 12-minute video that walked participants through the platform—coupled with office hours during the pilot—were sufficient. Avoid the tendency to make the training and change management overly complex as simplification drives user engagement.

| Implement the pilot and collect feedback via a survey. | • Your survey should measure the extent to which the platform(s) capabilities achieved the intended outcomes.
• If you have a people analytics team, involve them in the design and analysis of the survey.
• Sample survey statements we used include *"The platform was effective in inferring my skills when building my profile; the recommended jobs were relevant to my skill profile and career interests."*
• If you are testing more than one platform, compare the survey results of each and conduct a debrief session with stakeholders to determine which platform performed best. |

Strengthening AI's Inferences and Relevance to SWP

What factors will most likely improve the accuracy of the AI's inferences (e.g., skills and opportunities) so they are more useful for SWP?

| Ensure the skills taxonomy is relevant to the organization and determine if a skills definition is required. | • While ITM providers use a skills taxonomy to name, describe, and organize skills, these taxonomies vary by vendor. Some vendors use generic skills terms, such as 'leadership' whereas others use more specific terms (e.g., managerial courage).
• Also, not every vendor provides a definition that describes each skill. For our pilot, one vendor used a skill definition, and one did not. Surprisingly, the platform that did not have a skills definition performed better.
• Determine if a skills definition is important for your organization and if the additional complexity unlocks incremental value.
• The goal is to ensure that the skills taxonomy is relevant to your organization and is adequately described. |

An employee resume or LinkedIn profile is critical to inferring skills more accurately.

- Eighty-two percent of pilot participants uploaded a resume or a LinkedIn profile to the ITM platform.
- In comparing the survey results of pilot participants who uploaded a resume to those who used a LinkedIn profile, the former reported that the platform inferred their skills more accurately.
- The detailed information on a resume appear to generate more accurate AI-based skill inferences than a LinkedIn profile, which tend to be less descriptive. However, a LinkedIn profile helped the AI more accurately infer skills compared to uploading nothing at all.
- Since the inclusion of a resume as a data source disproportionately enhances skill inferences, employees should be encouraged to use resumes when possible.

Skill proficiencies have the potential to provide incremental value.

- Some ITM platforms offer a skill proficiency feature—where the assessor can indicate their proficiency level for the skill, such as foundational, experienced, or advanced.
- While both platforms we tested offered this feature, we did not turn it on for the pilot since it added more complexity. We also did not want the skill proficiency feature to feel like a performance evaluation.
- Not using the skill proficiency feature for our pilot could have detracted from the AI's ability to match employees and their skills to the most relevant job and development opportunities. It may have also led to a less accurate estimation of the business unit's skill supply.
- Organizations might want to test two pilot groups where one uses the skill proficiency feature and the other does not. This approach can determine if skill proficiencies allow organizations to better assess skill levels.

Consider having the manager validate the employees' skills.

- Our pilot used AI to generate an initial skills profile for employees based on various data inputs (e.g., resume, learning history, etc.).
- Employees then reviewed their AI-based skills profile and adjusted as needed (e.g., added and removed skills).
- While we did consider having the employees' manager validate the skill profile, we did not include the manager validation for the pilot due to it adding more complexity.
- Although self-assessment can result in workers overestimating their competence (Scott and Pearlman, 2010), a Conference Board (2022c) survey shows that manager evaluation of employees' skills is used only slightly more than employee self-evaluation.
- Organizations can test both approaches (self-assessment and manager validation) during their pilot to determine if there are meaningful differences in outcomes.
- One alternative to having a manager validate an employee's skills in the platform is to have the manger provide feedback to the employee during a performance check-in or career discussion. Employees can use the feedback as an input to update their skills profile.

The quality of opportunity descriptions (e.g., jobs, projects, learning) matters.

- An analysis from our pilot showed that the AI's job matching and development recommendations were more relevant when the descriptions of those opportunities were of higher quality and more robust (e.g., they clearly described the opportunity, requirements, etc.).
- Organizations should audit their job, project, and learning descriptions—as well as any other opportunity data sources—to determine where there are gaps and how to close them.
- Since this is a massive undertaking, it's recommended that organizations start with one area of their business and then gradually expand.

| Identifying employees' career interests can make AI recommendations more relevant. | • Most ITM platforms—including the two we tested—have a feature that allows employees to indicate their career goals and motivations.
• While there is value in this feature, it was not turned on for pilot since it required additional investments of time and resources (e.g., mapping BMS career terminology to the platforms' terminology).
• Including this feature would have likely led to the AI suggesting more relevant opportunities to our pilot group by factoring their career interests—not just skills—into the ITM's algorithms.
• It is recommended that organizations use the career preferences features to improve the AI's recommendation engine. Doing so will provide a more accurate estimation of an organization's bench strength for a given area of work since it factors in both skills and preferences. |

Overcoming Nontechnological Barriers to Implementing an ITM

What are a few of the nontechnological barriers to overcome to realize the full potential of an ITM as an enabler of SWP?

| Evaluate policies, guidelines, and processes that inhibit the internal movement of talent. | • While technology is a critical enabler of SWP and internal mobility, it would be remiss to not mention a few nontechnological factors that impact an organization's internal mobility practices.
• For example, many organizations have internal mobility policies and guidelines that impede internal mobility by overly regulating the "rules and conditions" under which these moves occur.
• A few of these policies include (1) *conditions on how long an employee should be in a role or with the company (e.g., 12 months) before applying to other internal opportunities*; (2) *requiring employees to request and receive permission from their managers before they can apply on an internal opportunity*; and (3) *restricting employees from moving more than one level in the organization.* |

	• While policies and guidelines are important, practitioners should evaluate various policies and guidelines that affect internal mobility and determine where changes are needed.
Minimize the tendency for managers to hoard talent.	• An organization can have the best technology, practices, guidelines, and practices, and employees who want to take on new internal opportunities, but internal mobility will be impeded if managers don't actively support talent sharing.
	• Talent practitioners will need to develop and implement strategies to reduce talent hoarding—a *manager's tendency to prevent or discourage employees from pursuing internal opportunities.*
	• A few tactics to reduce talent hoarding include *helping managers gain self-awareness when they are engaging in talent hoarding, findings ways to recognize and reward managers who share talent, including talent sharing as key expectation of managers and leaders.*
Help to remove the stigma associated with lateral job movement.	• One finding from our pilot was that AI-based lateral job opportunity recommendations (job opportunities that are the same job level as the employee's current role) were not viewed as positively by employees (i.e., a lateral move did not equate with career progression or development).
	• One tactic for reducing the stigma of lateral job moves is awarding a pay increase or financial increase or benefit—something that is not a common practice in many organizations.
	• Given that workers rank compensation and financial rewards as top priorities in evaluating opportunities (LinkedIn Talent Solutions, 2022), organizations should determine if they will provide a financial award to incentivize workers to make lateral job moves.

Tapping the Expertise of I-O Psychologists to Increase the Likelihood of Success

How can I-O psychologists help organizations overcome the challenges to implementing SWP through AI, skills, and ITM?

Develop a valid approach for deconstructing work beyond the confines of jobs and roles.	• Since only one in five organizations is effective at decomposing work beyond jobs or roles (Institute for Corporate Productivity, 2021), I-O psychologists can help organizations develop valid ways to fractionalize work into tasks and then link those tasks to required skills. • I-O psychologists can help answer: *Should work be structured around the problems to be solved and then the skills needed to solve those problems? Should work be organized by broader units of analysis, such as roles, jobs, and projects? What factors determine which approach to organizing work should be used?* • The answers to these questions have important implications, particularly since many organizations have well-established jobs architectures, levels, and grades that continue to fuel job-based talent practices. • Although jobs won't completely go away, the future of work will require firms to take an expanded and multi-faceted approach to how they organize work beyond jobs. I-O psychologists can play a critical role in this effort.
Guide organizations to select AI tools that are fair, ethical and reduce bias.	• I-O psychologists have been instrumental in helping organizations detect and minimize bias found in selection tools and assessments and ensuring that assessments are legally defensible. • Yet, despite the issue of bias being one of the biggest concerns about the use of AI for HR, I-O psychologists involvement remains limited when it comes to developing and evaluating AI for talent purposes (Gonzalez et al., 2019). • Although guidelines are emerging on how organizations can identify and understand risks through "explainable AI," this topic is complex, and organizations need help in navigating it. • I-O psychologists can help organizations ask the right questions, create awareness of potential AI risks, and provide stakeholders with fully informed recommendations for applying AI tools effectively and ethically.

Determine which data sources provide incremental value in accurately inferring employee skills.	• One observation from our pilot is that the employee resume disproportionately enhances AI's ability to infer employee skills. However, this observation is anecdotal. • I-O psychologists can help test which data sources provide both incremental and disproportionate value in making AI inferences and recommendations.
Provide guidance on which stakeholder groups should validate employee skills.	• For our pilot, we relied on AI to infer employees' skills; employees then had an opportunity to review their AI-generated skill profile and adjust as needed. • While many employers still rely on workers self-reporting their skills and proficiency levels, this approach might yield a less accurate view of an employee's skills compared to manager and multirater assessments. • I-O psychologists can provide guidance on the added value of having managers—as well as other stakeholders—validate an employee's skill profile.
Provide guidance on how managers and leaders can use AI to augment "human" decision-making—rather than replace it.	• While AI-based talent platforms can provide several insights that inform decision-making, one risk is that managers and decision-makers may allow the AI to disproportionately influence their talent decisions. • As leaders look at how to incorporate AI data into their analyses and decisions, I-O psychologists can provide decision frameworks that better enable managers and leaders to apply human judgment to AI-based data and recommendations.

While there are other questions and answers that can be added to this list of suggestions, these insights provide practitioners with a variety of considerations as they create opportunities to enable aspects of SWP through skills, AI, and ITM.

Personal Reflection and Conclusion

This chapter's title intentionally includes the word "enabling" since skills, AI, and ITM alone are insufficient for SWP. Instead, these individual components are part of an ecosystem that, collectively, enables SWP. For example, while there is a shift toward using skills as the preferred unit of analysis for SWP, skills by themselves are too atomic to sufficiently inform the demand side of SWP. Organizations cannot simply say, "We need X number of skills," since this approach doesn't fully operationalize the demand side of SWP. Operationalizing work demand usually requires a broader unit of analysis, such as roles, jobs, projects, and tasks. These broader work units help quantify work demand (e.g., "We have X number of projects that require this number of people"). Then, organizations can identify the skills needed to carry out those different units of work, assuming the work must be performed by people (e.g., some work can be automated, etc.). ITM and AI platforms support this effort by using a common skills taxonomy and helping organizations identify internal talent (one source of talent supply) to meet demand. This capability enables organizations to more quickly and effectively flow talent to work demand—a critical capability of SWP. This capability, however, requires an interplay of skills, roles, jobs, projects, AI, ITM, etc. to enable SWP.

As mentioned at the beginning of this chapter, AI, skills, internal talent marketplace, and SWP are complex topics. This complexity requires practitioners to experiment with different approaches to determine which SWP practices best fit their business. Approaches will vary depending on several factors, such as organization size, business model, and the type of work performed. Organizations with more stability in the work being performed are likely to rely more heavily on job-based SWP. Firms in which work is more fluid might find that project- or gig-based SWP is more suitable for their needs. Many organizations will take a hybrid approach, where they conduct SWP for a core set of roles that disproportionately impact their strategic capabilities and then use project-based and task-based SWP to meet work demand. Regardless of the approach, skills, AI, and ITM are key enablers. As practitioners help their organizations take the next step on their SWP journey, I hope this chapter has paved the way for accelerating those efforts.

References

Bersin, J. (2022, August 29). The HR tech market is going crazy: What to look for in 2023. https://www.youtube.com/watch?v=qbheWL4SHbU

Boston Consulting Group. (2021, June). The future of people management priorities. https://web-assets.bcg.com/16/b1/c25cb9e2471c81c355c9dccb8d4f/bcg-creating-people-advantage-2021-jun-2021.pdf

The Conference Board. (2022a, August). Agility and innovation are fueled by a skills-based talent strategy. https://www.conference-board.org/topics/future-of-work/skills-based-talent-strategy#

The Conference Board. (2022b). C-suite outlook 2022: Reset and reimagine. https://www.conference-board.org/pdfdownload.cfm?masterProductID=38504

The Conference Board. (2022c, October 7). Employees are central to a skills-based talent. https://www.conference-board.org/topics/future-of-work/employees-are-central-to-skills-based-talent-strategy

Deloitte. (2021, October, 26). Beyond the job. https://www2.deloitte.com/us/en/insights/topics/talent/new-work-models.html?

Deloitte (2022, September, 8). The skills-based organization: A new operating model for work and the workforce. https://www2.deloitte.com/us/en/insights/topics/talent/organizational-skill-based-hiring.html?

Gartner. (2022, June). Plan your workforce without the limitations of roles. https://emtemp.gcom.cloud/ngw/globalassets/en/human-resources/documents/hr-monthly-magazine-june-2022.pdf

Gonzalez, M, F., Capman, J. F., Oswald, F. L.,Theys, E, R, and Tomczak, D. L (2019). Where's the I-O?" Artificial intelligence and machine learning in talent management systems. *Personnel Assessment and Decisions*, 5(3), article 5. https://doi.org/10.25035/pad.2019.03.005

Heger, B., and Aulbach, A. (2019). Building the foundation for strategic workforce planning at Bristol-Myers Squibb. *People + Strategy Journal*. https://www.shrm.org/executive/resources/people-strategy-journal/fall2019/pages/heger-aulbach-feature.aspx

IBM Institute for Business Value. (n.d.). The enterprise guide to closing the skills gap. https://www.ibm.com/downloads/cas/EPYMNBJA

Institute for Corporate Productivity. (2021a, September 30). Only 30% of companies say their employees have needed skills, but few understand workforce capabilities today. https://www.i4cp.com/press-releases/study-only-30-of-companies-say-their-employees-have-needed-skills-but-few-understand-current-capabilities

Institute for Corporate Productivity. (2021b). Accelerating total workforce readiness. https://www.i4cp.com/survey-analyses/accelerating-total-workforce-readiness

Jesuthasan, R., and Boudreau. J. (2021, January 5). Work without jobs. *MIT Sloan Management Review*. https://sloanreview.mit.edu/article/work-without-jobs/

Lightcast. (2022, May). Shifting skills, moving targets, and remaking the workforce. https://www.economicmodeling.com/wp-content/uploads/2022/05/BCG-Shifting-Skills-Moving-Targets-and-Remaking-the-Workforce-May-2022.pdf

LinkedIn Talent Solutions. (2022, October). Global talent trends report. https://business.linkedin.com/talent-solutions/global-talent-trends?

Mercer. (2022, April). Mercer's 2022 global talent trends study. https://www.mercer.com/content/dam/mercer/attachments/private/global-talent-trends/2022/gl-2022-global-talent-trends-report-eng.pdf

Nair, J., and Pasala, B. (2021). Unilever`s AI-powered internal talent marketplace unlocks workforce capacity. IBS Center for Management Research. https://www.thecasecentre.org/products/view?id=175665

PwC. (2022). PwC pulse survey: Executive views on business in 2022. https://www.pwc.com/us/en/library/pulse-survey/executive-views-2022.html

Ransbotham, S., Khodabandeh, S., Fehling, R., Lafountain, B., and Kiron, D. (2019). Winning with AI. *MIT Sloan Management Review* 61180. https://sloanreview.mit.edu/projects/winning-with-ai/

Scott, J. C., and Pearlman, K. (2010). Assessment for organizational change. In J. C Scott and D. H. Reynolds (Eds.), *Handbook of workplace assessment* (pp. 553–575). Society for Industrial and Organizational Psychology.

Ulrich, D. (2020, February 16.) Talent Q. From workforce to work-task planning. https://www.talent-quarterly.com/from-workforce-to-work-task-planning/?

World Economic Forum. (2020, October). The future of jobs report. https://www3.weforum.org/docs/WEF_Future_of_Jobs_2020.pdf

World Economic Forum. (2021, December). Human-centred artificial intelligence for human resources: A toolkit for human resources professionals. https://www3.weforum.org/docs/WEF_Human_Centred_Artificial_Intelligence_for_Human_Resources_2021.pdf

9
Strategic Work-Task Planning

David Creelman, Alexis A. Fink, and David Ulrich

Workforce planning has been practiced for many decades to close the gap between the talent available and the talent required to deliver the strategy within a given timeframe. If there are gaps, then business and human resources (HR) leaders need to figure out how best to hire or develop employees to fill those gaps. Conversely, if the needs of the business are changing such that the firm has an oversupply in some areas, organizations need to build plans to reskill, redeploy, or otherwise reduce their workforce in those areas.

Workforce planning typically sees work in terms of headcount within specific locations, levels, and positions. As an alternative, work can be analyzed in terms of the *tasks* that need to be done and the skills required to execute those tasks. Instead of seeing the work of organizations as being comprised of a set of jobs, the work of the organization can be seen as being comprised of a set of tasks. From this perspective, *work-task* planning ensures the tasks get done, as contrasted with *workforce* planning, which ensures jobs get filled.

This alternative perspective provides insights and opportunities for talent management that workforce planning might overlook. It also introduces new complications. For example, in workforce planning, the simple unit of organizational analysis of "a job" matches tidily with the simple human unit of "an employee"—one position is filled by one employee. When analyzing tasks, one employee might do many tasks, and tasks can easily be moved from one employee to another. Additionally, tasks do not even necessarily need to be done by an employee; they may be automated or contracted out.

For example, when a company pivots its strategy from product innovation to customer service, it will clearly require new work to be done. Workforce planning focuses on new jobs in customer service and the employees who will fill those newly created jobs. Work-task planning focuses on the new tasks to be done and will consider which tasks can be automated, contracted out, distributed among part-time employees, and/or accomplished in the traditional way: by full-time employees in jobs.

David Creelman, Alexis A. Fink, and David Ulrich, *Strategic Work-Task Planning* In: *Strategic Workforce Planning*. Edited by: Marc Sokol and Beverly Tarulli, Oxford University Press.
© Society for Industrial and Organizational Psychology 2024. DOI: 10.1093/oso/9780197759745.003.0010

John Boudreau and Ravin Jesuthasan have written a significant amount on the disaggregation of jobs into tasks. Their most recent book on this topic is *Work without jobs: How to reboot your organization's work operating system*. They believe there is a great opportunity in shaking off the limitations of packaging work into discreet 40-hour/week jobs and instead opening our eyes to the great range of options that appear when we disaggregate jobs into tasks that can be reaggregated and executed in many different ways.

In this chapter, we build on their ideas to look at work-task planning, how it is being practiced now, and some ideas on how it could be leveraged even more in the future.

Before we proceed, it's worth considering the relationships among employees, jobs, tasks, and skills. Just as we can see jobs as being comprised of tasks, we can see employees as having a bundle of skills. By looking at employees as bundles of skills, it can be easier to see how they would fit into a job that, in terms of its title, is dissimilar to one they are in now on the basis of a similarity in the skillsets needed to execute the required tasks. We include *skill-task* as a subset of work-task since a task requires a set of skills as part of the unit of analysis (see Table 9.1). Skills focus on the individual employee's knowledge and ability; tasks focus more on the requirements to accomplish a business agenda. When skills deliver on tasks, the two come together to deliver business outcomes.

Table 9.1 Comparing workforce and work-task planning

	Workforce	Work-task
Unit of analysis (organizational)	Jobs	Tasks
Unit of analysis (human)	Employees	Skills
Emphasis	Role clarity (position description)	Responsibilities and accountability
Leaders ask	Did the employee do their job?	Did the work get accomplished?
Pros	Easy to understand	Flexibility, efficiency
Cons	Overlooks alternative ways to organize work	Requires fine-grained analysis
View of talent	Seeks employees to do jobs	Seeks people and technology to get work done

Increased Attention to Work-Task Planning

Work-task planning is of increasing interest because of the pace of change, automation, the rise of gig workers, and the power of natural-language processing to analyze tasks. With respect to the pace of change, consider the challenge to organizations suddenly faced in designing hybrid work (i.e., partly in the office, partly remote). It can be difficult to know how to handle this when so many jobs have, at least at times, a need to be in the office. Boudreau has suggested some of the difficulties may melt away if you disaggregate the jobs into tasks then recombine them into bundles that can be done fully remotely and other bundles that are best done in the office. This makes it easier to have fully remote jobs and others where you know you'll need office space for them most of the time. At the individual level, a worker can organize their own tasks between those that need to be done in-person and those that can be done remotely and arrange their days accordingly. The flexibility that work-task analysis brings allows organizations to react to change with more agility.

Automation may be the biggest reason organizations want to do more analysis at the task level. While the media tends to fret about automation replacing jobs, generally, whole jobs are not replaced by automation. Rather, it's more often the case that automation replaces some tasks within a job. If an organization is to respond to the opportunities (and challenges) of many tasks being automated, then it needs to be able to analyze work at the task level.

The rise of gig workers presents another interesting dimension. Companies have long used contractors and consultants who were not employees, but the role of these workers is usually best described as working on projects. With gig workers, who are typically remote, it's easier than ever to outsource tasks to workers who are not employees. This creates an opportunity for organizations to outsource tasks currently done by employees that could be done better, faster, or more cheaply by a gig worker. For example, taking a draft PowerPoint deck and making it ready for a presentation may be better done by a gig worker than by the manager who created the draft slide deck. Once again, gig workers push us in the direction of seeing work as being a collection of tasks rather than a collection of jobs.

Finally, it's worth noting the potential of artificial intelligence (AI) to make work-task planning a manageable project. Whereas a company might only have a few hundred distinct jobs, it might have many thousands of distinct tasks. Working through all the tasks manually is likely impractical; however, with natural-language processing it's possible to have a machine read through vast numbers of job descriptions and resumes and, from there, create a taxonomy of tasks—we'll see more about how this is done in the case of a large technology company.

To make this all more concrete, let's consider a few cases in a little more detail.

Work-Task Planning in Hospitals, Consultancies, and Manufacturing

Once you start looking for it, you will see that work-task planning already appears in many guises in different industries. Consider, for example, consulting companies, whose work is organized around projects; these companies would be alert to tasks that could not be handled by the project team and will find ways to fill that gap. For example, the consulting team might recognize that one of the tasks required in a project is projecting cash flows. If no one on the core team is able to do that task, the company would need to see where it could bring in an extra resource for that one task.

If we look at hospitals, we see work-task planning in another guise, one aimed at cost savings. The hospital would look at tasks done by high-wage workers (such as a doctor) and investigate if they could be done by a more cost-effective worker (such as a physician's assistant). This version of work-task planning isn't concerned with filling the kind of gap we saw in the example of a consulting team; instead, it's concerned with getting the tasks done as cost-effectively as possible.

In manufacturing, factories often can be productive if they can momentarily move workers from their main job to help out with a task somewhere else. For example, if there is a bottleneck upstream in the assembly line, some of the downstream people can leave their own tasks behind temporarily and pitch in on whatever tasks will help resolve the bottleneck. In fact, there is a manufacturing approach called MAMO, which is an acronym for *mouvements automatic main-oeuvre* (automatic movement of people). MAMO seeks to optimize the movement of people from task to task as needed. This is yet another flavor of work-task planning.

Work-task planning allows tasks to be accomplished anywhere in the world and frequently shows up in the form of *offshoring*. Often this can be done at the level of jobs with, for example, whole factories being moved overseas. In other cases, it involves looking at the tasks being done and moving those that are perhaps more routine or not affected by time zones overseas. A US-based people analytics function might pull out tasks like standard reporting, data cleaning, and data entry to a low-cost location while leaving tasks like interacting with line managers in the United States.

In retail, many have experienced work-tasking with self-service. The tasks related to checking out of a store can be performed by an in-person employee or, through technology, by the customer. Focusing on the task of checking out allows customers multiple options to meet their needs.

You will notice that already we see quite a variety of ways that work-task planning is used in organizations. It can be used to deal with a one-off situation, as in the consulting context; it can be part of a long-term plan to minimize costs, as in the hospital or with offshoring; or it can be a moment-by-moment strategy for optimizing production.

Work-Task Planning at a Distribution Center

Let's look at one case of work-task planning a bit more closely. Modern distribution centers are a hive of frantic activity, with boxes coming in, being unpacked, and items put on shelves. At the same time, workers are pulling items off shelves, packing them in boxes, and shipping them off. The amount and nature of work to be done vary from month to month, even week to week.

The planning process starts with quarterly demand planning—quarterly, at this operational level, is considered long-term. The planners project how much demand there will be for the area and then percolate that down to what's required of each warehouse.

In response, each warehouse will, by looking at the number of machines, the number of stations, expected attrition and attendance, and so on project its ability to meet (supply) the demand. At this point, the warehouse has a supply–demand gap for the quarter. From there it goes to weekly planning and again the question becomes the gap between supply and demand and what the warehouse can do about it.

Some of what the warehouse management does about it is traditional workforce planning, where they hire additional workers (sometimes full-time, but often on contract or part-time) or increase overtime. However, it seamlessly moves into work-task planning where sometimes the gap is at the task level (e.g., not enough people to pack boxes) and the solution is to move people from one task to another to fill the gap. HR, recognizing the need for this flexibility, provides the needed cross-training.

The ability to go from quarterly to weekly to even daily planning, identifying, and addressing gaps at the job or task level leads to highly efficient operations.

While at the level of an individual distribution center quarterly is long-term, elsewhere in the organization planning is looking a year or years ahead. In terms of distribution center operations, the big issue is automation. The automation team looks at which tasks can be automated, and it turns out quite a few can. At current levels of technology, an automated warehouse can be run with only 25% of the number of staff on a nonautomated operation.

The takeaway is that work-task planning is not a standalone project. Within a quarterly or weekly timeframe, the work-task planning flows seamlessly from strategic planning that impacts workforce planning as the planning gets more granular and short-term. In a year or multiyear timeframe, work-task planning is folded within planning around automation and the multitude of effects that has on how the company runs the operation.

> **Practitioner Tip!**
>
> Is work-task planning applicable to all jobs? A natural question is whether work-task planning is equally applicable to all jobs or whether it's best deployed for certain kinds of jobs. For example, it may be that the work in some kinds of jobs is so interconnected that it's difficult to disaggregate into tasks.
>
> However, in a business setting, it's better to start at the strategic level and ask where work-task planning will have the biggest impact. Work-task planning is likely to have more impact in the strategic positions and in jobs that differentiate an organization's success in the marketplace. More routine jobs would require more predictable skills since the tasks of those jobs are less likely to change. But jobs that differentiate an organization in the marketplace are more likely to change as the requirements of customers change. The tasks associated with these jobs and positions also change and require more discipline so that the right tasks can be identified. In many settings, the tasks required of strategic positions

> require cross-job and even cross-functional collaboration, so the tasks would also focus on collaboration and cooperation.
>
> Hence, while it may be more difficult to disaggregate the tasks in a job that differentiates the organization's success, it's more important to do it there.

Issues in Doing Work-Task Planning

The concept of doing analysis at the task level rather than the job level is easy enough to understand. The difficulty comes in implementing the concept in the workplace. Four common issues need to be considered anytime we want to apply a "task" lens to work in the organization.

1. How to disaggregate jobs into tasks
2. How to determine the best way to get a task done
3. Where work-task planning should sit in the organization
4. How to ensure the work-task plan is executed

We will consider each question, but before that let's review a little context.

How to Disaggregate Jobs into Tasks

It would be a disaster to take a workforce planning team and tell them to simply shift to do work-task planning this year. Workforce planning deals with jobs, and there are a relatively finite number of jobs in an organization, typically a few hundred. Tasks, to the contrary, can exist in vast numbers. Not only that, but whereas a job is a relatively well-defined unit of work (essentially the work one person can do), a task can be large ("Do heart surgery") or small ("Clean the medical instruments prior to surgery"). Before we can begin work-task planning we have to address how we can deal with the unruly world of possible tasks.

This problem may not be as difficult in a specific context as it is in general. As we saw from the distribution center example, the tasks the company needed to plan around were self-evident to it. In that operation, there were clear tasks around the main steps in shipping and receiving that the company needed to plan for. Similarly, in the case of hospitals looking at which tasks they might move from a doctor to physician's assistant, the tasks were reasonably self-evident to anyone working in that environment. We might call this the "self-evident" approach.

However, there are two more general approaches to deciding which tasks to focus on in a large enterprise:

- A *strategic approach*: One can take an approach that uncovers which tasks are most important. That strategic thinking can unfold by examining questions such as:
  o What key roles or positions in the company will deliver value to customers in unique ways?
  o Describe the key tasks of the strategic position(s). What does the role or strategic position do?
  o Partition tasks into specific subtasks.
  o What are the key activities for accomplishing the tasks?
  o Delineate these tasks in terms of specific behaviors or actions.

  These questions can be answered by a facilitator interviewing the individuals doing the tasks.

- A *systematic approach*: The most systematic method for work-task planning is to create a hierarchy of broader level tasks at the top and progressively narrower skills underneath. For example, near the top of the hierarchy you might have "Financial work" and at a much lower level "Reconcile bank balances." This provides a framework to make thinking through the issues manageable. It also means you only dive down into smaller-level tasks where you need to.

The takeaway is that there isn't a "right" way to approach strategic task planning. When you are dealing with a particular area, like a distribution center, then the "self-evident" nature of the tasks to be considered makes the question of disaggregation moot. In the enterprise-wide situation, organizations will always best start with some elements of the strategic approach. There should be a strategic issue that work-task planning is focusing on. The systematic approach revolves around the question of whether it is worth the effort of creating an overall taxonomy of tasks. Creating that taxonomy of tasks is hard work, although it is more practical now than in the past thanks to new AI tools. We can see how this is done by seeing how a large technology company created a skills taxonomy and how those same methods could be applied to creating a taxonomy of tasks.

A Systematic Approach to Disaggregating All Jobs into Tasks

A large technology company wanted to create a systematic skills taxonomy—one that deconstructed a job into the skills required—to improve internal mobility. Technology is a fast-moving industry, and it's common for groups to become redundant. This means that the people in those groups would be faced with layoffs leading to cyclical hiring and firing. The company does its best to find jobs for those people within the company, but too often nothing panned out.

The particularly troubling aspect of this was that often those same employees would be rehired by the company at some time down the road. Thus, the organization had gone through the expensive and time-consuming process of laying off an employee only to go through an expensive and time-consuming process of rehiring that same person a short time later. From the employee's point of view, it was an emotionally draining experience that felt completely unnecessary. From HR's point of view, the takeaway was that jobs did exist for most of the employees whose groups were being shut down—it was just that the mechanisms for matching employees to other jobs were inadequate.

The solution the company pursued was to create a skills taxonomy so that it would be able to look at an individual's skills and match them to any job that required similar skills, anywhere in the organization. Creating such a taxonomy by hand would have been impractical, so the company used a variety of natural-language tools (LDA, Jaccard Indices) to search through around 300,000 job-related documents (e.g., resumes) and from there determine what skills existed in the organization and where they would fit in a hierarchy (e.g., Is this skill a daughter to another skill on the taxonomy and so should be slotted in below it?).

One issue that always arises with skill analysis, and one that is bound to occur in task analysis, is whether something is a "skill," "knowledge," "competency," or some other category. With tasks, you can imagine distinguishing between projects, tasks, activities, and so on. In practice, worrying about these labels is usually more trouble than it is worth. Certainly, in this case, the company did not fret over making the knowledge/skill distinction.

An additional benefit to this approach is that the company was able to identify similarities among jobs that may not have been immediately obvious, thus helping employees identify a larger number of possible jobs for which they had relevant skills. Where a keyword search for relevant jobs is often quite relevant, the ability to examine the full set of relevant skills and include adjacent skills in the search helped identify significantly more possible opportunities.

It took a team of professional data scientists about a year to create the taxonomy. That level of effort is fine for a very large organization but might seem daunting to other companies. However, it is now increasingly possible to use commercially available, AI-generated taxonomies. The methods of analysis used in this case, while by no means commonplace, have been mastered by several vendors, and we can expect to see more and more opportunities to use off-the-shelf taxonomies. In fact, Revelio Labs already has built an "activities" taxonomy derived from the bullet points on resumes that describe the content of each position and the responsibilities section of job postings. Both resumes and job postings can be found in the millions online, thus making it possible for AI tools to do a thorough analysis.

Once the skills taxonomy existed the next step was to estimate what skills individuals had. This was achieved by looking at the job titles an individual had held for the past several years and making inferences on the likelihood that they would have had to possess or develop some particular skill to successfully perform their jobs during that period. With this done it was then possible to use this technology to match individuals who were at risk of being made redundant to other jobs in the organization. The results were impressive, approximately 80% of these individuals were matched for a job, up from the well under the 50% that the company had achieved prior to this new technology.

The lesson from the work on skills taxonomies is that the methods exist to build similar task taxonomies. With a taxonomy in place, any other analysis of tasks becomes easier because not only is there a common language, but there are also clear levels of abstraction from broad-level task categories down to increasingly narrow particular tasks. Depending on the application of task analysis, different "altitudes" (i.e., which level of the taxonomy) will be used.

With such a taxonomy in place, one could identify which tasks are common enough that it would be worth considering automation or find which tasks are suitable for gig work.

> **Practitioner Tip!**
>
> *Framing the work-task discussion with leaders.* Work-task planning, just like regular workforce planning, needs to be properly framed. The key questions are:
>
> - What timeframe are we concerned about? This quarter? This year? Several years hence?
> - Is the outcome a formal plan for hiring and training, or insights about the workforce that inform decision-making without committing to specific actions?
> - Is the focus on a few strategic areas, or are we doing work-task planning across large parts of the organization?

How to Determine the Best Way To Get a Task Done

What makes work-task planning a particularly exciting approach to talent management is that we are now in a time when there are many different ways to accomplish a task. If there is a gap between the need for a task to be done and the capacity of the organization to do it, then a key part of work-task planning becomes deciding how to close the gap.

Let's step through some of the alternative ways of accomplishing a task.

o *Automation*: Perhaps the most important issue for work-task planning is to understand the potential for automation (e.g., automated processes, AI, robots). Automation has been given a huge boost by no-code and low-code systems that make it much easier to automate tasks by allowing the worker themselves to design and implement the automation. What's important in these worker-designed automations is that the worker can automate any repetitive tasks while keeping themselves in the loop for areas that are too complex to be easily automated. At a higher level of sophistication, machine learning allows the automation of some cognitive tasks (such as language translation) in an affordable way, which will likely increase with emerging technologies.

- *Gig workers (external freelancers)*: With traditional employees, even contactors, you are typically hiring someone for 40 hours of work a week. That's a job, not just a task. Even part-timers usually do a full job, just not for 40 hours a week. However, with gig workers—the kind you can find on Fiverr or Upwork—you can potentially hire someone to do a narrow task. If work-task planning shows that managers are spending too much time on the task of formatting PowerPoint presentations, then they can arrange to have gig workers handle just that task as needed.
- *Internal freelancers*: There is increasing use of platforms like Gloat or Hitch to create an internal marketplace where employees can volunteer to work on tasks they find interesting. In this case, the tasks would be those at a higher altitude. What's interesting about this approach is that it has all sorts of benefits beyond getting a task done. It can increase employee engagement, help an employee develop their skills, and build connections across silos in the organization. Even more interesting is that Unilever found that the tasks got done without having a deleterious impact on the employee's regular job. Given an existing task, employees were sufficiently motivated to find ways to get it done on top of their regular work. Just as work can expand to fill the time available, so, too, it appears that motivated employees can expand their efficiency to get all the work done in the time available.
- *Volunteers*: It's worth noting that there are creative ways to get tasks done beyond the well-known ones described here. Researchers who wanted help solving protein folding problems reached out to volunteers who were equipped with a tool called Foldit (https://fold.it) to support the research. It's also worth noting that this human work on a task is in the process of being replaced by an AI tool called AlphaFold.
- *Employees*: In our enthusiasm to find alternative ways to get tasks done, we should not lose sight of the fact that often the best way to fill a gap in the capability to get tasks done is to hire regular, full-time employees.

> **Practitioner Tip!**
>
> *An internal freelance talent pool.* Work-task planning is an especially interesting approach because, as we have discussed, there are many ways to get a task done—such as using freelance gig workers rather than employees.

One organization took a rather novel approach: some of their employees became freelancers.

A large technology company had dozens of employees who had been displaced from their jobs due to projects ending, yet these employees were talented professionals and the company was reluctant to let them go and get into a "leave then return" cycle. In a bold move, they created an internal freelance group. The project was run by a director and three talent champions who handled 65 employee-freelancers. The talent champions got to know the freelancers, understanding their competencies, personalities, and interests. They then sought out tasks and projects from different parts of the organization where extra help was needed. The champions could then match the freelancers to work and set them up for success.

Setting a freelancer up for success was much easier with internal freelancers than it would have been using external ones. The internal freelancers could be productive from day one, whereas external workers would need to learn the tools and culture as well as go through the formalities of nondisclosure agreements, getting a PC, and so on. The most important element of starting a freelancer on a project was to ensure clarity on deadlines, deliverables, tasks required, and the skills needed. The talent champion would meet with the customer and the freelancer to set expectations. They would also meet mid-project to ensure everything was on track and again at the end of the project to see what lessons could be learned for both the internal customer and the freelancer.

The projects varied in length from days to months and could be anything from creating a video to setting up an event to running a project. Initially, the internal customers were not charged for the freelancer's time, but later that was shifted to a negotiated rate. For the customers, it was a way to get tasks done quickly and easily by a skilled professional. For the freelancer, it was a way to take on interesting work and grow their careers.

The experiment ended after a few years as other priorities arose for HR. However, the experiment inspired several HR technology vendors to build tools to help other organizations create internal talent marketplaces. The concept of employees acting as internal freelancers doing tasks is in the process of going from a bold experiment to a normal way of deploying talent.

> There is of course the challenge of having different groups of employees having different employment relationships; the regular employees have a different "deal" than those in the internal freelance team. This challenge is familiar to HR professionals who handle the tensions that arise from the different deals that full-timers, part-timers, contractors, unionized employees, and so on have. There will always be tensions with workers feeling someone else is getting a better deal, but the fact that multiple, more personalized deals exist is ultimately good for employees. Certainly, in this case, the possibility of moving back and forth between regular employment and being on a freelance team is good for employees.

Where Work-Task Planning Fits in the Organization

Note that our chapter title is *strategic* work-task planning, which means aligning work tasks to strategy. Adding work-task planning to a strategic business planning process may be an appealing idea. However, to succeed at this, one needs to be aware of possible organizational barriers to adopting this approach.

Strategic business planning answers two questions: (1) Where will we compete (e.g., what industry, geography, or product/service)? And (2) how will we win (through differentiated capabilities like innovation, efficiency, agility)? By answering these questions, business and HR leaders can then define the key positions required to deliver the emerging strategy and then the key tasks to make the strategy happen.

Workforce planning suggests the jobs required to deliver strategy and the number of people to fill those jobs. Work-task planning moves from business strategy to work-tasks and often requires a team of work analysts from either inside the company or contracted from outside. As noted above, this work-task identification can be tedious, but, once done, the key tasks and the options for doing these tasks can be identified.

Work-task planning may require upgrading some of the workforce planning professionals who focus first on positions and jobs. Focusing on tasks comes from re-engineering the processes for doing work and delivering capabilities. The strategic workforce planning team may also struggle because work-task planning is substantially different from workforce planning in a number of ways as described in this chapter. Just to reiterate one major difference, jobs are relatively well-defined and small in number, whereas to thoroughly tackle work-task planning the organization needs to develop a task taxonomy.

These challenges for the workforce planning team are not insurmountable. It's merely a practical question of whether the team is given sufficient time to take on a challenging and substantial task. It's not a simple add-on to the existing planning process.

Another problem may be overlapping accountabilities with other teams. While the work-task planning team may be looking at tasks and considering which could be automated; another technology team may be looking at automating processes and wonder why this work-task planning team is doing essentially the same work. Again, this is not an insurmountable problem; it simply requires coordination between teams whose accountabilities may overlap, but, in large organizations, this kind of coordination can be difficult. It is common in large organizations for the left hand to not know what the right hand is doing.

Something else enthusiasts for work-task planning should consider is the possibility that the project may not turn up anything new and useful. If we consider the warehouse case, it may be that the tasks themselves, the possibilities of automation, and the importance of cross-training are all well-understood by supervisors on the warehouse floor. Those places in the company where work-task planning has the greatest importance may have already been discovered.

Another challenge for work-task planning are the skills and background of those doing the work. Often, industrial psychologists focus on individuals and how to design jobs to improve employee experience, motivation, and productivity. Work-task planning starts with business and defining the tasks required to deliver business outcomes. The mindset is not just about giving the individual employee a positive experience at work, but a positive experience *so that* the business succeeds.

One possibility for HR leaders is to consider work-task planning as more of a mindset than an ongoing process. Whereas organizations typically run workforce planning on an annual basis, it may be the case that HR professionals simply need to be aware that analyzing work at the task level can occur when strategic choices are being made. If the strategy is changing, then the work-tasks may need to be analyzed for accomplishing the strategic agenda. When they run into situations where analysis is best done at the task level, they will lead a project to do just that. Workforce planning can (and is) done annually and with strategic reinvention. Work-task can be the same.

Planning, such as we find in workforce planning, is very closely linked to action. If our workforce plan projects that our organization will need extra accountants, then we will go about hiring a certain number of accountants or find some other solution. With work-task and work-skill planning, the results may be less closely tied to a specific action. Let's consider a case of work-skill planning where an HR department recognizes it will need to be more "data-savvy." In the workforce planning mindset, that will lead us to ask if we need a job called "HR Data Analyst" and how we might fill that position. However, it's not that HR needs that job; it's that—all across HR—employees need to be more data-savvy. We want more data-savvy recruiters, trainers, and HR business partners. The insight that we have a skill gap will mean that we lean toward hiring people with more data acumen, even if it's not one of the key job responsibilities. We will provide more training on being data-savvy and hope it sticks to varying degrees. It's not nearly as clear as having a fixed number of "HR Data Analysts"—it's more a matter of a CHRO observing that, across HR, we have enough skill in managing data so that, as tasks arise, there will be someone on the team who can do them. From a practitioner's point of view, it's a reminder that we don't always need to prescribe actions (i.e., a plan) following work-skill or work-task planning. It may be that awareness of the issues will be sufficient to direct managerial attention to handle whatever skill or task gaps we have uncovered.

> **Practitioner Tip!**
>
> *Work-task planning and remote work.* Work-task planning could be used to reconfigure work so that more jobs can be done remotely (i.e., all the tasks that must be done on-site are moved to a different job). This leads us into the debate about whether fully remote workers end up being second-class citizens. While companies will want to minimize the chance that talented remote workers are not overlooked, perhaps it's best to see this as a chance for employees to personalize their relationship with the organization to best meet their own needs. Ideally workers will be able to access the tradeoffs that come from different work relationships and make their own decisions about which deal is right for them at that point in their career.

How To Ensure the Work-Task Plan Is Executed

We have found that innovative ideas often are not implemented and thus do not accomplish the potential of the idea. In our work on making change happen, we have identified seven key factors that can be applied to implementing a work-task agenda. These seven keys are identified in Table 9.2. They can be monitored over time as a disciplined way to make work-task planning happen. They are somewhat sequential, with leading, creating a shared need, and defining direction done first. Mobilizing stakeholders requires that those affected by work-task planning participate in making it happen. The decision-making and allocating resources steps suggest getting started, even in small settings, to test the ideas. Finally

Table 9.2 Keys for implementing a work-task agenda

Keys to successful change	Requirement for change: Work-task requires...	Actions to take
1. Leading	Selecting a sponsor who supports work-task and a champion who is accountable	Assign an accountable leader for work-task planning who creates a team and reports to a senior leader
2. Creating a shared need	Preparing a business case for why work-task planning will help deliver strategic goals	Do a cost/benefit of the work-task planning agenda with outcomes and costs
3. Defining a direction	Establish a clear goal and outcome of the work-task planning initiative	Create a shared vision and measurable goals for the work-task planning initiatives
4. Engaging stakeholders	Engage those affected by work-task planning to have a common agenda and team	Identify those throughout the organization who can contribute to work-task planning; broad participation
5. Making decisions	Identify specific decisions to make and have clear accountability for decisions	Prepare a decision protocol of what decisions need to be made, when, and how for 90-day actions
6. Dedicating resources	Allocate money, time, and technology to work-task planning agenda	Make sure that the work-task planning team has the resources (money, people, technology) to make progress
7. Learning, adapting, measuring	Track results to learn what is working and not working, and adapt	Create a measurement system to track the results of work-task planning and build in a learning process to improve

measuring, adapting, and learning implies continuous improvement in the work-task agenda.

Attending to these seven keys helps ensure that the aspirations of work-task planning turn into actions.

The Future of Work-Task Planning

No one doubts that the "future of work" is changing and is no longer the "future" but the present. Where people work is increasingly varied, with hybrid work including work in an office as well as work done in remote locations. How people work is changing, with technology replacing and supplementing face-to-face interactions. These trends shift work from a job–person match to a strategy–task match. When strategic aspirations can be defined in terms of specific tasks, those tasks can be accomplished in many settings (e.g., hybrid) and in many ways (e.g., virtual or in-person). The flexibility of work-task planning will help organizations deliver on strategic promises with agility because tasks are easier to change than are jobs or people and because there are many ways to accomplish a task. Traditional and full-time employees can maximize their skills on tasks they can accomplish and learn to do. Other tasks can be accomplished with other "talent" resources (automation, part-time, contractors, etc.). In the future, when someone asks "What do you do for work?" the answer may be less about a role or job, which is likely defined as a noun (market researcher, manager, or teacher), and more about tasks to be accomplished by focusing on verbs (seek insights about customer preference through data, coordinate work of others to accomplish goals, or share information with students). The limitations of a workforce plan focused on a person in a job become unshackled because tasks may be accomplished through a variety of "talent" resources.

Reference

Jesuthasan, R., and Boudreau, J. (2022). *Work without jobs: How to reboot your organization's work operating system.* MIT Press.

10
The Job as Work Role and Profession

It's More Than Skills

Andrea Fischbach and Benjamin Schneider

We propose that when companies have in place the strategic workforce planning (SWP) that the new world of work requires, then a culture and climate for professionalism will exist that fits this new world of work roles. Our dynamic, interdependent, and increasingly complex work world changes the role of workers from narrow (the job) to broad (the work role). The reality of this work role world is that workers must necessarily exhibit increasing discretion over what they are responsible for, what they feel accountable for, and how they carry out their roles—they must be professionals. From carefully delineated and prescribed task activities, the new work role requires more than doing immediate tasks; it also requires being adaptable and flexible and being dependable, self-controlled, ethical, and so forth. In addition, the expansion of the work role requires employees to deal across functional boundaries, to work with people both inside and outside of their companies, to work with different teams under different leaders—and to experience and cope with the role ambiguity and role conflict that accompanies such work roles. If SWP is going to be effective, companies must have in place the various human resources (HR) tactics (job and work role design and analysis, selection, education/training, socialization, performance management, and leadership) that are focused on the work role as profession. The combined focus of these many HR tactics on work roles as professions will create a climate for professionalism that will promote the employee behaviors necessary for these new work roles.

SWP tends to focus in on the P—the planning. That is, the emphasis is on having the right number of people to fill jobs and determining whether the talent has the right skills, when those talents will be needed and where, and so forth. And, while some considerable attention is now being paid to "upskilling" as automation and artificial intelligence (AI) penetrate the

Andrea Fischbach and Benjamin Schneider, *The Job as Work Role and Profession* In: *Strategic Workforce Planning*. Edited by: Marc Sokol and Beverly Tarulli, Oxford University Press.
© Society for Industrial and Organizational Psychology 2024. DOI: 10.1093/oso/9780197759745.003.0011

workplace, this appropriate focus on the knowledge, skills, and abilities (KSAs) has inadvertently missed the necessity to focus on the "Os" in KSAO—those too-frequently ignored "Other" characteristics. Our position is that these Other characteristics are a key to professionalism in modern work roles. To be specific, our chapter is about what professionalism is and what it requires in the form of work styles and the SWP actions that should be taken via selection, training, socialization, performance management, and leadership to create a culture and climate for professionalism that will serve both workers and organizations well.

Professionalism in the New Work Role

Table 10.1 provides definitions of professionalism at work as obtained from a Google search using the term "professionalism at work." There you can see that various firms (Indeed, Insperity, Pinterest) see professionalism as a combination of various styles of behaving: being conscientious and reliable, being ethical and competent, being respectful and considerate of others, and so forth. Table 10.1 emerged from accessing various consulting firms' websites—firms obviously interested in and concerned about creating professionalism in their workforce. Obviously, we are not the first or only ones to think that the professionalism of work and work roles may have important implications for the future of talent management.

Table 10.1 Examples of professional behavior

Indeed[a]	Insperity[b]	Pinterest[c]
Reliability	Behave in ways that command respect of others	Be on time
Humility		Become a resource to others
Etiquette	Be reliable, ethical, competent, and mindful of others	
Neatness		Dress professionally
Consideration	Maintain composure despite challenges	Show respect for others
Dedication		Avoid office politics and gossip
Organization	Build business relationships to further skill and career development	
Accountability		Never be afraid to ask questions
Integrity		
Expertise		Take appropriate breaks

[a]Based on https://www.indeed.com/career-advice/career-development/the-ultimate-guide-to-professionalism
[b]Based on https://www.insperity.com/blog/professionalism-in-the-workplace/
[c]Based on https://www.pinterest.com/spjb01/professionalism-in-the-workplace/

A search of O*NET revealed a more comprehensive listing of these attributes under the heading of "Work Styles" that fits well with our thinking on professionalism; this listing is presented in Table 10.2. There is some overlap with the definitions in Table 10.1, especially with those from Indeed.[1] While O*NET does not explicitly get at issues like role ambiguity and role conflict, it does address some difficulties workers may encounter (see Self-Control and Stress Tolerance). Obviously, the wide-ranging nature of contemporary work roles can produce discomfort and difficulties, and this is why it is so important for companies to do what they can to ensure that people understand what these behaviors are (more on this later), that they have the KSAOs for the specific tasks they must do (KSAs) and how they do them (Os), and that the leadership they observe and experience as role models enact and support the development of these behavior styles.

Our fundamental proposals are these: (1) If workers at all levels of a company do not consider themselves to be professionals, they will not act the way

Table 10.2 O*NET listing of work styles that can characterize work roles

1. *Achievement/Effort*: Establish and maintain personally challenging achievement goals and exert effort toward mastering tasks
2. *Persistence*: Persist in the face of obstacles
3. *Initiative*: Willing to take on responsibilities and challenges
4. *Leadership*: Willing to lead, to take charge, and offer opinions and directions
5. *Cooperation*: Be pleasant with others and display a good-natured and cooperative attitude
6. *Concern for Others*: Be sensitive to others' needs and feelings and be understanding and helpful to others
7. *Social Orientation*: Prefer to work with others rather than alone and be connected to others on the job
8. *Self-control*: Maintain composure, keep emotions in check, control anger even in difficult situations
9. *Stress Tolerance*: Accept criticism and deal calmly and effectively with high-stress situations
10. *Adaptability/Flexibility*: Be open to change (positive or negative) and to considerable variety in the workplace
11. *Dependability*: Be reliable, responsible, and dependable, and fulfill obligations
12. *Attention to Detail*: Be careful about details and thorough in completing tasks
13. *Integrity*: Be honest and ethical
14. *Independence*: Develop one's own ways of doing things, guiding oneself with little to no supervision, and depend on oneself to get things done
15. *Innovation*: Creative and alternative thinking to develop new ideas for and answers to work-related questions
16. *Analytical Thinking*: Analyze information and use logic to address work-related issues and problems

*https://www.onetonline.org/find/descriptor/browse/1.C/1.C.1/1.C.4/1.C.5/1.C.3/1.C.7/1.C.2

professionals should; and (2) companies that employ their SWP practices to focus on the professional nature of work roles will reap the benefits in employee behavior and organizational success. It is the emphasis given professionalism as the way to behave across the variety of SWP that will yield work roles with appropriate standards for who occupies them and will contain people who have the appropriate KSAOs to carry out their roles and who will be in step with the nature of contemporary work.

The need for such professionals in everyday work roles is great. That is, the new world of work is dynamic, uncertain, complex, and ambiguous (Howard, 1995). In this new work world, it is increasingly less possible to precisely prescribe and directly manage the behavior, responsibilities, and outcomes of work. Consequently, the reality of the modern work world is that workers exhibit increased discretion over for what they take responsibility and for what they don't. We propose that an organization's aggregate level of professionalism—relatively autonomous work roles focused on doing the right things in the right ways given the organization's goals and objectives—is crucial to personal and organizational success.

Figure 10.1 shows that there are three major sets of organizational practices that must be in place to achieve a professional workforce. First is work-design and continuous redesign that focus directly on the work role breadth we see as characterizing increasingly large portions of future work. Second is HR management practices (including selection, training, and performance management) that focus directly on workers' fit with professional work-role

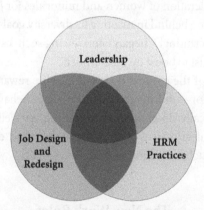

Figure 10.1 The culture and climate for professionalism is comprised of three interacting attributes: leadership, job design and redesign, and human resources management practices that all focus on professionalism.

requirements and responsibilities. That is, by behaving in the ways shown in Table 10.2, workers will be more effective, more committed, and more highly engaged in carrying out those roles. Third, all levels of leadership must continuously serve as role models to communicate through word and deed their support for professional behavior in all that is done both internally and externally (as with customers, suppliers, and so forth). A combined focus on all three of these diverse yet integrated policies, practices, and procedures will produce a culture and climate for professionalism within an organization. We deal with each of these in turn in what follows.

Prior to moving on to more details about the new work roles we see, this issue of role modeling and professional behavior will benefit from an example of how it can go wrong. The case concerns unprofessional behavior by various layers of workers and managers at Wells-Fargo.[2] Millions of fraudulent checking and savings and credit card accounts were created at Well-Fargo by account representatives working in various branches. Initially, individual branch employees and managers were accused of impropriety, but the blame was later shifted to top-down pressure from higher management to open as many accounts as possible through what is known as "cross-selling." Huge fines were levied against the bank, and there is still ongoing litigation. This scandal occurred in 2016, the CEO was fired, and Wells-Fargo ostensibly went about renewing its previous reputation for stability. In 2022, however, Wells-Fargo was again in the news for unprofessional behavior, this time for conducting "fake" interviews.[3] In this case, company managers were forced by senior management to interview people for jobs that had already been filled, the purpose of which was to build up statistics regarding the consideration of women and minorities for job "openings." That is, the bank was falling behind in meeting its diversity goals, and to build up its statistics vis-á-vis recruiting, it began interviewing such "candidates" even after the job was filled—just to boost up the numbers.

The point is that if the context does not provide rewards for and support professional behavior—and indeed punishes such behavior by firing those who do not unethically do enough cross-selling, as Wells-Fargo did—then the idea of the professional worker is nonsense, and even the finest HR attempts to create such a workforce will fail.

The New Work Roles

Job-role differentiation theory (Griffin et al., 2007; Ilgen and Hollenbeck, 1991) is very useful for grasping the difference between jobs and work roles.

A *job* consists of established and predefined elements in a formal job description that defines task requirements and the responsibilities of the job holder. However, today's jobs, because they exist in dynamic, turbulent, and ambiguous circumstances as well as across teams and levels, have far more responsibilities than previously, including working with automation, working across levels of the organization, working on different teams to accomplish goals, and working both within and without the boundaries of the organization. In short, work roles consist of established task elements ("the job") plus emergent task elements ("the role") that are more dynamic and constantly being changed. Emergent role elements are communicated by different social sources, including supervisors, colleagues, customers, and the job holder themselves. Sharon Parker (2014, p. 664) puts it well: "[J]ob characteristics have become salient as a result of changes in work organization. For example, the rise of dual working parents highlights the need to consider autonomy over working hours; the growth in service work identifies the need to consider emotional job demands; the rise of individuals working from home highlights the role of social contact during work; and changes in career structures bring to the fore opportunities for skill development."

Jobs with their established tasks are seemingly objective because there is a shared consensus about the tasks that comprise them. The source of this consensus is the formal job description. *Roles*, with their emergent elements on the other hand, are more subjective because there are several changing possibilities in the elements that comprise them. As Hackman (1969) noted early on, role occupants must recognize, understand, accept, and integrate frequently changing external role expectations into their personal role understanding. Consequently, while the boundaries of a job can be relatively precisely defined by the formal job description of the tasks involved, the boundaries of a role—role breadth—are not so easily specified (Parker, 1998, 2000).

Jesuthasan and Boudreau (2022) are ahead of the curve in contemplating the new world of work. Their book has achieved best-seller status for a *New York Times* business book because, we think, it is real and offers ideas for action as companies and employees grapple with the "new work." They provide the four principles for this new world of work, as shown in Box 10.1, obviously a new perspective on work and the people who do it—and the companies in which this is all happening.

And companies are not just standing on the sidelines with regard to this new world of work. IBM, for example, has created what it calls "The New Collar Program," one which seeks people for their talent and not for degrees

> **Box 10.1 The Jesuthasan and Boudreau (2022) New Work Operating System**
>
> 1. Start by focusing on the tasks for a job, not the whole job, which is likely to change as technology/automation is adopted; focus on the task elements.
> 2. Combine people and automation that optimizes the capabilities of both; do not assume automation will replace people—it will do tasks that optimize the talents of both people and automation.
> 3. Consider all manner of work and workers to accomplish what needs doing: traditional employment, gig workers, freelancers, specific project-based, and so forth.
> 4. Encourage employees to flow where they are needed, releasing their instincts to be useful and to craft work to get it done.

people may have obtained—and then trains them for specific roles. Box 10.2 is a description of this program from the IBM website.[4]

It is obviously essential for modern job analyses to address the work role attributes shown in Table 10.2 so that selection, training, and performance management focus on these professional behaviors. We have been unable to locate such job analyses although we have contacted several industrial-organizational (I-O) practitioners who work in the areas

> **Box 10.2 The IBM New Collar Program**
>
> The New Collar initiative is all about addressing the skills gap that we face in a world of fast-paced technology. A significant number of roles at IBM don't require a traditional education or career path. What matters most are the skills and experiences to perform a role.
>
> New Collar jobs are roles in some of the technology industry's fastest growing fields—from cybersecurity and cloud computing to digital design. These jobs require skills that can be gained through "earn while you learn" apprenticeships, returnships for professionals who have been out of the workforce and wish to re-enter, and innovative public education programs like P-TECH, which IBM pioneered, as well as coding camps, professional certification programs, and more.

of selection and job analysis. Such work role analyses would need to identify what Gordon Allport called "life as it is lived" (Allport, 1942, p. 56). In I-O, we refer to the issues raised in Table 10.2 as "competencies," and these can be contrasted with KSAs—which are obviously more specific in content and need to be generated through job analysis techniques such as the Critical Incident Technique (Flanagan, 1954) or diary methods (Bolger, Davis, and Rafaeli, 2003).

Let us be very clear: the KSAs required for excellent performance serve as a central issue in the professional behavior of people in work roles, while the style with which they display those KSAs—the "Os"—completes the picture of professionalism. A very talented air conditioning repair person who is not constantly learning (Achievement/Effort), who quits in the face of frustrations (Persistence), who fails to anticipate questions customers might ask (Initiative), and who fails to offer assistance to co-workers (Cooperation) is not being a professional.

Of course, some might argue that professionalism is more important in some work roles than others. Our opinion is that this is like saying manners are more important in some settings than in others. In some work roles, it may seem more obvious that what people feel responsible for and hold themselves accountable for is more serious (medical personnel, psychotherapists, teachers, bus drivers, and airline cabin attendants), but it is obvious from the list that a slippery slope exists where all of those jobs must be professionally accomplished but they differ in the hierarchy of the so-called professions: Are bus drivers and cabin attendants professionals? Of course they are: life and death depend on such workers. AC repair people control air pollution, and cleaning personnel and garbage collectors support health and well-being—the point is that the more these workers identify with these larger facets of their work roles and do so professionally, the more likely they are to be engaged and carry out those roles effectively. The point is that when the larger work role and the larger effects that performance in those roles can have are not considered, the less likely it is that the people in those roles will think of themselves as professionals.

It is the emergent quality of task elements as part of the work role that seem to us the most challenging issue for work design and redesign. That is, since workers will be operating more autonomously than in the past due to role expansion, natural job crafting (Bakker and Oerlemans, 2019)—a central feature of the new world of work—will occur. Autonomy has been a central feature of understanding worker involvement in work since the early

1980s (Hackman and Oldham 1980), but it takes on an increased importance the more flexible and fluid work roles become. We turn to the issue of work autonomy in some detail next.

The New Autonomy in Work Roles

At the root of our notion of the work role is the idea that workers will necessarily be relatively autonomous as they carry out their expanded work role in this new era of work. The construct of autonomy has long been a central focus of studies of jobs and job characteristics. In the Hackman and Oldham (1980) early job description work, autonomy was one of the five most central constructs underlying the meaningfulness of work. In addition, in Ryan and Deci's (2003) self-determination theory (SDT), peoples' identities are formed by their needs for autonomy, competence, and relatedness. Indeed, research shows clearly that people will act autonomously in any job that offers an opportunity for it (Bakker and Oerlemans, 2019), and, if the COVID-19 pandemic has taught us anything, it is that people who are given the opportunity to work autonomously will do so with vigor, dedication, and absorption—the three fundamental facets of engagement (Schaufeli and Bakker, 2010).

Acting autonomously to accomplish tasks associated with the role and doing so in keeping with the styles associated with professionalism need not compromise one's own autonomy as long as one has internalized those prescribed behaviors and responsibilities. Thus, work roles offer an important mechanism by which one can live out one's own autonomous identity (Ashforth and Schinoff, 2016). In what follows, we review the common solutions used in SWP (selection, training, socialization, performance management) as ways companies can hire and develop a work force that will foster and take advantage of this autonomous work motivation so necessary for workers and their organizations. In short, we agree with Barrick et al.'s (2013) notion of "purposeful work behavior." Their idea is straightforward: it is through selection of the right people plus the creation of the appropriate context that organizations achieve the motivation and performance of the workforce that matters. We call this "appropriate context" a climate for professionalism and develop it later in the chapter.

Selection/Staffing

One way that organizations can achieve this autonomous motivation in their people is by attracting, selecting, and keeping people who have it (Schneider, 1987). Of course, this is above and beyond the KSAs required for effective performance. Some might imagine that the "O" in "KSAO" is a way to conceptualize and thus assess this autonomous motivation, which we see as a predictor of the work styles noted in Table 10.2. Indeed, Table 10.3 presents one way to organize the work styles as correlates of the five-factor model of

Table 10.3 Hypothesized links between the five-factor model of personality and O*NET work styles

Five-Factor dimension	O*NET work styles facets
Conscientiousness	Achievement/Flexibility
	Persistence
	Dependability
	Attention to detail
	Integrity
Openness to experience	Adaptability/Flexibility
	Innovation
	Analytical thinking
	Initiative
Agreeableness	Cooperation
	Concern for others
Emotional stability	Self-control
	Stress tolerance
	Independence
Extraversion	Leadership
	Social orientation

Note: Extensive reviews of the personality research literature reveal that the professionalism work styles shown in this table are consistently and significantly predicted. Many of the reviews appeared early in the 2000s (cf. Ones and Viswesvaran, 2001) and subsequent reviews have replicated the significant findings (c.f. Barrick and Mount, 2013; Hough and Dilchert, 2017). There is also personality research on counterproductive behavior (indifference, distrustful, inconsistent, mischievous) with similar results, especially via personality measures focused on the so-called dark triad (O'Boyle et al., 2012). Few studies have used compound personality measures—combinations of Big 5 attributes, for example—to predict outcomes, but when they do the results are quite impressive with meta-analyses in the .40–.50 range (Hough and Dilchert, 2017; Barrick and Mount, 2012); a key example has been the prediction of theft behavior by employees in what is known as "integrity testing" (Ones et al., 2012). We encourage the use of compound personality traits to predict professionalism defined by the compound ratings of the likely interrelated work styles in this table.

personality so popular in I-O psychology research and practice (e.g., Hough and Dilchert, 2017). Table 10.3 presents our conceptual model of how the "O" in KSAO might be linked with the professional work styles that will characterize work role behavior—and the footnote to that table provides lots of evidence for the presumed validity of such personality attributes—especially as compound attributes—as predictors of those professional work styles.

There is mounting evidence that reveals it is through external selection that organizations most often obtain the specific kinds of personality in the people they have (Oh, Han, Holtz, Kim, Kim, 2018). Indeed, there is also evidence to suggest that the people in an organization tend to fit it, and, the better the fit, the more superior is organizational performance (Schneider and Bartram, 2017). We hypothesize that because of the kinds of people hired by and who work in them, organizations will differ in the extent to which they will be seen as a *professional organization*. So, in the aggregate, organizations that attract, hire, and develop those with higher levels of the personality characteristics shown in Table 10.3 will be seen by those inside and outside as being more professional organizations. That is, organizations in the attraction–selection–attrition (ASA) model are not seen as characterized by "a" (single) personality characteristics but by a bundle or package of personality characteristics. One might indeed think of this bundle of personality characteristics in the people in an organization and the professionalism it reveals as a potential attractor to future employees via Glassdoor, for example.[5]

Obviously, different jobs will have different tasks that make up the role, and different roles will have different needs for the professional styles shown in Table 10.2—and that is why we have work role analysis. That is, when the tasks involved in the role and the ways those tasks are carried out have been identified, then the KSAs and styles (Os) needed will be in hand and procedures for assessing them can be designed. Table 10.3 is an expanded version of Table 10.2, revealing for each style some examples of the kinds of behaviors that will contribute to work role performance as a professional. The importance of the style variables required for any role will vary, just like the KSAs will vary, and it is the package that will be necessary for the design of a potentially valid and legal selection process.

Conducting the kinds of work design/job analyses we previously discussed can help identify the KSAOs desired at entry and on which different selection procedures can be focused. Given our emphasis on the turbulent and ambiguous nature of modern work it is critical that the selection procedures used focus not only on the KSAs that might be required for a specific job/role but also on the Os—which define the motivation to work independently, be adaptive/flexible, take initiative, be cooperative, and tolerate stress well—see Table 10.3 for more possibilities. Some call this selecting for "person-organization (P-O) fit," and that is a useful construct to have in reserve when making finalized decisions so long as there is an explicit focus on evidence and not just recruiter or interviewer feelings (Barrick and Parks-Leduc, 2019).

Education and Training

Professionalism does not exist in the abstract but in the reality of doing. People may be selected who have the KSAOs to be professionals, but it is what happens to them after they are hired that determines the degree to which those KSAOs become operationalized in situ. Education and training explicitly provide the formal standards and values as well as an introduction to the unwritten norms of the company that serve as the foundation for how to behave—and thus professionalism (Grus et al., 2018). We think, for example, of the people in the medical fields (doctors, nurses, and so forth) as a metaphor because it is what happens to them early in their education and training that helps make them professionals. Of course, there are other critical experiences—like socialization, working with others, and the general culture and climate of the setting in which work is done that are also important—but we deal here with education and training now and those later.

The Education and Training Context

Who the trainers and educators are, how they behave, and what they emphasize are as critical to creating a sense of professionalism in newcomers as the content they provide (Andresen, Boud, and Cohen, 2000). In addition, many companies during COVID-19 moved from in-person to video-based training due to many different constraints. There is little research that compares video-based versus in-person training but we hypothesize that specific content (KSAs) is well-learned via video-based methods; however, unless the video-based learning involves two-way observation and feedback of the behavioral facets of professionalism, especially those involving other people, these are better accomplished via in-person modes. The role of education and training, then, is not only the teaching of KSAs but the provision of values and norms about behavior—doing the right things in the right ways, both of which are more difficult to accomplish in the absence of feedback. The earlier this values-laden training happens the more likely it is that professional behavior becomes the newcomer's norm (Ashforth and Anand, 2003). As we note again later, what is important in training is that workers be exposed to not only what to do but how to do it, plus be exposed to the consequences of what they do and how they do it.

Education and Training Goals and Process

Along with the acquisition of KSAs in training, the goal is the reinforcement of the motivations that people bring with them to the workplace—the motivations as in the hoped-for work styles we previously discussed. As will be clear throughout, it is this combination of context and person that is essential for SWP to produce the professional work-role behavior desired. The education and training system thus must provide conditions for the acquisition of the ways to draw inferences, make predictions, understand work issues, and decide which actions to take in the frequently ambiguous work situations trainees will encounter. The goal, then, is to provide future role players with the mental models that serve as a framework for the professionalism behavior desired (Jones, Ross, Lynam, Perez, and Leitch, 2011; Pfeffer, 2005), mental models that include what to do, how to do it, and the consequences of doing.

Obviously, we see this kind of education and training as being highly behavioral in type, as in experience-based learning with feedback (Andresen et al., 2000). Such education and training programs make use of structured and directed experiences in role-plays, games, or experiments. Instructional designers, teachers, trainers, and so forth must create and implement these experiences in a safe environment by (a) supporting the autonomy of learners in this process, (b) providing constructive and explicit feedback, and (c) acknowledging the importance of others in work role performance. This process of experiential learning should also include explicit attention to how to engage in ongoing self-reflection and self-development. Trainees can be encouraged and taught how to seek feedback and reflect on accomplishments and disappointments by oneself as well as with the help of others (co-workers, supervisors, counselors, and coaches) (Nesbit, 2012).

One example of an experience-based training program is an exercise developed for master's-degree students at the German Police University. The exercise is based on a simulation designed by Florian Klonek and Sharon Parker from the Centre for Transformative Work Design.[6] Box 10.3 summarizes the experimental conditions that are created for the students so that they get to have both positive and negative experiences. The goal is to experientially show trainees that it is context and not just people's own personal attributes that lead them to be professionals—and to be engaged and productive. Of course, this is to sensitize them to the impact they will have as leaders—the consequences—when they are out in the field (Parker, Andrei, and Van den Broeck, 2019).

The idea behind this exercise is to get trainees involved in positive experiences, to discuss how those differ from negative experiences, and to do this by teaching positive actions, not only teaching to avoid negative ones. Police work obviously can confront workers with situations that are ambiguous and require actions/reactions that make it crucial to have an awareness of what the positive options are and their consequences. Awareness of the consequences of behavior style choices is, of course, not only important for police, as we have unfortunately learned (e.g., as when airline cabin attendants are forced to confront unruly passengers).

Box 10.3 The Job Design Experiment for German Police University Leadership Training

1. Participants are randomly assigned to one of two conditions: (1) highly structured, with low chances of cooperation among team members and centralized control over how to proceed and (2) flat decision-making with high opportunities to discuss strategies and high worker autonomy to suggest ways to proceed.
2. The idea is to get students to experience different forms of job design and leadership and how those different forms influence their interpersonal behavior, their engagement, and their success. After the exercise, the two groups meet to reflect on how they felt as individuals and what their experience of being in the group was like.
3. The future police leaders learn to feel responsible for the roles they play and the roles their co-workers play as a task unfolds.

Socialization: Informal Education and Training

Socialization concerns how well early experiences (as a new employee or in a new work role) reflect the norms and values of the company. Earlier we noted how the context for learning and education/training is critical to how training will be received; socialization of newcomers is critical to how the larger organization will be perceived and is a cue to the behaviors that will be rewarded, supported, and expected. Most organizations have formal training programs to which they devote astonishing amounts of time, effort, and money yet these same organizations pay little attention to the onboarding and socialization experiences of new employees or of employees new to a work role. Yet the research on socialization is abundantly clear about its potential impact (Chao, 2012). The key concept here is one of a blank slate: newcomers are a (relatively) blank slate about the company and its norms and values, so any and all early experiences will determine what people believe the organization believes in and values—and how work roles are carried out in daily life. SWP can be excellent in the details and miss the bigger picture of ensuring that early newcomers have correct images of the organization and of their roles as professionals in it. Socialization is a time for newcomers to understand, accept, and be encouraged by co-workers to be professionals in carrying out their roles.

A supplementary idea here is very important: existing employees who are newcomers to new work roles receive even less attention than newcomers to the company! This is obviously silly since newcomers to work roles are also in need of the support and help associated with newcomer entry to the company.

A good example of the importance of socialization concerns the potential conflict between training and socialization on the job with police newcomers. Police in training typically learn about what the law requires of them as professionals, but, when on the job, they may unfortunately sometimes encounter what is called "Dirty Harry" unprofessional practice, achieving essential ends by tarnished means (Fekjær, Petersson, and Thomassen, 2014). Thus, it is crucial to invest in positive onboarding experiences for newcomers at all levels of the organization. This can be accomplished by assigning one of the most professional co-workers to be a newcomer advocate who is responsible for early information and experiences about how the work role is "really" done and who can be counted on for informal contact throughout the day, including being a lunch partner (Chao, 2012; Feldman,

1989). It is one sad detail of the murder of George Floyd by Dereck Chauvin in Minneapolis that Chauvin was serving as a field training officer despite the fact that he had been the subject of several prior complaints, including three shooting incidents (National Academies of Sciences, Engineering, and Medicine, 2022).

Performance Management

In the SWP process, is performance management first or last in what requires attention? We really thought about putting it before selection in our review—and before training—and before socialization. That is, the target of SWP needs to include the behavioral characteristics on which employees will be evaluated, judged, reinforced, and rewarded. Look at Table 10.2. These are the kinds of issues requiring attention in performance management if a company is going to achieve professionalism in work roles. As such, these items constitute a partial list of the issues on which SWP can focus. The list is partial because it fails to contain all of the other KSAs required for success and effectiveness in the work role, of which there are many examples (cf. Pulakos and Battista, 2020).

Work role performance is not only a function of the design of work roles, education/training, and socialization but also a result of the continual monitoring of work role behavior on the job. Every work role will have its own set of behaviors against which performance will be monitored and assessed, and we of course want it to contain the work style elements shown in Table 10.2, amended as appropriate for a specific setting. While the record of performance management techniques' impact on organizational-level performance is not what we would hope for, there is no doubt that it can be improved and that work role occupants pay attention to it (Pulakos and Battista, 2020). That is, the behavior that people observe being rewarded, supported, and expected in their work units and in the whole organization is crucial for their own decisions on how to behave (cf., Cleveland, 2020) and what they deduce is important for obtaining rewards. Thus, leaders must promote, support, recognize, and reward such professional work role behavior and recognize, address, and sanction failures to do the right things in the right ways. It is essential that employees who in any way violate these professional styles of work role behavior *not* be rewarded because everyone will notice such recognition. We propose that performance management systems (i.e., the evaluation itself, pay, promotion, and other reward systems) that consider these positive work role behaviors will shape and develop workers' professionalism and thus contribute strongly to the climate and culture of the organization.

The Culture and Climate for Professionalism

Organizational culture has to do with the *values* that characterize a setting for the people there; organizational climate has to do with the *focus* of the policies, practices, and procedures and the behaviors that are rewarded, supported, and expected in an organization (Ehrhart, Schneider, and Macey, 2017). Climate and culture are in reciprocal relationships, with the focus or foci of the climate signaling what is valued and what is valued dictating the focus of policies, practices, and procedures (Schein, 2010). When professionalism is valued in an organization, its SWP policies, practices, and procedures will, in the aggregate and across practices, focus on it.

The point is that there is no silver bullet to the creation and maintenance of professionalism in work role behavior for a company, but that many facets of HR management must be in place to get across that message. As Ed Schein has repeatedly noted in his writings on culture (e.g., Schein, 2010), what organizations devote scarce resources to helps to determine the culture of that organization. This focus on professionalism needs to be incorporated into all facets of SWP planning. That is, behavioral expectations for professional attributes starts with identifying them as characteristics (along with KSAs) that should be explicitly targeted when doing SWP and identifying gaps to be filled for the future—the essence of SWP. By devoting time, effort, and money to a focus on professionalism through selection, training, socialization, and performance management the message will get across that this way of behaving is valued by the company.

At least five critical HR tactics must be in place to show that there is a climate and culture for professionalism.

1. *Work roles must be explicitly designed and defined* for the new world of work that requires performance in turbulent and ambiguous times and that will require increased autonomy in carrying out the work

role—and for the people who will do this work. And it will require not only the KSAs (more than just the skills on which there has been so much focus) but the Os, too.
2. *New work role definitions must be converted into formal selection procedures* when "buy" is an identified solution to filling gaps. Such procedures will yield the KSAOs necessary as a foundation to carry out those roles.
3. In a "build" solution to filling gaps, *experiential-based education and training programs that focus on both technical skills and professionalism as required by the work role must be designed and implemented* that focus on doing things the right way.
4. *Socialization of newcomers by the most professional current members of the work force is essential.*
5. *Performance management processes must signal that professionalism on the job is rewarded, supported, and expected.*

Who will ensure these are in place? Business leaders who are key stakeholders and sponsors in SWP must not just designate: they must be role models by behaving in ways that indicate to all how critical SWP is to them for the future of the company. Of course, it is the SWP professionals who must ensure the necessary discussions occur, but it is the business leaders who must ensure SWP is being accomplished—the future depends on it. And all involved must expand their horizons beyond "skill development," to include knowledge, ability, and those other characteristics as well. As we noted earlier, Schein (2010) summarizes the issues well: it is to what leaders devote scarce resources and pay attention that reveals what they value. And it must always be remembered that, for leaders, time is a scarce resource. So, how they spend their time—on what they focus their time—sends the message about what is valued.

Leadership must focus on success as well as failures so that workers understand the difference. Failures may remain undetected by leaders if they are not paying attention to how things are being done (Aquino, Lewis, and Bradfield, 1999), and such failures can become the norm and a way of life. The Wells-Fargo case is an example of rewarded, supported, and expected unprofessional behavior. At Wells-Fargo, employees were punished if they failed to achieve unreasonable goals for cross-selling, so they were actually rewarded for creating false customer accounts to achieve these unachievable goals (Flitter, 2020). Leadership that creates these kinds of conditions for employees is apparently and unfortunately not that unusual (see Hagler, 2021, for a description of leadership issues at Volkswagen-Audi in what is known as "Diesel Gate"). While earlier we focused on the selection of employees and did not focus on the selection of leaders, we know that "pseudotransformational," "personalized charismatic," or "dark personality" types can hold leadership positions that they use to maintain their power rather than for the good of their companies or their employees (Den Hartog, 2015). People with high levels of "the dark side of personality" (Hogan et al., 2021) obviously will not be wanted in companies desiring their employees to be professionals.

Recently there have even been attacks against Jack Welch because he stopped focusing on doing the right things in the right way and instead focused on manipulating financial records to make GE look profitable—at all costs (Gelles, 2022). In short, leaders must devote their efforts to creating and monitoring organizational policies, procedures, and practices that focus on professionalism and the variety of stakeholder outcomes achieved.

Leadership is most crucial for shaping and enforcing professional standards and values. Leaders do this first as role models since everyone either is watching or hears about what leaders are paying attention to—and doing themselves. They must maintain their technical knowledge so that they are viewed by their people as up to date with the latest research and techniques (Pfeffer, 2005; Rousseau, 2006), and they must feel responsible and hold themselves accountable for the welfare of their people, the organization, and the various stakeholders of the organization (Voegtlin, 2012). The most critical thing the top management team can do is understand that all they do displays the values they hold, and they can enforce the value of professionalism in their people by ensuring it is focused on professionalism when conducting SWP.

Table 10.4 presents interview quotes from the diagnosis of a service firm—a bank—conducted by Schneider et al. (2003); the quotes reveal how climate and culture for service professionalism exists in the experiences of employees. Table 10.4 reveals the many ways the message is sent: by who gets hired, how leadership serves as a role model, how people are socialized and trained, relationships with customers, and so forth (many more examples can be found in Schneider et al.). The message is that all these facets of organizational functioning, in combination, are the message.

Table 10.4 Climate and culture for service: employees speak

- The CEO of the bank more than anyone embodies the service culture
- The culture of the bank is the way it is because management keeps employees focused on service
- At other banks they enforce rules by the book. Here we do what we have to do without doing it by the book. We're empowered.
- If customers do not see enough people meeting their needs, they are unhappy. That is why cross training is important; to be able to fill a lot of positions with very few people
- The older people here were taught customer service at the beginning and the younger people learn by watching the older people.
- We have monthly coaching sessions. We get ratings and we talk about them. We talk about next month and how they can be better, and everything is out in the open.
- [The CEO] sends each employee a note thanking them for accomplishments that make him look good. The message is that we are all equal.
- When we interview potential applicants, we tell them that our primary goal is customer service. Developing relationships with customers is part of the job description.
- Service is the standard on Day 1 so we hire people who believe in good service.
- [The bank] hires good people, people who want to learn.

From Schneider et al. (2003)

A Future Focus for Professionalism as an Integral Part of Your SWP Process

Our goal has been to tell you why professionalism is necessary when thinking about work roles in the new world of work and to show how, through an integrated set of lenses as shown in Figure 10.1, a culture and climate for professionalism can be created to make this happen. We conclude with some questions you can ask yourself as you think through how to put into practice this issue of a professional orientation for your people and your company. Developing answers to these questions will start you down the path of professionalism.

1. Is professionalism identified as a need and incorporated into the role descriptions during your SWP? Our experience is that professionalism can easily be missed when selection, training, socialization, and performance management tactics are implemented.
2. Are there some work roles in your company in which a professional mentality is critical in carrying out those work roles? Our experience is that these roles are invariably customer contact roles because they are so autonomous—and the evidence is clear that a focus on those Os for

customer contact through HR practices can pay dividends in customer satisfaction and profits (Hong et al., 2014).
3. How well are your HR practices collectively focusing on the professionalism issue? Our experience is that some practices (say, selection) have (a) an appropriate emphasis and focus on KSAs (mostly skills) but not the Os, and (b) that focus gets washed out because training focuses on technical skills, leadership is absent as a professional work role model, and performance management practices focus only on numbers and not on professional work styles. An unintegrated multifaceted approach to planning for future people needs will fail to produce a culture and climate for professionalism.
4. Do you overemphasize KSAs in who is hired, and ignore—and have no validity evidence for—those work style issues summarized in Tables 10.2 and 10.3? Who gets hired has long-term consequences for employee engagement and effectiveness—and long-term consequences for the reputation your company will have as an employer. Do you want to be known as the home of professional style? You can make it happen. For a company's selection process to meet both professional and legal standards, engaging I-O psychologists is essential.
5. On the issue of evidence (a) Are you tracking who you hire and how they work out? (b) Are you tracking how effective your training programs are in achieving the goals you (should) set for them? (c) Do the results from your performance management systems track with the engagement of employees and with customer satisfaction?

In short, in an era of data availability, companies can focus their data systems on the kinds of professionalism issues we have raised and track both employees and the effectiveness of HR practices and leadership in producing the kind of workforce and company you want to be.

Conclusion

As work organizations become increasingly flat and as jobs become increasingly complex employees are confronted by numerous decisions about what they should be focusing on and how they should behave. We propose that jobs be reconceptualized as work roles with all the expanded issues such roles require. In addition, we propose that those who perform work roles be the subject of all SWP, thus leading to them seeing themselves and being seen as professionals. As a result, we propose that the SWP professionals conducting these analyses and the basic HR systems and practices in organizations focus their efforts not only on the KSAs required for job performance but also on the professional styles with which such work roles are carried out. When business leadership intensively emphasizes professionalism in who gets hired, the socialization and training they receive, and the standards against which their performance is managed, a culture and climate for professionalism is possible. We emphasize the role of leadership in serving as role models for such professional behavior by (a) their own behavior and style and (b) their explicit devotion of time, effort, and resources to the SWP imperatives necessary to further the development of a climate and culture of professionalism.

Acknowledgments

Volume editors Marc Sokol and Beverly Tarulli made significant suggestions to improve the readability of our chapter and we greatly appreciate their careful attention to what we hoped to accomplish. We also appreciate the suggestions of Leaetta Hough, Fred Oswald, and Nancy Tippins on the ways personality issues might be reflected in professionalism in work roles.

Notes

1. These work styles are not to be confused with what O*NET lists as "Generalized Work Activities" (https://www.onetonline.org/find/descriptor/browse/4.AO) or what Hunt (1996) calls "Generic Work Behaviors."
2. See https://en.wikipedia.org/wiki/Wells_Fargo_account_fraud_scandal
3. See https://www.nytimes.com/2022/06/06/business/wells-fargo-fake-job-interviews.html
4. See https://www.ibm.com/us-en/employment/
5. See https://www.glassdoor.com/blog/guide/a-guide-to-professionalism-in-the-workplace/
6. This is an ongoing intervention study we are conducting together with Florian Klonek and Sharon Parker from the Centre for Transformative Work Design, Curtin University, Perth, Australia.

References

Allport, G. W. (1942). The use of personal documents in psychological science. *Social Science Research Council Bulletin*, 49, xix, 210.

Andresen, L., Boud, D., and Cohen, R. (2000). Experience-based learning. In G. Foley (Ed.), *Understanding adult education and training* (pp. 207–219). Allen and Unwin. https://doi.org/10.1007/978-1-4419-1428-6_4046

Aquino, K., Lewis, M., and Bradfield, M. (1999). Justice constructs, negative affectivity, and employee deviance: A proposed model and empirical test. *Journal of Organizational Behavior, 20*(7), 1073–1091. http:// doi.org/10.1002/(SICI)1099-1379(199912)20:7%3C1073::AID-JOB943%3E3.0.CO;2-7/full

Ashforth, B. E., and Anand, V. (2003). The normalization of corruption in organizations. *Research in Organizational Behavior, 25*(03), 1–52. https://doi.org/10.1016/S0191-3085(03)25001-2

Ashforth, B. E., and Schinoff, B. S. (2016). Identity under construction: How individuals come to define themselves in organizations. *Annual Review of Organizational Psychology and Organizational Behavior, 3*(1), 111–137. https://doi.org/10.1146/annurev-orgpsych-041015-062322

Bakker, A. B., and Oerlemans, W. G. M. (2019). Daily job crafting and momentary work engagement: A self-determination and self-regulation perspective. *Journal of Vocational Behavior, 112*, 417–430. https://doi.org/10.1016/j.jvb.2018.12.005

Barrick, M. R., and Mount, M. K. (2012). Nature and use of personality in selection. In N. Schmitt (Ed.), *The Oxford handbook of personnel assessment and selection* (pp. 225–251). Oxford University Press.

Barrick, M. R., Mount, M. K., and Li, N. (2013). The theory of purposeful work behavior: The role of personality, higher-order goals, and job characteristics. *Academy of Management Review, 38*(1), 132–153. https://doi.org/10.5465/amr.2010.0479

Barrick, M. R., and Parks-Leduc, L. (2019). Selection for fit. *Annual Review of Organizational Psychology and Organizational Behavior, 6*, 171–193. https://doi.org/10.1146/annurev-orgpsych-012218-015028

Bolger, N., Davis, A., and Rafaeli, E. (2003). Diary methods: Capturing life as it is lived. *Annual Review of Psychology, 54*, 579–616. https://doi.org/10.1146/annurev.psych.54.101601.145030

Chao, G. T. (2012). Organizational socialization: Background, basics, and a blueprint for adjustment at work. In S. W. J. Kozlowski (Ed.), *The Oxford handbook of organizational psychology* (pp. 579–614). Oxford University Press. https://doi.org/10.1093/oxfordhb/9780199928309.013.0018

Cleveland, J. N. (2020). Context matters. In E. D. Pulakos and M. Battista (Eds.), *Performance management transformation: Lessons learned and next steps* (pp. 233–263). Oxford University Press.

Den Hartog, D. N. (2015). Ethical leadership. *Annual Review of Organizational Psychology and Organizational Behavior, 2*, 409–434. https://doi.org/10.1146/annurev-orgpsych-032414-111237

Ehrhart, M. G., Schneider, B., and Macey, W. H. (2017). *Organizational climate and culture: Research, theory and practice*. Routledge.

Fekjær, S. B., Petersson, O., and Thomassen, G. (2014). From legalist to Dirty Harry: Police recruits' attitudes towards non-legalistic police practice. *European Journal of Criminology, 11*(6), 745–759. https://doi.org/10.1177/1477370814525935

Feldman, D. C. (1981). The multiple socialization of organization members. *Academy of Management Review, 6*(2), 309–318. https://doi.org/10.5465/amr.1981.4287859

Flanagan, J. C. (1954). The critical incident technique. *Psychological Bulletin, 51*(4), 327–358. http://www.ncbi.nlm.nih.gov/pubmed/13177800

Flitter, E. (2020). The price of Wells-Fargo's fake accoount scandal grows by $3 billion. https://www.nytimes.com/2020/02/21/business/wells-fargo-settlement.html

Gelles, D. (2022). Jack Welch and the rise of CEO's behaving badly. https://www.nytimes.com/2022/05/21/business/jack-welch-ge-ceo-behavior.html

Griffin, M. A., Neal, A., and Parker, S. K. (2007). A new model of work role performance: Positive behavior in uncertain and interdependent contexts. *Academy of Management Journal, 50*(2), 327–347. https://doi.org/10.5465/AMJ.2007.24634438

Grus, C. L., Shen-Miller, D., Lease, S. H., Jacobs, S. C., Bodner, K. E., Van Sickle, K. S., . . . Kaslow, N. J. (2018). Professionalism: A competency cluster whose time has come. *Ethics and Behavior, 28*(6), 450–464. https://doi.org/10.1080/10508422.2017.1419133

Hackman, J. R. (1969). Toward understanding the role of tasks in behavioral research. *Acta Psychologica, 31*(2), 97–128. https://doi.org/10.1016/0001-6918(69)90073-0

Hackman, J. R., and Oldham, G. R. (1980). *Work redesign*. Addison-Wesley.

Hägler, M. (2021). Wie Ex-Audi-Chef Stadler sich vor Gericht verteidigt. https://www.sueddeutsche.de/wirtschaft/rupert-stadler-prozess-audi-diesel-1.5172451

Hogan, R., Kaiser, R. B., Sherman, R. A., and Harms, P. D. (2021). Twenty years on the dark side: Six lessons about bad leadership. *Consulting Psychology Journal: Practice and Research, 73*(3), 199–213. https://doi.org/10.1037/cpb0000205

Hong, Y., Liao, H., Jia, H., and Kaifeng, J. (2013). Missing link in the service profit chain: A meta-analytic review of the antecedents, consequences, and moderators of service climate. *Journal of Applied Psychology, 98*(2), 237–267. https://doi.org/10.1037/a0031666

Hough, L., and Dilchert, S. (2017). Personality: Its measurement and validity for employee selection. In J. Farr and N. T. Tippins (Eds.), *Handbook of employee selection* (pp. 298–325). Routledge.

Howard, A. (1995). *The changing nature of work*. San Francisco: Jossey-Bass.

Hunt, S. (1996). Generic work behavior: An investigation into the dimensions of entry level hourly job performance. *Personnel Psychology, 69*, 51–83. https://doi.org/10.1111/j.1744-6570.1996.tb01791.x

Ilgen, D. R., and Hollenbeck, J. R. (1991). The structure of work: Job designs and roles. In M. D. Dunnette and L. M. Hough (Eds.), *Handbook of industrial and organizational psychology* (vol. 2, pp. 165–207). Consulting Psychologists Press.

Jesuthasan, R., and Boudreau, J. (2022). *Work without jobs: How to reboot your organization's work operating system*. MIT Press.

Jones, N. A., Ross, H., Lynam, T., Perez, P., and Leitch, A. (2011). Mental models: An interdisciplinary synthesis of theory and methods. *Ecology and Society, 16*(1). https://doi.org/10.5751/ES-03802-160146

National Academies of Sciences, Engineering, and Medicine. (2022). *Police training to promote the rule of law and protect the population*. National Academies Press. https://doi.org/10.17226/26467

Nesbit, P. L. (2012). The Role of self-reflection, emotional management of feedback, and self-regulation processes in self-directed leadership development. *Human Resource Development Review, 11*(2), 203–226. https://doi.org/10.1177/1534484312439196

O'Boyle, E. H., Jr., Forsyth, D. R., Banks, G. C., and McDaniel, M. A. (2012). A meta-analysis of the Dark Triad and work behavior: A social exchange perspective. *Journal of Applied Psychology, 97*(3), 557–579. https://doi.org/10.1037/a0025679

Oh, I., Han, J. H., Holtz, B., Kim, Y. J., and Kim, S. (2018). Do birds of a feather flock, fly, and continue to fly together? The differential and cumulative effects of attraction, selection, and attrition on personality-based within-organization homogeneity and between-organization heterogeneity progression over time. *Journal of Organizational Behavior, 39*, 1349–1366. https://doi.org/10.1002/job.2304

Ones, D. S., and Viswesvaran, C. X. (2001). Integrity tests and other criterion-focused occupational personality scales (COPS) used in personnel selection. *International Journal of Selection and Assessment*, 9(1-2), 31-39. https://doi.org/10.1111/1468-2389.00161

Ones, D. S., Viswesvaran, C., and Schmidt, F. L. (2012). Integrity tests predict counterproductive work behaviors and job performance well: Comment on Van Iddekinge, Roth, Raymark, and Odle-Dusseau (2012). *Journal of Applied Psychology*, 97(3), 537-542. https://doi.org/10.1037/a0024825

Parker, S. K. (1998). Enhancing role breadth self-efficacy: The roles of job enrichment and other organizational interventions. *Journal of Applied Psychology*, 83(6), 835-852. https://doi.org/10.1037/0021-9010.83.6.835

Parker, S. K. (2000). From passive to proactive motivation: The importance of flexible role orientations and role breadth self-efficacy. *Applied Psychology: An International Review*, 49(3), 447-469. http://www.redi-bw.de/db/ebsco.php/search.ebscohost.com/login.aspx?direct=trueanddb=aphandAN=3460386andsite=ehost-live

Parker, S. K. (2014). Beyond motivation: Job and work design for development, health, ambidexterity, and more. *Annual Review of Psychology*, 65, 661-691. https://doi.org/10.1146/annurev-psych-010213-115208

Parker, S. K., Andrei, D. M., and Van den Broeck, A. (2019). Poor work design begets poor work design: Capacity and willingness antecedents of individual work design behavior. *Journal of Applied Psychology*, 104(7), 907-928. https://doi.org/10.1037/apl0000383

Pfeffer, J. (2005). Changing mental models: HR's most important task. *Human Resource Management*, 44(2), 123-128. https://doi.org/10.1002/hrm.20053

Pulakos, E. D., and Battista, M. (Eds.). (2020). *Performance management transformation: Lessons learned and next steps*. Oxford University Press.

Rousseau, D. (2006). Is there such a thing as "evidence- based management"? *Academy of Management Review*, 31(2), 256-269. https://doi.org/10.5465/amr.2006.20208679

Ryan, R. M., and Deci, E. L. (2003). On assimilating identities to the self: A self-determination theory perspective on internalization and integrity within cultures. In M. R. Leary and J. P. Tangney (Eds.), *Handbook of self and identity* (pp. 253-272). Guilford Press.

Schaufeli, W. B., and Bakker, A. B. (2010). Defining and measuring work engagement: Bringing clarity to the concept. In A. B. Bakker and M. P. Leiter (Eds.), *Work engagement: A handbook of essential theory and research* (pp. 10-24). Psychology Press.

Schein, E. (2010). *Organizational culture and leadership*. Vol. 2. John Wiley and Sons.

Schneider, B. (1987). The people make the place. *Personnel Psychology*, 40, 437-453. https://doi.org/10.1111/j.1744-6570.1987.tb00609.x

Schneider, B., and Bartram, D. (2017). Aggregate personality and organizational competitive advantage. *Journal of Occupational and Organizational Psychology*, 90, 461-480. http://dx.doi.org/10.1111/joop.12180

Schneider, B., Godfrey, E., Hayes, S., Huang, M., Lim, B. C., Raver, J. R., and Ziegert, J. (2003). The human side of strategy: Employee experiences of strategic alignment in a service organization. *Organizational Dynamics*, 32, 122-141.

Voegtlin, C. (2012). Development of a scale measuring discursive responsible leadership. *Responsible Leadership*, 98(1), 57-73. https://doi.org/10.1007/s10551-011-1020-9

11

Beyond the Theory

Adaptive Workforce Planning Approaches That Are Business-Led

Adam McKinnon and Kanella Salapatas

Kanella Salapatas and Adam McKinnon, like many professionals in recent years, first met over Zoom in 2020—Kanella joining the meeting from Melbourne, Australia, while Adam was in Bucharest, Romania. Since that time the duo have had the opportunity to work together and collaborate on several people analytic initiatives as peers, friends, and fellow pragmatists. Kanella is currently the Group Head of People Analytics for QBE and has worked for other large financial institutions in Australia. Adam currently leads the People Analytics Capability at Reece Group and has previously worked for several multinational organizations in both Europe and the United States. Both are based in Melbourne, Australia.

This chapter comprises two unique stories written from the professional experiences and perspectives of Kanella (a journey into repeatable and sustainable strategic workforce planning [SWP]) and Adam (a novel approach to SWP—informing mergers and acquisitions). The project stories are notably different in terms of:

- Time frames in which they were performed and the business objectives they supported. It is important to note that SWP can support in-year activities and outcomes while also delivering longer-term results—for which SWP is better known.
- SWP can comprise a multitude of different datasets and methods which, when effectively used, can result in significant benefits to both employees and employer. Irrespective, the human change component, best exemplified in Kanella's story, is crucial for maximum benefit.

- Existing processes can be utilized to jump-start and accelerate the use of SWP and ultimately result in embedding it as part of the regular business planning cycle.

What is consistent across both stories is the criticality of the data and insights derived through analytics to inform SWP that drives business outcomes.

A Journey into Repeatable and Sustainable SWP

By Kanella Salapatas

SWP involves aligning an organization's workforce changes with its business goals and objectives to ensure the organization has the right employees with the necessary skills in place to achieve success and mitigate future risks. Although discussed across the organization and recognized as important, in late 2021, the organizational momentum was amplified with a new executive joining who had prior experience with SWP. As a result, SWP was included in the global organizational strategy as a must-do program with a commitment to evaluate its feasibility and benefits.

The organization's journey to implement SWP was understood to be a multiyear undertaking. With a global presence in 34 countries and varying business needs, choosing the right approach was crucial. It was also important to partner with an area of the business that recognized SWP as a critical component to creating a competitive advantage and was willing to invest resources and time in design and implementation. At this point, the organizational approach to planning was predominately a financial process focused on headcount and cost, with human resources (HR) being considered only in the final outcomes. The process lacked consideration of HR metrics and impacts when forecasting workforce demands for the business.

Recognizing the importance of SWP first came from the European and Asian continents. The CEO and CPO of the organization in question were aware of their workforce challenges and the need for better management. They also recognized the future strategy's need for an augmented workforce and the ability to plan years ahead. The CEO and CPO agreed to focus on delivering results quickly by partnering and creating a minimum viable product (MVP) to prove its value.

Jointly sponsored by Finance and HR, the MVP's goal was to replace and enhance the current financial planning process. This would be achieved by transitioning the financial planning to a new tool, adding HR metrics to the process, and involving the HR team in both the planning and actioning of information about workforce movements. The new approach would allow for workforce modeling and real-time assessment of the impact on HR metrics during planning.

Structuring the Team

A project team was established centrally to define the MVP's parameters, including technology, vendors, and stakeholders. The organization partnered with a consultancy firm for guidance and support while also utilizing internal resources to create a "workforce planning squad." The squad consisted of the group head of SWP and organizational design, a program manager, a technology lead, a change and communications lead, and a product owner who would oversee the technology and operation in a business-as-usual capacity. The goal was to balance local needs while delivering a scalable solution. The squad served as the central team to lead the business through the MVP.

Discovery and Framing the Opportunity

The project team partnered with European and Asian stakeholders and conducted discovery sessions to understand the current challenges that SWP could solve and determine the MVP's success measures. The discovery sessions involved business subject matter experts from Finance (Finance Financial Planning and Analysis [FP&A], Business Partnering) and HR (HR Business Partners, HR Data Analytics).

The first key observation was that although financial planning was a well-established, recurring activity with business involvement, it was only focused on headcount and cost planning. Improving this process and considering its impact on people would bring crucial HR dimensions to the forefront of consideration within an established process. The first opportunity was to embed critical HR metrics for impact and visibility and move to the first step on our multiyear maturity model, one focusing on connecting the people and finance planning processes (Figure 11.1).

The discovery process also revealed that financial processes were disconnected from HR systems. Changes to workforce plans were therefore not

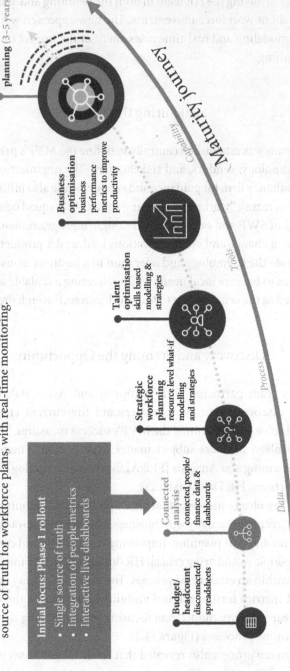

Figure 11.1 What needs to change? Our initial focus is to connect our disconnected data and processes to create a single source of truth for workforce plans, with real-time monitoring.

reflected in the human capital management (HCM) system. This disconnection caused numerous challenges, identified as pain points by business SMEs during planning:

- Lots of manual, high-effort checks were necessary for data accuracy and the validation of a plan.
- The current process was completed using Excel and was only uploaded into a finance system when finalized.
- Core HCM data did not match the approved plans, making it difficult to measure deviations and understand the reasons for them.
- There was an inability to determine an accurate total employee cost at an employee level.
- Finance users did not have access to actual worker-level details for accurate planning (i.e., worker salaries, existing vacancies).
- Financial planning focused only on headcount and cost and did not take into account the impact on people of issues such as diversity, retention of high performers, and capability.

The goal was for the new planning tool to address the pain points by automating manual checks, integrating systems, and providing access to HR data and metrics. It would also allow consideration of people impacts in financial planning, thus enabling informed decision-making. The implementation of this technology was the key solution to improving the existing financial planning process and delivering an MVP that would improve the way we delivered business-critical processes.

Key opportunities detailed are as follows:

- *Process enhancement*
  o Reduce manual effort associated with the maintenance of multiple systems and establish a systematic process to conduct variance analysis at a granular level linked to source changes (HCM).
  o Establish one source of truth to perform planning.
- *Data quality*
  o Automate integration between core HCM and planning tools to remove manual handling of data.
  o Incentivize managers to maintain data in HCM through utilizing planning data directly from the source system.

- Identify core HCM data that must be cleansed as part of the program and define integrations for sustainable maintenance (i.e., cost center hierarchies and manager hierarchies).
- *Improve user experience*
  - Deliver user-friendly self-service dashboards with metrics that will support business users as part of the annual budgeting and reforecasting processes.
  - Provide additional reports to managers, Finance, and HR to enable continuous and efficient monitoring of the plan.
  - Provide Finance business partners with the ability to view worker-level salaries.
  - Develop a security model that restricts access to only those parts of the business the planner is accountable for.
- *Workforce planning*
  - Enable business to better control workforce spending and assist in making informed decisions backed by data.
  - Set foundations to enable HR to model workforce requirements for longer-term business goals and different scenario modeling.
  - Create the ability to measure against HR metrics (e.g., diversity and inclusion) and future data, such as skills.

Having HR lead a redesign of the financial planning process is unconventional but can be effective with strong collaboration and trust between departments and clear sponsorship from both the CPO and CFO.

Challenges and Lessons Learned

Our goals for delivery and achievement were well-defined, but we encountered some obstacles along the way:

- *Replacing versus creating a new process.* Revising an established process within an organization is quite different from introducing a completely new one. Existing processes come with a history of technological difficulties and procedures that need to be understood. In the case of financial processes, a set methodology existed for calculating costs and making assumptions to produce financial forecasts as accurately as possible. With access to more employee data, we were able to

challenge the current assumptions and calculations and propose more precise calculations at the individual level. For instance, Finance previously calculated costs for training, bonuses, etc. at an overall level and allocated a sum to a cost center. However, we were able to break down these costs to the individual employee level. Improving cost calculations will remain a priority for us, with the goal of creating a more accurate total employee cost for use in planning, reforecasting, and scenario modeling.
- *Beginning with financial planning.* Financial planning is crucial in all organizations. The transfer of a vital financial process and technology ownership from Finance to HR elevated the significance of the HCM system and necessitated an evaluation of all maintenance procedures (such as release management and blackout periods) and the disaster recovery plan.
- *Data cleaning: Do it or be prepared to search for dirty data.* Preserving data quality is crucial for ensuring the usefulness of data in SWP. Having an accurate list of employees and information about their role, cost, location, performance outcome, and whether they are a flight risk or have high potential will help articulate the organization's current state and enhance the accuracy of planning. Data quality and accuracy can be a barrier for many organizations but should never be the reason to not commence SWP. Data cleansing is unavoidable, and the momentum of an organization to start SWP will be a catalyst for overall quality improvements. Given the inclusion of Finance data, data cleansing also extended beyond just HR and required multiple data sources to be considered.
- Several techniques can be used to improve the usefulness of data, including identifying and correcting errors, standardizing values, creating alerts at entry to flag the end user when incorrect data are entered, and creating audit reports that can be run for critical data checks and corrections ahead of planning kick-off.
- SWP doesn't need all data at once and can gradually be enriched over time with new data points if the task is too daunting at the start.
- *Hierarchies.* The biggest downstream impact was created by changing planning from a cost center view to a supervisory organization hierarchy. The decision was made early in the MVP process to allow for a connection to HR metrics. The change was necessary but underestimated. All costs that were allocated into cost centers needed

to be redesigned into a supervisory organizational hierarchy, which required us to ingest raw payroll and build costs from bottom up. This change required replicating the mapping of payroll data into expenses and building integrations to automate the process moving forward.
- *Waterfall versus agile versus prototyping approach.* The project initially used a waterfall approach for technology implementation but switched to an agile approach with multiple iterations of prototyping, feedback, building, and testing. The end users, especially Finance, were more suited to experiencing a smaller part of the functionality and providing feedback. This required a project plan redesign and adjustment to timelines. Testing duration was condensed, and a more fluid stakeholder engagement approach was created with check-ins and walkthroughs of the design. These meetings became working meetings where the solution was adjusted in real time, leading to a faster build and test process and a sense of co-development and ownership, which resulted in confident sign-off and better understanding of the platform.

Achievements and Next Steps

We had initially planned to deliver a workable solution using the MVP version for our annual planning process. With adjustments to our solution and delayed milestones we moved to deliver a month late. Instead of a go-live, we engaged parts of the business to perform parallel runs of their annual planning cycle, which required the planners to double-key the plan in our system to validate accuracy and sign-off.

The Finance team signed off with plans to go live for the next year's reforecasting and planning cycle, allowing time to fine-tune the solution and stabilize the operating model.

Other parts of the business showed interest in future implementation and discovery. The ultimate goal is to adopt a uniform foundational approach in financial planning that takes into account the impact of people, with a global playbook serving as the guide for the system's capabilities and methodology. In the future, the emphasis will shift toward resource-level modeling, talent optimization strategies, with the objective to elevate SWP maturity across all business areas through increased insights and functionality.

A Novel Approach to SWP: Informing Mergers and Acquisitions

By Adam McKinnon

In 2020, I sat down with the Chief Strategy Officer (CSO) of a European multinational organization—a company at the time of 57,000 employees in 66 different countries. The CSO quickly got to the point, stating: "I need your help finding a specialist to head up a new business we're looking to establish in Plant Photonics. The opportunity is ripe—so we need to get started as soon as possible. Could you help me identify a possible business leader from among the employee population within the next week?"

I knew this to be a challenge. The company had no centralized repository of employee skill data and was currently aggregating subject matter expertise through a centralized, opt-in repository that experienced low employee participation. I responded candidly, "I honestly don't know. I can certainly reach out to some contacts and look at the different datasets available internally, but I'm not 100% certain that I can find someone with the precise skillset that you're looking for."

The CSO considered this for a moment and asked "What about externally? Can you find me someone from outside the company?" I was relieved to hear the question, replying, "definitely—I can give you a detailed shortlist of specialists by close-of-business tomorrow." Upon hearing this the CSO smiled and asked: "How is it though that you can't find me someone from our global employee population of 57,000, but you can provide me a list of people in 24 hours among a global population of approximately 8 billion people?" Having considered this problem intensively over recent months, I answered instantly: "It's all down to the quality of data at my disposal."

This anecdote illustrates a common problem among companies of all sizes—most organizations are unaware of the full range of talent (i.e., skills and capabilities) residing within their employee population. Perhaps the bigger problems include:

- Limited focus on data that HR organizations have held, which has impacted the quality of data they have curated over time.
- Limited expertise resident in HR organizations to extract full value from the disparate data sources (think engineering, analytics, and interpretation).

These challenges have limited the opportunity for HR leaders to lead with data and insights. The remainder of this chapter explores a practical case study of using publicly available data, coupled with advanced analytic methods, to inform the decisions made within the context of a company merger. In addition, some practical insights and future directions for practitioners are proposed.

Using Strategic Workforce Data to Inform Company Acquisitions

Company acquisitions occur from a variety of motivations—realizing performance synergies such as reduced costs, improved margins, and cash flow; generating economies of scale; rapidly acquiring and growing market share (i.e., eliminating competition); accelerating development or access for the target's products; acquiring technologies faster or at lower cost than can be developed; or transforming one or both companies. Irrespective, most motives gravitate toward financial, product, or market factors, which has resulted in an underdevelopment of practice surrounding employee due diligence (during acquisition) and strategic integration practices (post deal).

The following sections focus on the use of open-source data, coupled with network analysis, to inform merger and acquisition (M&A) activities preclose and integration post deal.

External Data Informing Internal Decisions

In 2019, I had the good fortune to support HR colleagues leading the employee integration component of a company acquisition. In the 6 months prior to closure of the deal, the HR colleagues from the acquiring company were unable to access employee data from the acquired company, which was US based. US antitrust regulations require that acquiring companies who are competitors not have access to sensitive information prior to close of the deal. Consequently, HR colleagues from the acquiring company were limited to manually trawling public data sources such as LinkedIn to learn detailed information about the new employee population they would need to integrate.

The company being acquired was a technology company and was being acquired for its intellectual property (IP), specifically acquiring technologies (and market share) faster than could be developed. Due to the technological heritage of the acquisition company, my proposal was to use an unorthodox, publicly available dataset that indirectly related to employees and analyze the data using social network analysis. The dataset was patent data.

Why Patent Data?

Patent data was proposed for the following reasons:

- The data is freely accessible to the public across multiple international jurisdictions (e.g., United States Patent and Trademark Office, European Patent Office, Japan Patent Office, etc.) and is often aggregated by third-party data resellers. Consequently, the availability of data can expedite analysis. The key benefits of open-source data are:
  o There are no privacy concerns associated with the use of the data—its public. Therefore, no consent is required, which expedites the analysis and removes any legal liability associated with the data.
  o Open data is readily available—no consent, minimal to no cost, no time-consuming collection processes. Collectively these characteristics mean it is quicker to obtain the data and analyze it, thus significantly reducing the time to insights.
- Each patent lists the inventor(s). Many companies financially incentivize inventors to file patents (i.e., reward inventors and pay for the patent filing process). Therefore, when companies file patents, the inventor(s) often represent employees or contractors. Patents can therefore identify current (and former) employees and provide insight into their historical IP generation and the individuals they have collaborated with over time. In addition, collaboration patterns provided a greater understanding of the social fabric of the scientific community within the acquired company—specifically social influence, communication flows, and communities of practice. Such insights can inform retention contracts during mergers, future leadership roles, and change management practices.
- Patents list the many technologies associated with the patent, which can in turn characterize the inventors. By analyzing patents filed by both the acquiring and acquired companies, an understanding of both common and unique technologies was identified. Furthermore, the individuals

associated with common technologies could be systematically brought together in working teams to facilitate knowledge sharing and next-generation innovation.

Practitioner Tip!

There are more data available today than at any other time in history (I expect this comment to remain timelessly true)! The academic model unfortunately prioritizes the study of analytic methods. Learn to prioritize ongoing self-education in both *data* and *methods*. A comprehensive understanding of available data sources (both internal and external) can greatly expand what practitioners can do (i.e., questions asked, hypotheses generated and tested, analytic methods employed, and speed to insight—among others). Greater appreciation for data will greatly enhance the ability for HR functions to lead through data and insight.

Practitioner Tip!

Consider open-source datasets, both free and paid, when performing analyses. Data providers sometimes curate the quality of the data they collect, which can save analysts significant amounts of time and subsequently reduce the time to insight!

The data used in this analysis was obtained from a paid data subscription. Consequently, the quality of the data was high, aggregated from all global patent offices (i.e., comprehensive) and therefore enabled immediate analysis. I had proposed that network analysis be used to analyze the data and generate insights that exceed traditional descriptive methods.

What Is Social Network Analysis, and Why Use it?

Social network analysis is the process of studying the relationships and connections between individuals or groups in a social network. Social network analysis can include looking at who is connected to whom, how often individuals communicate, and the strength of connection. This information can be used to understand patterns of past behavior, identify key individuals in a social environment, and predict how information or ideas might spread through a group in the future. The integration has specific questions to address, including the following:

- *Which colleagues (i.e., employees and/or contractors) had generated the most intellectual property in previous years?* The analysis of patent data immediately shed light on those who had been important scientific contributors to the organization over time and therefore likely to be future contributors. This insight, coupled with insights regarding social influence and expertise (see below), helped prioritize use of available money for retention contracts.
- *How socially influential were inventors?* Very few of the patents filled by the acquired company had only one inventor listed—generally multiple individuals were listed. Social network analysis enabled quantifying the social influence of scientists. Social influence provided insight into who should be considered for leadership roles, current or future, from the acquired entity.
- *Social influence also identified who were the communication amplifiers in the scientific community.* Network analytics allowed us to quantify how critical to the flow of information through the network each inventor was (i.e., called *betweenness centrality*). On a practical level, it showed who should be engaged with on a personal level to amplify messaging within the scientific employee community during integration. Moreover, quantifying the social reach of inventors allowed the identification of an optimal group of scientists (i.e., the smallest group size of most socially influential) who could be engaged with to seed certain messages and maximize proliferation of communication throughout the network.

Figure 11.2 is a visual representation of a social network. Each circle in the network is known as a *node* and is representative of a scientist employed by the acquired company. It is important to collectively consider three node characteristics when interpreting the network visualization.

- *Size*: Nodes were sized according to the number of times a scientist was listed on a patent. Smaller nodes represent fewer patents generated by

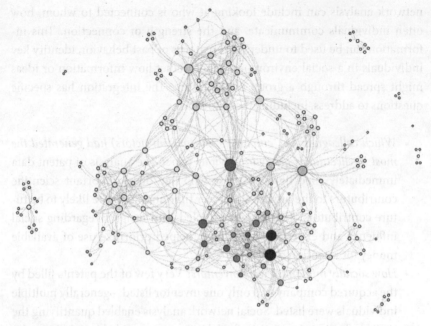

Figure 11.2 A social network analysis of inventors listed on patents. This information could be used to understand social dynamics within the scientific community of the acquired company and prompt further data collection in open-source platforms such as LinkedIn.

- the scientist, while larger nodes are indicative of scientists whose names were present on many patents.
- *Position*: Nodes closer to the center of the network are generally representative of more social influence and are considered more important to the flow of information across the network.
- *Color*: Node color is indicative of a network metric called *eigenvector centrality*, which is a network measure of social influence. In this example, eigenvector centrality scores ranges from low social influence (grey) through to high social influence (darker color).
- Color representation is not displayed in Figure 11.2 but is normally included in data visualization.

In addition to studying social dynamics, the patent data also enabled systematic identification of those scientific domains and technologies in which scientists were considered expert. By analyzing the International Patent Classification (IPC) codes and the technologies listed on patents from both companies, the HR integration team was able to supplement organizational design questions through data and insights. Specifically, the HR colleagues were able to identify which individuals or teams should be brought together to actively collaborate and synergize in the future (see Figure 11.3).

The patent data utilized in this analysis represented an imperfect representation of the scientific community in the acquired company. However, answering the above questions informed an understanding of which employees would be considered critical to retain. When the insights generated were complemented by LinkedIn data, it removed some of the uncertainty associated with the merging of two employee populations and enabled planning. Furthermore, it is important to note the unexpected accuracy of the data. The analyses, performed 6 months prior to closure of the acquisition, identified several socially influential and intellectually prolific scientists in the acquired company (i.e., high-value employees), one of whom was promoted to lead the merged R&D organizations.

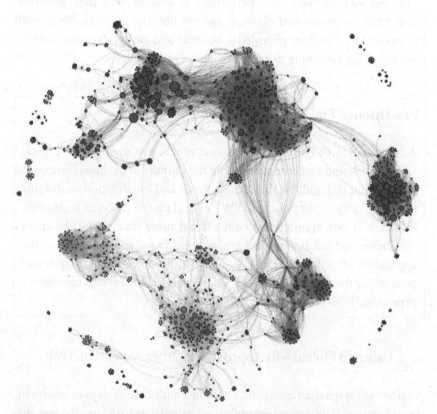

Figure 11.3 Network analysis of IPC codes to identify domains and technologies unique to each company; blue nodes (would be color coded and presented) to highlight the technologies consistent across both companies.

In short, there are no perfect datasets. However, any data, when properly analyzed, that reduces uncertainty and risk at such a strategic level has value to both organizations and employees.

Tools of the Trade

Several tools are beneficial in the analysis of open-source data such as patent data. In this project, the tool OpenRefine, open-sourced by Google, was used to perform data wrangling. This was particularly valuable for performing advanced methods, such as fuzzy matches (i.e., matching name variations—full name with surname and first initial) in a graphical user interface (GUI) that recorded steps and could be readily replicated by staff who did not possess expert knowledge.

The network analyses were performed in another GUI tool, Kenelyze. While many open-sourced network analysis libraries are available in both Python and R, Kenelyze provided a no-code and easily accessible tool for team members beginning their journey in network analysis.

Practitioner Tip!

A combination of PowerPoint and Beautiful.ai was used for the critical act of visualizing and communicating the outputs in business forums. It is important to highlight that the synthesis and presentation of insights remains a critical component of SWP and all people analytics endeavors. In fact, it is our opinion that equal, if not more time should be spent visualizing and practicing "pitching" insights to stakeholders than on the application of analytic methods. Effective communication of insights and positioning the subsequent call to action is critical to moving from theory to practical business benefit.

Using an Outside-In Approach in Other Aspects of SWP

A variety of external datasets can be used in a multitude of ways to inform internal practices. The current example used patent data to inform the merging of two scientific communities. However, a variety of different SWP-related activities can be performed with external data, including:

- *Strategy inferencing/acquisition selection*: Infer the future strategic direction that competitors are looking to move. This understanding can be further informed through publicly available documentation, such as annual reports, regulatory reporting, or press releases. The following questions can be addressed by studying the recruitment activity (i.e., jobs ads) and employee populations within competitor organizations:
  o What does the current skill make-up of their employee base tell us about their strategy and performance ambitions?
  o What does the current rate of skill attainment suggest about the timing of competitor ambitions? What is the likelihood of the company realizing their strategy?
  o Does the competitor strategy impact the likelihood of realizing our own strategy?
  o How do we distinguish ourselves from competitors when competing for employees and skills?
  o Which competitors, if acquired, provide the greatest acquisition of employee skills
    - in which we are underdeveloped?
    - to establish market authority?
    - that insulate intellectual property from external threat?
- *Site selection*: Perform due diligence to inform the identification and selection of geographies to establish new organizational sites or to relocate existing sites. Questions to be addressed include:
  o Which geographies are considered most favorable to existing staff?
  o What do cost of living and other livability metrics (e.g., housing, transport, education, health, safety, etc.) infer about the possible venues?
  o Which geographies afford greatest access to appropriately skilled candidates to realize business aspirations? Where does an organization experience less competition for skills required in the future?
- *Strategic workforce plans*: Connect external market data with internal data and insights to determine:
  o Whether business lines, services, and geographies have the talent supply and requisite skills to support business performance?
  o To the extent that internally cultivating skills is considered a viable option, to which external/internal learning resources and on-the-job opportunities should staff be connected?

- o Which employee skills are at risk of potential automation? How can employees acquire new, future-ready skills that leverage their current skills?
- o Can we quantify the expense (i.e., market price) associated with skills and in turn forecast future workforce costs?
- o What do workforce plans mean in a practical sense for operational HR teams that deal in volume activities, such as talent acquisition, leadership development, global relocation, and training and development?

While this list of questions is not exhaustive, it does illustrate the practical insight and utility afforded by external datasets when addressing workforce topics at strategic business levels and tying those insights back to current practices.

Conclusion

The chapter presents two successful cases of SWP that delivered tangible business results. Despite their differences, the examples demonstrated practical applications and positive outcomes that can be achieved. Key insights from the case studies discussed in the chapter include:

- *Real-world application*: The examples showcased the practical implementation and successful outcomes of SWP. SWP can inform both short- and longer-term business objectives. The critical requirement is to inform decision-making at scale through a comprehensive range of considerations, thereby embodying the term "strategic." The key is to ensure you are responding to a definitive business need.
- *Embed SWP into existing processes*: Embedding SWP into existing processes can generate instant momentum and help ensure sustained application, thereby driving better outcomes for the organization. Integrating SWP into day-to-day operations can ensure that workforce planning considerations become a routine part of decision-making processes for the organization. This can lead to a more integrated and effective approach to workforce planning and yield greater alignment between workforce planning and business goals.
- *Pragmatism driving innovation*: A strong focus on business challenges can lead to unconventional solutions that generate clear business and

employee benefits. While these solutions may not be rooted in traditional theories or practices, a focus on pragmatism can be the catalyst for adopting solutions that reduce risk and uncertainty and thereby improve organizational decision-making quality.

- *Data are critical to future HR success*: It is our position that HR functions will need to manage two critical resources—(1) people and (2) data—to achieve future success. While the HR function is historically stereotyped by "people" people, that is now changing. HR will require specialist skills in the future to architect disparate technologies in a manner that drives positive employee experiences at scale. In addition, HR practitioners will require a minimal standard of data literacy to make optimal use of available technologies and drive evidence-based decisions.

12
The X-Factor in Strategic Workforce Planning
For CEOs, Context Is King

David Reimer and Adam Bryant

Strategic workforce planning (SWP) is a specialized sport, a fact that represents both the greatest strength and also the vulnerability of the profession. The depth of planners' knowledge and their skillset means they get to add value and help shape and drive C-suite discussions that are central to the long-term prosperity of the organization. But, as with any deep expertise, SWP specialists may also be met with skepticism when they walk into a room of operations and finance executives. Leadership teams, and CEOs in particular, are not specialists, and so they may be skeptical—fairly or unfairly—that any specialist-generated plan can fully account for the complex realities of the business.

The challenge for the specialist is to drive the right conversations with or among business leaders to ensure that the resulting plan is *not the specialist's plan, but the leader's plan.* This is particularly important for CEO buy-in and requisite support. The best SWP conversations inform both sides of the table, helping each stakeholder clarify the problem set that they must solve together. Where such discussions in the past rested to a great deal on expertise—some version of the 2000's mantra, "content is king"—content is now table stakes. The differentiating factor for CEOs today is context. *Can I have confidence that the expert on the other side of the table has the ability to fully understand and adapt to my organization's specific challenges?*

The goal of this chapter is to provide a how-to guide for meeting the CEO where he or she is—and learn how to extract and integrate some of their thinking and assumptions into the resulting plan. This helps to ensure that everyone is aligned on the goals, challenges, and strategy in the broader

---

David Reimer and Adam Bryant, *The X-Factor in Strategic Workforce Planning* In: *Strategic Workforce Planning.*
Edited by: Marc Sokol and Beverly Tarulli, Oxford University Press.
© Society for Industrial and Organizational Psychology 2024. DOI: 10.1093/oso/9780197759745.003.0013

contextual landscape. That is the first step in building a successful and productive relationship between the executive team and the SWP function.

This step requires an up-front acknowledgment of fundamental changes in the macro environment. As Shawn Layden and Jeanette Gorgas (former Chairman of Sony Playstation Worldwide Studios, and former private equity Chief Strategy Officer and Chief Human Resources Officer [CHRO], respectively) wrote in 2021, "For most of the past two decades, organizations continued to use their industrial strategic planning, forecasting and analytical tools of the prior era. [For leaders], the 21st century began in earnest in February 2020."

Against this new, truly 21st-century backdrop, fundamental assumptions—particular Western assumptions—about stability and predictability have shifted. Globalism and the march of democracy via market forces are not "givens." Broad collaboration between economic systems cannot be taken for granted. The role of the CEO is more complex than just delivering for shareholders—in the 21st century, everyone is a stakeholder.

In the fact of such complexity, this chapter's framework and question-sets should be taken as directional guides for the SWP professional to adapt to his or her operating reality, not a literal playbook to be replayed in any and every organizational setting. Even when a part of the SWP process is to simplify complexity, it's crucial to attempt to grasp how that complexity manifests in each organization's and each leadership team's context.

To help emphasize this variability, we present three different, real-world case studies in which the CEO and the company faced unique challenges both inside and outside their companies. Each CEO brought a different level of openness to and understanding of SWP to the conditions they were trying to navigate. After setting up those cases, we share the practical and actionable playbook that we have refined in our consulting work over more than two decades and many shifts in the macro environment. We conclude with how each of those three case-study companies successfully generated insights and turned them into action.

Before we share those examples, it's worth noting that case studies tend to look neat and tidy in hindsight—as if the right moves were preordained and obvious from the start. But what we know from military history is also true for business—that the most successful battles are often extremely messy on the ground, hour to hour. Plans and strategies that make perfect sense in theory often have to be torn up early in the process. Strategic workforce planners know this. CEOs, however, don't always recognize it. Because the chief executive role is focused on future performance and strategy, it is understandable that new CEOs, especially, will be very clear on the desired state while also displaying limited patience for the "how" of getting there. An important part of the entire SWP CEO management process is figuring out the right cadence for refreshing the plan as organizations encounter the situational realities that come at the leadership team from all sides over time.

The Problem of Access: Two Obstacles and Tapping into Urgency

The problem of access, what we think of as coming down to two obstacles and tapping into urgency, is that SWP professionals do not always get direct access to the top leader in the normal course of their work. Therefore, let's take a moment to diagnose the "why" of this up front, based on our CEO interviews. The net outcome is that SWP professionals may often have to work through proxies—again, it may be easiest to think of this at the outset as a project reality. However, one of the goals of this framework is to embed questions within your diagnostic approach that will raise the profile of SWP within and up to the very top of the organization.

In our experience, SWP is underappreciated as a leadership discipline by CEOs and their top lieutenants for a few reasons. First, they may understand its importance intellectually, but they often think of it as downstream work carried out layers below them in the organization, more of a key function to keep everything moving but not really something for them to take on. Given the opportunity to sit a CEO down and help them start connecting the dots, they likely will recognize that SWP is a direct path toward delivering on the commitments of the strategy. They will understand that it is intimately tied to how decisions are made in the organization, how capital is allocated, how incentive and total rewards are structured, and how culture integrates and retains critical talent and divergent points of view. Ultimately, in the new world of stakeholder capitalism, this means that effective or ineffective SWP is going to impact almost every stakeholder that a CEO must manage.

Second, the art of the challenge for strategic workforce planners may stem from a simple branding problem. "Strategic workforce planning" can sound like an academic function to those not already in the know. CEOs are battered daily by thousands of variables that are vying for their attention. The way to focus a CEO's attention is through asking a handful of succinct, clear questions that strike at the heart of their job—to be effective stewards of the company's near-term financial performance and long-term strategic viability.

A useful comparison for SWP professionals lies within the finance department. There, whoever holds the financial planning and analysis (FP&A) role is highly visible to the entire C-suite and sometimes to the board during every budget cycle. FP&A personnel must overtly link financial planning and capital allocation to the company's strategy—which in turn is likely to significantly impact executives' compensation. Even though executive compensation lies completely outside the purview of FP&A, the underlying connection between these conversations and the impact to "me" is readily apparent to the C-suite and CEO.

For SWP, that link is not always as clear. Further, in their attempts to occupy a similar chair as FP&A personnel, SWP professionals can sometimes hamstring themselves by using a specialized vocabulary. While the intent is to drive specificity (and perhaps to demonstrate professionalism in the field), the net effect is to drive a wedge into those conversations. What CEOs need is for somebody to speak the language of the strategy and performance metrics of the organization and come to them with smart *business* questions. Strategic workforce planners need to meet CEOs where they are.

Borrow a lesson from supply chain, where advisors often struggled to have a voice at the table in the 20th-century world of relative stability. As Ernest Nicolas, the Chief Supply Chain Officer for HP Inc. has noted, that conversation shifted not merely due to external conditions, but due to the best supply chain professionals' ability to tap leaders' anxieties about those conditions in a calm and productive manner. "The combination of planning for complexity and operationalizing empathy," Nicolas (2023) wrote, "are muscles that every leader must bring to bear now. This is more than just being lean and it's more than just being agile. It becomes a way of constantly scanning the horizon and the organization for factors that could impact the way we source, build, and deliver".

Real-World Cases and Context

Our insights are based on experience. In our consulting work at The ExCo Group, we have worked side-by-side with hundreds of leaders since 2010 as they have driven organizational transformation. Our dataset also includes insights based on in-depth interviews with thousands of leaders in hundreds of companies. We've seen positive and negative versions of the CEO's attention to SWP. In the best cases, human resources (HR) personnel and strategic workforce planners are not only at the table, but they also are integral to discussions about the entire business: how the transformation will succeed, what must change, what must stay the same, what structural and talent moves will be required to not just keep the gears turning but to also help the company move further faster. There should be no separation between the business conversation and the strategic workforce plan discussion.

In cases with poor outcomes, the CEO and the top financial and operational leaders define an exciting vision, align on how they'll share that narrative with the market, and then turn to HR to figure out how to implement their bold vision. Structure, talent sourcing, resource deployment, and impacts on employees thus become a kind of afterthought. Predictably, that approach often ends with underperformance if not outright failure of the strategy, as well as significant cash and time lost for the organization. More pointedly, such an approach can prematurely end a CEO's tenure. But no SWP professional has the luxury (or the arrogance) to tell a CEO, "If you ignore my advice, it will likely shorten your time in the role."

The question becomes, "How do I engage the right level of attention?" The following three case studies are intended to bring to life three different challenges that organizations and the SWP professionals within them faced, and to provide insights that may help inform smart CEO question-sets in other contexts.

Case Study 1

A global manufacturing business had long pursued a strategy based on scaling through inorganic growth, with a foundational belief that a bigger footprint would inevitably lead to success. The strategy played well with investors and banks and provided a good run for the charismatic CEO who developed it—until it didn't. The promised cash bonanza from his investments failed to materialize over a 7-year period, and the board terminated his contract. The incoming CEO, a trained economist who had been with the company for a decade, faced two fundamental crises in the organization she now led.

The first was purely financial. The performance metrics of the organization were weak compared to competitors. The company had burned cash, accumulated debt, and failed to integrate all its acquisitions into a single operating platform. To manage the diverse businesses that it was running across 26 countries, the company required a sprawling infrastructure with several thousand people at headquarters, not to mention country-level headquarters in each of its major geographies. This added an overhead administrative cost that further dampened profitability and weakened cash flow. As one board member had said to the CEO shortly after she accepted the job, if the debt structure of the company weren't so complex, they would be breaking up the business and selling it for its component pieces.

The second challenge was more strategic. A trained economist, she was a broad thinker and reader and was concerned about the company's contribution to global warming. This was not simple altruism. The organization's legacy business made it one of the top carbon dioxide polluters on the planet. No one had attacked them publicly for this fact just yet, but she understood that it was only a matter of time before companies in her industry faced growing societal and regulatory pressures to change. She felt that meant her organization could be a laggard (or worse, a villain) or else could be the change leader in the global sector. For her, this created both a moral and an economic imperative to act.

Her challenge on both these fronts was that the entire leadership team had grown up in the legacy way of working and thinking. They—and her, too— had been promoted to their positions for their thinking within the old ways of working.

In searching for a partner to help her navigate these challenges, she turned to her CHRO. Newly appointed to that role, the CHRO had been with the company for only a few years and had come to the organization from a different industry and a smaller, nimbler environment. He brought an outside-in perspective that the CEO wanted for the company, even though HR had historically been relegated to a purely administrative function.

Together, they started to grapple with foundational questions: If we were to move toward greener technologies, what would that require of our top leaders? What about our culture would have to change—and what needed to remain core to company identity? What capital investments must we make? What talent will be required, and how will that talent affect our traditional "how" and "where" of decision-making?

The talent supply they needed to build the next generation of the business had a very different profile from the company's manufacturing legacy— which needed to remain high-functioning through years of transition.

Should they start thinking about their workforce in a bifurcated way, or get innovative in how they integrated their talent planning?

A successful transformation would require technologies that didn't yet exist. Their conversations were difficult, wide-ranging, and had to be kept relatively secret. After all, most of the CEO's direct reports were likely to be initial resistors of this magnitude of change—either actively or passively. They had to enlist people a couple layers down in the organization who were already thinking several years ahead to help work on the new plan. For the CHRO, this included numerous sidebars with an SWP professional to continuously provide him with questions he might have missed—angles on change or unintended consequence that he or the CEO might have overlooked.

These sets of overlapping contexts, along with the SWP professional's ability to ride the complex waves, gave the conversation a robustness and the solutions a kind of built-in resilience and adaptability too often missing from prior plans. The principle, "zoom out before you zoom in" is often helpful grounding. In addition, each new infusion of viewpoints add to and change the SWP requirements. In this case, a critical moment of reckoning came when the CEO, CHRO, and CFO presented the overall strategic plan to the board. While the directors approved it, the discussion revealed a further complexity: the board itself, not just the C-suite, had been built to serve the legacy business model. While the initial board approval of the new strategy gave them the right to pursue the business model of the future, it did not reflect unanimous support. There were also directors and investors who had signed on to the company based on the investment thesis that the CEO had inherited, and they would be scrutinizing every step of the execution of the CEO's and CHRO's work, looking for a reason to reverse course.

Case Study 2

An innovative corporate executive had stepped away from a C-suite job at a Fortune 100 company to co-found a niche financial services organization. His insight was to offer complex financing to a segment of the market that had never used financing before. Just as with any entrepreneurial venture, the risk was high and the demands of the job all-consuming, but the rewards over the company's first decade had been significant. From a two-man operation, the company had grown to 150 people with more than $3 billion in revenues—it dominated the market that it had created. Not surprisingly, competitors emerged, offering variations and attempting innovations on the founders' original market insight and their business model. The CEO, whose entrepreneurial streak had led him to start the company, now had to worry about being outmaneuvered if he couldn't master scaling his organization while staying as nimble as possible.

Scaling came with two challenges. First, part of the business's success had come from organic global expansion. As a financial services firm, the company was subject to regulations in each new market, and the varying frameworks had added increased levels of complexity to its deal analysis. Despite this, the two co-founders remained the primary mental horsepower on the investment committee. Brilliant as they were, trying to fully analyze the risk–reward differences between returns in a Singapore environment versus London versus New York was becoming inordinately time-consuming.

The second major challenge they identified was scaling their people—those they had and also those they needed to recruit to help sustain their growth trajectory. The founders were quirky and acknowledged it. Additionally, they had promoted several equally quirky people into core leadership roles—each technically brilliant and highly relevant in the marketplace. But, as a team, they were not aligned on what good leadership looked like or the kind of talent and culture the firm needed to successfully scale.

These two elements—scale and talent—came together in a range of stress points within the firm. The founders ended up deeply involved in matters ranging from the next round of fundraising to the color and style of the pillows in the lobby. They nonetheless recognized that they needed to free up time for strategy and stakeholder management, including starting to invest time on the culture now that they had passed the 100-employee mark.

Further complicating this picture, the company had recently completed its first acquisition of a competitor—a fellow start-up. This opened a new geographical and market niche, but it also created unique cultural challenges. The acquired firm's niche was highly specialized, operating with a special set of processes and regulations. It therefore came with a technical learning curve. Moreover, it also had a culture that was more rooted in the technology pace and mindset of the West Coast, while the acquiring company, though innovative, thought and moved with a more a Wall Street-centric culture.

The next evolution of both strategy and scale had to look different. The CEO understood the challenge with remarkable clarity. That was fortunate because, as is often the case with founder-led organizations, the CEO and his co-founder controlled the vast majority of the firm's equity. This placed the board in more of an advisory role than a true governance role—so constructive thinking about scaling, talent, and planning needed to come from the founders themselves. Few boards with hyperscaling founding CEOs in place will have the courage to pressure the CEO to slow down and become more planful.

This case study traces a familiar pattern of innovative founders who have a great idea, want to disrupt things, and are often deeply opposed to hierarchy and structure, seeing it as antithetical to the agility they believe is crucial to success. With that success, however, they typically grow to a point where their ad hoc structure and personality-driven management approaches become constraints to further growth. Intellectually, such founders often still look down on infrastructure and talent planning discussions as mere process that they don't want to be bothered with. The impulse is understandable. They have been successful to date in part because they didn't need process and structure to execute their ideas. Selling founders on the idea that their company needs more structure to grow requires patience and care. Part of the SWP challenge in this instance was to create just enough structure to streamline the organization for the founders' clear benefit, but not one iota more—the "just enough" principle.

Because the CEO effectively had no internal HR function, he reached out to our firm for help. We together contemplated the core philosophical challenge he faced: How can the company have the conversation that it needs to have about preparing for its next phase of growth, despite the personality-driven leadership culture and deep-rooted resistance to process and structure?

Case Study 3

A prominent media company faced a stark reality—status quo was not an option. The legacy business, based on expensive print advertising, had been disrupted by the internet, and the content for which they had charged subscribers was being made available on the internet for free. As a legacy organization, one of its many strengths came from adhering to standards and processes for delivering its products. But that strength also represented a weakness because the culture was resistant to changing what had been a successful formula for decades and that helped set it apart from competitors.

Faced with a falling stock price and a clear need to do something more than make incremental changes, the company reached outside its ranks to hire a new CEO. By his own admission, the new CEO was somewhat wary of the opportunity at first. People in his network were warning him to stay away because they felt the company was too resistant to change. But he was intrigued by the opportunity—he believed that if the organization could, in effect, get out of its own way, there was enormous upside.

He took the job knowing that he did not have the answers. He also understood media organizations well enough to know that if he went in with a clear plan and issued a memo that dictated the new strategy, he would likely face quick organ rejection. Instead, he adopted a couple of guiding principles. One was that the answer was going to come from the organization itself, and particularly from the newsroom. He needed the newsroom to be a partner because, as with most legacy media organizations, there was a thick metaphorical wall established between the newsroom and the business side so that the journalists remained free of any internal financial pressures that might compromise their journalism (such as aggressive reporting on a big advertiser). Because of that wall, there was a reflexive skepticism among the journalists for any idea that came from the business side. The CEO asked the newsroom for help, which it provided by setting up its own committee to seek answers for navigating the structural industry trends that most media companies faced.

Another of the CEO's guiding principles was that he was going to bring leaders from across the organization together on a regular cadence for open-ended, hours-long meetings. There was no set agenda other than to continue to talk until they had an answer.

A surprising development occurred in the newsroom's effort. A committee of journalists worked for 9 months, interviewed hundreds of people inside and outside the organization, and ultimately wrote a 100-page document that was full of blunt language about the challenges the company faced and how it was falling behind competitors in digital skills. Importantly, the document was free of any opinions and was based only on facts and charts and graphs that nobody could dispute. That report was meant for an internal audience only of the top leaders of the company. But, just days after it was shared with that group, it was leaked to an outside media organization. The initial reaction was shock and self-protection—wouldn't the report tarnish the gold-standard reputation of the organization? However, the unforeseen exposure turned out to be a key inflection point because it started productive conversations internally about the future of the company. It woke up people who had been skeptical of the need for change.

The subsequent changes in the organization would mean a marked shift for the role of HR. Historically, the company, particularly the newsroom, didn't want HR to have a significant voice and certainly didn't feel that an SWP discipline could add value to the business of journalism. Up to this point, HR had neither a voice nor a chair at the table.

The Stakeholder Playbook for SWP Professionals

These three cases serve as a simplified sample set of the endless variety facing both CEOs and SWP professionals. The economic disruption caused by the pandemic prompted wholesale changes across the business landscape. One 2021 survey of CEOs, by the Predictive Index, showed that 96% of chief executives shifted their strategy in some way since the start of the pandemic. Yet that same survey also showed that fewer CEOs believed that employees fully understood their strategic shifts.

The findings speak to an almost universal truth of leadership—that it is the primary role of the CEO to define big-picture threats and opportunities and to think about ways their organization might navigate or capitalize on those. But chief executives are not superhuman, and rarely do you find leaders who can both zoom out to the see the big picture and also zoom in to think through the granular implications and requirements of their strategy.

The structural and organizational details of building and adjusting the talent pipeline—as crucial as they are to implementing the overarching plan—can easily fall beneath the radar of CEOs and be relegated as work to be considered by others. As the CEO of a large institutional investment firm told us, "I'm not a scale operator. I hate scale operations. It's not interesting to me."

The challenge for SWP professionals is to elevate the conversation to an altitude at which the CEO is likely to engage. Can you lay a trail of breadcrumbs that leads them to recognize the link between SWP and making their vision work? To be clear, that doesn't mean explaining to chief executives how the workforce plan will be implemented. For the conversation to land well, it must start with asking CEOs (or your proxy who will then be communicating with the CEO) the right questions. CEOs are by nature problem-solvers—smart questions are the way to engage them.

A key challenge of driving large-scale organizational and strategic transformation is that it typically must play out on two distinct tracks. One is the big bets that the company is making on its future business model—for example, the shift from hardware to cloud services. In the near-term, these bets require not only serious investment, but may also generate no, or reduced, revenues and eat into enterprise profitability. While everyone can agree that the end goal represents the best shot at a prosperous and sustainable future, the transformation requires time to implement. That theory of the future will likely consume most of the energy and interest of the CEO, the board, and investors.

The second track is the legacy business, which is often highly complex in its own right and is also facing its own external pressures to innovate and stay efficient. For example, consider the electric vehicle (EV) movement in the established automobile industry today. After decades of resistance, automakers today are all-in on the pivot to EVs. But, aside from Tesla, every EV line is at the moment unprofitable and will be for years to come. For legacy automakers, the success of their EV businesses relies on their internal combustion engine (ICE) models. Some version of this story is playing out in nearly every industry today.

While it may be considered yesterday's news, the legacy business is still crucial to the company. As such, it demands attention but also restraint—the temptation is that everyone becomes so excited by the glamor and potential of the future business model that they too quickly retool the whole organization. Consider the example of the ill-fated attempt by Ron Johnson, a former Apple executive who ran its retail strategy, to overhaul JC Penney stores when he took over as CEO in 2011. The pivot he announced—to make JC Penney stores more like Apple stores—was a bridge too far. He showed little respect or understanding of JC Penny's established business, and his "innovations" caused a collapse in legacy sales. In less than 2 years, he was ousted.

For CEOs and strategic workforce planners to have truly productive conversations, understanding those parallel tracks will help you outline the themes under which you can package your most crucial questions. It's possible—and we say this respectfully as people who often ask questions ourselves on topics that we don't fully understand in order to help our clients trigger their own new insights—that the average SWP professional may not fully understand the subject area that they're pressing the CEO to consider. That's ok. Your value is less about telling the leader what to think about than it is helping them realize the critical implications of the questions you have raised. To create shared alignment with the CEO, consider the following questions:

- *What is the desired pace of change?* An important starting point is to raise questions about the desired speed of the transformation. At what pace does the CEO envision the strategic overhaul unfolding? What signals has the company shared with investors, public or private, about how the strategy is changing and the accompanying timetable? What external industry disruptions are driving or informing the change and how fast are those forces moving? What structural or talent track record does the organization have for making major changes at a similar pace? If it has accomplished similarly ambitious transformations in the past, what lessons can be drawn from those experiences? These questions raise CEO anxiety in a constructive way. Establishing clarity on pace is crucial because, while the near-term tends to be very well-defined, longer-term transitions can easily become more amorphous, it's likely that the CEO and possibly the investor community has pacing expectations. That's why a conversation to time-bound the plan is a cornerstone for a successful transformation.
- *What are the leadership implications of getting this change right?* If the planned transformation requires new leadership muscles for the organization, then a crucial question must be put on the table: What will leaders have to do differently *right now* to make sure the long-term plan goes well? If they simply hand off the organizational design and talent work to others and then return to business as usual, then the plan will be doomed to fail. Other questions to ask of the CEO and the leadership team: How ready for change are people throughout the organization? Do employees understand that the new strategy will require different talent and different ways of working to deliver on the commitments? Is the required talent to lead those new initiatives in-house, or do people need to be hired from the outside? Part of the reason for asking these questions is to give yourself a glimpse into senior leaders' thinking before you get to the more direct workforce inquiry (below). Finally, before leaving leadership implications, consider asking how leadership practices or behaviors will likely be different on the other side of this transformation, if all goes to plan.[1]
- *How will we communicate with the different sets of stakeholders inside and outside the company?* Communication is critical during times of rapid change. Has the CEO explained to the entire organization why status quo is not an option? Is everyone clear on the macro market trends that make transformation and careful planning necessary? Has

the leadership described the vision in compelling ways that advance the company's purpose, values, and culture? How are we talking to employees about new talent and skill requirements in a way that keeps the current workforce engaged as we retool the organization for a different future?
- *Any major operational changes that we should be considering as we plan?* For instance, what is working well now in the organization, and what might come under stress because of the planned shift to a new business model? Does the strategy require changes in the way the company allocates capital? To be clear, operational questions do not require SWP professionals to have a deep understanding of how the company allocates capital. You will never know the organization's inner workings better than the senior operators whose conversations you need to influence. Rather, the reason to ask the question of the experts in the room is that it may lead to important insights for them because they have possibly come to take for granted the way things work today.
- *What's changing or staying the same about how we make decisions?* Another potentially fruitful discussion area is decision-making. Will decisions be made differently in the new part of the business? In different geographies? Does the legacy business stay the same, or are you looking to speed up the pace of decisions there? It's not uncommon in successful transformations for highly matrixed decision-making to continue for the legacy part of the business while a small subgroup of leaders is given enhanced decision rights to drive the transformation. It allows them to be more nimble and more decisive. An issue related to both operations changes *and* decision-making: How will the operational key performance indicators change over time? How might they be different for the old and new parts of the business?
- *What are the talent implications of the strategy?* You might have thought, given the subject of this chapter, that this would be the opening question. But we recommend using a specific path before arriving at this subject. Why? Because *most CEOs don't think about talent implications—they think about strategy, operations, and results.* So, now that you've walked them through strategic, leadership, and operational areas—most CEOs' collective wheelhouses—it's now time to begin exploring your own area of expertise. But a word of warning: don't rabbit-hole. You're far better off asking that top-line question (What

do you see as the implications of this strategy for talent here?) and then listening to how the leader wants to engage on the topic.

Many other talent questions exist within HR's purview, and there you *can and should* go deep. Topics like the current talent profile of the organization, the skills the company has in abundance and those that are missing—these you know well and probably better than the authors, so we won't script them here. But we will take a moment to suggest one specific additional talent trend that may be worth asking of a CEO:

- *How effective is the organization at retaining outside-in talent?* You will want to consider this from several angles. One aspect will be how effective the organization is at recruiting early-career talent that looks different from its legacy hiring process. This may be skills, diversity, new geography—let the CEO interpret your question rather than directing their answer. Second, how does the executive think about the company's effectiveness at recruiting and integrating senior-level talent? A current trend is that most organizations have become markedly better at recruiting a diverse workforce for entry-level positions. But many organizations remain challenged when they try to recruit senior-level talent, diverse or otherwise, because of the more complicated, visible, and politically charged ecosystems those new hires must navigate. Increasingly, this leads to their departure within 2 years. If the execution of the CEO's strategy hinges partially on bringing in new leaders in key roles, this question of how to integrate and hold onto such strategic hires will help you fully engage the CEO's attention.

- *What are the structural and organizational implications of the strategy?* Most organizations have built up their structures over time through a combination of strategic intent and cultural habits—sometimes further shaped by the personalities of those in charge. The second case study we described in this chapter was a classic example of a startup whose structure evolved over time to match the personalities of people in charge. Their matrix may not have made much sense on paper, but it worked in the early years because of the force of personalities of the leaders at the time and because the overall headcount was low enough to work through informal channels to get things done. A few questions to raise on this theme include: How does the current structure allow the company to accelerate into its planned future? Are there aspects of the current structure that are momentum-killers today and that will make the transformation difficult to execute at the intended pace? What is the ideal degree of separation between the legacy and new parts of the business? How much ongoing interaction between parts of the organization should there be to retain a broader enterprise lens? How will the company be organized to interact with its customers, and what steps should be taken to enhance those relationships? For example, should a technology company have a centralized engineering group or engineering groups embedded within the various business units to have a better feel for the needs of the customers of each segment? Helping bring such pragmatic questions into sharp focus for the CEO—even if the answer is clearly still under debate—will sharpen their understanding that SWP is hardly an academic undertaking. They will see you as a true thought partner.

There are perhaps dozens of other questions that could be asked of the company's leaders to probe their thinking on the implications of and levels of preparedness to pursue a transformation strategy. But a key point is that these questions should be used sparingly. Choose a handful of areas and questions that seem like the most relevant themes and stick to them. It's not in anybody's interest to have thoughtful questioning turn into what may feel like an interrogation. And the bad movie version of this approach is that it feels like the questioner is trying to prove how smart he is rather than asking to listen. The goal is to leave such meetings with some foundational answers and to help leadership consider one or two challenges in a new light.

After all, the senior leaders of an organization are continuously analyzing current performance of the business and trying to think about how to either avert risk or capitalize on risk to create the best future. Like all leaders, they will have their blind spots. The value that strategic workforce planners can provide is to raise smart but simple questions that will allow them to see an issue from a new angle. The overarching goal is to be seen as an ally who is helping them remain relevant, contemporary, and competitive in a fast-changing world. A secondary goal is to help surface any underlying assumptions about the business that may be working against clarity and alignment for the transformation.

Many of these themes inform how the three companies we discussed early in our case studies addressed their respective challenges. We return to those case studies here to explain how their transformations unfolded over time.

Case Study 1, Continued

For the global manufacturing business, the CEO, CHRO, and the leadership team assessed the implications of moving from a cash-intensive, high-churn mergers and acquisitions (M&A) growth-engine model to a more technologically advanced, greener, sustainable, cash-generating business. They asked themselves many of the questions we mentioned above. To improve their cash flows, they needed to pull out of certain countries, some of which they had only recently entered for M&A purposes that were marginally profitable at best. The company began a difficult process over a 7-year period of pulling out of roughly half the countries in which it operated.

It also became apparent that to deliver on some of its goals to move to cleaner technologies, it would need to incorporate some of the most leading-edge solutions, many of which were still being developed. In some cases, they would need to either partner with other firms or create the technologies they required to realize their strategy. SWP professionals helped conduct an overdue talent audit in the organization, which led to two important insights. First, they did in fact have people deep in the organization who were working on some of those technologies in far-flung parts of the company. They realized they could invest in and organize some of those people into collaborative groups, elevating them to create more of an internal innovation engine than the company had in the past. Doing so would require changes in how they allocated capital, and that was the story they presented to the CHRO and that he presented to the CEO.

The second key insight was that while the top leadership layers of the company were filled with executives who had built their careers in the legacy part of the business—and had limited skill when it came to the new, long-term direction the company—most of those top leaders were incredibly loyal to the business and embraced the CEO. They would do their part to make the transformation successful. They rolled up their sleeves to sustain revenues, improve cash flow, and grow profitability in the existing businesses. They stepped back to help the organization create the next generation of leaders who could build and operate a future company that looked very different from the legacy business. That included top leadership moving emerging talent to different roles in one another's geographies and parts of the business to round out their international experience and understanding of market contexts.

As the company started to shrink its global footprint, it also undertook broader integration of 10 years' worth of acquisitions into a single company-wide decision-making framework and consolidated many of their systems. The net result was a simplified structure, a drastic reduction in headcount at headquarters, and hundreds of millions in savings.

Not everything went smoothly. One of the unforeseen hurdles was that a large portion of the company's investor base had invested based on a thesis of M&A growth and the legacy business model. The changes introduced by the CEO and the leadership team rattled that community at first, which required more time than the leadership expected to manage investors. It also required changing out some board directors who were wedded to the legacy model. During this period, when the CEO and CFO were consumed by investor relations, the CEO relied heavily on HR and strategic workforce planners within the organization to keep the operational trains moving on the change. To put those changes in effect, HR and operational leaders partnered closely to identify executives in the field who were much closer to innovative technologies and greener solutions and started to fast track them in leadership roles around the organization to get them ready for broader enterprise leadership. Those emerging leaders thought differently about the business, and, because the company encouraged them to keep doing so, they tended to continuously bring a more innovative lens to the organization's new direction.

The plan has largely succeeded. The organization has made the transition from a high-polluting past to a much greener present, and its future will be greener still. Along the way, it has built clean-energy technologies through joint ventures or stand-alone innovation. Two of those have spun out as public companies, creating billions of dollars in additional market capitalization. From its past as a cash-negative, high-polluting, strategically ambiguous organization, it has evolved to being viewed as one of the most innovative companies in its space.

Case Study 2, Continued

The co-founders of the niche financial services organization knew they had to solve their various leadership challenges to expand globally and maintain their first-mover advantage over newly emerging competitors. But when they were presented with a SWP professional's plan for structure and talent, they reacted with skepticism. They couldn't see it working for the nontraditional leaders they'd assembled in the firm who were not going to fit neatly in the prescribed boxes. They rejected the good counsel on creating structure and decided instead to invest more time and energy managing those individual personalities and navigating around inevitable conflicts.

It was all-consuming for the CEO. Yet, for 3 more years, the company continued to experience strong growth. They executed some smaller acquisitions but found that they ran into consistently high turnover rates after each of them because the individual quirks of the firm's leaders and its amorphous organizational structure made it difficult for outsiders to assimilate. As a result, they recognized that they were squandering elements of the strategic goals that were driving their acquisitive plans. In the middle of all this, the pandemic forced everyone to shift to working remotely.

With more time to reflect on big-picture questions, the founders decided, in late 2021, to revisit the SWP conversation. The CEO said he realized that while the revenues were scaling, the company was constrained in the near term because the structure was built to accommodate individual personalities rather than to enable growth. He recognized that he was never going to be able to see the company realize his longer-term vision either, if he didn't take a different approach. He also recognized that, while he and his co-founder were still relatively young, he needed to be able to hand off the organization to a next generation of management. That meant building that next-generation team now so that they could align on and co-own the desired culture. Doing all of this would mean creating some structure.

In other words, his adoption of the SWP plan was almost complete—it just took 3½ years. The result was the formation of a management committee, which led the shift of some of the key personalities out of leadership and into individual contributor roles where their specialized skills could be deployed to great effect but their negative impact on management and decision-making were eliminated. The company then recruited people into the firm who did not have the subject-matter expertise of the firm's niche business but had strong management and organizational skills and could help with the recruitment and retention of talent. In the wake of that change, the company completed another acquisition, and the integration unfolded much more smoothly because reporting lines were now clear, and the tensions that they had in different offices around the world started to ease. People are thinking much more as one team, rather than focusing on building and protecting their silos or trying to anticipate the varying moods of various leaders on various days.

Case Study 3, Continued

For the legacy media organization, the challenge at a very high level was clear—to shift from a print-focused business model to an uncertain digital future. Everybody understood the goal and the urgency required to make that shift. The leadership conversations about that necessary transformation also led to an important strategic shift—to focus more on digital subscribers than advertisers—with profound implications for the structure of the company and its workforce planning.

The reason that shift was so powerful is that it addressed deep cultural and organizational impediments to operating as one company. As we noted earlier, the company was effectively two companies with a metaphorical wall between them, and there was deep skepticism on the news side about any ideas or initiatives that came from the business side. By reorienting the company strategy around adding more subscribers, everybody in the organization could sign on to that goal because it made sense for both the newsroom and the business side. The effect was to enable conversations that never happened before, with leaders from the business side and the newsroom side now working side by side to build a loyal and growing base of subscribers.

That shift had important implications for the HR function, which for decades had been kept at a distance by the newsroom. With the new model, HR now had a much bigger seat at the table, and there was a growing realization that the tough-editor newsroom management style of the past wasn't going to work. The organization has started to reward leaders who are team players first and foremost, with enterprise mindsets, rather than people who were more interested in building their parts of the business. This was a key lead-in for SWP. Understanding how the leadership culture was changing, it became much more viable to have realistic conversations about building the needed workforce of the future.

Now HR had the opportunity to play a vital role in recruiting digital specialists to help the company realize its strategy. Those recruiting efforts were challenged by the fact that the media company was now competing with every other firm that was battling over a limited supply of top tech talent. But it was helped by the power of its brand, a strong draw for many people who were inspired to help with its journalistic mission. The new strategy has paid off, with sharp and steady growth generating profits that the company could reinvest to solidify its position as a leader in the field.

* * *

It is hard to overstate the importance of successfully navigating these conversations. And we recognize that in smaller organizations this might be a direct discussion between an SWP professional and the CEO, while in larger organizations the SWP advisor may be working through proxies. Either way, those discussions can mean the difference between an organization evolving and taking advantage of macro trends—Apple and Disney come to mind— or a company going the way of, say, a Blockbuster or Blackberry.

As you reflect on these cases, the macro environment you yourself are navigating, and your own client experiences, remember that your greatest skill is not your content, but your ability to ask rich questions that ground and contextualize whatever planning happens next. Consider these core areas and prompts in Table 12.1 as a starter kit and adapt and evolve with your own rich insights.

The urgency to get these conversations right is heightened by the fact that every organization today is on some form of a digital transformation journey and is wrestling with how to best evolve or revolutionize its business model. Furthermore, the actual jobs of the future are at best only partly defined. In

Table 12.1 Helping CEOs plan for the future: A playbook for strategic workforce planning professionals

Area of focus	Helpful prompts
Understand what the strategy requires of leadership	Before diving into the workforce of the future, what do top executives think the strategy requires of *them as leaders* that will be different from their past experience?
Create resilience, not sameness	In each part of the business impacted by SWP, ask: what outputs must this business drive? What are we trying to protect along the way? What is the balance we need to strike between lean (and low-cost) vs. robust and agile?
Use the matrix to create value	How strong are the organization's cross-functional thinking and execution skills, and to what extent will the workforce of the future need to collaborate?
Anticipate shifts in the world of people who work	The world of work is different and evolving quickly. The blend of on-site and remote, contract and outsourced, not to mention adaptive artificial intelligence (AI) are in flux. What are the CEO's aspirations and hard limits when imagining the distribution of a future workforce?
Build in metrics for measuring organizational design effectiveness	What will good look like, and how will the organization measure that it's tracking on its desired SWP outcomes? Where might existing incentives and structures conflict with those goals and measures?

addition, all public, and many private, organizations are still navigating the implications of the emergence of stakeholder capitalism.

The table stakes for leaders have changed, just as they have for SWP professionals. That challenge to the status quo presents a major opportunity because it means your questions of a CEO are vital. It's the very simplicity of your prompts that will force a leader to pause, reflect, and possibly come back with something like, "Interesting. I have to think about that." That's an emotional and intellectual buying signal that you've shown them that they can't just hand off SWP and not worry about it—they need to truly sponsor and co-own this work.

In many ways, this moment is an important evolutionary step for the HR function itself, which for many years faced the challenge of getting a proverbial seat at the table. During the pandemic, HR not only got its seat, but in many ways had to chair the table. This new reality provides an opportunity for the profession and the function of SWP, too. CEOs face leadership challenges and implications that may be outside the traditional remit of SWP. The next step is for SWP professionals to demonstrate an understanding of this new set of realities. It opens the door to becoming a true partner to the CEO, helping make everyone at the leadership table better by ensuring that the right questions are being asked and answered.

Note

1. An equally—and sometimes more—effective approach is to run a pre-mortem exercise. "If this effort fails and an MBA program uses it as a case study of how not to lead a transformation, what would be the core leadership lapses that fueled breakdown?"

References

Layden, S., and Gorgas, J. (2021). The gift of creating a new future. *People+Strategy*, 44(1), 5.

Nicolas, E. (2023). How to operationalize resiliency. *People+Strategy*, 46(3), 40–43.

13
Scenario Planning
The Secret Sauce to Making Strategic Workforce Planning Agile

Edie Goldberg

In this chapter, I share the strategic workforce planning (SWP) approach I used to help MyoKardia, a high-growth biotech company (now a wholly owned subsidiary of Bristol Myers Squibb), prepare to launch its first product. The organization was anticipating significant year-over year growth (~30%/year) leading up to approval by the US Food and Drug Administration (FDA) and launch of its first therapy. The planning that took place to create a workforce plan for the next 3 years relied on no traditional formula regarding expected growth trajectories, nor did it try to emulate the growth trajectories of other companies as MyoKardia prepared for the commercial launch of its first product. While we did benchmark against peer organizations, we strategically deviated from typical growth trajectories given the organization's specific strategies designed to outperform the competition.

For many organizations SWP has been an Excel spreadsheet forecasting exercise that felt like a necessary evil but was rarely engaging. Planning was usually approached in a linear fashion that assumed that growth would follow the same trajectory as it had in the past. Most companies assume the status quo will remain, and there will be little change in the company's talent needs other than those related to growth. Given today's volatile, uncertain, complex, and ambiguous (VUCA) business environment, companies need to adopt new approaches to SWP that are more agile and that help organizations to quickly shift strategies and tactics based on emerging business dynamics. While the COVID-19 global pandemic probably could not have been predicted in advance, it laid bare the need to be agile as an organization. The need for companies to be able to rapidly pivot resources and business priorities became more apparent than ever.

The approach outlined in this chapter provides one example of an emerging trend of building agility into traditional human resources (HR) processes. Any SWP process must begin with a strong understanding of the business strategy as well as the capabilities needed to execute on that strategy. By integrating scenario planning into the process, organizations can create alternative visions of what is possible in the future and understand the organization's capacity to maximize their opportunities and minimize their risks.

Scenario Planning

Scenario planning helps organizations plan for the future and consider other possible outcomes. This in turn helps them create flexibility in plans to accommodate alternative outcomes or identify indicators to watch for and which signify that changing conditions are emerging. In scenario planning, an organization begins with a deep understanding of the business strategy and then considers trends and uncertainties the organization is facing to help refine its plans for a specific issue. The development of scenario planning is often attributed to Herman Kahn who created the technique of telling possible future stories about the business in his work in both the US military and at RAND Corporation. One of the first well-documented uses of scenario planning was conducted by Royal Dutch/Shell in the 1970s to predict oil price scenarios. Previously the consumer held the power in oil markets. The scenario planning conducted at Royal Dutch/Shell considered a possible scenario where the power in the markets shifted from consumers to oil-producing nations. Sure enough, shortly thereafter the Mideast oil embargo and global energy crisis emerged, shifting the power in the markets. Shell was more prepared for this possibility than their competitors. Their ability to act quickly was largely credited to their prior scenario planning work which caused them to consider how they would react in such a scenario.

In scenario planning, organizations consider known facts about the future—such as demographics—along with key unknowns that could impact the company's future (e.g., social, technical, economic, environmental, and political [STEEP] trends). Sometimes organizations consider other issues that are important within that industry (e.g., supply chain stability). The idea is to get people to consider extreme scenarios that could impact the threats or opportunities faced by the business.

Scenarios are not predictions about what *will* happen in the future, but rather they are theoretically possible stories about what *could* happen. The purpose of a scenario is to break leaders of the habit of assuming that the future will look much like the present or that business will continue to grow at the same trajectory and have the same competitive forces it has always experienced. Scenarios allow leaders to consider the uncertainty of the future.

Scenario planning imagines how various elements might interact to create different conditions. For example, from 2015 to 2018, I was part of a project that was focused on understanding the future of work and how HR needed to change to meet the changing nature of work. The project was called CHREATE (The Global Consortium to Reimagine HR, Employment Alternative, Talent, and the Enterprise; see Boudreau, Rearick, and Ziskin, 2018). In this project, we identified five forces of change that would influence the future of work (social and organizational reconfiguration; an all-inclusive, global talent market; a truly connected world; and exponential pattern of technological change; and human and machine collaboration). With these forces in mind, we articulated two core themes that would greatly change the dynamics of business.

- *The democratization of work*: A more highly democratized future is characterized by new "employment" relationships that are shorter in duration, with a greater power balance between individuals and the company. A shift toward a more agile and responsive view of work will deliver results by activating purpose-built networks.
- *Technological empowerment*: Technology is transforming the way we live and work. Machine learning, 3D printing, mobile, wearables, and algorithmic analytics are some of the many technologies that promise to improve individual empowerment.

By putting this into a 2 × 2 matrix, we produced four potential scenarios for the future that we could further define. This helped people to imagine the complexity of multiple events unfolding at the same time (Figure 13.1).

Deeply defining the scenarios is an important step so that everyone has the same mental model of the possibilities for the future. In the CHREATE Project (Pryor, 2018), we defined these four scenarios as follows:

1. *Today, status quo*: Consistent with its label, this scenario suggested that the world of work in 2025 would bear a striking resemblance to when

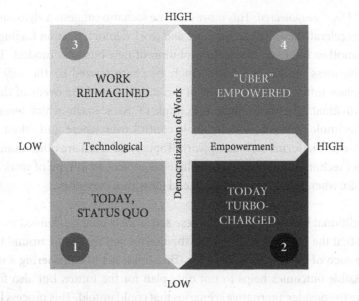

Figure 13.1 Scenarios for the future.

the analysis was completed. This scenario suggests that through a general slow-down in the evolution of technology or management science or a significant set-back, the world of work remained similar to the current state. This scenario may also be the result of a political, social, climatic, or economic catastrophe.

2. *Today, turbo-charged*: This scenario suggests the continued evolution and empowerment of technology-empowering business, but with little advances of evolution in business or management models. This scenario is characterized by similar employment relationships but in a faster, better, cheaper business paradigm. For example, companies still primarily hire full-time employees, but artificial intelligence and 3-D printers dramatically increase the speed of work while reducing costs.

3. *Work reimagined*: In this scenario, the future sees the evolution into new business and employment models without significant advances in technology. The current level of connected technology provides both individuals and collectives of employees' greater agency to make demands that create an optimal experience for themselves. The rise of remote and hybrid work arrangements is a prime example, as is the greater use of independent contractors.

4. *"Uber" empowered*: This more extreme scenario suggests a virtuous and accelerated cycle of technology *and* work democratization fueling one another to create the rapid evolution of new business models. These business models will increasingly be characterized by the way they place into balance the needs of the company and the needs of the individual. Uber is an obvious example of this scenario which leverages technology to allow individuals control over where and when they work. Platforms such as Upwork, Toptal, and Guru are other examples of technology enabling individuals to control what type of work they do, when and where they do it, and for whom they work.

In traditional scenario planning, these scenarios would be defined in such detail that the reader could imagine themselves and the world around them under each of the possible scenarios. The simple act of considering a range of possible outcomes helps to not only plan for the future, but also forces leaders to consider alternative scenarios that could unfold. This process helps overcome the natural tendency to plan for what we hope will happen and not give enough thought to alternative futures. Executives who consider a wide range of possible outcomes and their impact on the business, and who then maintain vigilance in tracking signals regarding which outcome is unfolding over time, will be in a better position to take advantage of unexpected opportunities and will be able to pivot more quickly when adjustments in strategy need to be made based on unexpected events (Schwartz,1991; van der Heijden,1997).

Because scenario planning considers the extremes of a situation (work is not democratized and the employer remains in control vs. democratization of work with employee having greater agency), it helps begin a conversation about a range of possibilities and considering outcomes that may not have previously anticipated.

Critics of scenario planning argue that it has not been studied extensively and there is no real evidence that the value of the process outweighs the effort and resources required to do it well. Some credit Shell's experience to luck and argue that, since 1970, this process has not created any competitive advantage for the organization. Anecdotal stories would suggest that the reason there is no "evidence" of scenario planning having a significant positive impact on a firm's financial performance is simply because this type of activity represents a company's strategy, and companies are unwilling to share any reports on the process, findings, or its impact.

As an industrial-organizational (I-O) psychologist, I view scenario planning as testing a hypothesis. By explicitly stating a possible (yet plausible) outcome of the future, we can gather evidence and test to see if this outcome is likely to unfold. But more recent research points to some very important impacts that the process has on the company and its leaders.

In one study (Rohrbeck and Schwartz, 2013), researchers examined 77 large multinational firms to assess the value derived from a "strategic foresight" activity, such as scenario planning. While this research has its flaws and limitations stemming from field work, their research points to the fact that while few firms report any evidence of getting a strong return on investment for strategic foresight activities, there are four ways that this type of activity can bring value to an organization.

1. *An enhanced capacity to perceive change*: This was the most prominent contribution of this type of strategic planning activity.
2. *An enhanced capacity to interpret and respond to change*.
3. *Influencing other actors*: One of the strongest findings in their study was that high-performing companies were most likely to use scenario planning to identify opportunities and threats to their product/technology portfolio. With this information, they could influence others in the organization to take action to improve the firms positioning.
4. *Enhanced capacity for organizational learning*: While only a small number of companies indicated they used scenario planning to shape their future, this was more prominent in high-performing companies.

Other research has demonstrated that scenario planning can positively impact organizational resilience, creative climate, and perceptions of being a learning organization (Chermack et al., 2017; Chermack et al., 2015; Haeffner et al., 2012). "Scenarios change our mental models and the way we perceive the world around us. This opens us up to seeing new possibilities and that had an impact on business success" (T.J. Chermack, personal communication, January 21, 2022).

To get a conceptual overview of one step-by-step model for how to conduct a scenario planning process the reader should consider Peter Schwartz's 1991 well-referenced book, *The Art of the Long View*. While scenario planning has traditionally considered macroeconomic and macropolitical factors, *Porter's Five Forces Model* (Porter, 1979) is another popular model used in scenario planning. Porters Five Forces include threat of new entrants, bargaining power of suppliers, bargaining power of customers, competitive rivalry, and threat of substitute of products or services. It is important to note that Porter's work asserts that the proper unit of analysis is really the industry and not macro factors. This was the point of view taken in the situation described below.

Our Agile Approach to SWP

In 2018, I took a scenario planning approach to SWP with my client, MyoKardia, because we knew that the organization had to anticipate several possible future outcomes. We began the process by ensuring that all members of the executive team had a clear understanding of the current business strategy, known internally as Vision 2020. (The executive team had already been discussing what changes they need to make to create a new Vision 2025—an evolution of their current vision.) With this as our foundation, we began discussing the potential forces of change that could impact the company's future.

While I originally encouraged the executive team to consider more macroeconomic factors or even extreme industry-focused scenarios (e.g., major changes in regulatory policy or disruptive new technologies) or more typical STEEP issues, they ultimately chose to focus on a few critical areas of uncertainty that would have a significant impact on the company. For example, the outcomes of current clinical trials would determine the trajectory of the company. Initially I pushed back and wanted to take a more traditional approach to scenario planning. However, as our conversation progressed, I realized that the company had several very specific uncertainties they were facing and that they would get the most value out of the process if we limited our scenarios to those critical uncertainties.

Prior to our first scenario planning meeting we prompted the executive team with questions that were designed to help them consider the possibilities and uncertainties they face as they view the future of MyoKardia. To give you a feel for the questions we asked, we list a sample of the questions utilized.

1. What are the most important forces impacting MyoKardia going forward in the next 3–5 years (e.g., trial outcomes, regulatory changes, innovations in drug discovery, partnerships, etc.)?
2. If you could see into a crystal ball, what would you most like to know now regarding the state of MyoKardia in 3–5 years?

3. What is the most optimistic picture of the future of this organization? What are the major factors driving that point of view?
4. What is the most pessimistic scenario for the organization in the next 3–5 years? What are the factors driving this outcome?
5. What are some important upcoming decisions you need to face or make as an organization? Over what period will these decisions, and their consequences, play out?

Each executive individually submitted their responses to the questions asked so that we could content-analyze their responses. With this information we were able to identify the biggest sources of uncertainty for the organization and then define the range of likely outcomes. Other organizations might ask other questions using either STEEP issues or a model such as Porter's Five Forces as a starting point for this type of exercise. Although initially we identified six critical uncertainties facing the organization, one (Changes in Regulatory Policy) was eliminated as being highly unlikely within the next 5 years, two were identified as being a more granular subset of other forces of change, and one did not have enough assumed variation to be meaningful in this exercise. With the two remaining forces of change in mind—Clinical Trial Outcomes and Alliance Partnerships—we were able to identify four potential scenarios for the future.

Next, the executive team agreed on the most likely scenario for which we would plan while recognizing that different scenarios could emerge. Thus, we identified key indicators that could be tracked to understand which scenario was emerging as events unfolded (e.g., business partner relationships, drug trial results, etc.). The team agreed on a process and schedule to track key indicators to understand if or when adjustments needed to be made. Given how dynamic business environments can be, we agreed on a quarterly review process to track performance indicators. Going forward they would plan for the most likely scenario but keep a constant eye on the performance indicators that would tell them if the situation was changing and a different scenario would play out.

Defining Capabilities for the Future

The next step in our process was to identify which organizational capabilities would be needed to achieve the best possible outcome for each given scenario.

Note that this is a slightly different focus from traditional SWP, which focuses on roles and headcount versus capabilities. We used this approach because we knew that not only were new skills emerging in the industry the company needed to develop, but also that, as the company moved into commercialization, entirely new capabilities would be needed as a company, and these roles did not yet exist within the organization. For each scenario we asked, "If this scenario were to emerge in the next 3–5 years . . .

1. What capabilities will you need to acquire or build to help you execute? By when will you need to have these capabilities?
2. Are there strategic partnerships you would need to form to be able to execute on this scenario? If yes, by when?
3. What additional resources will you need to be effective under this scenario?
4. What capabilities do you have that will become less important?"

It was through this process that we were able to understand the pivot points the organization would need to manage if its target scenario did not turn out to be the future reality. That is, while it might not need certain capabilities because of strategic partnerships it had, should anything change, what new capabilities would the company need to acquire and how likely was it to accomplish this? This facilitated organizational resilience to adapt to change.

These questions enabled the team to conduct a capability gap analysis to understand what type of investments needed to be made to achieve their desired outcomes under different scenarios. A year before this SWP exercise, MyoKardia had conducted an extensive Organization Capability Analysis (OCA) to understand its strategic positioning. The executive team identified 51 critical capabilities they needed to execute on their business strategy. They then evaluated each capability along two dimensions: performance relative to competitors (worse, equal, better) and importance for winning in the marketplace (needed to play, needed to compete, and needed to win). We were then able to chart these ratings in a 2 × 2 matrix to see which capabilities were aligned to where the company needed to be competitively, which capabilities represented strengths that may be unnecessarily utilizing resources, and which capabilities were not as strong as needed to lead in the marketplace (Figure 13.2).

Because this was a relatively young, high-growth company, it only had a few capabilities that were identified as a potential surplus. However, those

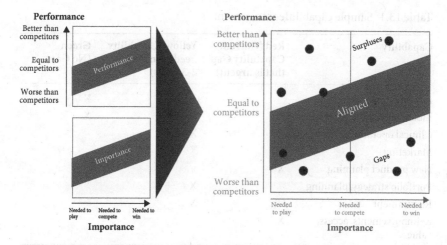

Figure 13.2 Organization capability assessment.

items were a competitive advantage for the firm, so it did not believe it was overinvested in those capabilities.

Other organizations would find value in assessing if there are surpluses of resources where the capabilities they have are of declining importance to the organization. Then the discussion would be on what to do with this talent. This is going to be of growing importance to companies because all industries are going through massive business model and technology-based disruptions. Very few organizations have had aggressive plans to reskill their workforce to ensure they are ready for the future of work. However, with the talent supply shrinking in many fields, organizations will need to turn to reskilling rather than simply laying off people with outdated skills. Not only is this the right thing to do, but organizations will increasingly not be able to find the talent they need to hire because of limited supply in the labor market.

To conduct the SWP capability gap analysis we began with those items previously identified as gaps from the OCA. For the purposes of this exercise, we did not discuss capabilities that had already been identified as a strength in the OCA. In addition to the previously defined gaps, we identified new, emerging capabilities that would be important for the company's success looking forward. This SWP capability gap analysis was very focused on identified gaps as well as new capabilities that needed to be built to support the Vision 2025 strategy. We listed the capabilities and then identified where the company stood in terms of having the capabilities it needed. Table 13.1 provides an example of how we evaluated each of the capabilities.

Table 13.1 Sample capabilities assessment

Capability	Red (Current Capability Gap that is urgent)	Yellow (Capability needed in next 2-3 years)	Green (No Gap)
Alliance management			X
Biochemistry and biophysics			X
Clinical operations		X	
Marketing		X	
New product planning	X		
Portfolio strategy/planning		X	
Recruitment		X	
Reimbursements, access, value	X		

In this example, each capability was rated as either: No gap (Green), Capability needed in the next 2–3 years (Yellow), Current Capability Gap that is urgent (Red). As indicated previously this assessment started with capability gaps we knew the organization already had. Some gaps that were identified in the previous assessment had already been closed, and thus were now rated as "Green," meaning they were no longer a perceived gap. However, we were not surprised that only a few areas were rated "Green."

The purpose of this assessment with the executive teams was to identify what areas represented a significant threat to executing on their strategic plan today (Red capabilities) and which capabilities they needed to begin planning for how they would be developed or acquired to remain on track in the next 2–3 years.

For every Red and Yellow gap identified we dove deeper into a discussion about the specific knowledge, skills, abilities, and technologies needed within that broad capability and how quickly they would be needed, as well as how many resources would be needed to fill the current gap. For example, at the start of this exercise the organization had no commercialization capability. As it looked forward to launching its first drug, it would need to build this capability internally. The leadership knew that to meet their goals they needed this talent within 2–3 years. Specifically, they identified the need for a Chief Commercial Officer and additional roles to build out a commercial team. Thus, in these discussions, we began to get granular in terms of what type of talent was needed (both skillset and at what level; executives, managers, individual contributors), how many, and by when.

Given that our goal was to be agile and anticipate potential future changes that would impact the business, we spent a fair amount of time discussing what new emerging technologies could impact the business and how the organization could best plan for this undefined future (e.g., digital health and health monitoring technologies). These items were identified as capabilities that would be needed in the next 2–3 years, but this process forced a dialogue to consider the importance of beginning now to build this capability for the future.

Analyzing the Current Workforce

While the executive team focused on the business strategy, scenario planning, and identifying the capabilities needed to execute on their vision, when it came to understanding the workforce's ability to deliver on their plan, we turned to functional leaders to help us understand the talent they had on their teams. In larger organizations, this would have been done with managers or directors of large teams. We asked them questions such as

1. Did their current staff have the right skills and competencies to meet their current and future needs (beyond hiring for new, additional roles)?
2. What challenges did they foresee in obtaining these capabilities?
3. What training/development was needed for their current staff to build the skills needed as the company grew?

We had one scenario option that was very uncertain for MyoKardia, so leaders were also asked, If this condition changed, what additional capabilities would they need and in what time frame? Current talent gaps were identified by analyzing the data and insights collected from each of the functional leaders.

Labor Market Impacts on SWP

An important part of SWP is understanding the labor market and its impact on gaining access to critical pools of talent. We scanned the external market to identify which roles, if any, would present a challenge in terms of attracting the talent needed to execute on both the scenario we thought would be most likely as well as alternative scenarios. While one approach to doing this external scan could be the use of technologies that have labor market data (e.g., LinkedIn, Emsi Burning Glass, etc.), we conducted independent research with the most well-established search firms to gain their insights into both our local market as well as the markets from which most competitors are drawing talent. It was quite clear that there was a great deal of competition for talent in clinical, biostatistics, medical affairs, and regulatory affairs roles. While the company had an advantage of being in a biotechnology hub (South San Francisco), which provided a relatively large pool of talent from which to draw, the high demand for these roles resulted in not enough qualified talent to fill all the available roles. Furthermore, the high cost of living in the San Francisco Bay Area and long commute times posed a challenge for attracting talent from outside this geography. To exacerbate the challenge, technology giants (e.g., Alphabet) have increasingly become new competitors with very attractive offerings for prospective candidates.

Our research of the external market and current time-to-hire statistics pointed to the fact that planning to acquire talent needed to be done well in advance of the company's actual need because there would be a long hiring cycle for these roles. All of this had to be considered for when they would begin the search to fill critical capability gaps as the organization moves toward the launch of its first product.

It is interesting to note that, considering post-pandemic acceptance for remote working, we did discuss the possibility of creating either a satellite location or hiring individuals who would be 100% remote. The leadership team was a bit reluctant to consider the viability of these options at the time. Research does require sophisticated equipment, and this makes many remote roles implausible. However, it was determined that the strategy could be included in subsequent SWP plans depending on different business scenarios.

Creating a Staffing Forecast

Having completed all the above steps, we were able to create an initial staffing forecast for the next 5 years based on input from individual functional heads and in collaboration with the executive team. Bringing the executive team together to gain a bird's-eye view of the plan in its entirety was important because, up to this point, they had individually been considering the growth of their own respective parts of the business. While we knew that certain new capabilities were needed, we found that different executives assumed those capabilities would be part of their organization. By sharing the big picture with everyone, we were able to decide the best place for those capabilities to exist, and we were able to ensure that multiple executives were not building overlapping capabilities in their individual functions.

It also allowed us to discuss how growth in one function would have an impact on other functions. For example, if Biology is producing two molecules per year, the Clinical Development Team needed to be staffed appropriately to support the new studies that would support the advancement of these potential future drugs.

Once the executive team had agreed that the initial staffing plan was directionally correct, we further vetted the initial plans with the finance organization to ensure the growth plans were feasible based on current and projected funding. This also had implications for office space planning, and we wanted to ensure we brought the finance organization into the conversation early.

Strategies for Building the Organization of the Future

As skills shortages intensify and competition for top talent intensifies, determining the ideal mix of employed and contingent talent is essential. The optimum mix allows the company the flexibility to expand and contract its workforce with changing market and business needs. We considered the following strategies to close the talent shortages the organization had to address to achieve its target scenario (Figure 13.3).

Time and resources are the two biggest factors in making the decision whether to buy, build, rent, or borrow. MyoKardia was mainly considering

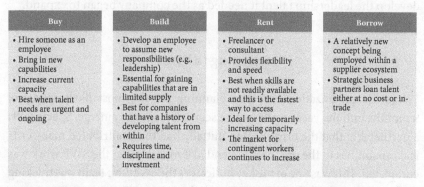

Figure 13.3 Options to bring in talent: buy, build, rent, or borrow.

buying new talent as the organization needed ongoing capability and capacity. However, it is interesting to note that currently 20% of its workforce was contingent (rent). The rent strategy was being utilized for two reasons: (1) it was the only way they could access some highly sought-after talent who were not interested in taking a job, but were interested in project-based work; and (2) the long-term need for the skills and capacity being provided by contractors was unclear. Thus, accessing this talent on an as-needed basis seemed prudent.

When an organization relies heavily on contractors, it is highly recommended that it track its use of this type of talent to determine if or when these contractors should be made into full-time employees. We recommended that the company keep a record of the capabilities contractors are providing, the number of hours they work, and their hourly rate. We advised that the organization continuously review its long-term strategy to determine when to bring capabilities in-house instead of leveraging the incorrect strategy, which was more costly, for the growth phase of the organization.

Finally, because we were planning for significant growth in the organization, it was clear that existing organizational structures would need to change to support anticipated growth. Although each function would not be making immediate changes, the growth of the organization also had implications for broader leadership development. We needed to understand if the firm already had high-potential talent that just needed to be developed, or if leadership talent needed to be part of the strategic workforce plan to fill a previously unrecognized capability gap. We identified the specific leadership positions and skill gaps the organization needed to close and then presented a build strategy with recommendations for how it could develop the leadership talent it needed as the company began to expand.

Learning to Pivot

While the organization executed planning for the most likely scenario, 9 months into the year an alternative scenario began to emerge. Specifically, a partnership that the organization initially had that contributed many critical capabilities to the organization ended 4 months after the SWP work was completed. This was one of the key indicators the executive team was tracking to determine if a different scenario might emerge. Because the executive team had previously discussed which capabilities would be needed under different scenarios—including this one—they were prepared to pivot. Given the work we did during our scenario planning discussions, they knew exactly which capabilities they needed under this scenario and thus they were able to quickly adjust their workforce needs. This demonstrates how considering alternative scenarios enabled the leaders to see a different potential future, and, as a result, they were able to quickly adapt and adjust their plans to fit the new reality.

At MyoKardia, the SWP provided a roadmap of long-term headcount projections and was not an approval for hiring all positions. It did, however, inform the annual planning cycle and budget, and the 2019 headcount was very much aligned with the headcount projections of the SWP. In addition to periodic review(s), going forward, executives were committed to conduct the SWP exercise along with scenario planning annually to ensure that it reflects any changes in the business. They saw the strategic workforce plan as a continuous living document that would help inform their growth, capability, and talent investments.

Useful Tips for Using Scenario Planning in SWP

This chapter has covered several tips you might keep in mind as you begin your SWP effort. For ease of reference, we provide this summary.

1. Scenario planning considers the extremes of a situation, and one role of the consultant is to facilitate creative thinking on part of stakeholders.
2. Collaborate with the client to find the unit of analysis (industry, company, business unit, etc.) that they are motivated to address.
3. Even if there is a most likely scenario, strive to explore a range of scenarios including some that may be unlikely but significant if they occur. You can also have the client assess and rate the likelihood of different scenarios.
4. During scenario planning for SWP, include a set of questions about the unique talent implications of each of the scenarios.
5. Conduct scenario based SWP in close association with asking about organizational performance implications and achieving/risking overall company competitive advantage. This reminds stakeholders SWP is about business performance, not just roles and headcount.

6. Added attention to labor market insights helps complete the picture *and* opens discussion of options to secure needed talent and capabilities (build, buy, borrow, etc.) as well as other strategies to access talent (e.g., location-based strategies, use of remote work).
7. Bringing stakeholders together from across the company helps surface and align their assumptions and allows them to see the interdependencies across their parts of the business.
8. Each approach to securing talent (build, buy, borrow, etc.) has different implications for how you on-board, manage, engage, and retain talent. In other words, you aren't done just deciding on what talent procurement strategy to use; you must also plan how to execute it effectively over time.
9. Reframe SWP from headcount projection (and project) to being part of company aspirations for nimble business leadership.

Epilogue

Due to the strong positioning of the company and its continued scientific success, MyoKardia was acquired by Bristol Meyers Squibb at the end of 2020. Being acquired was never part of the company's strategic plan, thus this scenario was never one they considered.

Acknowledgments

Parts of chapter article were adapted from Goldberg, E. L. and Boyes, I. (2019). Using scenario planning to facilitate agility in strategic workforce planning, *People + Strategy Journal*, 42(4), 57–61.

References

Boudreau, J. B., Rearick, C. L., and Ziskin, I. (Eds.). (2018). *Black holes and white spaces: Reimagining the future of work and HR with the CHREATE Project*. Society for Human Resource Management.

Chermack, T. J., Coons, L. M., O'barr, G. and Khatami, S. (2017). The effects of scenario planning on participant reports of resilience. *European Journal of Training and Development*, 41(4), 306–326.

Chermack, T. J., Coons, L. M., Nimon, K., Bradley, P., and Glick, M. B. (2015). The effects of scenario planning on participant perceptions of creative organizational climate. *Journal of Leadership and Organizational Studies, 22*(3), 355–371.

Goldberg, E. L., and Boyes, I. (2019). Using scenario planning to facilitate agility in strategic workforce planning. *People + Strategy Journal, 42*(4), 57–61.

Haeffner, M., Leone, D., Coons, L. and Chermack, T. (2012). The effects of scenario planning on participant perceptions of learning organization characteristics. *Human Resource Development Quarterly, 23*(4), 519–542.

Porter, M. E. (1979). How competitive forces shape strategy. *Harvard Business Review, 57*(2), 137–145.

Pryor, G. (2018). Future states. In J. B. Boudreau, C. L. Rearick, and I. Ziskin (Eds.), *Black holes and white spaces: Reimagining the future of work and HR with the CHREATE project*. Society for Human Resource Management, 20–21.

Rohrbeck, R., and Schwarz, J. O. (2013). The value contribution of strategic foresight: Insights from an empirical study of large European companies. *Technological Forecasting and Social Change, 80*(8). doi:10.1016/j.techfore.2013.01.004

Schwartz, P. (1991). *The art of the long view.* Doubleday, 1593–1606.

van der Heijden, K. (1997). *Scenarios: The art of strategic conversation.* Wiley.

Further Reading

For those interested in learning more about scenario planning the following resources may be helpful.

Bryan, L., and Farrell, D. (2008). Leading through uncertainty. McKinsey and Company. https://www.mckinsey.com/business-functions/strategy-and-corporate-finance/our-insights/leading-through-uncertainty

Chermack, T. J. (2011). *Scenario planning in organizations: How to create, use and assess scenarios.* Berrett-Koehler.

Young, M. (2014, May). Scenario planning for human resources and strategic workforce planning. Conference Executive Board Research Report. https://www.conference-board.org/publications/publicationdetail.cfm?publicationid=2760

14
Moving Mountains

Stamina and Resistance in Just Workforce Planning

Juliet R. Aiken and Tori Glascock

The just workforce. What is a "just workforce"? Workforce planning is targeted toward specific goals and pain points. While these goals often have productivity, performance, or financial underpinnings, organizations in general share one pain point: to be more diverse, equitable, and inclusive. No organization we have ever worked with is fully equitable simply because the world we live in is not equitable. A critical side point in *just workforce planning* (JWP)—and *justice, equity, diversity, and inclusion* (JEDI) work in general—is that the work of planning for and building toward a just workforce is not ever done. No check box or list of tasks will ever enable an organization to be at a place where it can say, yes, we no longer need to strive for equity. The work of JWP and JEDI is the work of many lifetimes, and it is the work most worth doing.

Introduction

In the early 1970s, Montmore County Government was put under a consent decree for alleged discrimination based on race and gender in hiring decisions. For the reader unfamiliar with the concept of consent decrees, these legal decisions require behavioral change on the part of the organization in question (which can include recompense to affected parties) without the admission of guilt. To exit this decree, Montmore was tasked with three requirements. First, Montmore needed to develop a proactive diversity recruiting function to improve the diversity of its applicant pools. Second, Montmore needed to implement unbiased selection processes. Third, Montmore needed to provide regular quantitative reports on its progress toward these goals. In short, Montmore was asked to develop recruiting, hiring, and reporting processes that enabled a more just workforce. After over 30 years, a massive workforce reduction, *and bankruptcy, Montmore was placed in contempt for failing to meet the requirements of this decree.*

Strategic workforce planning (SWP) encompasses many things, some we are taught in our formal education as industrial-organizational (I-O) psychologists and some we are not. Encompassed in the idea of SWP are recruiting, hiring, training, workflow, and organizational structure. Essentially, SWP concerns itself with how people should be deployed most effectively to accomplish not just what the organization needs at this moment, but what it will need in the future. As I-O psychologists, we are given some of the pieces of this puzzle in our formal training. Often, we are provided with a background on quantitative methods and analysis and selection. Sometimes, we are provided with a background on training. Very rarely, our formal training may touch on recruiting, strategy, or organizational structure. We are usually given building blocks related to the individual and, less frequently, building blocks related to the organization in its wholeness. For more on the teaching of SWP—both as it is and as it could be—we encourage the interested reader to dive into Chapter 16 in this volume, "Teaching Strategic Workforce Planning: Hit the Ground Running."

Practitioner Tip!

Diversity. Diversity refers to the amount of variety (or differences) among the members of a defined group or organization with respect to a common characteristic or attribute (Harrison and Klein, 2007). Diversity is a group-level phenomenon; individuals cannot be diverse, only groups. Diversity focuses on differences in one or more attributes; these differences can be *demographic* or *deep* attributes. Demographic attributes refer to those that are considered more visible, such as race, ethnicity, age, etc. Deep attributes refer to attributes that are considered less visible, such as cultural diversity, background, and neurodivergence (Harrison, Price, and Bell, 1998).

Exposition

When Montmore was placed in contempt, the federal judge overseeing this case appointed a Receiver to oversee the needed workforce changes. Conceptually, a Receiver is an individual who takes financial, strategic, and tactical responsibility for (in this case) all human resources (HR)-related decisions. They have the power to appoint, hire, promote, or fire anyone for any reason; determine and change the budget; and make structural decisions and changes to their organization. The Receiver essentially takes top leadership control of the organization—only for the duration of the Receivership—then turns responsibility back over to the county leaders after the Receivership has been exited and the consent decree closed out.

While we come into SWP with some building blocks, we are often taught these building blocks in silos. We learn each topic in a separate class, and it is rare that we enroll in classes that embed us in the rich interconnections between these human talent processes and frameworks. When we enter SWP practice, we therefore run the risk of becoming task- or process-focused and losing sight of the larger picture: What is the underlying issue that the organization needs to address? Complicating this further is that the theoretical underpinning of planning for a *just* workforce is lacking. Most of our theories and research on SWP have been developed by those who are dominant in our academic settings; our Western, educated, industrialized, rich, and democratic (WEIRD) samples have been collected by WEIRD researchers (Meadon and Spurrett, 2010). Therefore, the theoretical groundwork we *do* have not only insufficiently addresses developing just workforces, but also comes from one dominant perspective. There may be schools of thought and assumptions underlying these theories that we have not fully questioned. Part of constructing a just workforce will require taking this anti-oppressive lens and exploring who benefits, who makes decisions, and what assumptions underlie theoretical, empirical, and practical SWP (c.f., IO Coffeehouse, n.d.). This does not mean our existing theories are not useful—it simply means we cannot adhere to them without independent thought and flexibility, leveraging what is useful in each workforce planning project and letting go of what is not.

Practitioner Tip!

Equity. Equity means recognizing that individuals have distinct circumstances and calls for the allocation of resources and opportunities to address existing imbalances. *Equity stands in contrast to equality*, which is providing equal treatment to everyone regardless of their unique

> circumstances (Rodriguez, 2016). *Inclusion* means allowing members to share their unique characteristics while also helping them develop a sense of belonging at work (Mor Barak, 2014). In an inclusive organization, people can be themselves and are recognized and appreciated for their unique contributions. The concept of inclusion is a dynamic one that addresses the extent to which diverse individuals are empowered to participate and have voice in organizational contexts, receive access to material resources, are treated equitably within institutional processes, and are valued and respected in terms of behavioral interactions within the normative culture (Chun and Evans, 2018). *Inclusion is all about there being more than one right way.*

The Receiver overseeing Montmore conducted a thorough internal analysis of the HR needs of the county. He assessed recruiting, selection, training, reporting, performance management, benefits, and HR Information Systems (HRIS), and more. He noted that changes would need to be made throughout the entire county, to all HR processes, and to leadership hiring, promotion, and philosophy, for Montmore to become an employer of choice. He correctly identified that the foundational need of the county would not be fixed by meeting the letter of the consent decree. The county did not need recruiting practices, hiring, and reporting. Montmore needed a cultural transformation to enable more diverse talent to enter, develop, stay, and thrive—and for its reputation internally and externally in a diverse community to advance.

Regardless of the overarching goal and need, we must begin an SWP process somewhere. Some part of the SWP universe must be identified as a priority and a starting place to feed efforts. Ideally, the first process tackled should provide early wins, engender confidence in internal and external stakeholders, and begin to seed buy-in even among those resistant to change. And who among us can claim to be unresistant to change? The first process tackled—and how it is approached—lays the foundation for all future efforts.

And here we digress. So far, in a chapter that is clearly titled "Just Workforce Planning," we have not used that term a single time. And here is why: it is our philosophy that SWP and JWP are one and the same. Talent management, done right, requires diversity, equity, and inclusion to be fully centered in all decisions and considerations and by all leaders in the organization, not just one designated with this charge. Unfortunately, many organizations view JEDI as a box to be checked, just one part of work. Effective JWP requires the practitioner to see that JEDI isn't a part of work—it is all of work. Everything that leaders do either moves the organization toward or away from diversity, equity, and inclusion. Talent *is* equity, full stop. You cannot have an optimized talent lifecycle if you have any inequity in your human systems. It is as simple, and as extraordinarily difficult, as that. So, while JWP is SWP specifically for a just, diverse, and equitable workforce, we contend that all SWP should be JWP. Nonetheless, so the reader can stay focused on our topic, we use the acronym "JWP" in place of "SWP" for the remainder of this chapter.

> **Practitioner Tip!**
>
> *Justice. Justice* sits at the intersection of equity, equality, and inclusion (Greenberg and Colquitt, 2013). For those who exist on the margins of society, given that our systems are often led from an equality and not an equity lens, the presence of justice means that the wrongs that marginalized groups have endured will be recognized and learned from. As a result, actors in the systems we live in transform their actions to embody equity and inclusion. *Justice* stands in contrast to *reparations*. Whereas *reparations* are an action to help make up for a wrong, *justice* is a way of being, a way of embodying in which those who are otherwise overlooked are treated in an equitable and inclusive way. *Justice* must be entrenched into the fabric of organizations.

Rising Action

As part of the initial assessment the Receiver conducted—and of every follow-up evaluation on progress—he calculated core statistics to provide a view into how Montmore was operating in its human talent practices. The report covered data around background checks, hiring processes, discrimination complaints, budgets, staffing levels in HR, and a training needs assessment survey, among others. In addition to leveraging archival and survey data, the Receiver drew on deep qualitative and content assessment in his report. However, his recommendations projected well beyond the data gathered, recognizing that, inherently, Montmore needed to be entirely reconstructed. The Report, grounded in data, projected a dream for a healthier county government.

JWP requires revolution not evolution. When we commit to building just, equitable, and diverse workplaces, we commit to a future that is not mirrored in our past. How do you consider future talent needs when you want a more diverse workforce but do not currently have one? While quantitative analysis and SWP are deeply entwined, data inherently are backward looking. We cannot measure what we do not have. This is akin to the statistical concept of *range restriction*. For nonstatisticians reading this chapter, range restriction describes a phenomenon whereby models made on restricted variability datasets do not generalize sufficiently to broader populations (Hunter, Schmidt, and Le, 2006). The practice of creating a just workforce requires that we pull from what we know and create a path into a future where there may be many unknowns simply because we have never been there before. JWP is a creative and hopeful exercise, one grounded in what we *do* know as fully as we can honor that as a foundation for a different future.

The Receiver dedicated significant financial and human resources to accomplish the needed JWP transformation. The Receiver initially engaged consultants to develop selection processes according to best practices in creating valid and fair (unbiased) procedures, addressing one prong of the consent decree. These consultants worked in parallel to an internal team of I-O practitioners who were likewise developing selection procedures. In total, Montmore had over 200 different job classes for which selection procedures may have eventually been required. And, with the recent reduction in workforce, the need to hire in a large majority of these classes—often more than 100 at a time—was urgent. The Receiver engaged one consultant (the first author of this chapter) to lead the internal team of I-O practitioners toward completion of this prong of the decree.

All organizational change efforts require resources (financial, human, accountability) to be successful. Unfortunately, most organizations treat JEDI—and JWP—as a "nice to have" not a "need to have" and commit insufficient resources to the complete talent transformation that is required for true JWP. Many organizations who have JEDI officers do not provide authority to those officers. The authority to drive JWP almost never lies with JEDI officers; instead, it typically lies with top leadership or HR who may delegate JWP to JEDI specialists but rarely provide resources or authority for them to do so effectively. Resourcing these functions and providing them with formal authority enables JEDI practitioners to make significant impact; without this authority and without the explicit support of key stakeholders, JEDI practitioners otherwise rarely have the latitude to drive the kinds of changes their organizations ask them to make (Chrobot-Mason, Ruderman, and Nishii, 2014).

Top leaders often delegate ownership of JEDI down the chain of command, typically to these JEDI practitioners. This not only undermines accountability, but also makes JEDI appear less important to the organization because top leadership itself is not boldly championing the cause. Moreover, the people doing JEDI work are often Black, Indigenous, and People of Color (BIPOC), who are often reporting to a White person, thus increasing the load on internal JEDI practitioners not only around accountability but also around implicit requirements to educate. The "fix" for this is straightforward, and we have already set it forward: organizations—and top leaders—need to view all talent as JEDI and allocate resources to, own, and champion those efforts accordingly.

Conflict

As hiring began to pick up pace and the pool of talent hired into the county became more diverse, a rift formed almost immediately between new hires and existing employees. Many existing employees—predominantly White—had been demoted during the RIF and were working their old jobs as well as their new for reduced pay. Incoming employees—more racially diverse in their composition—were now hired either alongside or above those existing employees. For some existing employees, resentment built. Some were now training new employees on their old jobs, while they continued to get paid less. To some other employees, these new employees were not seen as hired for their qualifications but for their race or gender. Even in the best managed change management process, no organization is a monolithic entity; all organizations are comprised of individuals who have different needs, fears, and motivations. Resentment is almost inevitable in organizational change—the primary question is whether the organization is aware of it as it happens, and the secondary question is how the organization deals with it.

There is the unfortunate belief by many that diversity and qualifications are fundamentally at odds. In many JWP efforts, employees and leadership believe that hiring and promoting more diverse talent requires "lowering" standards, and that when Black applicants are hired, for example, they are hired because they are Black. The first author of this chapter had the dubious honor of getting sucked into such an argument at an office Christmas party in 2016. Consider how our own field plays into this dynamic and this belief, with our fixation on the "diversity-validity" tradeoff, for example (Ployhart and

Holtz, 2008). JWP requires that we question our assumptions. From where did our ideas of what "success" or "performance" look like? What are the underlying values embedded in those ideas? Why were those constructs created in the first place? Sir Francis Galton, the first person to measure general intelligence, also coined the term "eugenics," for example (Aubert-Marson, 2009; Galton, 1883). Our assumptions that there is a diversity–validity tradeoff rely on the idea that the architecture underlying how we assess validity is unbiased. Perhaps instead of feeding into a narrative that continues to harm people belonging to traditionally underrepresented groups, it is time for I-O practitioners to ask the bigger question: What are we really measuring when we measure performance and its predictors? And, what other perspectives might we take instead?

Initially, the consultant appointed to lead the internal selection team worked to bridge the gap between the internal I-O practitioners and the consulting team, facilitating processes that aligned their approaches in designing and validating selection procedures, including their reporting templates. Over time, the consultant worked to assess and chart a path forward for training and development, reporting, and other parts of HR. As she moved between functional areas, she strove to integrate their workstreams more naturally to align resources, aims, and outcomes. For example, job analysis data from selection was used to populate onboarding sheets coming out of training and development; recruiting priorities informed and were reciprocally driven by the stated needs of leaders and the priorities and commitments of the selection team.

Just as I-O practitioners are often taught in silos, critical human talent functions in many organizations often operate in silos. You will not drive effective JWP processes if you operate this way. Success only comes when you recognize and honor the interconnectedness of all human talent systems. Like the systems in a human body, the talent systems in every organization rely on and feed into each other. If any system truly fails, regardless of the functioning of the other systems, the entire organization will fail in its efforts. If we consider specifically JWP, many organizations do what Montmore was formally tasked with doing—recruit and hire *diverse* talent. However, these same organizations often overlook the fact that their climate and internal environment is hostile to the talent that they are bringing in. Without considering talent processes overall—as the Receiver wisely did in this case—organizations hiring diverse talent without consideration of inclusion, equity, and justice internally are bringing in diverse talent to be abused. Is it so surprising that these organizations struggle to retain their new employees?

Climax

As the selection and training teams began working together, opportunities emerged to catch potential inconsistencies between what jobs needed and what supervisors wanted. For example, training staff working on onboarding documents could quickly detect when the requirements demanded by direct supervisors for their new employees were misaligned with the information provided in the job analysis. At times, these discrepancies may have been due to inconsistencies between how direct supervisors and others viewed the job requirements at entry and therefore presented an opportunity for education. At other times, these discrepancies may have been due to deliberate attempts to discourage new employees when leaders were unable to make the hire they personally wished to make.

Organizational systems disconnect sometimes by oversight and sometimes by design. Not everyone in the organization(s) you work with will be a friend to JWP—or, really, to any change you wish to implement. Organizations are beasts made of individuals, and individuals do not as a whole align. They do not share the same wants, needs, fears, insecurities, and personal constraints. Even if you feel you have buy-in from key stakeholders, they may undermine your efforts—and the buy-in you do *not* have can also undermine you. This is a particularly salient challenge in JWP because JEDI efforts are often taken very personally on the part of top leadership. Many top leaders going through JWP see the very act of JWP as a criticism of them as a human being and their own perceived "failings" in fostering a just workplace. Unfortunately, it is difficult to get these decision-makers to understand, as our executive director often says, "it's not about you." The only hope of getting to this point with those who are resistant is to first understand their insecurities. Push-back comes from a place of fear. Understanding this fear does not guarantee buy-in, but you certainly cannot overcome push-back without understanding the fear that drives it. For those familiar with Schein's (2010) work on cultural transformation, Schein outlines three stages of cultural change: (1) unfreezing the current culture, (2) cognitive restructuring to enable movement to a new culture, and (3) freezing the new culture. Schein's description of cultural change likewise hearkens to complexity theories of change, wherein discontinuous emergent system (e.g., organization-level) change occurs as the system moves from one state of being to the next (for those interested in complexity theory and change, Uhl-Bien and Marion's 2007 book, *Complexity Leadership Part I*, provides a wonderful foray into the world of complexity theory and organizations). Considering both Schein's work and complexity theory, a focus on uncovering the underpinnings of resistance and addressing them is necessary for successful unfreezing and cognitive restructuring; without these efforts the organization cannot move from one state to the next.

Falling Action

The Receiver faced with this effort did not interface directly with the training or selection staff working on these processes. He was not involved in job analysis, design, or review of onboarding forms or in discussions unearthing any discrepancies. Nevertheless, when discrepancies did arise, he was able to guide the staff through the successful resolution of each challenge. When education was needed, he facilitated information-sharing and supported staff in how and what to provide employees. When necessary, he would greet new employees personally, galvanized by the entire picture of what was happening in his organization and prepared to ensure that they had the resources they needed to be successful.

The official drivers of most JWP processes sit at high levels of the organization—these are decision-makers who take a strategic orientation, plan for the future of the organization, and avoid (ideally) getting into the weeds of day-to-day work. Nonetheless, JWP planning efforts will absolutely fail unless they are catalyzed by the knowledge, experiences, and needs of those even in entry-level jobs. JWP must be bottom-up as well as top-down and must be fed by a constant flow of information from throughout the organization. JWP decisions cannot be made from only one mindset and only one perspective. They must be infused with the perspectives of the manifold constituents within the organization. We strongly encourage the interested reader to explore the thinking presented in *Toyota Kata: Managing People for Improvement, Adaptiveness, and Superior Results*, which operates similarly: change must be driven from the bottom up, as those on the front lines know where their pain points are most intently (Rother, 2010). To succeed, leaders of JWP must stay in a receiving posture. All information is new information. Information comes from everywhere, and those sharing their experiences are valued. Even when some information flowing to you may appear to be in direct contrast with other information, become comfortable holding multiple realities in your head at once: even directly conflicting information may reflect the truly believed and lived experiences of those sharing that information with you.

None of this was planned—there was no way for the Receiver to know which onboarding documents would misalign with job analysis results and which supervisors might have different expectations from their new employees than outlined in those job analyses. The Receiver, consultants, and internal team members pushed forward daily—business as usual, in so much as there is ever business as usual in a massive, federally backed change effort—when on occasion, the training staff would discover and surface these challenges. Regardless of their emergent nature, he moved quickly and decisively along a previously unplanned course of action to ensure that progress toward revolutionizing the county workforce continued.

Organizations are alive. The plans we lay and intend to execute will constantly run into the reality that, as we move, so, too, does the organization. Unlike when we perform surgery on a human body, an organization cannot be anesthetized. We all are familiar with a (paraphrased version of) Helmuth von Moltke's (1993) saying, "no plan ever survives the first encounter" (Gibson, 2021). As Gibson notes, JWP is dynamic. It requires us to often run on three or more tracks at once, rapidly switching between tracks as conditions change. Even contingency planning alone does not guarantee success. The JWP practitioner must be like water. They must be able to adapt to the unexpected, keeping the goal—an equitable, inclusive, just, and productive workforce for the future—constantly in focus. Rigid adherence to one given path fails. Staying magnetized toward your goal enables success.

Resolution

Over the course of nearly half a decade, the Receiver, consultants, and internal staff interlocked to drive cascading changes across county leadership and HR. Leveraged in this process were I-O psychologists, HR professionals, technology specialists, engineers, financial experts, and so on. A deeply and demographically diverse team of dedicated professionals worked hand in glove to enable systematic, lasting, powerful change for Montmore County. Mornings at Montmore started early—typically by 7 AM—and consultants and the Receiver often worked into the evenings. There were days where the embedded consultant would work on a required report until 2 AM, turn it over to the Receiver who worked on it until 6 AM, and then picked back up immediately at 6 AM to ensure that a deadline was met. Five years on, this transformation may have seemed like a long time. As a helpful grounding, the federal judge overseeing this case once declared that he did not think he would see it done within a decade. In this light, 5 years was a heroic lift.

As we look at the incredible effort that a committed JWP process requires, we acknowledge two things. First, JWP teams themselves must be diverse. In order to plan for a future we cannot pull out of our past, we must have out-of-the-box thinking and planning that stretches beyond what the organization has done before. Second, JWP is a marathon, not a sprint. Committing to justice and equity is not the work of a moment; it is a daily commitment to do hard internal and external work. It requires broad, sweeping, systemic change and a universal professional and personal commitment among committed staff to continuously grow and improve. The JWP practitioner must temper their own and their organization's or client's expectations. There are no grand gestures in JWP, just enduring commitments that are carried through every day. There are no shortcuts; trust and transformation take time.

Over the course of 5 years, the internal and external JWP practitioners grew close. Work trickled into friendship, babies were born and celebrated, some employees changed jobs, relationships dissolved, some planned for retirement. Half a decade later, those involved often still text and email each other, not just to reminisce on the experience but to hear about each other's lives and families. During what was an effortful and challenging process, staff and consultants leaned into each other for support.

JWP is brutally personal. Many practitioners engaged in any JEDI work took up the mantle because it is personally meaningful to them, often because of their own lived experiences. It wears on the soul to strive to drive change in a personally relevant area in the face of pushback, evasions, and outright denials that any change is needed. JWP is hard work physically, emotionally, and mentally. As a JWP practitioner, you must take care of yourself. Set boundaries, engage in self-care, and partner to hold organizations accountable for creating life-giving environments for this critical work. The very nature of these efforts places unbelievable pressure around getting things "right." You are, ultimately, human. Embrace the reality that you will not always say or do the right thing. Seek community for support, feedback, and accountability. All JWP practitioners need shoulders, basins of strength to refill our wells, and true friends who hold our feet to the fire so that we, too, learn, grow, and do better every day.

After years of concerted efforts, the Receivership ended, and the Receiver transitioned organizational decision-making power back to Montmore County. After a period of monitoring, the Consent Decree was concluded a full 45 years after it entered this decree. Prior to the receivership ending, the consultants had pulled back considerably from their prior embedded roles. Prior to the consent decree ending, HR was already considering other ways to approach selection and to begin to reintegrate leaders into some selection processes while preserving fairness. The Montmore County that went into Receivership is not the Montmore County that came out of Receivership; the Montmore County that exists today is different from both.

No system survives the toll of time. No matter how thoughtfully JWP is conducted, the systems will eventually drift. Change in the environment is inevitable, and the organization must respond accordingly. Worst case: decision-makers in the organization change or drift from their commitment to the principles that originally guided their efforts. Best case: once thoughtful decisions become nonoptimal. Either way, JWP practitioners must account for and plan for this drift. JWP must go above and beyond the initial goal or benchmark to account for drift and backsliding—our goal is to accomplish *more* than we intend, to prepare for the impact of time on our carefully designed systems. In doing so, one key challenge is this: do not develop systems around any one person, and do not create systems or processes that one bad actor can undermine. Set up systems around *organizational* needs, not individual convenience, and create checks and balances to thwart attempts to derail progress. This is particularly essential in positions related to risk management, HR, JEDI, and legal functions.

Epilogue

Montmore's story is obviously deeper, more complex, more dynamic, and more personal than space would ever allow us to do justice to. Hopefully, even in this short space, the reader can see clearly that creating a just workforce pits us against formidable, imposing, dynamic mountains of tradition that are so deeply rooted and entrenched that they become the unquestioned, immutable "given" status quo in workplaces and in our discipline, training, and theories.

In closing, we offer the JWP practitioner the following insights, which were woven throughout the story of Montmore's JWP transformation. These insights are hardly exhaustive but will hopefully provide you with both security and freedom as you drive JWP revolutions in your or your clients' organizations (Table 14.1).

Table 14.1 Guidelines for Just workforce planning (JWP)

1. The processes that need to be changed are not the same thing as the change that needs to be made. What is the need that knits those tactical changes together? What is the underlying force? What isn't yet equitable, right, or just? When making these decisions, absolutely pull from but do not only rely on data—data provide you with critical insight into the past and present but cannot alone drive a future that is unknown to any of us.
2. The work of justice, equity, diversity, and inclusion (JEDI) never ends. It is not a box to be checked. It is daily, unsexy, grueling internal effort and accountability on the part of all leaders in an organization. There are no short-cuts; the only solution is to show up daily, put in the self-work, and consistently follow through.
3. The head bone is connected to the neck bone. Our practices are not siloed, and JEDI is not siloed from talent. You cannot do JWP piece by piece; attend to the internal world not just the hiring or you set your hires up to fail. Organizational systems are interconnected; talent IS JEDI.
4. Begin JWP thoughtfully in places where impact is maximized and buy-in can be gained. Where are the biggest gains in equity available for the least (relative) lift? Where can you plant seeds for support, help the organization, and demonstrate value?
5. Leaders: JEDI work and JWP is not about you. It isn't personal. Put your money where your mouth is and resource JEDI efforts fully. Embrace the messiness of self-work. You have the choice to be comfortable or uncomfortable. Not everyone does—it is your duty to make the choice to be uncomfortable for the betterment of your organization and your employees.
6. When assembling JWP teams, make sure you put together both deeply and demographically diverse teams to enable breakthrough thinking. The same thinking that got us here will not get us there.
7. When conducting JWP, we need to think of the theories and methods we learn as frameworks and mechanisms, not straightjackets. They should provide us with guidance and direction but we should not adhere to theory so rigidly that we cannot flex to what is truly needed in practice. We must likewise question our assumptions of what makes for strong performance and what might predict it.
8. Effective JWP requires bottom-up change, not just top-down. When working to get buy-in at all levels of the organization, you must understand where stakeholders' insecurities and fears come from to have any hope of overcoming resistance.
9. JWP is not just task work, it is also hard emotional labor. Be sure to identify, cultivate, and maintain your well to challenge you, support you, and make sure you do not go empty. This well should—ideally—span both your personal and professional lives.
10. JWP is a marathon, not a sprint. The work is long and often discouraging, and, when a project is "done," drift is inevitable. Plan to finish ahead of where you want to so that the toll of time is less likely to truly set you back.

This chapter presents an ethos and a way of being that enables workplace revolution. Because we offer an ethos, the reader may be wondering what they can do *right now*, in existing SWP functions and businesses, to begin the good work. The answer to this is simple, profound, and profoundly difficult: set your ego entirely aside. As you do so, the following recommendations in Table 14.2 become remarkably actionable.

Table 14.2 What next?

1. Come to terms with the reality that you are not yet doing just workforce planning (JWP). Our strategic workforce planning (SWP) frameworks and approaches are not grounded in justice, equity, diversity, and inclusion (JEDI) either in theory or practice. You may *want* to do JWP but it is nearly a certainty that you are not yet doing it in your current place of work.
2. Form a strong relationship with any JEDI professionals and human resource business partners (HRBPs) in your organization. This relationship must be one in which you are open to their expertise and guidance. Do not go to them as a checkbox at the end of a decision or process; do not go to them presenting yourself as an expert. Go to them at the *beginning* of any of your processes and weave them in as core experts throughout building and implementing any interventions.
3. Make yourself open to information. Information comes from everywhere, and you will be most effective if you know everything that is happening throughout the organization. Be grateful for the information you receive. Act on it and keep it in confidence. Always listen to the same information told from multiple viewpoints without rushing the process—it is not possible to hear or know enough.
4. Relax any current fixation you have on viewing SWP as *process change* and view it instead as *people change*. This reframing will enable you to approach each step of the process with respect for the dignity and diversity of the people in the organization who must live with every decision you and your team make.
5. Do the self-work every single day. Read books and consume media that help you challenge your own assumptions about the world and your own biases. We all have them. Surround yourself with people who challenge and annoy you, who push you to be the best version of yourself. Open yourself every day to the liberation that comes with accepting that you are not yet at your peak—you have the beautiful opportunity to grow daily. Seize it.

Acknowledgments

We want to celebrate and appreciate several brilliant, beautiful minds who contributed to the ethos and observations shared in this chapter. Deep appreciation and gratitude to Lorren Oliver, Tonya Dawson, Katelyn Ford-Bey, and our colleagues Sakinah Muhammad, Domonique Edwards, and Paul Hanges. Like many movies, please note that the following story is based on a true story. Names (including the organization name) and details have been adapted in creating this chapter.

References

Aubert-Marson D. (2009). Sir Francis Galton: le fondateur de l'eugénisme [Sir Francis Galton: the father of eugenics]. *Medical Science (Paris), 25*(6–7):641–645. doi:10.1051/medsci/2009256-7641. PMID: 19602363

Chun, E., and Evans, A. (2018). *Leading a diversity culture shift in higher education: Comprehensive organizational learning strategies*. Routledge.

Chrobot-Mason, D., Ruderman, M. N., and Nishii, L. H. (2014). Leadership in a diverse workplace. In D. V. Day (Ed.), *The Oxford handbook of leadership and organizations* (pp. 683–708). Oxford University Press.

Galton, F. (1883). *Inquiries into human faculty and its development*. Macmillan.

Gibson, A. (2021). *Agile workforce planning*. Kogan.

Greenberg, J., and Colquitt, J. A. (2013). *Handbook of organizational justice*. Psychology Press.

Harrison, D. A. and Klein, K. J. (2007). What's the difference? Diversity constructs as separation, variety, or disparity in organizations. *Academy of Management Review, 32*, 1199–1228.

Harrison, D. A., Price, K. H., and Bell, M. P. (1998.) Beyond relational demography: Time and the effects of surface- and deep-level diversity on work group cohesion. *Academy of Management Journal, 41*, 96–107.

Hunter, J. E., Schmidt, F. L., and Le, H. (2006). Implications of direct and indirect range restriction for meta-analysis methods and findings. *Journal of Applied Psychology, 91*(3), 594–612. https://doi.org/10.1037/0021-9010.91.3.594

IO Coffeehouse (n.d.). Anti-racism fact sheet. https://pufferfish-synthesizer-snts.squarespace.com/s/Anti-racism-two-pager-01-11-2021.pdf

Meadon, M., and Spurrett, D. (2010). It's not just the subjects: There are too many WEIRD researchers. *Behavioral and Brain Sciences, 33*, 104–105.

Mor Barak, M. E. (2014). *Managing diversity: Toward a globally inclusive workplace* (3rd ed.). Sage.

Ployhart, R. E., and Holtz, B. C. (2008). The diversity–validity dilemma: Strategies for reducing racioethnic and sex subgroup differences and adverse impact in selection. *Personnel Psychology, 61*(1), 153–172.

Rodriguez, A. J. (2016). For whom do we do equity and social justice work? Recasting the discourse about the other to effect transformative change. In N. M. Joseph, C. Haynes, and F. Cobb (Eds.), *Interrogating whiteness and relinquishing power: White faculty's commitment to racial consciousness in STEM classrooms* (pp. 241–252). Peter Lang.

Rother, M. (2010). *Toyota kata: Managing people for improvement, adaptiveness, and superior results*. McGraw Hill Education.

Schein, E. H. (2010). *Organizational culture and leadership* (vol. 2). Wiley.

Uhl-Bien, M., and Marion, R. (Eds.). (2007). *Complexity leadership: Part 1: Conceptual foundations*. IAP.

Von Moltke, H. (1993). *Moltke on the art of war: Selected writings*. D. J. Hughes (Ed.). Presidio Press.

15

Zero Hour for Jobs

How One Company Helped Others Adapt Their SWP when COVID Roiled the Planet and Learned to Adapt Itself

Michael N. Bazigos

This chapter begins with a unique instance of a spontaneous strategic workforce planning (SWP) innovation born of disruption of labor markets by the global pandemic of 2019. That moment is chronologically sandwiched between its past and its future. The story goes backward in time to describe the origins of the capability that met the moment in early 2020. It proceeds forward in time to describe some of the other SWP innovations that foundational capabilities enabled. The entire arc illustrates the essence and value of developing agile, sense-and-respond ability in SWP. Last, the chapter describes a number of differentiating human abilities the author calls out as important for any industrial-organizational (I-O) psychologist to have impact on organizations.

Imagine This Scenario

It's April 2020. Much of the world is entering the pandemic lockdown phase. You head recruiting for the US division of a global retailer. Customer demand for products is exploding. However, you cannot find enough employees to staff your registers at point of sale.

Your SWP challenge is a labor shortage. People leaders in your company convene, and the situation's parameters are strategically assessed.

1. *Shuffling workers will not work*. Stores are geographically separated by distances that defy commuting. Therefore, surplus employees in stores

where demand is lower cannot be redeployed easily or at all to the larger mass of stores where help is needed most.
2. *Prior fixes will not work.* Pushing known methods harder (e.g., retention bonuses for hourly workers and affordable wage increases to attract new hires) is assessed to have limited utility. The latter will take critical time to put into place.
3. *The problem is bigger than your company.* Your company cannot solve the problem alone. But it can't look more broadly within its sector either. Other retailers of your type are experiencing similar issues. There are few active employees with the right skillsets, even if they could be lured away.

Although you do not yet know it, a global hospitality chain that operates hotels in areas where your company's stores reside has the opposite SWP issue: a labor surplus. COVID has frightened clientele away, resulting in mass furloughs and layoffs of staff, including most check-in staff.

One company has too few employees, another too many. Is there an opportunity to solve both problems? There are obvious benefits to each organization and their people from a potential fix that streams surplus workers into in-demand positions. There are also corresponding complexities. However, each has a potential fix, resolving the paradox for the greater good.

First, while the two companies share few similarly titled positions, many of them require similar levels of preparation. Especially for roles at lower levels of preparation, workers could potentially be fungible across specific job titles. For example, furloughed hotel receptionists and retail cashier positions share Zone 1 level of preparation in the O-NET taxonomy.

Another complexity for the retail chain is background check requirements that would ordinarily delay onboarding and time-to-hire. However, the hospitality organization is well-known for the rigor of it background checks. With appropriate arrangements (i.e., pooling nonconfidential and aggregated workforce information by such categories as location and experience) companies could accelerate hiring furloughed and laid-off people and avoid future job losses.

Taken together, this solution could make the hotel employees qualified for open retail positions due to minimum onboarding and training effort. Their job descriptions share similar knowledge, skills, abilities, and other characteristics (KSAOs, e.g., greeting customers, processing transactions, etc.).

The final complication, however, could be a dealbreaker: How can you broker a deal if there isn't one on the table? Your organization doesn't have a working relationship with the hospitality chain, and therefore no visibility into—or recognition of—the opportunity. The solution is available in theory but invisible in practice.

A Philanthropic Thunderbolt

In late March 2020, a group of Chief Human Resources Officers (CHROs) convened to address issues of mutual interest or concern. In this meeting, they were laser-focused on a single objective: addressing disruptions wreaked on workforces by the pandemic and negotiating around a jigsaw puzzle of regional regulations, infection rates, and wildly variable responses to the global health emergency.

An overview of labor supply and demand validated the relevance of the question. As Figure 15.1 makes plain, while many organizations were reducing workforce, others were hiring at scale.

The CHROs were inspired by the idea of sharing information between companies. They aspired to foster employment and productivity during a once-in-a-century, exogenous, and uncontrollable "black swan" event.

The emergent initiative was labeled People + Work Connect ("Connect"). Four organizations came together as founders: Accenture, Lincoln Financial Group, Verizon, and ServiceNow.[1] (The wider founding company coalition was larger.[2]) Its specific objective was to facilitate increased employment by rapidly deploying people across industries and organizations around the world, enabled by an analytics-driven technology platform codesigned with CHROs and leaders across Accenture.

The agreed approach was to form a CHRO and C-suite coalition to develop and manage the platform to help facilitate the process of keeping people employed and ensuring business continuity. The workforce matching platform would enable global organizations to connect available workers to open jobs based on select criteria such as location and experience.

Because speed was of the essence, high-level design principles emphasized parsimony:

1. Open to all
2. Simple and scalable
3. Progress over perfection
4. Evolutionary and fit-for purpose

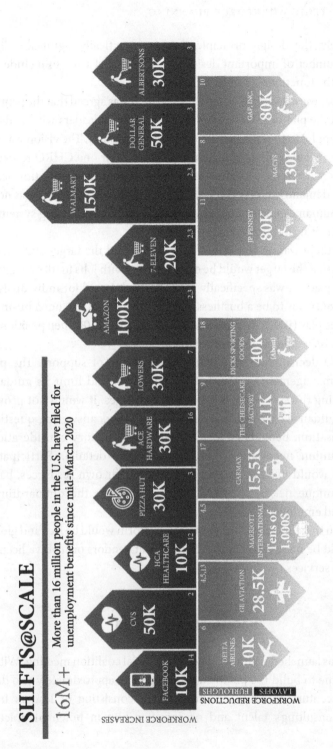

Figure 15.1 Workforce increases and reductions by company as of April 8, 2020.

Ultimately, the design principles became practically significant. They guided a number of important design decisions about what to include and exclude in the functional design.

First, there were decisions around the intent. It was agreed that the primary function of the platform was to connect organization leaders with available workers (supply) to those that needed workers (demand). The vision was that the platform would supply sufficient information for one CHRO to decide whether there was reason to contact a peer from another organization across the supply–demand boundary. It was also agreed that the platform was not to become a human capital management system, applicant tracking system, or provide recruiting or outplacement services.

Second, there was an important decision around the target audience. It was agreed that the target would be organizations with jobs to fill or available workers to place. It was specifically not to be a job board for individuals. In short, Connect was to be a business-to-business play (B2B), not a business-to-employee play (B2E). Any organization with at least 100 open positions or workers at risk would be encouraged to apply.

The third decision set was defining the scope of support. The platform and management system built around it would limit its guidance to confirming the suitability of resource exchanges. It would not provide "how to" guidance on executing the exchange (e.g., answering questions of compensation, benefits changes, legal and regulatory considerations, potential union negotiations, or myriad other details). Participating companies would need to answer these with their own resources, based on their unique needs. It would also not manage the onboarding of transitioned employees.

Finally, in the spirit of philanthropy, the platform would be free and global. There would be no involvement with for-profit vendors or involve licensed software or services.

Backstory of the Build

Connect was launched within 14 days of the initial coalition meeting. Within that, the time to build the platform prototype was approximately two days. Within Accenture, a multidisciplinary team consisting of leaders from Strategy Consulting's talent and organization/human potential practice, organizational analytics, and applied intelligence, and the organizations sprinted together for the platform build.

One important consideration for the functional design was, "What is the minimum information required to suggest a useful person–role match?" One idea was to harness an existing proprietary capability within Accenture that uses natural language processing (NLP) and an artificial intelligence (AI) capability trained to read job descriptions and return a numeric indication of how much overlap exists between any two job descriptions. For example, one pair of job roles might share 82% of KSAOs while another pair may only overlap by 13%. (For a general description of this approach, see Duan and Bazigos, 2022).

The team consulted with coalition designees to provide perspectives and nine external partners to provide input into this question as well as other questions that arose.[3] Honoring the principle of parsimony, the decision was to match workers to roles based on the skill preparation level ("Job Zone") in the public domain job analysis system, O-NET (Peterson et al., 1997), and their zip code. Consequently, participating organizations with job roles to fill or workers to place completed a spreadsheet with a simple text-matching option that provided the closest O-NET roles to the job title a particular organization assigned and enough information to select the best equivalent. The O-NET job role's corresponding Job Zone information would then autopopulate the spreadsheet.

Zip codes for available positions and work locations of surplus employees were similarly uploaded. That distribution of available talent was displayed on a geographical map of the world and was visible to CHROs of participating organizations.

Results

Company engagement was gratifying. Within a few months' time, more than 1,500 organizations engaged with Connect. More than 240 organizations in 89 countries loaded over 400,000 roles.

Process metrics, however gratifying, tell only part of the story. What if you ran a manufacturing operation and needed workers? Nestlé, corporate parent of such better-known brands in the US as Nespresso, San Pellegrino, Purina, and Gerber, saw its food supply chain threatened. This was a typical issue for many companies. (Accenture research found that 94% of the Fortune 1000 reported COVID-19–related supply chain disruptions, and 75% reported negative or strongly negative impacts to their business).

With increased demand for its food products from people newly "sheltering in place" at home, the platform helped the company identify regions, industries, and organizations that had available talent. Through new connections made on the platform, 600 people furloughed or laid off from other companies joined Nestlé's online talent community, enabling the company to fill a broad range of positions quickly. That, in turn, enabled the company to fill 70 positions at a pizza processing factory in just 45 days. Other participants experienced similar results. John Seward, Talent Acquisition Manager at Nestlé, saw wider benefits, as well.

> With the help of People + Work Connect, we're getting some phenomenal talent coming through the door, and talent that we might not historically have pursued. The ability to use the platform to search for people by either skill set or location has enhanced our ability to hire for a broad range of job types. But for me, the real value has been in helping us create a community of talent partners, one that gives us a real competitive advantage in the job market (Accenture, 2020).

Invention of the "Remote Work Indicator"

Shortly after Connect's platform build was completed, Accenture's Organizational and People Analytics practice learned more about participating organizations' emerging and unmet pandemic-inspired needs. Many large organizations, each with thousands of job titles, sought guidance on which jobs could be performed fully or partially remotely.

Using the approach of training an NLP-based model to analyze job descriptions, the team developed an automated capability to estimate the percentage of tasks within a set of job roles that required physical presence. The output was used as input for optimization equations useful for reallocating tasks among team members and workforce scheduling. By doing so, workers most vulnerable to infection could remain productive from fully remote locations while enjoying the protection of a self-managed environment.

What We Learned

The agility behind this initiative emerged naturally. It was philanthropic, mission-driven, and the goodwill cross-cut ordinary barriers of organizational identity and superseded competition dynamics. It's important to briefly note what went right, to better prepare for an undesired next challenge of pandemic or even endemic proportions. The pace of viral and bacterial threats at scale to humans has increased in recent decades, putting a premium on preparation.

If we were to extract useful and adoptable principles from Connect for reuse, the author's list would include the following:

1. *Network thinking is superior to go-it-alone.* A wholesale mindset shift was required because the level of magnitude shifted. Conventional approaches have been shaped by competitive mindsets and corporate structures that focus on single companies as the "unit of analysis" as it were. But no single company could make the Connect platform work. Like owning the first and only telephone or fax machine, the invention is worthless if there's nobody on the other end; nor would investing in the invention's development be justified without reasonable confidence in its rapid adoption by a network of significant partners and size. (The power of a given network size is approximated mathematically in Metcalf's Law, summarized as the geometric expansion 2^n where n is the number of "network nodes," in this case, network partners.)

2. *Founder credibility matters.* The four founding members were well-known among the community of people leaders for, if for nothing else, the size of their workforces. Accenture, for example, currently has more than 700,000 employees. While not a founding member, Wal-Mart, with a global workforce of millions, was among the initial consortium members. Initial coalition members served as Connect ambassadors, reaching out to invite other organizations into the community.

3. *Occam's Razor (a.k.a., the law of parsimony) is enormously valuable.* At first glance, the "design principles" mentioned earlier may seem light to the point of uselessness. Those who are inclined to technical precision and accuracy may have chafed. Yet, the "lightness" of the design principles clearly enabled speed by avoiding unnecessary complexity. As important, they enabled agreement among large, complex

companies with large, complex needs and requirements. The design set emerged not despite but because of the myriad unique requirements that required avoidance. The least common denominator—the one that got the consortium to "yes"'—was the rule set at the highest level of abstraction.

4. *Future potential abounds.* We will continue to scale and evolve Connect because this type of workforce exchange could set a new norm to manage future labor market volatility. Envisioned future uses include steering talent to in-demand job roles in the not-for-profit community and, equally, the reverse: connecting unemployed service recipients of not-for-profit organizations (NPO) to organizations that value recruiting people from underrepresented communities.

Evolution of Connect and Related Branches

Once the decision to build Connect was made, we did not start from scratch. We had been building significant new organizational analytics capabilities before the pandemic, continued to evolve them in parallel with Connect, and continue to this day. This section provides an inside look at what came immediately before, during, and shortly after the Connect platform.

Job Analysis Undergirds Everything

"Job analysis is the driest topic in your program; but it will also be the most useful in your career," I was fond of telling my graduate students in the Human Resource (HR) Management course at Columbia University's program in social-organizational psychology. It was an anchor chapter in the textbook I was using at the time (Noe et al., 2023).

What was true during my tenure as adjunct faculty in the early naughts through the early teens of this century was no less true in 2020. Job analysis is critical to establishing the link to virtually any HR process (e.g., establishing the job-relatedness of a selection battery and the rating dimensions of performance management systems). It is equally relevant to SWP in documenting both the skills and tasks that a given role requires.

O-NET, the US Department of Labor's job analysis system, is a useful way to standardize analysis within and across companies. First introduced in 1997, and updated continuously through 2022, its taxonomy organizes occupations into 1,016 occupational titles, 923 of which represent O-NET "data-level occupations" (i.e., 93 occupational titles including military roles for which no additional corresponding data are provided; i.e., tasks and skills).

The content model focuses on worker-oriented information (essentially KSAOs) and occupational requirements (tasks, activities, and labor market information and trends).

For purposes of illustration, an excerpted example of an O-NET description for the familiar role of "Industrial-Organizational Psychologists, 19-3032.00" follows. The 25 tasks that typify the work appear in Figure 15.2, listed in descending order of their importance rating. (The full analysis appears in the Appendix.)

> Apply principles of psychology to human resources, administration, management, sales, and marketing problems. Activities may include policy planning; employee testing and selection, training, and development; and organizational development and analysis. May work with management to organize the work setting to improve worker productivity.
>
> *Sample of reported job titles*: Consulting Psychologist, Industrial Psychologist, Industrial/Organizational Psychologist (I/O Psychologist), Management Consultant, Organizational Consultant, Organizational Development Consultant (OD Consultant), Organizational Psychologist, Research Scientist

Our SWP Journey Began by Estimating the Probability of Workforce Automation

Two years before our Connect journey began, we began attacking the SWP question of workforce automation. It was a long-established principle that, to address a labor gap, solutions included buy, borrow, and build (respectively hire, contract, or train/upskill employees). But what, exactly, was the opportunity to automate the work? We now had a fourth "B": bot.[4]

Management teams across industries and geographies began asking a pervasive question: What is our automation opportunity? We set about addressing that question at a very specific level of detail. Accurate answers would impact organizations' capital investment decisions in automation

Tasks

Importance	Category	Task
82	Core	Formulate and implement training programs, applying principles of learning and individual differences.
81	Core	Conduct research studies of physical work environments, organizational structures, communication systems, group interactions, morale, or motivation to assess organizational functioning.
81	Supplemental	Participate in mediation and dispute resolution.
79	Core	Conduct presentations on research findings for clients or at research meetings.
78	Core	Provide expert testimony in employment lawsuits.
77	Core	Study consumers' reactions to new products and package designs, and to advertising efforts, using surveys and tests.
75	Core	Review research literature to remain current on psychological science issues.
75	Core	Develop interview techniques, rating scales, and psychological tests used to assess skills, abilities, and interests for the purpose of employee selection, placement, or promotion.
74	Core	Conduct individual assessments, including interpreting measures and providing feedback for selection, placement, or promotion.
74	Core	Write articles, white papers, or reports to share research findings and educate others.
74	Core	Develop new business by contacting potential clients, making sales presentations, and writing proposals.
69	Core	Develop and implement employee selection or placement programs.
69	Core	Identify training and development needs.
69	Core	Train clients to administer human resources functions, including testing, selection, and performance management.
69	Core	Facilitate organizational development and change.
67	Core	Analyze job requirements and content to establish criteria for classification, selection, training, and other related personnel functions.
66	Core	Assess employee performance.
66	Core	Observe and interview workers to obtain information about the physical, mental, and educational requirements of jobs, as well as information about aspects such as job satisfaction.
66	Supplemental	Provide advice on best practices and implementation for selection.
65	Core	Coach senior executives and managers on leadership and performance.
64	Core	Study organizational effectiveness, productivity, and efficiency, including the nature of workplace supervision and leadership.
63	Core	Write reports on research findings and implications to contribute to general knowledge or to suggest potential changes in organizational functioning.
59	Supplemental	Counsel workers about job and career-related issues.
54	Supplemental	Advise management concerning personnel, managerial, and marketing policies and practices and their potential effects on organizational effectiveness and efficiency.
48	Supplemental	Analyze data, using statistical methods and applications, to evaluate the outcomes and effectiveness of workplace programs.

Figure 15.2 Screenshot of detailed O-NET tasks with importance ratings for industrial-organizational psychologists (2023).

technology. In some cases, the opportunity could have shareholder impact for those organizations that elected to capture the efficiencies that automation could provide. For other organizations, the opportunity to redesign work to bring more "human" into the tasks executed by humans was attractive.

Frey and Osborne, researchers at the University of Oxford, published two papers estimating the impact of automation on jobs (Frey and Osborne, 2013, 2017). They concluded that 47% of US employment was at high risk (probability of more than 70%) for replacement by automation. An additional 19% of US employment was at medium risk (30–70% probability). They also concluded that the probability of automation was negatively correlated with the level of educational attainment and income. The paper crashed like a tsunami around the world, triggering concern and debate that continues today.[5]

The analysis itself was performed with automation of a kind. NLP, an emerging approach to mine insights from language interpreted in its natural context by a machine, was used to read the O-NET occupations.[6] Their model consisted of a differentially weighted assessment of nine job characteristics in O-NET subsumed under three categories: Perception and Manipulation (finger dexterity, manual dexterity, working in cramped spaces and awkward positions), Creative Intelligence (originality, fine arts), and Social Intelligence (social perceptiveness, negotiation, persuasion, assisting/caring for others). Machine readings output from the O-NET text were compared to human labeling for the 70 occupations the NLP algorithm was trained on.

After an 89.4% accuracy estimate was achieved, there was sufficient confidence to apply the algorithm to the remaining occupations of the 702 for which O-NET provided data. (O-NET provided no data for military and certain other occupations.) Applying the same algorithm uniformly to all occupations protected the analysis from human subjectivity. Results appear in the appendices of both papers. To provide a sense of results, the occupation ranked safest from automation risk was recreational therapist (0.28% automation probability), followed closely by first-line supervisor of mechanics, installers and repairers, and emergency management director (0.30% automation probability for each). The analysis established a nine-way tie for occupations at highest risk (99% automation probability): data entry clerks, library technicians, new account clerks, photographic process workers and processing machine operators, tax preparers, cargo and freight agents, watch repairers, insurance underwriters, mathematical technicians, sewer workers, title examiners, abstractors and searchers, and telemarketers.

(Readers may be comforted to learn that the I-O psychology occupation ranked 57th of 702 for safety from automation, with a predicted probability of 1.2%.)

We became intrigued by the methodology and adopted it with two significant refinements. Our goal was different than Frey and Osborne's: rather than a societal-level estimate, we wanted to help our clients understand their opportunity to have machines do what they do best (e.g., calculation, perception), thus liberating time for humans to do more of what they do best (e.g., leading, creating, persuading).

Consequently, we adopted two differentiating principles. First, we hypothesized that the *job level* was a less practical unit of analysis than the *task level*. We adopted a task-based analysis and sought to estimate what percentage of time within each role could be automated. We ultimately proved our hypothesis correct after succeeding in estimating the percentage of tasks within every one of O-NET's occupational titles for which data were provided.

Second, we hypothesized that it was possible to train the analytic capability to identify tasks that could be automated by *available technology*. This represented a second departure from the original research. Frey and Osborne made no representation about the timeframe for any particular job to become automatable. The actual availability of the occupation-specific technology was not a constraint in their model. Consequently, the automation could occur anytime up to two decades hence.

To assess which tasks were automatable with existing technology, we convened a panel of experts in technology, industries, and functions who rated the automatability of role-related tasks within a sample of occupations. Similar to Frey and Osborne, we developed an algorithm that accurately "predicted" the human assessments. That algorithm was then applied to occupations outside the training dataset. Subsequent sampling and review of task automation estimates by the expert panel were deemed accurate at the 70% level of probability or better.

An example of the output is provided in Figure 15.3. The occupation is Customer Service Representative (CSR), which subsumes a plethora of similar titles wherever the essence of the role is deployed. O-NET describes the occupation's activities as

> Interact with customers to provide basic or scripted information in response to routine inquiries about products and services. May handle and resolve general complaints. Excludes individuals whose duties are primarily installation, sales, repair, and technical support.

Associated job titles run the gamut: Account Representative, Call Center Representative, Client Services Representative, Customer Care

JOB ROLES ARE BEING DECOMPOSED INTO COMPONENT TASKS

COMPANY TITLE	STANDARD TITLE	TASK DESCRIPTION	TASK TYPE	AI?	GIG?	RECOMMENDATION
CUSTOMER SERVICE ANALYST	CUSTOMER SERVICE REP	Compare disputed merchandise to records	REASON & PLAN	Y		Intelligent Process AUTOMATION
		Record customer interactions	REASON & PLAN	Y		Intelligent Process AUTOMATION
		Refer out unresolved customer grievances	PERCEIVE & SENSE	Y		AUGMENTED Human Intelligence
		Solicit sales	KNOW/ LEARN	N	Y	ADAPTIVE Internal
		Order root cause tests	KNOW/ LEARN	N	Y	ADAPTIVE External Managed

Figure 15.3 Illustrative task decomposition of O-NET role: Customer Service Representative, 43-4051.

Representative (CCR), Customer Service Agent, CSR, Customer Service Specialist, Customer Support Representative (Customer Support Rep), Guest Service Agent, and Member Services Representative (Member Services Rep).

In the Figure 15.3 example, an organization has defined the role as Customer Service Analyst. This label appears under "Company Title" in the figure. A role matching algorithm links it to our analysis of the CSR role, for which there are 15 tasks listed in O-NET. Because the organization's management deselected 10 of these, five remain. The CSR role is listed in the second column of the figure under "Standard Title." Task descriptions of the five tasks appear in the third column under the eponymous label.

The fourth column, labeled "Task Type," lists the task type using the O-NET task taxonomy. (This information was incorporated into our automation estimation algorithm as supplemental to other variables it considered.)

The fifth column, labeled "AI" in the figure, is a binary assessment of the automatability: Yes (Y) or No (N). This is based on a 70% probability estimate. In the version we deploy with clients, the Y/N threshold is configurable. A more ambitious management team might, for example, set the probability for a Y to a minimum of 60% (or any other number) at their discretion.

In this example, three of the five major tasks for this company's Customer Service Analyst role are likely automatable, and two are not. On an unweighted basis, therefore, 60% of the role can be automated if the investment is made. This figure is close to the Frey and Osborne estimate of the probability that the whole role would be automated within the next two decades: 55%.

The sixth column is labeled "Gig." Of the two tasks that were assessed as unlikely to be automatable today, both were reassessed for fulfillment by contract labor or borrowed internal talent from other job roles or areas of the company. (This is the "borrow" term of the buy/build/borrow/bot alliterative taxonomy.) The Gig algorithm was developed by a different panel of humans with deeper expertise in industries and functions, similar to the method used to develop the automation algorithm.

The final column, "Recommendations" recommends the type of automation or "gig" labor. *Intelligent process automation* is a descriptive category. It is most commonly operationalized as *robotic process automation* (RPA), which trains an automated capability to learn tasks that are typically finite, routine, and repetitive. Typical training data are digital recordings of humans performing those tasks, like screenshots of a CSR (in this case) looking up a record to determine whether there is a match or recording the time, type, and outcome of a customer interaction.

The term "Adaptive" is applied to human labor other than from the traditional full-time employee hired into a specific job title, Customer Service Analyst in this case. Adaptive (Internal) indicates that a different employee without a Customer Service Analyst title could handle the sales task. Adaptive (External Managed) indicates that gig labor as it is traditionally understood—temporary contract labor source on a platform or (historically) from an agency—could perform the "triage" task of determining whether to refer the problem for further diagnosis or not.

A final point: NLP was recently used by the US Department of Labor (DOL) itself to facilitate its periodic updates of the taxonomy. An excellent discussion that sheds more light on how the process works is posted on the O-NET site (Dahike and Putka, 2021).

When the Pandemic Arrived, We Were Prepared

Acquiring expertise with NLP and training machine learning (ML) models to categorize natural language against a taxonomy like O-NET proved valuable when the call to create the Connect platform arrived. It allowed us to bring to the table a wide range of options. Because of the multiparty nature of the stakeholders it would serve, the simplifying principle of parsimony was honored. We included only the minimum functionality necessary for one people leader to signal to another over the platform the information required to establish a potential match and subsequent direct contact. No more, no less. (Perhaps, considering this criterion, we were overprepared.)

Of all the functionality that we had at our disposal, we elected only two: a simple term-matching methodology and a postal zone code (zip code) lookup table. The matching process consisted of each organization entering the job title it used into a table, then selecting the O-NET occupation that best matched the role from a drop-down menu of alternatives. The zip code lookup consisted of a simple embedded geolocation function, the primary purpose of which was to display a point on a map graphic for purposes of visualization and ease of use by the people leaders.

O-NET provided us with one additional benefit to standardization. Using O-NET's rating of the degree of preparation and specialization of any given occupation ("Job Zone"), the platform would automatically tag each listed occupation that participating companies uploaded—on both the supply and demand sides of the community. We hypothesized that lower Job Zone levels would have both greater populations of employees and far fewer training issues in the event of robust yet inexact matches. For example, it seemed likely that a registration desk employee from a hotel could, after a brief orientation session, serve customers on a retail checkout line. O-NET confirms these are both Zone 2 level occupations, requiring between 3 months up to a year of preparation and a high school diploma. Salaries in the latest available year (2021) were similar: $27,260 for cashiers and $28,080 for the hotel, motel, and resort desk clerk occupation.

The Other Big Pandemic Question: Which Job-Role Tasks Are "Remote"?

With the arrival of workplace lockdowns and employee health concerns, many companies scrambled to adapt. For organizations for which all or almost all work had traditionally been performed on site, remote work was completely new. According to one study at the time, 74% of organizations surveyed planned to shift some of their people to remote work permanently, and three in four CFOs planned to shift at least 5% of their onsite workforce to permanent remote status (Gartner, 2020).

The initial question was, "Which *workers* can work remotely?" However, like the automation question framed in terms of whole jobs, we suggested that a more useful framing would be, "What *work* can be performed remotely?"

If we could accurately distinguish between role-related tasks that demanded physical presence from those that could be performed remotely, we suspected the information could inform job redesign and scheduling. For the former, we speculated that jobs could be decomposed into remote versus on-site components and reassembled into jobs where most or all tasks could be performed only on-site and jobs for which most or all tasks could be performed remotely.

This led to the invention of the Remote Work Indicator. We set about applying a similar approach to the one described for estimating the percentage of work that could be performed through automation, gig, and adaptive workforces to create two new metrics:

1. Percentage of work tasks that can be done remotely
2. Percentage of time that individual can work remotely with additional technology support

Returning to the CSR occupation that formed the basis for an automation illustration, we arrived at Figure 15.4. Two-thirds (67%) of the task distribution were assessed as performable remotely with no further technological enablement than telephone and laptop connection. Another 20% could be performed remotely with additional technological enablement.

All told, this equates to roughly 3 or 4 days of remote work. If the work were redistributed in a way that redesigned CSR positions consisted of (1) tasks that can performed remotely and (2) tasks that can be performed remotely through additional technology support, or (3) work that cannot be done remotely, then individual employees could be assigned more closely to the workplace they preferred.

All other things equal and proportional, perhaps only 13% of the CSR workforce would be ultimately required onsite. This would clearly impact facilities use and workforce scheduling in ways that were responsive to the moment.

Complementing Task Analysis with Skills Analysis

Near-Fit Roles Based on Skills

In the context of solving the SWP labor shortage issue for particular roles, the build component of the 4-B (or 6-B) model typically means providing

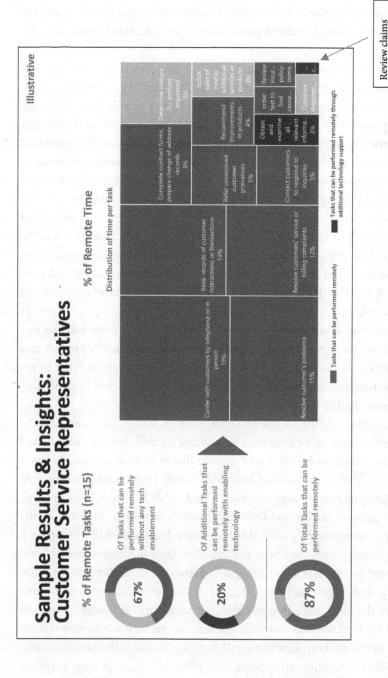

Figure 15.4 Percentage of tasks performable remotely with and without additional technological support.

new training for current employees in low-demand roles to migrate to unfilled in-demand roles. Critical to this is assessing the degree of skill distance between any two roles to understand the effort and budget involved, assuming that enough individual employees are interested in making the switch.

Skill-based analyses are typically difficult to perform at scale because only a small minority of organizations have invested in (a) creating a role-based skill taxonomy and (b) creating an inventory of employee skills, including proficiency levels. In an ideal world, they would, and skill-gap closure plans could be created from the ground up (i.e., at the individual level and then aggregated at a meaningful unit level for planning purposes). However, approximations are possible by assuming that, for incumbents in roles codified by a position description, they can be assumed to have the skills implied by the position description. Skill proficiency is estimated by using length of tenure in the position as a proxy indicator. This has the benefit of leapfrogging over a potential multiyear, expensive process to catalogue skills and inventory the workforce on skill acquisition and proficiency. It has the disadvantage of assuming that all incumbents hold all skills the role requires at an acceptable minimum level of proficiency. It also relies on an assumption that multiple versions of the same job role can be somehow standardized. For example, "truck driver" in US English and "lorry driver" in UK English are essentially the same position. Due to regional customization, however, they may never be considered together unless a process to link them is established.

A contextual reading of the skills required in either, however, can analyze them jointly and compute a percentage of skill overlap. Automated capabilities based on ML and NLP can do this at scale at acceptable levels of accuracy. If the organization has a sufficiently large number of job role descriptions including responsibilities and KSAOs, those descriptions, linked to name of the business unit (BU) and department, can provide sufficient context to identify roles that have high degrees of skill overlap and, conversely, roles with very little skill overlap. Unit identifiers like BU and department are required to distinguish between ("disambiguate") similar sounding skills. For example, "diagnose problems" means something different for the auto mechanic and process consultant. Although many job descriptions lend themselves to automation, the reason is not sample size (to train the automated capability) but rather utility. A unit with a small number of job roles can use human experts. And while ML requires large corpuses of data to learn, a useful workaround can be to cross-walk an organization's roles to a preanalyzed job role taxonomy like O-NET. Assuming the capability has already learned the O-NET roles and corresponding tasks and skills, only matching and overlap computations are required. These operations are much lighter in their data demand. A simplified analysis appears in Figure 15.5.

An early test of a trained capability in role-based skill overlap analysis considered seven roles. Of these, six existed and one, versatile analyst of the future (VAF), was aspirational—and the target. Solid arrows depict high skill similarity, while dotted arrows depict low skill similarity. The saturation level of each indicates degree of similarity within "high" and "low" designations.

Results are useful from a planning perspective. They show a strong direct connection between programmer/analyst (a potential feeder role) and VAF (the receiving role). There are 36 programmer/analyst FTEs. Depending on the speed and size of the demand for VAFs, some or all programmer/analysts could be trained into that role.

The largest pool of incumbents are systems analysts, with 82 FTEs. However, they share only some skills with programmer/analysts, suggesting this is an indirect route to addressing the presumed VAF shortage. At a directional level, we can hypothesize that some training in programmer/analyst skillsets would be required in addition to other skills defined in the VAF role. (This would need to be confirmed at the next level of detail.)

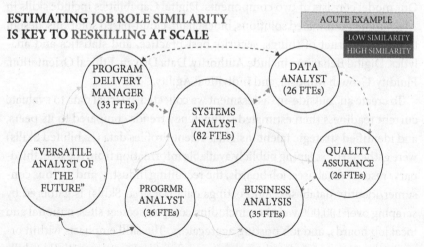

Figure 15.5 Illustration of a skill-based near-fit role analysis.

Shifting from "Static" JA to Dynamic Market-Based Skills Analysis

The preceding analysis was performed and viewed as useful by the organization that owned the roles. Underlying the analysis was an assumption that the role descriptions developed by the organization considered skills that were relevant to its success and were continuously updated at the speed of business.

However, this is rarely the case. From observation, many organizations fail to update role descriptions, thereby promoting their obsolescence, eroding their utility, and implicitly denying guidance to their employees about dynamic shifts in the external market affecting their skillsets' relevance. These organizations typically gather and maintain little organized intelligence about what people who leave do, and for whom. Skill trends and market demand of competitors are rarely researched. The new data science of *web scraping* public job postings wherever they appear (among other data sources), organizing by industry and competitor, and understanding de facto emerging career paths using market data are all useful to enhanced market-based SWP.

An example of the result of one such analysis, skills comprising our "Digital Dexterity" assessment, makes clear the relationship of skills to competitive advantage. The implications for SWP are self-evident. Digital Dexterity is a validated assessment of people's digital skills and behaviors to leverage existing and emerging technologies for better business outcomes. Our model consists of two components. Digital Capabilities include skills in AI solutions, automated solutions, blockchain, cloud-based solutions, design thinking, internet of things, security best practice, and statistics and analytics. Digital Behaviors include Authority, Data Driven, Ethical Orientation, Fluidity, Growth Mindset, and Individual Agility.

To create an "outside-in" assessment we collected external data to evaluate current readiness then estimated competency trends compared to its peers, and identified strategic talent insights. Talent Profiles data (Exhibited Skills) were gathered by scraping publicly available information from the web, third-party resume databases, job boards, the recruiting industry, and various consumer/identity databases. Job Postings data (Desired Skills) is gathered by scraping over 100,000 websites, including company career sites, national and local job boards, and job posting aggregators. The skill emphasis within organizations is evaluated as the percentage of profiles/postings with that skill.

The result was a readout of digital dexterity gaps between desired versus exhibited skills. When we performed this analysis on a peer set of five large energy companies, we were able to demonstrate to one of them why a key competitor was on track to dominate, digitally speaking. It turned into a wake-up call for that organization's SWP and recruiting functions.

Critical Practitioner Skills

My current role as the global managing director of organizational and people analytics in a large global consulting firm relies on critical practitioner skills built over several decades in internal corporate roles and external consulting roles with large management consulting firms.

Throughout my career, my driving passion has been evidence-based organization development and change (OD&C), including talent and culture. The complexity of building a career based on this is that, very often, business executives (and even I-O psychologists) are skeptical that such a thing exists. As many understand it (and with some merit), a historical lack of quantitative rigor makes managing these areas somewhat mystical, or "woo-woo." For this reason, I have researched the linkage of hard outcome variables like financial outcomes of businesses (earnings before interest, taxes, depreciation and amortization [EBITDA], return on invested capital [ROIC], total return to shareholders [TRS]) to soft predictors like results of organizational health, organizational agility, leadership, and change management diagnostics. When enough evidence was accumulated, I developed the following syllogism to convert skeptics into partners:

1. *Behavior equals money.* (Reference is made to the equation for productivity, where inputs are total workforce cost or headcount, and outcomes are revenue or profit.)
2. *Money lags behavior.* (Quasi-experimental designs using cross-lagged panel methodology strongly suggests behavior causes economic outcomes.)
3. *Therefore, companies should measure and manage behavior, including talent and culture, with the same rigor as their financials.* (But—warning!—nobody ever measured their way to success: be prepared to act or don't measure in the first place.)

I learned over time that analytics were the best route to convince skeptics to invest in OD&C, including talent and culture. I also learned that certain skills were more important than others in getting to a place where I could enjoy the privilege of working with clients to make work better for people and companies more successful.

These skills roughly fit into the three sets shown in Figure 15.6. Hitting the trifecta is living at the intersection of the three, labeled here as "Ideal Balance." In my experience, all three are required to have company or client impact.

Overweighting any one of the three in career preparation would limit effectiveness. For example, data science is a very broad field with many definitions. However, at their core, almost all data scientists are very deeply skilled at analyzing data. But context is important, too. Without a grounding in basics of organizational psychology (and its related science), it is impossible to consistently create analyses that are relevant to an issue concerning people and organizations. To the contrary, it is possible to create an impressively deep analysis that concludes the opposite of what is true. (This happens more often than it should.)

Similarly, overweighting consulting skills could nudge someone into roles that major in client relationship management. Done right, these roles are extremely valuable to consulting firms because they deepen client relationships.

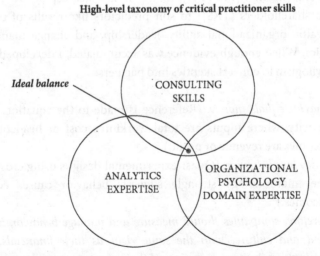

Figure 15.6 Skills for impact as an organizational analytics practitioner.

There is less of a premium on any particular domain of expertise, and analytical issues are often fobbed off to "the data scientists."

Overweighting knowledge of organizational psychology risks continuously emphasizing "how things should be done." This is particularly a tendency of new graduates, eager to demonstrate the value they bring to a new setting. Even absent new graduate phenomenon there is a risk of being perceived as a very capable expert in an extremely narrow area, albeit "not strategic," a dreaded career-limiting sobriquet.

The following areas contain some skill-based observations. They're not intended to be a complete list, but rather KSAOs that struck me as differentiating and characteristic of highly effective practitioners.

Consulting Skills

Three characteristics are necessary but not sufficient without the basics. Effective summary writing, effective sequencing of messages (e.g., along the lines of Minto, 2021), sensing when to intervene (talk) and not, stakeholder management, facilitation, managing win-win outcomes in discussions about negative surprises, and negotiating resources and financial considerations are all table stakes.

- *Empathy*. There is no success without it. This took me time to learn because I wrongly thought that seeming smart was the key to success. Never forget to take the other's perspective, whether it's a colleague peer, boss, direct report, or consulting client. Ask yourself, "How does my analysis/deliverable/statement/attitude jibe with the other's concerns?" The best consultants work backward from this consideration. At a bare minimum ask, "Did I/we 'answer the mail'?" (i.e., address the burning issue)?
- *Flexibility*. We all have our favorite techniques, language, and a set of expectations about how things "should" be done. We are always concerned about scientific integrity and have our red lines about values. (We may all draw them differently, but they are important to have.) When those clash with others' expectations, it becomes necessary to find methods to finalize the work or perhaps its presentation in a way that resonates with all stakeholders.

- *Centeredness.* Viewed through the lens of consulting, this goes beyond the ability to maintain personal composure when others are not. The ability to resist taking on the emotions of the other in an interaction is critical. There are practitioners who take on their client's or boss's anxieties, inferred or explicitly stated. There are practitioners who take on the other's ego or perceived invulnerabilities when they serve the CEO or chairperson. Maintaining separation of self from other is the common thread that unites these examples. It is essential.

Analytics Expertise

These characteristics are necessary but not sufficient without the basics. These include generating audience-relevant insights from the data, finding and communicating the story that the data tell, survey design and development, NLP/text analytics, ML approaches, and popular, business-accessible visualization platforms like Power BI and others.

- *You don't have to be the coder.* But you do have to learn how to communicate with data scientists who are not classically trained I-O psychologists. (They form the majority in many settings.) The ability to translate I-O analytic terms into data science terms is important. For example, both a classic linear multiple regression (an I-O classic) and random forest analysis (from data science) can be used to determine which of multiple predictors/conceptual independent variables (IVs for I-Os, known as "features" in data science parlance) are most important to the dependent variable (outcome).
- *How to frame a problem and corresponding research design.* Understanding the root cause of any issue to be diagnosed helps to identify the most relevant analysis. For example, analyzing the relationship between company training expense and business outcomes only by correlating those two variables lends little insight. It is far better to understand what proportion of the participants trained actually apply new behaviors on the job. Knowledge of the causal chain naturally suggests the addition of the moderating variable.
- *Facility with proxy markers for dynamics within passive data.* Organizations are increasingly willing to engage in unobtrusive observation. Practitioners have the responsibility to ensure it is

used ethically (e.g., pre-agreements on levels of aggregation in reporting). But they should also be aware of and active in suggesting opportunities. For example, Howson (2021) examined the incidence of microaggressions along gender and racial lines using an objective yet passive metric: number of interruptions in recorded online meetings. ("Manterruptions" could be an example.)

Organizational Psychology Domain Expertise

These characteristics are necessary but not sufficient without the basics. These include essential knowledge and applied techniques in change management; leadership and culture assessment and recommendations; talent development and strategy; and diversity, equity, inclusion, and belonging (DEI&B); and related social psychology and intervention effectiveness literature.

- *Ability to educate on key organizational psychology differences.* Explaining the difference between individual- and organization-level analysis to others is especially important for those who are attracted to work with organizational culture, leadership, change management, and DEI&B, among other areas. Because these areas are assumed by most to lack an empirical evidence base, articulating the difference between analysis of individuals and organizations or their units will be important to the work of those in people and organizational analytics. A small but growing number of publications expand on this point (e.g., Bazigos and Sokol, 2022, and Schneider and Pulakos, 2022).
- *Detecting threats to validity.* Explaining what can and cannot be concluded based on the implicit research design is essential. Data are analyzed in different ways by people from different disciplines. Maintain vigilance on internal and external threats to validity (e.g., selection bias, mortality, regression to the mean) and explain the plausibility of rival hypotheses that less rigorous designs create.
- *Ability to match any research question with the right design and analysis.* Real life is rarely textbook. If methodology needs to be compromised, one needs to be able to size the error range and reassess whether the study is worth conducting under those circumstances.
- *Understanding and explaining bias in measurement and historical datasets.* Machine learning requires that very large datasets ("corpuses")

be gathered and fed to the capability ("ingested"). If the data contain a historical bias, particularly along race and gender lines among others, the machine will replicate that bias extremely efficiently. Be your own trust and ethics officer in any work that you do.

Conclusion

This chapter covers much ground. It follows the evolution of one consulting practice unit's journey applying a variety of analytic approaches to important questions in SWP. This journey has been informed and accelerated by the special questions that a once-in-a-century exogenous global event inspired.

We began with ML applications to estimate the automation potential of job role tasks. Understanding what work can or should be automated will vary by company and role. But the ability to apply evidence to the estimation is critical. (This aligns with SWP's "bot" term.) We also estimated what work could be performed by contracted, external, task-specific gig labor (SWP's "buy" term) and internal slack resources (SWP's "borrow" term.)

Through the technologies we developed to serve our automation analyses, we were equipped to rapidly apply matching algorithms when the pandemic came. They made efficient the standardization of roles across different companies participating in the Connect collaboration. (This also informed SWP's "borrow" term.)

In parallel to Connect, we were asked by our clients to provide counsel on the separation of "remotable" work versus on-site work. We adapted analytical techniques refined during our automation studies to the new question. The analytical output informed work redesign and created scheduling and infrastructure efficiencies.

To help address labor shortages in key areas, we extended our NLP journey and applied it to companies' internal data to address the question of skill proximity between job roles within client organizations. To help companies understand their competitive posture with respect to skill acquisition, we created "outside-in" analyses using market data that were necessarily external to the organizations. This required new capabilities and partnerships with external data providers.

Both internal and external approaches align with SWP's "build" term. It may indirectly affect a fifth term, "bind," based on research indicating that development can increase employee retention.

***

The inside views of the type provided in this chapter are in no way a claim of uniqueness. There are many other organizations tracking along the same routes. They are advancing the same inquiries for the benefit of their own organization and their clients' if they offer those services. For all of us, the learning journey continues.

Future directions of SWP analyses will be, as they have been, influenced by macroeconomic issues and demographic and social trends. In the medium term, issues affecting labor supply and demand include rising income inequality, demands for alternative wage structures like universal guaranteed income, a trend to reverse offshoring of work to low labor cost locations ("onshoring"), and the rise of automation technologies capable of performing complex nonroutine work like writing novels, legal briefs, and computer code through generative AI vehicles such as ChatGPT.

The latter will impinge on the professional class, which could eventually lead to political action and legislation protecting jobs and professions by limiting applications of the new advanced technologies. (Disclosure: This chapter was entirely sourced from a human!) All of this may well be accelerated by the rise of quantum computing (technology that harnesses the laws of quantum mechanics to solve problems too complex for classical computers) as opportunities to capture labor efficiencies become better understood.

It's not difficult to see automated work becoming commoditized, reducing the cost of replaceable labor. Released from traditional labor forms, new forms will emerge for humans. One will be work performed by human–machine dyads or teams. Applied research on implanted brain chips for human–machine interface has already arrived. It's been the case for years that managers supervise teams of robots in warehouses, and single humans run factories populated by robots. It's conceivable that these trends will eventually generalize to other work forms.

If it does, SWP will need to include robots in its headcounts. Computing capacity depends on processors, and those data will need to be included in supply–demand planning cycles, which may become themselves fully automated.

Against this *mise en scene*, humans will adapt and prevail. Our species contains an extra wrinkle that our ancestral forebears did not: a genetic predisposition to collaborate. Hunting in groups, for example, resulted in bigger and more consistent payoffs than go-it-alone individual efforts. Species that lacked this advantage like, Neanderthals and Denisovan hominins, are now extinct, victims of the inexorable march of selection bias. Given that, the future may consist of work that consists of wholly human-to-human services and commercial interactions: humans collaborating with each other. In this brave new world, competitive advantage and premiums would migrate to those who can create, negotiate, persuade, lead, and provide personal services, to name a few.

Acknowledgments

The collaborative efforts of other Accenture leaders in the creation of the products and services described in this chapter are gratefully acknowledged. Dr. Lili Duan, Managing Director ("Partner"), has global responsibility for Organizational Science within the Organizational Analytics practice and led development of a wide range of offerings, only some of which are described here. The assistance of Subramanya Mohan Udagani, a Management Consulting Senior Principal, was vital to these efforts. Tanushree Guha, now Managing Director ("Partner") and former leader of the HR analytics team, provided important support for the matching algorithm of People-Work-Connect platform.

Notes

1. Respective people executives at that time were Ellen Shook, Lisa Buckingham, Christy Pambianchi, and Pat Wodors.
2. Initial coalition members included ADM, Baxter, Blue Apron, Cargill, Frito-Lay, Marriott, Mondelēz International, Nordstrom, Walmart, and Zenefits, in addition to the founding four.
3. External partners included Business Roundtable, Center for Advanced Human Resource Studies in the ILR School at Cornell University, Center for Executive Succession at the Darla Moore School of Business, Gallup and the CHRO Roundtable, HR Policy Association, Institute for Corporate Productivity, National Academy of Human Resources, Society for Human Resource Management, and World 50.
4. Two additional B's are currently in SWP parlance: "bounce" (removing low-performing performers or noncritical roles) and "bind" (retaining high performers).
5. Among the first evidence-based retorts was a report by the Organisation for Economic Cooperation and Development (OECD) in 2018 using a different approach and different job analysis (Survey of Adult Skills [PIAAC]), which estimated that 14% of jobs in 32 OECD countries participating in PIAAC were at high risk (probability of greater than 70%) of being automated based on current technological possibilities. An additional 32% of jobs had a probability of being automated of between 50% and 70% and could face significant changes in their job content.
6. Data scientists refer to this as NLP. I-O psychology refers to this as *computer-aided text analysis* (CATA). The terms are, for most purposes, synonymous. The chapter uses NLP because that is the term most practitioners in the business community use, in my experience. Most do not have an I-O psychology background.

References

Accenture (2020). *People + Work Connect helps Nestlé meet unprecedented demand through increased hiring.* https://www.accenture.com/content/dam/accenture/final/a-com-migration/pdf/accenture-nestle-casestudy-v6.pdf

Bazigos, M. N., and Sokol, M. (2022). An expanding organizational mindset benefits all I-O psychologists. *Industrial and Organizational Psychology, 15*, 408–412. doi:10.1017/iop.2022.41

Dahike, J. A., and Putka, D. J. (2021). Streamlining the identification of emerging tasks in the O*NET system using natural language processing (NLP): Technical summary. National Center for O*NET Development. Raleigh, NC. Subcontract Number (through RTI International): 1-312-0207142--41224L. https://www.onetcenter.org/dl_files/EmergingTasksNLP.pdf

Duan, L., and Bazigos, M. N. (2022). Sensing without surveys: How new data science helps companies respond to their people. *People + Strategy Journal, 45*(1). https://www.shrm.org/executive/resources/people-strategy-journal/winter2022/Pages/feature-sensing-surveys-accenture.aspx

Frey, C. B., and Osborne, M. (2013). The future of employment: How susceptible are jobs to computerisation? Oxford Martin Programme on Technology and Employment. https://www.oxfordmartin.ox.ac.uk/downloads/academic/The_Future_of_Employment.pdf

Frey, C. B., and Osborne, M. (2017). The future of employment: How susceptible are jobs to computerisation? *Technological Forecasting and Social Change: An International Journal, 114*, 254–280. doi:http://dx.doi.org/10.1016/j.techfore.2016.08.019

Gartner. (2020). CFO survey reveals 74 percent of organizations to shift some employees to remote work permanently. https://www.gartner.com/en/newsroom/press-releases/2020-04-03-gartner-cfo-surey-reveals-74-percent-of-organizations-to-shift-some-employees-to-remote-work-permanently2

Howson, C. (2021, August 27). To make real progress on D&I, move past vanity metrics. *Harvard Business Review.* https://hbr.org

Martin, J. P. (2018). *Skills for the 21st century: findings and policy lessons from the OECD survey of adult skills.* OECD Education Working Paper No. 166. Organisation for Economic Co-operation and Development. https://one.oecd.org./document/EDU/WKP(2018)2/en/pdf

Minto, B. (2021). *The pyramid principle: Logic in thinking and writing*, 3rd ed. Pearson Education Limited.

Noe, R. A., Hollenbeck, J. R., Gerhart, B., and Wright, P. M. (2023). *Human resource management: Gaining a competitive advantage*, 13rd ed. Irwin McGraw-Hill.

Peterson, N. G., Mumford, M. D., Borman, W. C., Jeanneret, P. R., Fleishman, E. A., Levin, and Kerry Y. (1997). O*NET Final Technical Report, vol. I, II, and III. Utah Department of Workforce Services. Contract Number 94-542. https://files.eric.ed.gov/fulltext/ED455452.pdf

Schneider, B., and Pulakos, E. D. (2022). Expanding the I-O psychology mindset to organizational success. *Industrial and Organizational Psychology, 15*, 385–402. doi:10.1017/iop.2022.27

Appendix

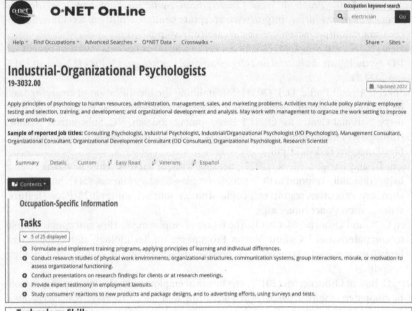

Detailed Work Activities

5 of 13 displayed

- Develop educational programs.
- Conduct scientific research of organizational behavior or processes.
- Mediate disputes.
- Prepare scientific or technical reports or presentations.
- Testify at legal or legislative proceedings.

Work Context

5 of 22 displayed

- **Electronic Mail** — 96% responded "Every day."
- **Telephone** — 83% responded "Every day."
- **Structured versus Unstructured Work** — 66% responded "A lot of freedom."
- **Freedom to Make Decisions** — 64% responded "A lot of freedom."
- **Face-to-Face Discussions** — 68% responded "Every day."

Experience Requirements

Job Zone

Title	Job Zone Five: Extensive Preparation Needed
Education	Most of these occupations require graduate school. For example, they may require a master's degree, and some require a Ph.D., M.D., or J.D. (law degree).
Related Experience	Extensive skill, knowledge, and experience are needed for these occupations. Many require more than five years of experience. For example, surgeons must complete four years of college and an additional five to seven years of specialized medical training to be able to do their job.
Job Training	Employees may need some on-the-job training, but most of these occupations assume that the person will already have the required skills, knowledge, work-related experience, and/or training.
Job Zone Examples	These occupations often involve coordinating, training, supervising, or managing the activities of others to accomplish goals. Very advanced communication and organizational skills are required. Examples include pharmacists, lawyers, astronomers, biologists, clergy, physician assistants, and veterinarians.
SVP Range	Over 4 years of preparation (8.0 and above)

Worker Requirements

Skills

5 of 23 displayed

- **Active Listening** — Giving full attention to what other people are saying, taking time to understand the points being made, asking questions as appropriate, and not interrupting at inappropriate times.
- **Reading Comprehension** — Understanding written sentences and paragraphs in work-related documents.
- **Complex Problem Solving** — Identifying complex problems and reviewing related information to develop and evaluate options and implement solutions.
- **Judgment and Decision Making** — Considering the relative costs and benefits of potential actions to choose the most appropriate one.
- **Speaking** — Talking to others to convey information effectively.

Knowledge

5 of 10 displayed

- **Psychology** — Knowledge of human behavior and performance; individual differences in ability, personality, and interests; learning and motivation; psychological research methods; and the assessment and treatment of behavioral and affective disorders.
- **Personnel and Human Resources** — Knowledge of principles and procedures for personnel recruitment, selection, training, compensation and benefits, labor relations and negotiation, and personnel information systems.
- **English Language** — Knowledge of the structure and content of the English language including the meaning and spelling of words, rules of composition, and grammar.
- **Administration and Management** — Knowledge of business and management principles involved in strategic planning, resource allocation, human resources modeling, leadership technique, production methods, and coordination of people and resources.
- **Education and Training** — Knowledge of principles and methods for curriculum and training design, teaching and instruction for individuals and groups, and the measurement of training effects.

Education

How much education does a new hire need to perform a job in this occupation? Respondents said:

- 48% Doctoral degree required
- 47% Master's degree required
- 5% Post-doctoral training required

Worker Characteristics

Abilities

5 of 16 displayed

- **Oral Comprehension** — The ability to listen to and understand information and ideas presented through spoken words and sentences.
- **Oral Expression** — The ability to communicate information and ideas in speaking so others will understand.
- **Written Comprehension** — The ability to read and understand information and ideas presented in writing.
- **Written Expression** — The ability to communicate information and ideas in writing so others will understand.
- **Deductive Reasoning** — The ability to apply general rules to specific problems to produce answers that make sense.

Interests

All 4 displayed

Interest code: **IEA**

*Want to discover your interests? Take the **O*NET Interest Profiler** at My Next Move.*

- **Investigative** — Investigative occupations frequently involve working with ideas, and require an extensive amount of thinking. These occupations can involve searching for facts and figuring out problems mentally.
- **Enterprising** — Enterprising occupations frequently involve starting up and carrying out projects. These occupations can involve leading people and making many decisions. Sometimes they require risk taking and often deal with business.
- **Artistic** — Artistic occupations frequently involve working with forms, designs and patterns. They often require self-expression and the work can be done without following a clear set of rules.
- **Social** — Social occupations frequently involve working with, communicating with, and teaching people. These occupations often involve helping or providing service to others.

Work Values

All 3 displayed

- **Working Conditions** — Occupations that satisfy this work value offer job security and good working conditions. Corresponding needs are Activity, Compensation, Independence, Security, Variety and Working Conditions.
- **Relationships** — Occupations that satisfy this work value allow employees to provide service to others and work with co-workers in a friendly non-competitive environment. Corresponding needs are Co-workers, Moral Values and Social Service.
- **Achievement** — Occupations that satisfy this work value are results oriented and allow employees to use their strongest abilities, giving them a feeling of accomplishment. Corresponding needs are Ability Utilization and Achievement.

Work Styles

5 of 16 displayed

- **Analytical Thinking** — Job requires analyzing information and using logic to address work-related issues and problems.
- **Initiative** — Job requires a willingness to take on responsibilities and challenges.
- **Integrity** — Job requires being honest and ethical.
- **Dependability** — Job requires being reliable, responsible, and dependable, and fulfilling obligations.
- **Achievement/Effort** — Job requires establishing and maintaining personally challenging achievement goals and exerting effort toward mastering tasks.

More Information

Related Occupations

5 of 10 displayed

- 11-3121.00 Human Resources Managers
- 13-1071.00 Human Resources Specialists Bright Outlook
- 13-1111.00 Management Analysts
- 11-3131.00 Training and Development Managers
- 13-1151.00 Training and Development Specialists

16

Teaching Strategic Workforce Planning

Hit the Ground Running

Steve Weingarden, Nikita Arun, and Juliet R. Aiken

We are excited to write about something we spend so much time thinking about and enjoy teaching. Each author is passionate about this topic and gains energy from the discussions and content that take place in the classroom when teaching strategic workforce planning (SWP). In this chapter, we think broadly about SWP as a cluster of potential courses within the industrial-organizational (I-O) universe. These may include but are not limited to SWP, organizational change, talent management, or business partnering. As soon as a student begins a course in SWP, they are not only a student, but also a practicing professional. Welcome to the SWP world!

In this chapter, we reflect on three general lessons: (1) striving for skill development related to critical and organizational-level thinking, (2) providing a practical SWP course experience through realistic contexts, and (3) coaching students to develop professional I-O identity. We end the chapter with advice for professors, students, and early-career professionals. Throughout the chapter, we sprinkle in what SWP students told us and what SWP professors can visualize as hoped-for comments from students in their SWP courses.[1]

Lesson Learned 1

When teaching SWP, provide graduate students the opportunity to build critical thinking competencies and diagnostic-driven approaches in SWP courses. Additionally, understanding how to take broad organizational knowledge concepts and applying those in one's specific organization is an invaluable outcome from an SWP course.

Steve Weingarden, Nikita Arun, and Juliet R. Aiken, *Teaching Strategic Workforce Planning*
In: *Strategic Workforce Planning*. Edited by: Marc Sokol and Beverly Tarulli, Oxford University Press.
© Society for Industrial and Organizational Psychology 2024. DOI: 10.1093/oso/9780197759745.003.0017

As demonstrated from the assembled chapters earlier in this volume, the needs of organizations continue to drive change in SWP processes toward becoming (a) more holistic, with improved consideration of the organizational development (OD) ecosystem; (b) increasingly focused on the current and future end-customer of the organization; and (c) sensitive to disruptive forces (e.g., COVID-19).

SWP is a discipline that presently falls between an art and a science, requiring significant tailoring and customization in its application to the specific work setting and sector in which a practitioner is working. Students may stubbornly root themselves to a sought-out and found linear model only to find disappointment when presented with messy scenarios that are nonlinear ("But the model says to follow these steps in this order!"). SWP incorporates planning based on what is known and what is expected but also relies on adapting to the unknown and the unexpected. Some students may be concerned about courses that teach and apply the concept of uncertainty, particularly uncertain outcomes (Roca, 2022). Professors must consider how best to teach a strong practical foundation and engage students through a lens of an *unknown and potentially unexpected* future. Therefore, SWP teaching is served well by providing students with overarching models geared toward critical thinking, specifically the use of logic and reasoning, that can then be applied to—and adapted to—specific circumstances. Here, we briefly touch on examples from two other parallel—and directly related to SWP—disciplines.

Nonlinear Courses: Critical-Thinking Principles and Models

Example 1: The Importance of Directional Accuracy as a First Step in Planning

One challenge with nonlinear courses is finding the best path to follow when so many choices exist. If a practitioner makes a less-than-optimal judgment on diagnosis, the choices that follow may be out of sync. Additionally, having the know-how to retrace steps and revise diagnoses is pivotal to success. Professors must stress the importance of applying organizational diagnosis *accurately* within the field of OD (McFillen et al., 2013). In fact, McFillen et al. tie the effectiveness of a well-conducted diagnosis to organizational effectiveness outcomes. Using an example of medical diagnosis as a proxy for evidence-based research, the authors developed a corresponding model for organizational diagnosis. In their model, the first and second steps involve collecting data (symptoms) to understand the organization's situation. Next, based on emerging patterns from the data, initial diagnoses (interventions to organizational systems) are proposed. Finally, in the fourth and fifth steps, organizational consultants test, evaluate, and revise their diagnosis.[2] This organizational diagnosis model is depicted in Figure 16.1.

McFillen and O'Neil (2010) describe how the graduate curriculum at their university is built on the application of organizational diagnosis, including preceding courses, following courses, methods for diagnosis, and a capstone-style case around diagnosis. We believe that skill development in organizational diagnosis is an all-important potential outcome in SWP courses—and, notably, across the entire graduate curriculum (i.e., diagnosis doesn't belong exclusively to SWP). We encourage drawing inspiration from this type of model to provide a powerful point of reference for guiding students on how to think critically about organizational diagnosis: from a common principle as well as an organization-specific perspective (McFillen and O'Neil, 2010).

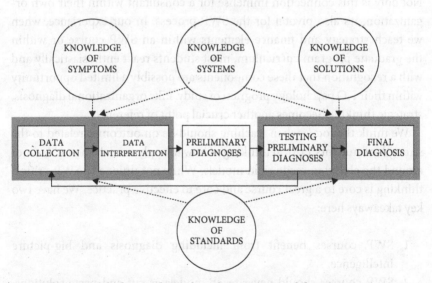

Figure 16.1 Model of an evidence-based organizational diagnostic process.
From "Organizational diagnosis: an evidence-based approach," by J. M. McFillen, D. A. O'Neil, W. K. Balzer, and G. H. Varney, *Journal of Change Management*, 13(2), p. 234, Copyright 2013 Taylor and & Francis Ltd. Reprinted with permission of the publisher (Taylor & Francis Ltd, http://www.tandfonline.com).

Example 2: The Importance of Financial Acumen

It seems that practitioners often engage in discussions about the importance and challenge of moving organizational members toward organizational-level thinking and consideration. In one example of this type of discussion, an argument is made that everyone in an organization, at all levels and in all positions, does better when they understand how financial success is measured and how they have an impact on the company's performance (Berman and Knight, 2013). Working in the managerial discipline, Berman and Knight asserted that the foundational curriculum for financial intelligence included understanding the basics of financial measurement (foundation), questioning and challenging the numbers (art), using the numbers to inform decisions (analysis), and considering the numbers within strategic context such as the economy, the competitive environment, regulations, changing customer needs and expectations, and new technologies (big picture). The way in which an organization defines financial success often varies, and so umbrella financial knowledge needs to be applied with consideration of context. Furthermore, organizational members who can link organizational financial performance and their job can find more enjoyment in their work and make a greater impact on their organization (Berman and Knight, 2013). Not only is this connection immense for a consultant within their own organization, it's also pivotal for the SWP process. In our experience, when we teach strategy and finance elements within an SWP course or within the graduate program curriculum, most students react enthusiastically and with a recognition that these components are possibly a limited opportunity within their I-O psychology program of study. Like organizational diagnosis, strategic thinking becomes another crucial point of reference.

We think the focus when teaching should be on outcomes related to the strength of students' critical thinking of how to apply models in practice, not around the ability to recite rigid models. While not unique to SWP, critical thinking is core to a great course and core to effective practice. We have two key takeaways here:

1. SWP courses benefit from including diagnosis and big-picture intelligence.
2. SWP courses should never teach models as cut-and-paste solutions, but rather as frameworks to be adapted through critical thinking in real time to real contexts.

In leveraging these examples in the development of an SWP course, overarching guideposts blended with organizational customization is preferred to standardized, regurgitated knowledge. Arguably, one distinction we're trying to achieve with I-O graduate students is to focus more on impact measurement, human resources (HR) analytics, and strategic business priorities rather than overreliance on HR metrics (Boudreau and Ramstad, 2005; Marler and Boudreau, 2017.)

"My first few months in my new role post-graduation involved hours of data entry that no one else had the capacity to do. Instead of thinking of this as just putting numbers into a database, I understood that I was learning about the records management software, the structure and composition of my company, the processes that required the data to be up-to-date, and I had the opportunity to identify a problem I could solve *(How did this data entry project get so behind to begin with?)*"

"Really think through important questions. What was the root of the challenges/resistance/setbacks? Where did it originate? What was missed? What wasn't planned for that showed up? How were things going throughout the change process – in the beginning, middle, and late stages? Not only that, but what was going well? What were our successes?"

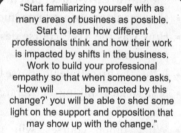

"Be mindful of the importance of systems thinking. Whether it is optimizing the workforce or implementing organizational change, one has to consider the impact your actions have at the organizational, team and individual levels, as well as the inter-relationship between all three."

"Start familiarizing yourself with as many areas of business as possible. Start to learn how different professionals think and how their work is impacted by shifts in the business. Work to build your professional empathy so that when someone asks, 'How will _____ be impacted by this change?' you will be able to shed some light on the support and opposition that may show up with the change."

Lesson Learned 2

Graduate students who receive a holistic SWP experience that simulates organizational scenarios or includes organizational consulting opportunities benefit more than when provided a "by the textbook" model of learning.

Recognizing that an SWP course should build high-level organizational knowledge, develop and exercise critical thinking skills, and apply I-O fundamentals related to diagnosis is crucial to course design considerations. In the following section, we share what we've learned about several aspects of designing and conducting an SWP course. Specifically, we discuss (1) curriculum content, (2) textbook choice, (3) the importance of practice and application, and (4) bridging the content gap between course and organization experience.

Course Versus Curriculum

Each SWP class will stem from a different perspective given the educational program (e.g., I-O psychology, business, master's, PhD, etc.) of which it is a part, and, as such, there is no one ideal syllabus to share across programs for SWP. Therefore, when developing a course of study, there are certain high-level program considerations we recommend a professor to reflect on.

- Where are students in their journey from graduate student in I-O psychology to early-career practitioner?
- How far along are graduate students in the overall program?
- How was the SWP course designed to fit into the architecture of the program?
- Is this the first strategic course that a graduate student is experiencing?
- Is strategic thinking an overarching skill covered in every course of the program?
- What other courses will graduate students be simultaneously enrolled in?
- What content will follow this course?

Answering these questions will enable the SWP professor to determine what needs to be incorporated into the course.

Professors must be aware of assumptions being made regarding a certain level of knowledge around a related I-O subject area, such as training and development or selection. If a cohort hasn't experienced that learning yet—or experienced it in a way much different from that anticipated by the SWP professor—then the speed and quality of coursework as well as learning retention could be affected. Another example—somewhat common—is that the SWP course is the first time that a graduate student is expected to apply the aforementioned critical thinking and "thinking big" skills. These are challenging skills to develop, and if the SWP course is a student's first exposure, they may struggle with the on-ramp of the new skill as well as the content of the course. We recommend SWP professors review the sequence of courses in the curriculum and their learning objectives; doing so may help the SWP professor design in alignment with the program-level developmental path.

Professors must also consider the composition of their potential student cohort when determining what to teach and how to teach an SWP course. A student cohort that arrives with extensive working experience in organizations will certainly have different needs and expectations of their SWP class as compared to newcomers who have yet to work in organizations or a cohort mixed with some students with polished working experience and other students with limited experience. This is particularly critical to address because many concepts in SWP are not ones that new practitioners will get to practice immediately. SWP practitioners—at least those driving the initiatives—are often more senior in their organizations. If an SWP class is comprised of students more junior in their organizations, or not yet employed, then teaching skills and content geared toward executive decision-making may be too removed to "stick" effectively. SWP professors may find themselves first needing to teach about executive roles and how executive decision-making may mirror and contrast with other forms of organizational decision-making. It is critical that professors scale their training not just to address what students will need in the future, but also to how they can help drive SWP-related change, possibly at an entry level.

Another point of differentiation in a student group is types of work experience. We've observed situations where one individual within a cohort is a newer performer at a small nonprofit and another individual is at a semi-senior level of a large corporate organization. While the range provides great opportunity for diverse discussions around SWP, it may also require increased time to make the course directly relevant to everyone. Then again, we stand by our earlier pronouncement of the values of overarching models and enabling students to imagine how each of these models applies to their specific situations.

The Textbook Conundrum

Several SWP and related textbooks seem to primarily present linear, top-down models for workforce planning and change management. This can be important to lay a step-by-step foundation but can feel insipid or removed from the reality of SWP in practice. As a result, much of the currently available written material for SWP does *not* provide early career practitioners with actionable guidance on how they can be part of SWP, even in entry-level positions.

Nevertheless, a professor may find a textbook that works for their particular course. For example, we know of one professor who finds *Agile workforce planning*, written by our volume co-author Adam Gibson (2021), to be an excellent resource. Other professors may wish to supplement or replace traditional texts with alternative resources to provide students with guidance that better aligns with their cohort's developmental path. All three professors writing this chapter eschew traditional textbooks because of the difficulty of aligning existing textbooks with their specific course objectives within the context of their program's curriculum. One professor specifically incorporated *The perfect swarm: The science of complexity in everyday life* (Fisher, 2009) to provide bottom-up models of decision-making to students in addition to the top-down models that traditional methods present. A different professor, looking to lean toward a cognitive and individual buy-in approach, selected *Pre-suasion: A revolutionary way to influence and persuade* (Cialdini, 2016) as the course text. Another professor, who was interested in applying a broader perspective, selected *Cases and exercises in organizational development and change* (Anderson, 2018), and business cases authored by various practitioners found through the SAGE Business Cases (https://sk.sagepub.com/cases/discipline) and Harvard Business School Publishing Education (https://hbsp.harvard.edu/home/) sites, utilizing a collection of case studies to supplement the material.

Another possibility for resolving the textbook conundrum would be the creation or identification of SWP simulations. Simulations high in psychological fidelity that follow established practices in instructional design (Salas et al., 2012) could feasibly provide the supplemental structure to increase the effectiveness of an SWP course. As an alternative to locating an existing SWP simulation, a professor could rely on the blueprints provided by Thornton, Mueller-Hanson, and Rupp (2017) in their book *Developing organizational simulations: A guide for practitioners, students, and researchers*. While an SWP simulation provides an insulated space for applying learning, there are other opportunities. As an SWP professor, find the resource or set of resources that integrates best in achieving your course objectives, which for SWP may mean looking beyond the textbook.

Practice and Application: The Course Consulting Project

It is critical for professors to consider *how* to impact *skills*, not only impart knowledge, as previously noted. Much of the SWP content typically presented encompasses idealized frameworks—however, students must be trained on how to apply those frameworks in practice. Professors, therefore, need to spend time considering how to demonstrate the messiness of SWP in practice. Multiple authors implement hands-on projects in their classes to enable students to practice. There are some challenges to implementing practice-oriented exercises with live clients. However, we have outlined four such considerations and proposed solutions below.

First, course projects are naturally tied to semester- or term-based deadlines. Clients are not. Therefore, students and professors can experience considerable stress during live projects as they feel dependent on client timelines and preferences rather than able to effectuate their projects fully outside of client influence. One way around this dilemma is, where possible, to have live clients who are more readily put under deadlines—for example, the graduate program itself may serve as a client for the purposes of the course.

Second, when working with live clients, professors need to coordinate the timing of when to bring students in on an initiative. If a professor brings the students in for organizational diagnosis, there is a risk that the project may not be as relevant to the course. If a professor brings the students in after organizational diagnosis, the students miss out on valuable experience. A workable solution tends to be for an initial high-level organizational diagnosis by the professor with a follow-up in-depth diagnosis by students.

Third, professors should consider the accountability of work. Students should be given a rough project plan at the start of term outlining their anticipated responsibilities as they relate to client work, with appropriate deadlines, with the understanding that these plans are fluid. If students are working on different workstreams of the project over the course of the term, expectations of high levels of communication may need to be discussed. This is a consulting project: clarity on expectations and specific project milestones over the course of the term as well as final deliverable deadlines apply.

Fourth, some organizations may have privacy issues in sharing data or strategies, especially with graduate students who are hoping to use the project as work samples. In instances where the professor can only locate organizations where privacy is an issue, an alternative is to have students select a public company, where strategies are often readily available and some data may be available via some effortful research. This approach will still provide much of the nonlinearity and messiness of applied work.

Despite the inevitable challenges of a class applied project, all of the authors recommend this approach. The real-world experience seems to serve students well in learning transfer to future work.

Bridging the Content Gap Between Course and Organization Experience

While there is considerable variation in SWP courses, there are a few themes that form the essence of an SWP learning experience. Not surprisingly, these themes build from the substance of earlier chapters in this book in that the themes are organizational more than technical. Specifically, an SWP syllabus probably includes coverage of:

- Understanding organizational life cycle
- Differentiating levels of the organization
- Defining organizational roles
- Communicating specifics of an initiative
- Gaining stakeholder buy-in
- Diagnosing SWP needs
- Analyzing organizational strategy

The combination of and focus on these themes suggest an I-O perspective toward SWP rather than a discrete management consulting or OD practitioner skillset. While all these themes help form the crux of an SWP course, some themes are of higher magnitude and may appear throughout a course (i.e., diagnosing SWP needs). As discussed in the "Course Considerations" section, the content coverage is guided by a calibration to student-needed outcomes. In other words, scrutiny must be given to what the learning outcomes should be and ensuring that higher-level learning is built early and dominantly into the course—learning which is anticipated to help the student most in the workplace—and governs the bulk of the course.

In our experience, students refer back to these consulting and practice skills as some of the most valuable obtained in the SWP course.

These skills tend to be highly applicable and foster self-awareness of balancing consulting skills with other aspects of I-O psychology training.

> "Case studies were especially helpful. Before learning about change management, it is easy to be unintentionally narrow-minded. We often think about how we would perceive a change and stop there. Case studies illustrated the many different perspectives and responses to change as well as encouraged us to empathize with the situation and think of how we would handle it."

> "The client consulting project where we had to diagnose and solve for realistic client challenges enabled me to reflect on and apply what I had learned in the course. The project allowed me to incorporate my learning throughout the semester by designing a strategy that would close the gaps between the current and ideal states across all levels of an organization."

> "Class discussion seemed to be the most effective way (for me) to glean information, as we often covered real-world topics or situations someone was encountering at work and discussed how to solve them."

> "I found the most helpful tool to reinforce understanding from the course were the scorecards we created to apply what we had learned from class lecture and assigned readings … The exercise is a practical application of how one might distill down information in a professional setting."

Lesson Learned 3

An underlying essential component of an SWP course is the cultivation of an emerging professional I-O identity of an SWP student.

Our discussions with alumni surfaced two consistent themes around developing an SWP practitioner identity and efficacy in practice:

1. Building confidence in one's skills around SWP and overcoming imposter syndrome
2. The importance of seeking internships and connections to continue building one's career in the field

These comments shared by alumni weren't often directly connected back to SWP courses, though some confidence-building might be built during the course. Specifically, the experience of the course, particularly if it includes hands-on components, can foster a sense of success after the course. Facing real organizational challenges appeared central to the ongoing confidence-building and comfort with connection that alumni sought and continue to seek.

Students tend to arrive in an SWP course without social comparison for what it means to be an SWP practitioner. While the Society for Industrial Organizational Psychology (SIOP, via its Guidelines for Education and Training in Industrial-Organizational Psychology (2016)), offers a robust view of the competencies related to being a professional in the field of I-O psychology, the specifics of what it means to be an I-O professional working specifically in SWP relies on the role modeling of the professor. We've realized that this process occurs through the focus of the course and how the course is taught. Additionally, the professor, through their approach, values, and energy, sets the tone for how students gain self-confidence.

More broadly, this is an ongoing recognized challenge for I-O. Possibly the best synopsis on this knotty problem for I-O is provided by Lefkowitz (2010) as he begins his article with a section title: "Another Identity Crisis: So What Else Is New?" Similar to Ryan and Ford (2010), Lefkowitz focuses on the importance of values and, at the time, the lack of a commonly agreed upon set of values for the I-O field. Since then, a SIOP Values Statement has been published. For example, as part of its 2021–2023 Strategic Plan, SIOP (2020) clearly states its organizational values.

At SIOP, we will:
- Promote the highest ethical standards in research, education, and evidence-based practice of I-O psychology
- Inspire individual and organizational health, well-being, and effectiveness
- Serve as the trusted authority for the science of psychology applied to the workplace
- Create and nurture an inclusive and collegial community through intentional action
- Encourage and embrace more diversity within our profession
- Respond in a timely and meaningful way to real-world problems
- Steward our human and financial resources for maximum positive impact

A SWP professor—at least an I-O SWP professor—can role-model these values in how the course is taught. Another opportunity is to share these values with students at the beginning of the semester and repeatedly throughout the semester. Doing so might help students to cement who they are as an I-O professional and as an SWP practitioner. In other words, as professors, we can help answer the question, "Who am I when in the role of SWP practitioner? And how am I different than other professionals?"

"It requires that you push past your insecurities, your doubts, your fears, your 'what ifs?'– especially as a student or early career professional. Yes, being early in your career or education is scary. ... intrinsically, you bring something to the table that is new, unique, never thought of – and that is valuable ... Being aware and accepting of your assets (don't argue with the people that identify one of your assets!) are big, important factors that help strengthen your confidence. Having that quality – confidence – will make sure you have long-term org. change and continuing, positive change in yourself – as a professional and a person."

"When I'm feeling under-qualified, I look back at my work from school. I think back to all the good feedback I received on work—especially from our external consulting projects. Hearing from a real business that I benefitted them in some way is a huge confidence boost. I/Os are needed so much right now. Remembering that I have essential skills that are sought after by companies gives me the courage to keep putting myself out there, even though I'm not fully confident yet."

"Starting a new job is, and should be, uncomfortable. I think that many new graduates feel compelled to show up as "experts" who can immediately solve complex, strategic problems. After all, that type of work is usually what is glamorized in the case studies we encounter in school. We incorrectly assume that others (i.e., new managers, peers, etc.) expect us to arrive knowing everything and be able to do everything."

"Consider how to use what you learn in class to interview for [SWP] jobs. It's good to know the steps for organizational change and the models, but each person needs to figure out how to apply this for themselves. I built a framework for myself for how I was going to approach organizational development job interviews. It's very qualitative, and each person needs their own individual flavor to apply the concepts."

Recommendations for Professors, Students, and Early-Career Professionals

As we conclude this chapter, we would like to provide a set of tips for the different roles within the SWP course (and slightly beyond).

Practitioner Tip!

For teachers:

Inspire:
1. Agree to teach an SWP course only when the passion is flowing in you—to *teach* and *learn* about this topic. It's a high-energy demand set.
2. Customize your course. Stay true to the foundational elements of SWP but arrange the approach so you can provide the most impact.
3. Role-model that you stay up to date on business and industry news and trends.
4. Share your own journey in I-O and SWP. Help students understand how your career path emerged over time. What was constant? What changed? What do you love about SWP? Why are you teaching this specific course?
5. Serve as an ambassador for the profession by providing additional or nontraditional resources. For example, communicate about an upcoming Society of Human Resource Management (SHRM) meeting focused on SWP, or make students aware of SWP resources offered by other disciplines at the school where you're teaching.
6. Provide plenty of feedback that challenges students to reflect on situational changes or what they would do next if their original plan doesn't accomplish what they intended—or, better yet, if it does!
7. Demonstrate care in always maintaining the people perspective of SWP. We are I-O psychologists.

Embrace uncertainty:
1. Look for an overarching model (or models) that can keep you centered, but don't rely on your models as a complete solution.

2. Provide scenarios ripe with uncertainty. Some students may grumble, but SWP consulting inherently requires being able to adapt.
3. Teach with the future in mind. Call out examples and possibilities of where the external environment has or may make a profound difference. Practicing with forecasting is a useful learning approach for SWP courses.
4. Supply data, preferably throughout the semester, to help develop diagnostic skills.
5. Use the Socratic method, and then adapt the Socratic method as needed to keep students thinking critically at an appropriate level.
6. Consider guest speakers, especially for topics where your expertise is less focused. For example, every professor should have a "strategy" friend.
7. Teach SWP from an organizational perspective. Understanding the different functions and departments of an organization matters.
8. Provide strategies and skills that enable SWP from the bottom up (for early career practitioners) as well as from the top down.

Plan:
1. Learn a lot about the program and how the course fits within the program. You may discover, for example, that your course may be the only course or the first course where students learn about senior-level consulting.
2. Learn about the cohort that will be taking the course. The cohort one semester may be very different than the cohort the previous semester (e.g., organizational experiences).
3. Select a textbook that ties to your SWP course objectives. If you can't find a textbook that moves you toward the course objectives, don't use a textbook.
4. Limit academic reading.
5. Build or capitalize on your relationships with organizations—especially nonprofit organizations—to offer consulting experiences for students. Ideally, you're in search of low-risk opportunities.
6. Make a list or a Venn diagram or a heat map or an audio recording (whatever you wish!) of the topics you cover in the course. The key

is that you have some way of organizing a snapshot of what you're really teaching in the course, such as strategic HR partnering. Whatever the flavor of your theme, make sure your content fits together and adjust to ensure fit. (This is also a way to discover or reinforce the higher-magnitude topics.)
7. Consider a checklist to test your topics—in the way you teach those topics—to applied settings.
8. Use rigorous teaching resources that are already available to you, such as the Bell et al. (2017) review of 100 years of training and development research.

Practitioner Tip!

For students:

Self-motivate:
1. Be open-minded about the SWP course. You may already be excited as the course begins, but even if the course description doesn't excite you, allow your professor a chance to bring the energy and understand that there is learning even in spaces of lower enthusiasm.
2. Own your learning. In all likelihood, there will be a lot of potential resources (e.g., readings, tools, speakers, etc.) provided throughout the semester, possibly more resources than other courses typically provide. It's up to you to engage at a graduate level where learning is the priority.
3. Push yourself to think broadly and creatively. Perhaps this is a strength you already have; if not, you will need to find a comfort level building this skill and competency.
4. Seek additional information beyond the resources. Ultimately, an SWP course—with your help—should position you to sustain SWP learning well beyond the course.
5. The people make the place.[3] While the professor may set the tone, how you participate in the SWP course—engaging in conversations involving critical thinking, speaking about broader aspects of

organizations, analyzing data but considering what additional data you would like to have, staying on topic—makes a difference in the course rhythm. The same is true of the rest of your cohort.
6. Be willing to recognize that you may be learning something, even if it doesn't follow a learning measurement approach of multiple-choice tests. Percentage correct is not the only measure of learning.

Embrace uncertainty:
1. Accept ambiguity as an exciting part of an SWP course.
2. Demonstrate comfort with syllabus and timing changes that help accommodate client consulting projects.
3. Open your mind to feedback that challenges you to think deeper and about questions that build off what you've said or written.
4. Realize that it's okay to lack confidence in consulting skills before, during, and after the SWP course. We're all learning and getting better with each project.

Seek learning opportunities:
1. Begin keeping up with business and industry news. Consider the news resources that your professor shares with you.
2. Unlearn—at least for the SWP course—the academic style of writing. Summaries and visuals will likely be part of the toolbelt you wear during the course.
3. Make connections between content earlier in the semester with content that occurs throughout the entire semester (yes, even finals week!).
4. Study your syllabus as if it has hidden puzzles, chockful of "Aha!" learning moments. Arguably, it does. (And if your syllabus isn't as fun as an escape room, it won't hurt you to review it.)
5. Each SWP course will be different and should be to be effectively taught. However, as a foundation for a student coming into an SWP course, you'll probably be able to tie in foundational knowledge to the new content areas you'll discover. Specific foundational knowledge that is likely relevant to your SWP course includes job analysis, recruitment, selection, and turnover. Hint: The foundational knowledge will tie into organizational effectiveness.

> **Practitioner Tip!**
>
> For the early-career professional:
> *Learn open-mindedness*:
> 1. Practice meaningful questioning and root cause analysis for everything (e.g., articles in the news, consumption choices, other courses) to keep your skills fresh and to enhance them.
> 2. Do not underestimate the value of data and information that may seem tangential to organizational systems.
> 3. Use the diagnostic data examples and approaches from your SWP course as a starting-point guide—and possibly as a foundation—for your own applications of critical thinking and diagnostics. Hint: You'll quickly go in different directions than only what was covered in your course. The types of data and number of ways to measure and analyze organizational phenomena are immense.
> 4. No matter how much you know—or think you know—about a specific organization's metrics, you probably aren't yet fully informed. Use your expertise on criteria to parse out even more information about what really matters in an organization.
> 5. A consultant—especially an I-O consultant—is a person relating to other people. Remember the human side.
>
> *Go beyond the course*:
> 1. Become an expert in the people analytics portion of SWP.
> 2. Become a student of strategic planning.
> 3. Find ways to continue to diagnose following the course, whether those opportunities emerge from your job, nonprofit work, passion projects, or from something else.
> 4. Understand the parts of the organizational consulting process—such as proposals, contracting, understanding client needs vs. your own wish list, implementation, cost, etc.—that aren't directly I-O related, or risk perishing in the consulting realm.
>
> *Become a professional*:
> 1. Network cross-functionally, not just to say "Hi!" but to learn and understand how different functions fit together within a

specific organization and how those functions connect the business processes to organizational outcomes.
2. There is something special—in terms of practitioner development and affirmation—when we learn via conversations with other consultants regarding similar and shared experiences in SWP consulting. In other words, our dreams and nightmares are often correlated.
3. Allot and spend time thinking strategically and future-oriented about an organization. Hint: This is a trouble spot, even for executives, at many organizations.
4. Reflect thoroughly and intensely on what consulting work to take on within an organization—your role should expand to nontraditional consulting work—and what work to turn down or redirect—ultimately, there will likely be parameters to your work and scope.
5. Use the low-risk opportunities from your course (the risk likely is moderately higher for your professor—yay!) to develop organizational consulting skills and to observe a role model's approach to organizational consulting. Also, consider case studies—such as the ones in this volume—as a developmental aid post-course.
6. Build your own curated resource stream of business and industry news and trends to ensure ongoing awareness around what is going on in the world of work and the world.
7. Continuously think about the communications plan.
8. Seek out and be open to new opportunities to build experience and carve out your unique niche within the SWP arena.
9. Curate a set of references from your classes and professional experiences to use as your guide during the early days of practice.
10. Create a portfolio (e.g., personal website or PDF document) to highlight your strengths and professional brand

Conclusion

Context matters when building an SWP course. Each professor will also bring a unique set of experiences and perspectives to the course that they are teaching. It is feasible, and even probable, that the course in one learning setting will have a fully different feel than a course in another learning setting.

Tied to this difference is the possibility of one or more different lessons learned than what we were able to cover in this chapter.

Regardless of the unique course differences that may emerge via individual differences in professors, a clearer set of considerations emerges for the development and implementation of an SWP course. Categorically, these considerations include skill-building focus around critical and organizational-level thinking, experiential opportunities for applying integrated knowledge and skills, and the cultivation of a professional identity within the subfield.

Underneath these broader considerations are a clearer image of what types of course outcomes that an SWP professor hopes for when students complete the course. Here are some example outcomes:

At the higher level, develop skills related to:

- Critical thinking
- Organizational diagnosis
- Strategic analysis

At the proximal level:

- Define and understand what is encompassed within the SWP universe of thought
- Frame and moderate the discussion within organizations around SWP
- Recognize the interconnections between organizational phenomena (e.g., business strategy, succession planning, selection, etc.) and SWP
- Thoroughly analyze how SWP plays a role in impacting overall organizational effectiveness, including financial, growth, mission, and social responsibility goals
- Thoroughly analyze how SWP plays a role in impacting more-specific people-related measures of organizational effectiveness (e.g., retention, turnover, diversity, equity and inclusion, engagement, culture, etc.)
- Evaluate the role of organizational ethics within the framework of SWP

These are the types of outcomes that are desirable at the conclusion of an SWP course. Ironically, the forecasting of student success mimics one of the thrills and challenges of SWP—seeing more clearly how people succeed now and in the future. What remains discoverable is how SWP courses contribute to success longitudinally.

In composing this chapter, we were pleased with our decision to reach out to alumni because of the rich contextual insights received. Informal as our collection of those insights may have been, there was a noticeable stream indicating that the efforts from SWP courses does, indeed, carry into professional practice and continue to influence students several years past course completion. Similar to Ford, Baldwin, and Prasad (2018), who point out that "We have a body of research that has generally treated training as an event, not an episode, and we thus have too little evidence regarding formal and informal learning and the trajectories of transfer," we would benefit from a more formal understanding of how SWP course structure influences student success in the long term, rather than only the powerful anecdotal evidence used to form a course (e.g., stories from alumni many years removed from a course describing how instrumental SWP and SWP-style thinking was to their career success).

Last, we thank you, the reader, for the opportunity to delve into this topic—we know our conversations in producing this chapter were energizing for each of us.

Notes

1. We benefitted incredibly in crafting this chapter from feedback provided by recent alumni of a course we taught. We're grateful for what their insights taught us about how to teach SWP courses. We thank and acknowledge our I-O colleagues: Erin Bailey, Christian Bastian, Shirley Han, Kelly Lariviere, Lauren Moretti, Mallory Smith, and Shannel Winslow.
2. Those familiar with agile methodology may notice some similarities, for example, with the iterative process.
3. (Wink.) This is a nod to Ben Schneider's (1987) article "The people make the place"—notably relevant to class discussion regarding SWP.

References

Anderson, D. L. (2018). *Cases and exercises in organizational development and change*, 2nd ed. SAGE Publications.

Bell, B. S., Tannenbaum, S. I., Ford, J. K., Noe, R. A., and Kraiger, K. (2017). 100 years of training and development research: What we know and where we should go. *Journal of Applied Psychology, 102*(3), 305–323.

Berman, K., and Knight, J. (2013). *Financial intelligence: A manager's guide to knowing what the numbers really mean* (revd. ed.). Harvard Business Review Press.

Boudreau, J. W., and Ramstad, P. M. (2005). Talentship, talent segmentation, and sustainability: A new HR decision science paradigm for a new strategy definition. *Human Resource Management*, 44, 129–136.

Cialdini, R. (2016). *Pre-suasion: A revolutionary way to influence and persuade*. Simon and Schuster.

Fisher, L. (2009). *The perfect swarm: The science of complexity in everyday life*. Basic Books.

Ford, J. K., Baldwin, T. T., and Prasad, J. (2018). Transfer of training: The known and the unknown. *Annual Review of Organizational Psychology and Organizational Behavior*, 5, 201–225.

Gibson, A. (2021). *Agile workforce planning: How to align people with organizational strategy for improved performance*. Kogan Page Publishers.

Lefkowitz, J. (2010). Industrial-organizational psychology's recurring identity crises: It's a values issue! *Industrial and Organizational Psychology*, 3(3), 293–299.

Marler J. H., and Boudreau, J. W. (2017). An evidence-based review of HR Analytics. *International Journal of Human Resource Management*, 28(1), 3–26.

McFillen, J. M., and O'Neil, D. A. (2010). *Building OD&C as an academic discipline: teaching organizational diagnosis* [Professional development workshop]. 2010 Academy of Management Annual Meeting, Montreal, Canada.

McFillen, J. M., O'Neil, D. A., Balzer, W. K. and Varney, G. H. (2013). Organizational diagnosis: An evidence-based approach. *Journal of Change Management*, 13(2), 223–246.

Roca, J. B. (2022). Teaching technological forecasting to undergraduate students: A reflection on challenges and opportunities. *Technological Forecasting and Social Change*, 180, 121684.

Ryan, A. M., and Ford, J. K. (2010). Organizational psychology and the tipping point of professional identity. *Industrial and Organizational Psychology: Perspectives on Science and Practice*, 3(3), 241–258.

Salas, E., Tannenbaum, S. I., Kraiger, K., and Smith-Jentsch, K. A. (2012). The science of training and development in organizations: What matters in practice. *Psychological Science in the Public Interest*, 13(2), 74–101.

Schneider, B. (1987). The people make the place. *Personnel Psychology*, 40(3), 437–453.

Society for Industrial and Organizational Psychology, Inc. (2016). *Guidelines for education and training in industrial-organizational psychology*. SIOP.

Society for Industrial and Organizational Psychology, Inc. (2020). *SIOP strategic plan 2021-2023*. SIOP.

Thornton, G. C. III, Mueller-Hanson, R. A., and Rupp, D. E. (2017). *Developing organizational simulations: A guide for practitioners, students, and researchers*, 2nd ed. Routledge/Taylor and Francis Group.

Conclusion
A Call to Action for Rethinking Workforce Planning

Beverly Tarulli and Marc Sokol

When we began discussing a book on strategic workforce planning (SWP), it was from the perspective of our academic and professional backgrounds in industrial-organizational (I-O) psychology. We both recognized that although we had never been formally trained in SWP, our education prepared us uniquely to do this work. We were also aware that few of those doing or leading this work in organizations are I-O psychologists. Additionally, I (Beverly) noticed a trend in my teaching: more I-O psychology master's students were taking my class in workforce planning at the New York University School of Professional Studies. It seemed as if the time had come for a SWP book geared toward I-O practitioners, academics who are interested in teaching it, and I-O psychology students who want to learn more about it.

Interest in SWP has appeared to wax and wane, as Dan Ward described in Chapter 1, on the legacy of workforce planning and its implications for the future. At present, we are seeing an upswing of interest in SWP and a paucity of people experienced in conducting it. There are many reasons for this. The demographics of the US working population are shifting, with more women, Hispanics, and workers over the age of 65 projected to make up the labor force by 2029 (US Department of Labor, n.d.). At the same time, organizations continue to have trouble in hiring and retaining qualified talent. Of course, the global pandemic had dramatic effects on organizations and the labor force. In March and April 2020, US companies quickly shed 22.4 million jobs (US Bureau of Labor Statistics, June 2021), with certain industries such as leisure and hospitality hit particularly hard because of the lockdowns. The pandemic has had a lasting impact on workers' perspective about work in many ways.

Beverly Tarulli and Marc Sokol, *A Call to Action for Rethinking Workforce Planning* In: *Strategic Workforce Planning*. Edited by: Marc Sokol and Beverly Tarulli, Oxford University Press. © Society for Industrial and Organizational Psychology 2024.
DOI: 10.1093/oso/9780197759745.003.0018

Where we work has become a point of contention between organizational leaders, who are demanding more people be on-site, and employees, who feel as though they have proved their ability to perform remotely and are loathe to give up the flexibility, time savings, and cost benefits of remote work. The quick pace with which technology is changing the world of work cannot be discounted. Artificial intelligence (AI) has been progressively changing how we work in human resources (HR) for almost 10 years, and, with the introduction of generative AI tools, these changes are occurring even faster than we had anticipated. The complexity wrought by these mega-events and gradual shifts has led HR leaders to seek more predictability in the workplace.

Historically, workforce planning has been primarily a financial and headcount exercise. We still see this today in some organizations. But the broad workplace changes described above mean that just planning for the number of employees is limiting. We need to consider where work gets done (location: on-site or remote), how work gets done (primarily by a person, augmented by technology, or totally replaced by technology), capabilities and skills needed across the workforce, and the right organizational structure. Adam Gibson and Nicola Oldroyd describe these when they present the "seven rights" of workforce planning in Chapter 6.

Given the myriad of forces driving the recent interest in SWP, it is an opportune time to take a critical look at its current state, consider its future, and engage our imaginations about the promise it holds to improve the organizations we work in and the societies we live and operate in. The following sections are intended to summarize emerging trends in SWP, expand our collective thinking as we address the future of work, and explain the skills that are required as a strategic workforce planner.

Emerging Directions for SWP: Tasks, Skills, and Professionalism

The clearest trend we see among practitioners of SWP is the move away from jobs as the primary unit of analysis. Jesuthasan and Boudreau (2021) have advocated a new work operating system that deconstructs jobs into their component parts and allows reconstruction of work based on worker skills and abilities. Their argument is that (a) we need greater agility in organizations to address disruptions within business and that (b) focusing on the job level has inhibited progress in digitization, augmentation, or substitution (e.g., gig work). They also believe that it has made it more difficult for organizations to identify skill gaps, which is a key component of SWP. From an SWP perspective, instead of asking what are the current and future *jobs*, planners should ask what are the current and future *work tasks*. This translates into the required capabilities to perform those tasks and, ultimately, into the best combination of options to achieve those capabilities (Jesuthasan and Boudreau, 2022).

Similarly, David Creelman, Alexis Fink, and Dave Ulrich describe workforce planning using a work-task approach in Chapter 9. From their perspective, work planning at the task level provides greater organizational flexibility to ensure that critical tasks get done without being excessively dependent on filling full-time jobs. Pivots in strategy can then be executed at the task level by automating some tasks as appropriate, distributing other tasks to part-time employees or contracted to external resources, or assigning tasks to people who hold full-time employment. Both Jesuthasan and Boudreau and Creelman et al. are shifting our focus to the *demand* side of the SWP equation by redefining the unit of analysis.

With respect to the *supply* side of SWP, we are seeing organizations attempting to create skills-based operating systems (see Brian Heger's Chapter 8) that make it easier to address skill needs. One of the challenges often faced by SWP professionals and the business leaders they work with is to identify the current skills employees have and project future skill needs, especially when the planning horizon is 3, 5, or more years out.

What is facilitating this new thinking about the supply and demand sides of SWP is all forms of AI. It is the enabler that allows organizations to infer skills more easily by feeding information from resumes, training completions, certifications, and so on into algorithms and then cull through multitudes of job descriptions to identify tasks. Dystopian views of AI might lead one to only imagine people being replaced by machines and software platforms, but the more optimistic view is that AI will allow organizations to augment the work of humans. Decomposition of jobs into tasks—also accomplished by AI—enables matching of tasks to wherever they are done best. It also allows the matching of talent with work opportunities via internal talent marketplace platforms, as Brian Heger's chapter illustrates. This in turn fosters a more fluid internal talent marketplace and enhances career movement and development.

SWP, whether utilizing job, task, or skill as the unit of analysis, is all about the "what" ("What jobs/tasks/skills do we need?"), "how many" ("How many people are doing job X with skills Y and Z?"), and perhaps "where and when" ("Where do we need them and when do we need them?"). Rarely does workforce planning (or most other human resources [HR] practices) concern itself with how work gets done. In Chapter 10, Andrea Fischbach and Benjamin Schneider make the point that rather than narrowly defining "the job," our increasingly complicated work environments require workers to have greater discretion, go beyond the tasks described, and be adaptable, dependable, self-controlled, and ethical. They call this *professionalism*, and we intuitively know how important this is for individual performance and organizational success, but rarely is it part of the conversation in SWP. This could be the eighth "right" of SWP: the right way.

Who (or What) Is Considered the Workforce

The long history of SWP has, as its name implies, been focused on the workforce, generally consisting of full- or part-time employees. *Workforce* has usually meant the people that we hire, train, engage, promote, and terminate from our organizations. But we have for some time had other ways to get things done. Organizations have long relied on contract, contingent and temporary workers, and consultants to meet peak work demands, as a temporary supplement to their permanent employees, or for specialized (but temporary) knowledge needs. Since the financial crisis of 2007-2008, we have added gig workers to the mix at scale, and several gig platforms have evolved to meet the needs of organizations for people with specific expertise. In SWP, these sources of talent are not typically considered when looking at supply and demand, so we have not considered them as part of "the workforce." A very practical reason contractors, consultants, and temporary workers are not included in SWP efforts is that it is often difficult to get data on their current state. Contractor management may lie within the procurement organization, and management of temporary workers or consultants might sit within individual managers' purviews and budgets. We have often heard strategic workforce planners deciding not to include them even if they are so inclined to do so for this very reason. Another reason strategic workforce planners may not consider temporary external sources of talent is reluctance on the part of their business leaders. Many are hesitant because of the difficulty of defining specific tasks that gig workers can work on, fear that permanent employees might have of their jobs being negatively impacted, or a concern for quality of work from unknown entities. We believe that including the entire workforce ecosystem (Altman, Kiron, Schwartz, and Jones, 2021) when conducting SWP will become more common as the way work gets done becomes more fractured and as more and more workers see the benefits of freelance employment.

As organizations continue to look for ways to improve productivity, we will see a greater reliance on technology solutions. From 1979 through 2019, US productivity increased 59.7% (Mischel, 2021), driven by a number of factors, including new productivity software and robotics. New AI tools are promising to profoundly change how we work in ways that we cannot precisely predict. In 2016, the World Economic Forum first introduced the idea of the Fourth Industrial Revolution, articulating the impact that emerging technologies would have on the future of jobs, and, in its most recent publication, "The future of jobs," they note that 34% of all business-related tasks are currently performed by machines, with the remaining 66% performed by humans (World Economic Forum, 2023). Although their survey found that the rate of task automation has slowed somewhat, they also found that traditionally "uniquely human" capabilities such as communication, coordination, and reasoning are expected to be more automatable in the future. They estimate that as much as 35% of reasoning and decision-making and 65% of information- and data-processing could be automated by 2027.

This leads to the question of what SWP will encompass going forward. If it is about how to help organizations determine how to get work done in pursuit of their business goals and strategies, can we ignore the parts of work that will no longer be the domain of permanent human workers within the four walls of our organizations? We don't think so. Luckily, several others provide us guidance. In his book, *Retooling HR* (2010), John Boudreau "challenges strategic workforce planning to go beyond predicting gaps in headcount needed for today's jobs. Instead, ask, 'Where are the significant pivot points in our strategy, and what new performance elements will become more pivotal as a result?'" These pivot points could be where technologies such as AI can improve organizational productivity by not requiring human resources to achieve it. Gibson (2021) addressed this under the topic of demand optimization. He draws from operations management to advocate for workforce planners to consider other ways to meet work demand before using the usual talent levers—buy, build, borrow—to address gaps. The two additional levers he described to address demand before considering talent are "bot" and "balance." *Bot*, of course, involves using technologies to either replace or augment work. *Balance* refers to looking at strategic realignment, quality, and organizational design as solutions to consider in addressing workforce gaps before we buy, build, or borrow. Both strategic alignment and organizational design are domains in which I-O psychologists have expertise. However, most strategic workforce planners are primarily, if not solely, focused on talent solutions to any gaps identified through the process. We argue that this may be one reason that organizations frequently find themselves in a "hire, then fire" employment cycle. Periods of overhiring are often followed by significant layoffs, which are good for neither the organization nor the employees.

Taking into consideration all these ways of identifying and addressing workforce gaps, we suggest that "SWP" may be a misnomer. Rather, we should be talking about *strategic work planning*.

The idea of strategic work planning allows us to more readily embrace both work-task planning and workforce planning around professional roles. As Andrea Fischbach and Benjamin Schneider note in Chapter 10, it doesn't stop with the plan. Sustainable execution of work requires a combination of HR and management practices and policies that foster organizational climates that define and support the behaviors that encourage professionalism.

SWP: A Force for Good?

There is discussion among SWP professionals about how to measure its success. A hard-nosed business perspective might suggest that financial controls and business outcomes are the appropriate measures. Yet a few of the authors made us consider incorporating other important criteria into our work. In Chapter 14, Juliet Aiken and Tori Glascock introduced us to "just workforce planning," where the word *just* refers to incorporating justice, equity, diversity, and inclusion (JEDI) goals into the workforce planning process, the organizational culture, and talent-management practices. It is worth thinking about how the work we do and the terminology we use, as well as how we integrate with other HR processes, can impact how effectively our organizations meet their diversity goals. When organizations set such goals, it is rarely with SWP in mind. Indeed, we wonder how many readers who have engaged in SWP activities have incorporated diversity goals into their plans. As an added benefit, Aiken and Glascock remind us that conducting SWP and handing off a plan is an incomplete action. Integration with other aspects of HR—talent acquisition, talent management, total rewards, and learning—is critical to executing the plans, and it is essential for moving the needle on diversity within organizations.

It may also be worthwhile to think more widely about how SWP can have a positive impact not only on diversity within organizations but also on the broader societal ecosystem. There has been a trend over the past several years to eliminate college degrees as a hiring criterion in certain jobs. In its place, companies are placing a greater emphasis on skills-based hiring. Despite this, companies often miss out on a pool of talent to fill jobs, especially entry-level jobs. A study done by Accenture and the Harvard Business School (Fuller et al., 2021) found that companies' hiring processes systematically exclude whole populations, which they call "hidden workers." These include caregivers, the formerly incarcerated, veterans, and people with disabilities. Speak to workforce planners and you will find that these populations are not on their radar screens as potential sources of talent to fill gaps. But what if strategic workforce planners brought this idea to the table when they work with business leaders and HR business partners? They may produce a win-win solution to talent shortages: the organization can more readily fill jobs, and the communities in which these organizations operate become healthier by providing family-sustaining work to segments of the population that often find it difficult to navigate the corporate hiring maze.

A concrete example of doing well by doing good is the one presented by Michael Bazigos, in Chapter 15. During the early days of the pandemic, when some companies were shedding large numbers of workers and others were struggling to find workers to meet business demands, several chief human resources officers created a way to reallocate talent across organizational boundaries. Called *People + Work Connect*, it was a technology-driven tool that helped keep people employed during a challenging time. It was undertaken during extraordinary circumstances; as workforce planners, however, we might wonder why it could not be done more broadly and more consistently. There are, of course, competitive concerns, but over the past years (2022 and 2023), we have seen massive layoffs, particularly within the tech sector, because of overhiring and a softening economy. What if there were better ways to access such talent to fill openings in industries where they are needed? The idea of using the knowledge and skillsets that I-O psychologists possess so that larger, systemic problems can be addressed is not new. Jones (2020, 2022) introduced the idea that research from cognitive, social, and developmental psychology could be brought to bear on issues of environmental sustainability. Similarly, I-O psychology can offer solutions to broader questions about workforce planning and workforce development beyond the four walls of the organizations they work for.

I-O Psychology Skills Required for SWP

Our premise for undertaking this book was that I-O psychology can provide an excellent foundation for conducting SWP. The Guidelines for Education and Training in Industrial-Organizational Psychology (SIOP, 2016) define the general knowledge and skills, core content, and related areas of competence that graduate programs in I-O psychology cover. We have highlighted the many that are relevant to the practice of SWP in Table C.1.

Beyond I-O Psychology Skills: Managing the Function

For those who manage SWP teams, there are also the knowledge, skills, and abilities required to establish and manage a center of excellence (COE) that encompasses SWP. Sheri Feinzig's Chapter 3, on operationalizing workforce planning provides advice on data collection, sourcing data and its responsible management, choice points regarding several types of analytics, and thinking about the type of SWP team you might create. She also addresses the topic of building buy-in among stakeholders, which we take up shortly in combination with the advice of other authors in this volume. In Chapter 11, by Adam McKinnon and Kanella Salapatas, the reader can find a rich narrative describing the thought process and actions involved in building and managing a SWP organizational capability. Such skills for managing an SWP COE go beyond basic education, but they should be on the radar screens for those who aspire to establish or lead such a function.

Consulting Practices That Foster SWP Progress

Because of its heavy reliance on data, it might be easy to think that SWP is a subset of people analytics and that the real practitioners are simply subject

Table C.1 Areas of competence for industrial-organizational (I-O) psychology graduate programs defined by Society for Industrial and Organizational Psychology (SIOP, 2016) and relevant to strategic workforce planning (SWP)

Category	Area of competence	Definition
General knowledge and skills	Professional skills	Communications: Using technology, writing, and presenting; Interpersonal, negotiation, and conflict-management skills to build and maintain relationships and an ability to navigate relationships in a politically savvy way. Business Writing: Characterized by brevity, action orientation, attention to the audience, and link to the organization's bottom line. Consulting: problem-solving and decision-making skills, communicating solutions in layperson's terms, selling products and services, developing and maintaining relationships with clients, and providing high-quality customer service. Project Management—The details of organizing work, including budgeting, scheduling, delegating, and managing/coaching others.
	Research methods	The scientific method; inductive and deductive reasoning, the generation and articulation of problem statements, research questions, and hypotheses; literature review and critique; the nature and definition of constructs; study designs (experimental, quasi-experimental, and non-experimental); psychometrics; technology-related skills (e.g., programming)
	Statistical methods/ data analysis	The various statistical techniques that are used in the analysis of data generated by empirical research; generalizations, inferences, and interpretations that can legitimately be made based on statistical evidence; translating research findings into theoretical and applied implications in layperson terms.
Core content	Human performance	Study of limitations and capabilities in human skilled behavior, with emphasis on the interaction of human behavior and tools, tasks, and environments.
	Individual assessment	Skills that are needed for assessing, interpreting, and communicating distinguishing characteristics of individuals for a variety of work-related purposes.
	Job/task/ work analysis	The theory and techniques used to generate information about what is involved in performing a task, a job, or work; the physical and social context of this performance; and the attributes needed by an incumbent for such performance.

(continued)

Table C.1 Continued

Category	Area of competence	Definition
	Organization development	The theory and research relevant to changing individuals, groups, and organizations to improve their effectiveness.
	Organization theory	Classical and contemporary theories of organizations, organizational structure, organizational design, organizational culture/climate, organizational change including change management, technology, and the process of organizational policy formation and implementation.
Related areas	Human factors	Psychological principles, knowledge, and research to improve technology, communication and information, decision making, and work settings. Includes areas such as workstation design, workload measurement, control systems, information display systems, health and safety, and human-computer interactions.

Definitions adapted from The Guidelines for Education and Training in I-O Psychology.

matter experts in all aspects of data handling and analysis. Although these skills matter greatly, all our contributors recognize how essential good consulting skills are to managing the competing perspectives, priorities, and values that surface during SWP projects.

Most practitioners are regularly faced with tradeoffs in how they approach SWP: task versus role; using a highly data-driven approach versus working with what is most readily available; focusing on senior sponsorship versus working on a small, pressing issue that creates a track record of small wins. Our seasoned authors tend to see these tradeoffs as sets of competing values where context and maturity of SWP practices serve as guideposts. It is one thing to advocate a "both/and" mindset, but it is another to hold to it when some stakeholders only see one side of the issue rather than different ideas in balance. Many contributors share hard-earned lessons of experience and practical tips.

In Chapter 2, Tanya Moore reminds us that different organizations can be at differing levels of maturity in SWP, and she defines four levels of maturity: budget-driven, focused on talent planning, incorporating workforce analytics, and fully integrated into business strategy and processes. Although the strategic workforce planner may want to introduce sophisticated data or a rigid framework, her advice is to meet the organization where it is. For example, if the organization is only interested in a budget-driven approach, it is best to start there. Finding a willing part of the organization to work with and act as a partner (e.g., the finance group) can expedite your learning and build on the skills you developed as an I-O psychology professional. David Reimer and Adam Bryant, focusing on the CEO and C-suite as key stakeholders in Chapter 12, remind us that the most engaging SWP conversations inform both sides of the table where the specialist and senior executives help each other clarify the path forward and come to see SWP as a challenge they must address together. They offer the reader several questions to help make the most of those meetings.

Laura Knowles and Samantha Adrignola work at the enterprise level of the federal government but recognize that their approach must also be one that enables agencies and departments to experience autonomy in local SWP practices. In Chapter 4, they describe how what might have been a tug of war over who has influence is instead transformed into a collaboration and exchange of best-practice guidance. In similar fashion, Christian Hobson and Paul van Katwyk, in Chapter 5, recognize that SWP and talent-management subject matter expertise at Saudi Aramco must be nested within national economic priorities of Saudi Arabia.

In Chapter 7, James Eyring, Andrew Newmark, and Sunil Setlur note that large and global organizations often include geographic, business model, and economic diversity such that no single plan is an ideal fit for all situations. What they refer to as "multispeed" planning is the ability to tailor an approach to various parts of the business. High- and low-growth environments have different business challenges and different growth strategies and thus require different skills and processes, and there are unique risks for each type of people strategy. You can expect that your stakeholders will be more engaged and responsive when your consulting approach includes an array of SWP and related talent strategies that demonstrate you understand where the business is economically and in relation to the external market.

The multispeed approach reflects consulting advice to tailor solutions to fit your firm rather than benchmark and copy another approach in its entirety. Among Brian Heger's recommendations in Chapter 8, he suggests bypassing the "easy" opportunity to buy AI-based SWP solutions even though they claim to work elsewhere or promise an all-in-one solution. He advocates designing your own pilot studies to discover what aspects of an AI SWP approach fit with your organization and its readiness for implementation. Yes, it is more work, as you can see from his multistep approach, but it also means that your eventual solution is customized to succeed in your company.

Several authors pay close attention to relationships, processes, and dynamics that surround and enable SWP. In Chapter 8, Brian Heger reminds us that the internal marketplace is often an underrecognized lever for surfacing hidden or trapped capacity. A close colleague of any SWP professional should be the HR business partners assigned to each business line or function because they will have more ready access to this internal marketplace. In Chapter 2, Tanya Moore advises practitioners to start with a business problem, conduct a small pilot, and demonstrate small wins. In a tight labor market, if you are losing as many people as you are hiring, leverage that data to start a new narrative with business partners. Edie Goldberg uses scenario planning in Chapter 13 to help highly dynamic businesses maintain an agile mindset. This approach, as outlined in her chapter, is likely to deeply engage stakeholders who are 24/7 in their attention to envisioning a competitive business strategy.

The idea of being agile is at the heart of a consulting mindset. Adam Gibson and Nicola Oldroyd offer a full set of such practices in Chapter 6, and several stand out for us. First, be ready to engage in discussion about the workforce and strategy along multiple time horizons: today, next year, several years out. Second, remember that interactions and relationships override processes and tools, especially if you hope to win the war not just the battle. Similarly, an agile approach is one marked by collaboration and flexibility, not reliance on only negotiated agreements. Last, plans matter, but responsiveness to change may determine whether your plan is a living document or a fine piece of work that sits on a shelf.

We should acknowledge that all SWP projects follow a common methodology. Although there are slight variations from source to source, this methodology generally takes the form shown in Figure C.1.

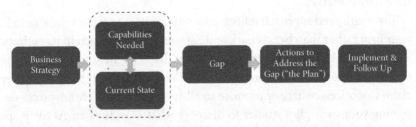

Figure C.1 A common strategic workforce planning methodology.

As ubiquitous and helpful as this methodology is, SWP is not simply a mechanical step-by-step process. Common to the authors of this volume is an understanding that, at its heart, it is a consulting process. As Wendy Hirsch, vice president of HR technology, analytics, and services at Eaton put it, "Sometimes, strategic workforce planning is like business therapy" (personal communication, April 4, 2022). We recommend readers consider some variation of the following four-step approach in their SWP consulting. To simplify with an acronym, follow your AIMS: that is, consider SWP as a cycle in which you assess, imagine, mobilize, and shape the results you aspire to achieve. When you *assess*, you conduct some type of baseline analysis, consider trends and disruptions impacting how work and work planning might occur, and test consensus with stakeholders around strategic business priorities. Once you assess, you can begin to *imagine* different future states. This can be accomplished through exploring various scenarios, analyzing options, and debating tradeoffs until consensus is achieved. Now that some plan is agreed upon, the SWP task is to *mobilize* stakeholders and processes, plan the journey (or journeys for various parts of the business), and gain agreement on responsibilities, timelines, and targets. As a skilled change agent, your next step in the process is to *shape* implementation over time, often following some cycle of plan-do-check-adjust around talent and work-planning process, capturing and sharing insights and lessons of what works in your company, and embedding the process into the company. Here again SWP becomes more sustainable to the extent that it is aligned with other HR COEs, with the daily work of HR business partners, with management expectations, and with company policies.

Within each of these four steps there are places to leverage analytic practices, places to engage stakeholders by telling a story, and times to test consensus and buy-in before moving to the next step. Figure C.2 illustrates this four-step consulting approach.

If you combine these two frameworks as shown in Figure C.3, it is easy to see how the assess and imagine components of the AIMS consulting model apply most readily to the "business strategy" through "gap" steps in the SWP methodology. The mobilize and shape components apply to the "actions to address gaps" or development of the workforce plan through implementation. This is a more complete equation that illustrates the complexity of SWP and the importance of the technical and consulting skills needed to be successful at it.

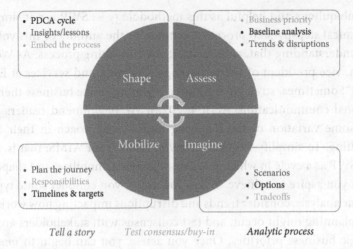

Figure C.2 A four-step approach to strategic workforce planning consulting.

A Call to Action: I-O Psychologists Trained to be Broader as Well as Deeper and to Integrate SWP into Their Vision of the Profession

Students graduating with a degree in I-O psychology should have confidence that they have the requisite skills to do SWP. We see several barriers that limit their ability to do so. The first is the lack of exposure to the methodology and practice of SWP in their curriculum. As we looked for academic I-O psychology professionals who teach it, we found very few programs that included it, even as an elective. Most of those were in master's level I-O psychology programs. A notable exception is described by Steve Weingarden,

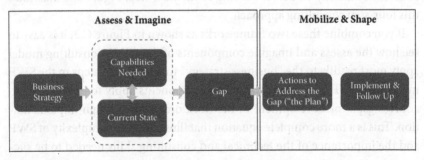

Figure C.3 Technical and consulting model for strategic workforce planning.

Nikita Arun, and Juliet Aiken in Chapter 16, on how they each teach this topic. They stress the importance of building critical-thinking competencies and a diagnostic mindset with respect to SWP. They ask students to take a holistic organizational approach, allowing them to later extend their actions to go beyond the textbook. Last, they note that to really embrace SWP, it must become part of one's developing identity as an I-O psychologist.

The broader lack of courses on SWP reflects several structural factors. The most prominent one is that modifications of curriculum typically require lengthy university- and state-level reviews and approvals. It is also likely the case that many academic I-O psychologists have never conducted SWP projects themselves and do not feel qualified to teach a course. Some may also feel that there is no "science" behind the topic, but we would argue that there is psychological science behind all the areas (listed above) that are core competencies of I-O psychology and are relevant to SWP. In our experience, an emphasis on change management/stakeholder management (which could be covered in consulting or organization-development courses), along with inclusion of scenario planning and deep dives into special topics such as how AI will change work, would be highly valuable in preparing newly minted I-O psychologists to do this work.

Because organizational psychology is a profession built on a science-practitioner model, we would also like to see our academic colleagues take on SWP as an area of research. It does not appear that this is on academicians' radar screens. In fact, a search on the website of the Society for Industrial and Organizational Psychology (SIOP) for the term *workforce planning* returns no results. Nor, at the time this volume was being prepared, was it an area of expertise that SIOP members could select when they set up their profiles. It would be hugely beneficial to practitioners to be able to utilize research-based techniques, approaches, and methodologies. In fact, this is an area that may be most amenable to research partnerships between academia and practitioners. In turn, this research could raise the profile of SWP as an area worthy of I-O psychologists' attention.

As is true for many disciplines, developing competency in SWP usually means becoming "T-shaped." I-O psychologists bring deep expertise in the competencies defined by SIOP but may lack more business-focused skill sets required to work effectively with business leaders. Becoming T-shaped means moving outside our psychologist comfort zone to learn from other disciplines. Two that stand out are finance and strategy, with whom we frequently partner in this work. If one has not been exposed to financial management concepts or strategy frameworks, it can be helpful to broaden one's knowledge in these areas. It also goes without saying that understanding the business that you are in and the business environment in which your organization operates is essential in doing SWP. This applies at the macro level as well as whatever level you are conducting your workforce planning (see Gibson's discussion of macro, meso, and micro levels in Chapter 6). Successfully guiding business leaders through the workforce planning process depends on bringing both deep expertise and broad skills and knowledge to bear.

We believe SWP is both valuable to organizations and an area in which more I-O psychologists should engage and become proficient. This book is intended to spark interest among current and future practicing I-O psychologists, whether working inside organizations or in consulting roles. It is even more important that I-O psychologists in academic roles teach SWP and conduct research on the methods that can drive true evidence-based approaches, underpinned by principles from our field. We hope we have provided the reader with best practices in SWP that they can apply, a more expansive view of the impact it can have, and a roadmap for how I-O psychology can play a larger role in this important organizational practice.

References

Altman, E. J., Kiron, D., Schwartz, J., and Jones, R. (2021). The future of work is through workforce ecosystems. *MIT Sloan Management Review*, 62(2), 1–4.
Boudreau, J. (2010). *Retooling HR: Using proven business tools to make better decisions about talent*. Harvard Business Press.
Fuller, J. B., Raman, M., Sage-Gavin, E., and Hines, K. (2021, September). Hidden workers: Untapped talent. Harvard Business School Project on Managing the Future of Work and Accenture. https://www.hbs.edu/managing-the-future-of-work/Documents/research/hiddenworkers09032021.pdf
Gibson, A. (2021). *Agile workforce planning*. Kogan Page.
Jesuthasan, R., and Boudreau, J. W. (2021). Work without jobs. *MIT Sloan Management Review*, 62(3), 5–8.
Jesuthasan, R., and Boudreau, J. W. (2022, Spring). Can't fill jobs? Deconstruct them. *MIT Sloan Management Review*, 63(3), 15–17.
Jones, R. G. (2020). *The applied psychology of sustainability*. Routledge.
Jones, R. G. (2022). *Sustainable solutions: The climate crisis and the psychology of social action*. APA.
Mischel, L. (2021, September 2). Growing inequalities, reflecting growing employer power, have generated a productivity-pay gap since 1979. Economic Policy Institute. https://www.epi.org/blog/growing-inequalities-reflecting-growing-emplo

yer-power-have-generated-a-productivity-pay-gap-since-1979-productivity-has-grown-3-5-times-as-much-as-pay-for-the-typical-worker/

Society for Industrial and Organizational Psychology. (2016). *Guidelines for education and training in industrial-organizational psychology*. SIOP.

US Bureau of Labor Statistics. (2021, June). COVID-19 ends longest employment recovery and expansion in CES history, causing unprecedented job losses in 2020. https://www.bls.gov/opub/mlr/2021/article/covid-19-ends-longest-employment-expansion-in-ces-history.htm

US Department of Labor, Women's Bureau. (n.d.). Labor force by sex, race and Hispanic ethnicity. https://www.dol.gov/agencies/wb/data/latest-annual-data/working-women#Labor-Force-by-Sex-Race-and-Hispanic-Ethnicity

World Economic Forum. (2023, April 30). The future of jobs report 2023. https://www.weforum.org/reports/the-future-of-jobs-report-2023/

Index

For the benefit of digital users, indexed terms that span two pages (e.g., 52–53) may, on occasion, appear on only one of those pages.

Tables, figures, and boxes are indicated by *t*, *f*, and *b* following the page number

Accenture, 318, 320–22, 323, 377
action planning case study, 136–37*b*
activities taxonomy, 207
adaptive planning
    challenges/lessons, 246–48
    data processing tools, 256*b*
    data quality, 245–46, 247, 249
    data sources, 250–51, 252*b*, 256–58, 259
    discovery process, 243–46, 244*f*
    financial planning, 247
    hierarchies in, 247–48
    mergers & acquisitions, 249–58
    overview, 12, 241–42, 378
    pain points, 243–45
    patent data, 251–52, 254–55
    pragmatism driving innovation, 258–59
    process enhancement, 245
    real-world application, 258
    repeatable/sustainable SWP, 242–48, 244*f*
    replacing *vs.* revising processes, 246–47, 258
    site selection, 257
    social network analysis, 252–56, 254*f*, 255*f*
    stakeholder messaging, 243–46
    strategic workforce plans, 257–58
    strategy inferencing/acquisition selection, 257
    teams in, 243
    user experience improvement, 246
    waterfall *vs.* agile *vs.* prototyping approaches, 248
    workforce planning, 246
Adrignola, S., 10, 381
agile workforce planning
    action plan case study, 136–37*b*
    action planning, 134–37
    AI application case study, 130–32*b*
    automated technology in, 134–35
    baseline stage, 124–27
    business model understanding, 122, 124
    capacity/capability requirements case study, 129–30*b*
    case studies, 125–26*b*, 127–28*b*, 129–32*b*, 133–34*b*, 136–37*b*
    critical function identification, 125–26*b*, 127–28*b*
    data/modeling, 130
    delivery stage, 138
    demand stage, 128–32
    factors affecting, 118–19
    five D's of, 118–19
    flexibility in, 117–22
    framework, 123–38, 124*f*
    gap analysis, 132–34
    gap analysis case study, 136–37*b*
    in growth environments, 156–60
    overview, 10, 382
    planning horizons, 117–18, 118*f*
    principles of, 116, 117*f*, 120*t*, 122–23, 382
    problem understanding, 126–27*b*
    siloed approach to, 117–18, 118*f*
    stakeholders in, 119, 121, 122, 125–27
    supply profile case study, 127–28*b*
    supply stage, 127–28
    target setting, 119
    teams in, 122
    traditional *vs.*, 120–23, 120*t*
    values of, 121–22
    waterfall *vs.*, 123*b*
Agile Workforce Planning (Gibson), 5, 356
Aiken, J. R., 13–14, 376–77, 384–85

AIMS acronym, 383
Allport, G. W., 222–23
Alphabet, 293–94
AlphaFold, 209
Alteryx, 66
analytics. *See* data analytics
applicant tracking system (ATS), 169
Art of the Long View, The (Schwartz), 287–88
artificial intelligence (AI). *See also* automation
    agile workforce planning case study, 130
    Bristol-Myers Squibb case study (*see* Bristol-Myers Squibb case study)
    in Connect initiative, 321, 343
    effort mobilization, 183, 184
    employee skill profiles, 168–69
    I-O psychologists roles, 183, 193–94
    impacts of generally, 371–72, 375
    inferences/relevance strengthening, 183, 188
    internal opportunities repository, 169–71, 170*f*
    internal talent marketplace (ITM), 168–72, 170*f*, 171*f*, 183, 191, 382
    maturity model applications of, 28, 33*f*, 33, 43–45
    nontechnological barriers, 183, 191
    overview, 11, 381–82
    pilot study implementation, 183, 185
    skills-based talent practices, 165–66
    in strategic worktask planning, 200–1, 205, 207, 209
    SWP implementation challenges, 165–66, 167*t*, 172–73
    talent intelligence platforms, 166–67, 167*t*
    vendor evaluation, 183, 185
Arun, N., 13–14, 384–85
AT&T Bell Labs, 18–19
attraction–selection–attrition (ASA) model, 226
automation. *See also* artificial intelligence (AI)
    in agile workforce planning, 134–35
    Connect initiative, 325–30, 329*f*, 334–35
    impacts of generally, 375
    intelligent process automation, 330
    robotic process automation (RPA), 330
    in strategic worktask planning, 200, 203, 207, 208

balance, 375–76
Bardot-Braddock cycle, 18
Barrick, M. R., 224
Bartholomew, D. J., 17–18
Bazigos, M., 13, 377–78
Beautiful.ai, 256*b*
Bechet, T., 16, 20
Berman, K., 352
Bersin, J., 166
BMS. *See* Bristol-Myers Squibb case study
bot, 375–76
Boudreau, J., 199, 221, 222*b*, 372–73, 375–76
brand perception data sources, 54*t*
Bright & Co., 38–39
Bristol-Myers Squibb case study
    actionable insights, 183–94
    AI capabilities of interest, 175, 176*f*
    background, 173–74
    data sources, 179, 179*t*
    development opportunity recommendations, 177*t*, 181*f*, 182
    employee skills profile, 179*t*
    executive support, 176–77
    Internet opportunity matching, 179*t*
    job matching, 177*t*, 181*f*, 181
    overview, 172–73
    pilot group selection criteria, 178
    proof of concept testing, 177–83, 177*t*, 181*f*
    results, 180–83, 181*f*
    skill inferences, 177*t*, 180, 181*f*
    talent capability workstream, 174–75, 175*f*
    user experience, 177*t*, 181*f*, 182–83
    vendor evaluation, 176–77
    workforce planning usefulness, 177*t*, 181*f*, 182
Bryant, A., 12, 380–81
Burack, E. H., 18
business strategy data sources, 36

capacity/capability requirements case study, 129–30*b*
capacity planning, 117

case studies
  action planing, 136–37b
  agile workforce planning, 125–26b, 127–28b, 129–32b, 133–34b, 136–37b
  benefits, limitations of, 261–62
  Bristol-Myers Squibb (see Bristol-Myers Squibb case study)
  capacity/capability requirements, 129–30b
  CEO engagement, 264–70, 276–81
  distribution center, 202–4
  Dutch Railway, 38–39
  gap analysis, 136–37b
  Gojek, 141–42, 155–60, 159f
  green technologies transition, 264–66, 276–77
  HIPO/succession management program, 39–40, 41f
  IBM, 43–45, 65
  internal freelance talent pool, 209–11b
  M. C. Dean, 39–40, 41f
  Marriott International, 141–42, 150–55
  maturity model, 38–45
  mergers & acquisitions, 249–58
  repeatable/sustainable SWP, 242–48, 244f
  Saudi Aramco (see Saudi Aramco case study)
  supply profile, 127–28b
  systematic skills taxonomy, 206–8
Cases And Exercises In Organizational Development And Change (Anderson), 356
centeredness skills, 340
Centre for Transformative Work Design, 229
CEO engagement. *See also* stakeholders
  access problem, 262–63
  buy-in/support, 260, 262–63, 270–71, 280–81, 280t
  communication, 272–73
  context, 263–64
  decision-making, 273, 277
  desired pace of change, 272
  financial services case study, 266–68, 277–78
  global manufacturing case study, 264–66, 276–77
  leadership implications of change, 272
  legacy business issues, 271, 277
  media company case study, 268–70, 279–81
  operational changes planning, 273
  outside-in talent retention, 274, 278
  overview, 12, 260–62, 380–81
  stakeholder playbook, 270–75, 280–81, 280t
  structural/organizational implications, 274–75, 278
  talent implications, 273–74, 278
ChatGPT, 343
Chief Privacy Office, 55
CHREATE, 284–85
Chuai, X., 147–48
compensation data sources, 37
competitive landscape data sources, 36
competitor information sources, 37
Complexity Leadership Part I (Uhl-Bien/Marion), 308–9
Connect initiative
  artificial intelligence (AI) in, 321, 343
  background, 318–20, 319f, 377–78
  design principles, 320–21, 323–24, 330–31
  evolution of, 324–25
  founder credibility in, 323
  functionality, 330–31
  intent of, 320
  job analysis, 324–25, 326f, 328–29, 331
  natural language processing in, 321, 322, 327, 330, 334–35
  network thinking in, 323
  parsimony in, 321, 323–24
  potential of, 324
  practitioner skills, 337–42, 338f
  Remote Work Indicator, 322, 331–32, 333f
  results, 321–22
  scope of support, 320
  skill-based analysis, 332–37, 335f
  standardization, 331
  target audience, 320
  task level analysis, 328–29, 329f, 331–32, 333f
  workforce automation, 325–30, 329f, 334–35

consulting/practice skills, 92, 201–2, 339–40, 358–59, 378–83, 379t, 384f
contractors. *see* freelancers; gig workers
course consulting project, 357–58
COVID-19 pandemic
　business revenue impacts of, 151–52
　business strategy impacts of, 270, 282
　data analytics on impacts of, 72–74
　impacts of generally, 50, 371–72
　labor shortage *vs.* surplus scenario, 316–18
　overview, 13
　People + Work Connect (Connect) initiative (*see* Connect initiative)
　supply chain disruptions, 321–22
　time horizon impacts of, 69
　work role impacts of, 224, 227–28
Creelman, D., 373
critical role identification
　agile workforce planning, 125–26b, 127–28b
　data analytics, 21f, 31, 39, 51, 55–56, 59t, 61, 63, 64b
　federal public sector, 81, 85, 88
　maturity model, 31, 39
　Saudi Aramco case study, 107–8
cross-selling, 220, 233–34

data analytics
　adaptations to process, 56b
　agile workforce planning, 130
　analytics expertise, 340–41
　associative analyses, 57, 59t
　Big Data analytics, 58
　buy-in/influence, 70–71
　challenges, 71–72
　computational analyses, 57
　context in, 63b, 69b, 70b
　correlational/regression analyses, 57–58
　cost savings, 70b
　COVID-19 impacts, 72–74
　critical role identification, 21f, 31, 39, 51, 55–56, 59t, 61, 63, 64b
　data sources, 52–67, 54t
　description analyses, 57, 59t
　expertise, skills, 340–41
　follow-through, 71
　governance process, 61–62

　headcount *vs.* skills focus, 62b
　HR data sets ethics, 55
　implementation, 71b
　method types, 56–58, 59t
　nonanalytical approaches, 62–63
　open-source data sets, 252b, 256
　outcomes predictability, 57b
　overview, 6, 9, 48–49, 378
　policies/regulations, 55
　predictive analyses, 57, 59t, 61b
　privacy/ethics, 55, 58
　scenario planning (*see* scenario planning)
　software tools, 66–67
　stakeholder interactions, 63
　strategy maps, 63
　SWP defined, 50–51
　SWP implementation, 51–52
　SWP operationalization, 67–71
　SWP scope, 67–68
　SWP team/skills, 68–69
　SWP time horizon, 69b
　talent analysis, 52b
　workforce assessment/analytics, 90–91
　workforce dynamics analyses, 57–58
　workforce planning accuracy, 58–62
　workforce planning role, 55–56
data fabric, 66–67
data sources
　adaptive planning, 250–51, 252b, 256–58, 259
　brand perception, 54t
　Bristol-Myers Squibb case study, 179, 179t
　business strategy, 36
　compensation, 37
　competitive landscape, 36
　competitor information, 37
　data analytics, 52–67, 54t
　economic trends, 54t
　education, training, 36, 356
　employee skill profiles, 168–69
　federal public sector, 91b
　financial, 54t
　government, 37
　human resources, 54t
　internal opportunities repository, 169–71, 170f

job analysis, 324–25, 326f, 329f
labor market trends, 54t
maturity model, 32, 35–37
O*NET, 330–31, 346–48
open-source data sets, 252b, 256
patent data, 251–52, 254–55
qualitative, 54t
talent acquisition, 36
workforce profile, 36, 54t
Deci, E. L., 224
demand optimization levers, 134–35
derived demand, 128–32
Development Sprints, 154
Diesel Gate, 233–34
directional accuracy, 350–51, 351f
distribution center case study, 202–4
Draup, 66
Dutch Railway case study, 38–39

economic trends data sources, 54t
education, training
　AI applications to, 43–45
　competency development, 89–93
　consulting/practice skills, 92, 358–59, 378–83
　content gap bridging, 358–59
　course consulting project, 357–58
　course vs. curriculum, 354–55, 385
　critical thinking competencies, 349–53, 354–55, 384–85
　data sources, 36, 356
　diagnostic-driven approaches, 349–53
　directional accuracy, 350–51, 351f
　early-career professional recommendations, 366–67b
　experience-based training programs, 228–29, 229b, 233
　financial acumen, 352–53
　growth environments initiatives, 153, 158–60, 159f
　holistic SWP experiences, 353–59
　I-O psychology, 94–96, 378, 379t, 384–86
　job analysis/competency modeling, 91–92
　just workforce/JEDI planning, 308–9
　New Collar Program, 221–22, 222b
　nonlinear courses, 350–53

organizational culture/climate, 227–31, 229b, 233
organizational theory, 93
overview, 13–14
practitioner skills, 337–42, 338f
professional I-O identity cultivation, 359–61
simulations, 356
student recommendations, 364–65b
teacher recommendations, 362–64b
textbooks in, 355–56
workforce assessment/analytics, 90–91
electric vehicles (EVs), 271
empathy skills, 339
employee skills profile, 168–69, 179t
Emsi Burning Glass, 293–94
eugenics, 306–7
Excel. See Microsoft Excel
ExCo Group, 263–64
Eyring, A. R., 142, 147–48
Eyring, J. D., 10–11, 147–48, 381

federal public sector
　agency best practices, 95–96
　best practices, 93–96
　budget cycle, 78b
　budget/hiring dynamic, 78–80
　centralized approach to, 83
　challenges, 78–80
　competency development, 89–93
　conceptualization, 81
　context in, 85
　coordinated approach to, 84f, 84–86
　data sources, 91b
　decentralized approach to, 83
　employment statistics, 76, 77t
　I-O psychologist best practices, 96
　I-O psychology benefits to, 93b
　inferences across agencies, 82
　mission-critical positions, 81, 85, 88
　overview, 10, 76, 381
　stakeholder connections, 81b, 83, 89
　SWP benefits, 80
　SWP defined, 80b, 86–88
　SWP implementation, 86–88, 97–98b
　SWP sustainment, 85–86
　tailoring/standardization of processes, 82–86

Fedscope.gov, 91*b*
Feinzig, S., 9, 378
financial acumen, 352–53
financial data sources, 54*t*
Fink, A. A., 11, 373
Fischbach, A., 11–12, 373–74
five-factor model of personality, 225–26, 225*t*
Fiverr, 209
flexibility skills, 339
Foldit, 209
Ford, J. K., 360
Fourth Industrial Revolution, 375
freelancers, 209–11*b*, 295*f*, 295–96. *See also* gig workers
Frey, C. B., 327–28

Galton, F., 306–7
gap analysis case study, 136–37*b*
General Electric, 146–47, 234
General Manager Certificate program, 154
Gerber, 321–22
German Police University, 229*b*, 229
Gibson, A., 5, 10, 356, 375–76, 382
gig workers, 200, 207, 209, 295*f*, 295–96, 330, 374–75
Glascock, T., 13, 376–77
Gloat, 209
Global Talent Trends study, 164
Gojek case study, 141–42, 155–60, 159*f*
Gojek Growth Leader Journey, 158–59, 159*f*
Goldberg, E., 12, 382
Google, 146–47
Gorgas, J., 261
government data sources, 37
green technologies transition, 264–66, 276–77
growth environments
 action planning, 160–62
 agile workforce planning, 156–60
 areas of focus, 149
 challenges of, 142–46, 143*t*
 core capability strategy, 147*f*, 148, 149, 151*t*
 cultural context in, 146–47
 education, training initiatives, 153, 154, 158–60, 159*f*
 Gojek case study, 141–42, 155–60, 159*f*

 innovation leveraging, 142–44, 143*t*
 key talent strategy, 147*f*, 148, 149–50, 151*t*, 154
 leadership strategy, 144–45, 158–60, 159*f*
 manager promotion/turnover, 149–50, 154
 Marriott International case study, 141–42, 150–55
 organizational culture, 144–45
 overview, 10–11, 381
 position planning strategy, 147*f*, 148–50, 151*t*
 SWP process relationship to, 140–42, 145–46, 151*t*
 SWP strategies, 155*t*
 talent management strategy, 144–45, 146–51, 147*f*, 151*t*
 talent pooling strategy, 147*f*, 148, 149, 151*t*, 154–55
Growth Leader Assessment (GLA), 158–59
Growth Leader Strategies Assessment, 158–59
Growth Leader Style Assessment, 158–59

Hackman, J. R., 220–21, 224
Harvard Business School, 356, 377
Hawkins, M., 19
Heger, B., 11, 381–82
hidden workers, 377
high-growth companies. *See* growth environments
high potential (HIPO)/succession management program case study, 39–40, 41*f*
Hirsch, W., 383
Hitch, 209
Hobson, C., 10, 381
holistic SWP experiences, 353–59
Howson, C., 340–41
HP Inc., 263
HR business partners (HRBPs), 68
HRForecast, 42–43
human resource planning process flow, 20*f*, 20, 21*f*
human resources data sources, 54*t*

IBM case study, 43–45, 65, 221–22, 222*b*
identity cultivation, 359–61

INDEX 395

if-then scenarios, 55–56
Iles, P., 147–48
intelligent process automation, 330
Interactive Flow Simulator (IFS), 18–19
internal opportunities repository, 169–71, 170*f*
internal talent marketplace (ITM), 168–72, 170*f*, 171*f*, 183, 191, 382

Jesuthasan, R., 199, 221, 222*b*, 372–73
job families, 34
job-role differentiation theory, 220–21
JOBFLO, 19–20
just workforce/JEDI planning
    consent decree, 300–1, 312
    cultural transformation processes, 308–12
    description, 308
    diversity, 301*b*
    diversity-validity tradeoff, 306–7
    education, training, 308–9
    equity/equality, 302–3*b*
    guidelines, 313*t*, 314*t*
    hidden workers, 377
    hiring/promotion, 306–9
    I-O psychologist roles, 301, 305, 307, 309, 310–11
    inclusion, 302–3*b*
    internal workforce analysis, 303, 304
    justice, 304*b*
    litigation historically, 19
    Montmore County Government case study, 300–12
    overview, 13, 376–78
    processes, 303–6, 307
    range restriction, 304–5
    receivership, 301–2, 304–5, 312
    reparations, 304*b*
    resources in, 305–6
    self-care necessity, 311
    theoretical groundwork, 302

Kahn, H., 283
Kenelyze, 256
key performance indicators (KPIs), 61–62, 63
King Fahd University of Petroleum and Minerals (KFUPM), 101
Klonek, F., 229
Knight, J., 352
Knowles, L., 10, 381

KSAOs, 216–17, 218–19, 222–23, 225–28, 232–33, 236

labor market trends data sources, 54*t*
Layden, S., 261
learning management system (LMS), 169
Lefkowitz, J., 360
Lewis, M., 18
Lim, A., 142
Lincoln Financial Group, 318
LinkedIn, 32, 58, 255, 293–94
low-growth companies. *See* growth environments

M. C. Dean case study, 39–40, 41*f*
Maki, W., 16, 22
MAMO approach, 201
Marion, R., 308–9
Markov manpower models, 19
Marriott Development Academy, 153
Marriott International case study, 141–42, 150–55
maturity model
    AI applications, 28, 33*f*, 33, 43–45
    areas of focus identification, 40*b*
    budget-driven planning, 30–31, 31*f*
    case studies, 38–45
    consultant firm selection, 43*b*
    critical role identification, 31, 39
    data sharing, 35*b*, 44–45
    data sources, 32, 35–37
    gap closure solutions, 38*b*, 44
    global labor shortage, 28
    global skills crisis, 28
    levels of, 31*f*
    overview, 9, 27, 380–81
    recalibration of values, 28
    scaling, 40
    skilled resources, 33–34, 44–45
    skills taxonomy, 34–35
    SWP defined, 29–30
    SWP implementation, 30*b*, 37–46
    SWP outcomes, 30*f*, 39, 43–44
    SWP process level, 31*f*, 32–33
    talent planning, 31*f*, 31–32, 39–40, 42–43
    workforce analytics/planning, 31*f*, 32, 38*b*, 43–45
    workforce trends, 28–29

396 INDEX

McFillen, J. M., 350–51
McKinnon, A., 12, 241, 249–58, 378
Merck Group case study, 42–43
mergers & acquisitions case study, 249–58
microaggressions, 340–41
Microsoft Excel, 19–20, 38b, 39, 66
modeling. *See also* maturity model
   agile workforce planning, 130
   ASA model, 226
   five-factor model of personality, 225–26, 225t
   job analysis/competency, 91–92
   organizational diagnosis, 350–51, 351f
   role models, 218, 219–20, 233–34, 235t
Monte Carlo study, 65
Montmore County Government case study, 300–12
Moore, T., 9, 380–81, 382
multispeed growth. *See* growth environments
MyoKardia. *See* scenario planning

natural language processing (NLP), 321, 322, 327, 330, 334–35
Nespresso, 321–22
Nestlé, 321–22
New Collar Program, 221–22, 222b
Newmark, A., 10–11, 381
Nicolas, E., 263

Occam's Razor, 323–24
Office of Personnel Management. *See* federal public sector
offshoring, 201–2
Oldham, G. R., 224
Oldroyd, N., 10, 382
O'Neil, D. A., 351
O*NET, 218, 218t, 225t, 321, 324–25, 326f, 329f, 330–31, 346–48
onshoring, 343
open-source data sets, 252b, 256
OpenRefine, 256
operational workforce planning, 117
organization capability analysis (OCA), 290–92, 291f, 292t
organization design/charting software, 66
organizational culture/climate
   adaptive planning and, 247–48

   appropriate context in, 224, 227–28
   autonomy in, 224
   CEO engagement, 264–70, 276–81
   competencies, 222–23
   education, training, 227–31, 229b, 233
   green technologies transition, 264–66
   jobs *vs.* work roles, 220–24, 222b
   KSAOs, 216–17, 218–19, 222–23, 225–28, 232–33, 236
   New Collar Program, 221–22, 222b
   New Work Operating System, 222b
   organization development/change (OD&C), 337–42, 338f
   overview, 11–12, 216–17
   performance management, 218t, 231–32, 233
   professionalism in, 217–20, 217t, 219f, 223, 232–36, 235t
   rewards, punishments, 220, 233–34
   role models, 218, 219–20, 233–34, 235t
   selection/staffing, 225–27, 225t, 233
   socialization, 230–31, 233
   task elements in, 223–24
   work styles, 218, 218t, 225t
organizational diagnosis model, 350–51, 351f
organizational psychology domain expertise, 341–42
Osborne, M., 327–28

Parker, S., 220–21, 229
patent data, 251–52, 254–55
People + Work Connect (Connect) initiative. *See* Connect initiative
PepsiCo, 146–47
Pepys, S., 16
personality, five-factor model of, 225–26, 225t
PESTLE forces, 113b, 124
police training, 230–31
Porter's Five Forces Model (Porter), 287–88
Positioned (Tripp/Ward), 5
Power BI, 66
PowerPoint, 256b
practitioner skills, 337–42, 338f
Pre-suasion: A Revolutionary Way To Influence And Persuade (Cialdini), 356

INDEX   397

Predictive Index, 270
Preece, D., 147–48
problem framing, 340
Produgie, 154, 158–59
professional I-O identity cultivation, 359–61
professionalism. *See* organizational culture/climate
projects/gigs database, 169
proxy markers facility, 340–41
Purina, 321–22
Python, 66, 256

qualitative data sources, 54*t*

R (software), 66, 256
RAND Corporation, 283
Reimer, D., 12, 380–81
Remote Work Indicator, 322, 331–32, 333*f*
remote work shift, 72–74
repeatable/sustainable SWP case study, 242–48, 244*f*
research design, 340
research/professional services companies, 37
resource management, 117
resource planning, 117
Retooling HR (Boudreau), 375–76
Revelio Labs, 207
revenue growth. *See* growth environments
Roberts v. Texaco, 19
robotic process automation (RPA), 330
role models, 218, 219–20, 233–34, 235*t*
Royal Dutch/Shell, 283, 286
Ryan, A. M., 360
Ryan, R. M., 224

SAGE Business Cases, 356
Salapatas, K., 12, 241, 242–48, 378
San Pellegrino, 321–22
SAP Analytics Cloud, 66
Saudi Aramco case study
    Aramco Production Training Program, 100
    collective culture importance, 108–9
    critical segments identification, 107–8
    digitization of roles, 107–8
    education, training initiatives, 100–1, 107, 111–12
    historical context, 99–105
    I-O psychology value/roles/impacts, 108–13, 111*f*, 113*b*
    leadership journey assessment, 109–11, 111*f*
    Master Gas System, 101–2
    maturity model, 106*f*, 106–8
    mega-projects, 101–2
    nationalization of, 101–2
    overview, 10, 381
    Saudization as priority, 100–1
    spending localization initiative, 103
    SWP drivers, 105–11
    talent diversity initiatives, 103–4, 111–12
    team-level talent, 112–13
    Vision 2030, 102–4, 105, 108–9
    workforce growth, 101–2
    workforce planning considerations, 104–5
scenario planning
    agile approach to, 288–89
    benefits of, 287
    capabilities, defining, 289–93, 291*f*, 292*f*
    capability gap analysis, 291, 292*t*
    current workforce analysis, 293
    data analytics in, 65–66
    democratization of work, 284, 285*f*
    description, 283–88, 285*f*
    forces of change, 284–86, 285*f*, 289
    labor market impacts/SWP, 293–94
    limitations of, 286
    organization building strategies, 295*f*, 295–96
    organization capability analysis (OCA), 290–92, 291*f*, 292*t*
    overview, 12, 282–83
    staffing forecast creation, 294–95
    technological empowerment, 284, 285*f*
    tips summary, 297–98
    today, status quo, 284–85, 285*f*
    today, turbo-charged, 285*f*, 285
    tracking, pivoting, 296–97
    uber empowered, 285*f*, 286
    Vision 2020/Vision 2025, 288, 291
    work reimagined, 285*f*, 285
scheduling, 117
Schein, E. H., 308–9

Schneider, B., 11–12, 234, 373–74
Schwartz, P., 287–88
Science Of Complexity In Everyday Life, The (Fisher), 356
self-determination theory (SDT), 224
self-service retail, 202
sensitive personal information (SPI), 55
ServiceNow, 318
Setlur, S., 10–11, 381
simulations, 356
Sinek, S., 122
SIOP Values Statement, 359–61
skill adjacency analysis, 66
skills-based operating systems, 373. *See also* artificial intelligence (AI)
skills taxonomy, 34–35, 206–8
Smith, A. R., 18
social influence, 253
social network analysis, 252–56, 254f, 255f
Sokol, M., xi–xii, 1, 371
Sony Playstation Worldwide Studios, 261
sources. *See* data sources
staffing cycles social consequences, 18
stakeholders. *See also* CEO engagement
    in agile workforce planning, 119, 121, 122, 125–27
    data analytics interactions, 63
    federal public sector, 81b, 83, 89
    strategic worktask planning framing to, 208b
STEEP trends, 283, 288, 289
strategic workforce planning
    applications, 1–3
    as area of research, 385
    areas of focus, 6–8
    career guidance, 24–25
    communities of practice, 23–24
    defined, 29–30, 50–51, 80b, 86–88
    formalization of, 17–20
    historical origins of, 16–17
    I-O psychology relationships, xi, 3–5, 4t
    methodology, 382f, 382–83, 384f
    organizational change drivers, 2
    perceptions of, 6
    process, 21f
    questions, 22–23
    standardization, 20f, 20
    talent acquisition/retention, 2–3
    technical/consulting model, 384f, 384–86
    terminology, 6
    thought exercises, 1–2
    tradeoffs in practice of, 6–7
    trends in, 372–74
    workforce defined, 374–76
strategic worktask planning
    applicability, 203–4b
    artificial intelligence (AI) in, 200–1, 205, 207, 209
    automation in, 200, 203, 207, 208
    benefits of, 200–1, 215
    best practices determination, 208
    in consultancies, 201–2
    disaggregation, 204–5
    distribution center case study, 202–4
    framing to stakeholders, 208b
    gig workers in, 200, 207, 209
    in hospitals, 201–2
    hybrid work designs, 200
    implementation of, 204, 214–15, 214t
    internal freelance talent pool, 209–11b
    in manufacturing, 201–2
    organizational fit, 211–13
    overview, 11, 373
    remote work designs, 200, 213b
    strategic approach to, 205
    systematic approach to, 205
    systematic skills taxonomy case study, 206–8
    volunteers in, 209
    workforce planning *vs.*, 198–99, 199t, 211–12
strategy maps, 63
SuccessFactors, 66
succession planning software, 66
supply profile case study, 127–28b
SWP. *See* strategic workforce planning
SWP Advanced Practitioners' Colloquia, 24
systematic skills taxonomy case study, 206–8

tactical workforce planning, 117
talent intelligence platforms, 166–67, 167t
talent management
    acquisition data sources, 36

CEO engagement, 273–74, 278
current workforce analysis, 293
data analytics, 52b
growth environments, 144–45, 146–51, 147f, 151t, 154
intelligence platforms, 166–67, 167t
internal freelance talent pool case study, 209–11b
internal talent marketplace (ITM), 168–72, 170f, 171f, 183, 191, 382
labor market impacts/SWP, 293–94
maturity model, 31f, 31–32, 39–40, 42–43
near-fit role analysis, 332–37, 335f
optimization levers, 135
organization building strategies, 295f, 295–96
outside-in talent retention, 274, 278
pooling strategy, 147f, 148, 149, 151t, 154–55
skills-based talent practices, 165–66
staffing forecast creation, 294–95
workforce defined, 374–76
Tarulli, B., xi–xii, 1, 371
Tesla, 271

Texaco, 19–20
Tripp, R., 5, 16, 22

Uhl-Bien, M., 308–9
Ulrich, D., 11, 373
Unilever, 209
Upwork, 209

van Katwyk, P., 10, 381
Verizon, 318
Vetter, E., 17
Visier, 66
Volkswagen-Audi, 233–34

Wal-Mart, 323
Walker, J. W., 16, 18
Ward, D. L., 5, 9, 15, 16, 22, 371–72
web scraping, 336
Weingarden, S., 13–14, 384–85
Welch, J., 234
Wells-Fargo, 220, 233–34
workforce profile data sources, 36, 54t

Young, A., 18